Contributions to Management Science

The series *Contributions to Management Science* contains research publications in all fields of business and management science. These publications are primarily monographs and multiple author works containing new research results, and also feature selected conference-based publications are also considered. The focus of the series lies in presenting the development of latest theoretical and empirical research across different viewpoints.

This book series is indexed in Scopus.

José Ramón Saura
Editor

Global Perspectives on AI, Ethics, and Business Economics

Charting the Future

Springer

Editor
José Ramón Saura
Department of Business and Economics
Rey Juan Carlos University
Madrid, Spain

ISSN 1431-1941 ISSN 2197-716X (electronic)
Contributions to Management Science
ISBN 978-3-031-88780-2 ISBN 978-3-031-88781-9 (eBook)
https://doi.org/10.1007/978-3-031-88781-9

This Springer imprint is published by the registered company Springer Nature Switzerland AG
The registered company address is: Gewerbestrasse 11, 6330 Cham, Switzerland

Preface

Few subjects today generate as much debate and transformative potential as Artificial Intelligence (AI). Once confined to highly specialized research labs, AI has rapidly entered the mainstream, reshaping how businesses operate, how individuals interact with technology, and how nations envision their economic and social futures. Yet, the breakneck speed at which AI evolves creates a correspondingly urgent need for reflection, dialogue, and consensus-building around the ethical and economic impacts that emerge when algorithms become part of everyday life.

This volume, *Global Perspectives on AI, Ethics & Business Economics: Charting the Future*, sets out to explore the profound influence of AI on the business landscapes, governance structures, and societal frameworks. While technical innovations in AI have garnered much scholarly and media attention, questions related to its ethical boundaries, business models, and real-world implementation have remained relatively understudied in a holistic manner. Drawing on contributions from experts across different regions and sectors, this book aims to fill that gap, offering a panoramic view of how AI reverberates through economies and communities worldwide.

One of the motivations behind this project is the realization that AI is not just another technological tool, but rather a complex ecosystem of data, algorithms, and human interactions that continuously evolves in response to shifting social, economic, and regulatory forces. Indeed, AI's ability to learn from massive datasets and adapt to changing contexts can be both a source of remarkable insights and a liability when biases, privacy violations, or opaque decision-making processes are embedded within it. These ethical tensions come to the fore in business environments, where AI's deployment may yield productivity gains, tailored consumer experiences, and cost savings. Yet, it also prompts concerns about surveillance, digital monopolies, and widening inequalities in access to data or high-level expertise.

In many respects, the emergence of AI and its swift adoption by corporations worldwide recast what we mean by "business economics." Traditional considerations, such as supply and demand, market competition, resource allocation, and profit maximization, take on new dimensions when augmented by machine learning, predictive analytics, and automated decision-making. Companies can now harness algorithms that forecast consumer behavior with striking precision, driving strategies that include hyper-personalized advertisements, dynamic pricing, and advanced supply chain management. Thus, such efficiency enhancements may seem unequivocally positive. However, deeper inquiry reveals a need for robust ethical guidelines related to how transparent should these predictive models be to the public? What are the implications for consumer autonomy when the next best "decision" is pre-calculated by an AI? Might the digital economy's benefits accrue unevenly, favoring large entities that have the computational resources to collect and analyze massive amounts of data?

Addressing these sorts of questions requires an interdisciplinary perspective that spans computer science, law, economics, philosophy, and organizational management, among other fields. Researchers and practitioners who specialize in AI often bring their own disciplinary lenses, focusing on narrower aspects such as model accuracy, computational efficiency, or algorithmic bias. While these specialized debates are crucial, they do not always capture the broader strategic and societal ramifications of AI adoption. This edited book, therefore, seeks to integrate these specialized discussions into a wider analytical framework that explicitly tackles how AI shapes human well-being, business competitiveness, and global economic structures.

Equally paramount is the geographic diversity of AI implementation. Different regions and countries have embraced AI in ways that reflect local resources, policy priorities, cultural norms, and market conditions. For instance, nations with stringent data protection laws may constrain the kind of data-intensive analytics that businesses can employ, whereas others might adopt a more permissive regulatory stance to spur innovation. In some localities, the costs of building reliable digital infrastructure may limit the extent to which AI can be deployed, creating disparities in access and opportunity. Meanwhile, global competition for AI talent and investment capital can widen gaps between technology hubs and regions that lag behind in digital readiness. These factors shape the speed of AI diffusion and how ethical principles manifest in real-world use cases.

Under this new paradigm, the chapters in this book have been carefully chosen to represent a range of topics and sectors. Readers will encounter discussions about data economies, ethical governance frameworks, the rise of digital marketing hyper-personalization, and the application of AI to public services, among other themes. Each chapter offers distinct insights into how machine intelligence interacts with business processes, policy considerations, and social values. While some authors tackle broad theoretical questions, others ground their analyses in detailed case studies that illuminate how AI-enabled innovations take shape in practice.

Despite the intellectual diversity in these chapters, a unifying message runs through them: AI, when harnessed judiciously, carries the potential to advance economic prosperity, spur innovation, and address complex societal challenges. From healthcare optimization to sustainable resource management. Yet, AI also presents risks when developed or applied in ways that undermine democratic norms, exacerbate inequalities, or disregard data privacy. Balancing these competing outcomes is at the heart of AI ethics, and by extension, at the heart of this edited volume.

In writing and editing *Global Perspectives on AI, Ethics & Business Economics: Charting the Future*, I have been repeatedly struck by the notion that AI is as much about human choices and values as it is about computational capabilities. Also, while AI can automate certain decisions, individuals and institutions remain accountable for setting the boundaries within which those decisions occur. Consequently, the very term known as AI might be a misnomer if it obscures the human agency behind AI's lifecycle, from design and training to deployment and oversight.

In this context, another feature that emerged strongly during the development of this edited book is the tension between localized ethical standards and the global ambitions of AI-driven businesses. Multinational corporations face the challenge of reconciling different legal frameworks, cultural expectations, and risk tolerances as they roll out AI solutions worldwide. Local stakeholders, for their part, may need to adapt AI tools to fit unique infrastructure or workforce requirements, while simultaneously adopting best practices from leading technology firms. The connection of these local and global dynamics shapes an evolving conversation that will continue as AI's capabilities and societal roles expand in unforeseen ways.

Above all, this edited book aims to spark deeper reflection and collaboration. Whether you are an executive evaluating how to responsibly integrate AI into your firm's strategy, a policymaker grappling with the complexities of AI oversight, an academic exploring theoretical paradigms, or a student eager to understand the future of AI-driven economies, this edited volume provides an invitation to think critically and creatively about AI's transformative power. The "global perspectives" words in the title are not just a nod to the multinational or multicultural nature of contemporary business, they represent a call to inclusivity, urging stakeholders worldwide to recognize their shared responsibility in guiding AI's trajectory toward ethical and equitable outcomes.

A key impetus behind this edited volume is the recognition that meaningful discourse on AI must not be confined to abstract theorizing or purely technical descriptions; it must also address how the technology intersects with pressing realities of business practice and societal well-being. As AI's capacity for real-time analytics and predictive modeling grows more sophisticated, private and public decision-making becomes increasingly data-driven. From forecasting supply chain disruptions and detecting fraud to influencing consumer preferences and managing public infrastructure, AI is built into the fabric of modern economies. Simultaneously, this expanded role brings heightened scrutiny. Regulators and civil society groups caution against potential abuses of algorithmic power, pointing to real-world concerns such as discrimination in automated credit scoring, invasive surveillance in public spaces, and digital monopolies that threaten market competition. When presenting these trends and controversies, the chapters in *Global Perspectives on AI, Ethics & Business Economics: Charting the Future* underline the necessity for robust ethical frameworks that transcend narrow technical "fixes," encompassing organizational culture, legal structures, and a broader societal consensus on acceptable AI usage.

This focus on the interplay between ethics, economics, and AI reflects a deeper philosophical question: How can innovation remain vibrant and market-oriented while honoring principles of justice, transparency, and human dignity? Throughout history, periods of transformative growth—such as the Industrial Revolution or the emergence of the World Wide Web—have triggered debates about the distribution of wealth, workers' rights, consumer protection, and societal well-being. Likewise, AI intensifies these discussions by reshaping productivity, employment patterns, and the fundamental ways in which users engage with digital environments. As data becomes the new currency of commerce, power can accrue to those entities most adept at extracting, analyzing, and monetizing information. Yet, this dynamic invites competing views on stewardship: some argue that maximizing data sharing and algorithmic experimentation can spur breakthroughs, while others insist that users retain control over their personal information and that companies be held accountable for potential harms.

In this way, bridging these views requires broad-based, inclusive conversations about how technology is steered, who benefits from it, and what ethical standards should guide its development. The chapters in this volume offer a diverse range of insights into these issues. While Section 1 introduces foundational questions of AI, data economies, and the corporate responsibilities accompanying advanced analytics, Section 2 provides concrete investigations of AI's application in fields like public governance, healthcare, and tourism. Through case studies and conceptual analyses, authors reveal that context truly matters: AI's pitfalls can be mitigated or exacerbated depending on local legal frameworks, cultural norms, resource availability, and stakeholder engagement. The examples illustrate, time and again, that genuine progress demands an approach encompassing the full spectrum of interests, from engineers and entrepreneurs at the design stage to policymakers, academics, and community leaders who oversee implementation and impact.

In preparing this edited volume, I have come to appreciate the collaborative spirit necessary to produce an integrated conversation on AI's ethical and economic implications. The authors have contributed not only their domain expertise but also a willingness to engage in dialogue that traverses the boundaries between research methods, professional cultures, and national contexts. Their contributions represent a collective effort to transcend disciplinary silos, recognizing that AI's problems and potentials are multifaceted by nature. Readers will find that while some chapters focus more narrowly on business models or regulatory challenges, others delve into qualitative experiences of AI adoption, highlighting, for example, how frontline staff respond to algorithmic decision-support systems or how city managers use data governance for climate initiatives. This balance of theoretical rigor and real-world practicality exemplifies the spirit of engagement that I believe is critical for pushing AI in responsible directions.

I sincerely hope that the synergy of these perspectives will resonate with a broad audience. Whether you are a seasoned academic researcher, a startup founder wrestling with data ethics, a public official eager to craft balanced AI legislation, or a student exploring the interdisciplinary domain of AI for the first time, the ensuing chapters aim to spark fresh insights. They may challenge existing notions about how technology is shaped—or should be shaped—within organizations and communities. They may also serve as a blueprint for more informed discussions and collaborations. The economy of the future will invariably be influenced by digital platforms, algorithmic systems, and machine learning techniques. Consequently, it is our collective responsibility to ensure these tools reinforce, rather than undermine, social and economic well-being.

With these thoughts in mind, I encourage you to read the specific arguments, case studies, and policy recommendations presented throughout the volume. Each chapter, in its own way, champions the idea that AI is at once a catalyst for progress and a lightning rod for deep ethical tensions. Through informed debate, empirical inquiry, and an openness to cross-sector collaboration, it is possible to harness AI in a manner that enriches global economies and upholds fundamental ethical standards. The goal, ultimately, is not to stifle innovation but to shape it, so that the dividends of AI-driven growth are distributed more widely, and the risks minimized for all stakeholders.

Thank you for joining me on this journey. It is my hope that *Global Perspectives on AI, Ethics & Business Economics: Charting the Future* will challenge assumptions, illuminate new pathways, and, most importantly, spark action. The future of AI depends on who participates in its shaping, the values they bring, and the dialogues they initiate. May these pages be a step toward a world where AI is embraced for its capabilities and capacity to uplift human endeavors responsibly and sustainably.

Madrid, Spain José Ramón Saura

Contents

Part I
Ethics and Business Challenges in AI Development

AI, Data Economy, and Behavioral Intention: Towards Ethical Paths

José Ramón Saura

Introduction

In the unfolding era of advanced digital technologies, Artificial Intelligence (AI) is at the epicenter of a profound structural transformation that affects global economies, cultural norms, political frameworks, and how individuals think and act in a world saturated with ubiquitous computing power (Agarwal et al., 2024). As we navigate the contours of the digital economy and, more specifically, the data economy (Einav & Levin, 2014), it becomes increasingly clear that conventional value creation and consumption paradigms are being redefined. Data has emerged as the world's most valuable resource, guiding decision-making processes across sectors and continents and pushing societies into new ethical and economic frontiers (Helfrich, 2024). This shifting landscape is not merely about machines making predictions or automating tasks, it is about the fabric of human intention, attention, and cognition being integrated, influenced, and sometimes manipulated by algorithmic processes on a massive scale (Saura et al., 2024).

The role of AI and data-driven business models opens powerful avenues for hyper-personalization, predictive analytics, and advanced behavioral targeting, allowing firms to anticipate desires, preempt choices, and shape consumer journeys (Jain et al., 2021). From streaming platforms that know precisely when to recommend a certain movie based on contextual signals (Häglund & Björklund, 2024) to e-commerce sites that deploy behavioral retargeting (Jiang et al., 2021), organizations use massive troves of user data to gain insight into micro-moments of decision-making. These micro-moments, intertwined with digital psychographics and shaped by real-time analytics (Hussain et al., 2024), can capture a user's shifting moods,

J. R. Saura (✉)
Department of Business and Economics, Rey Juan Carlos University, Madrid, Spain
e-mail: joseramon.saura@urjc.es

J. R. Saura (ed.), *Global Perspectives on AI, Ethics, and Business Economics*, Contributions to Management Science,
https://doi.org/10.1007/978-3-031-88781-9_1

emotional states, and contextual triggers. The resulting ecosystem, reliant on techniques such as social listening, context- and behavior-based segmentation (Zhang, 2011), and customer mood analytics (He et al., 2016), suggests a world in which marketing and behavioral economy exchange become deeply personalized, predictive, and behavioral, leveraging large-scale data to anticipate and influence future actions.

Likewise, central to this development is the concept of the data economy, a system in which data functions not just as an input but as a critical economic asset, an intangible commodity that can be packaged, traded, analyzed, and monetized (Nuccio & Guerzoni, 2019). This data economy underpins the digital economy's broader infrastructure, weaving together cloud computing, edge devices, IoT sensors, online platforms, mobile applications, and intelligent agents. As more aspects of daily life move online, leaving behind digital footprints (Golder & Macy, 2014), entire industries adjust their strategic postures. For example, banking, healthcare, retail, manufacturing, and entertainment all rely on data-driven insights to innovate and remain competitive. At the center of these activities are AI algorithms that sift through oceans of data to find patterns, correlations, and predictive signals (Kotras, 2020).

In this context, the analytics generated by AI models inform pricing strategies, product development, market segmentation, user interface tweaks, and countless other decisions that shape the modern business environment (González-Padilla et al., 2024). Yet, these transformative possibilities raise critical ethical questions about privacy, fairness, accountability, and the future of a connected society (Bauer et al., 2015).

While AI can optimize resource allocation, enhance efficiency, and enable hyper-personalization, it can also facilitate invasive surveillance (Zuboff, 2019), intensify digital manipulation, and contribute to phenomena such as digital fatigue (Zheng & Ling, 2021), where individuals feel overwhelmed by content and persuasive messaging. The ethical dilemmas here are not limited to consumer markets. Governments utilize AI for public services, security measures, and policy evaluations. Non-governmental organizations and advocacy groups leverage data analytics for social impact, but also risk marginalizing vulnerable populations if biases and unintended consequences lurk in their algorithmic architectures. The promise of AI, therefore, is interlocked with the peril of misaligned incentives and compromised ethical standards (Mittelstadt, 2019).

Therefore, at the heart of these issues lies the core challenge of governing AI and data in ways that preserve human dignity, autonomy, and social cohesion. The emergence of frameworks like the Privacy Sandbox (Geradin et al., 2021), a concept championed by leading technology companies like Google, reflects a growing recognition that user data cannot be managed as a free-for-all resource without protections. Instead, we require privacy-preserving architectures (Saura et al., 2023), differential privacy techniques, data clean rooms (Herbrich, 2022) that allow secure data collaboration, and policy frameworks that constrain how, where, and for what purposes data can be used. Similarly, data clean rooms provide a controlled environment where data from multiple organizations can be compared and analyzed without exposing sensitive information. These tools and concepts are part of a broader ecosystem of technical and regulatory solutions designed to create accountability and trust (Novelli et al., 2024).

However, the technological solutions alone are insufficient. In addition to strong regulation, ethical codes, and technical safeguards, there must be a cultural shift in how businesses, policymakers, and societies conceptualize data and AI. The concept of the Economy of Intention (Youssef et al., 2021) adds a compelling dimension to this conversation. This notion recognizes that human attention and intention have become scarce resources in today's interconnected digital environment. In this context, companies compete not only for market share or wallet share but for the very intention behind user actions. Each click, scroll, search query, or pause in reading time is a signal that can be mined, analyzed, and used to shape future behaviors. Aligning these intentions with ethical standards, respecting user autonomy, and avoiding manipulative design is essential for forging a future in which AI augments rather than diminishes human agency (Saura et al., 2022).

Thus, concepts such as digital cognition (Usmani et al., 2024), introduces another layer of complexity. As individuals interact incessantly with AI-driven platforms, their cognitive patterns adapt. The hyper-personalized feeds, behavioral retargeting techniques, and emotion pattern recognition (Ribeiro et al., 2017) embedded in these platforms do more than just react to user behavior; they also shape it.

Over time, user expectations, desires, and mental shortcuts evolve in tandem with the algorithms, producing a co-evolution of machine intelligence and human cognition. Users might not simply consume what is offered to them; they co-create the landscape of opportunities and constraints through their collective digital footprints. This mutual shaping process, while often beneficial, can lead to unintended consequences (Zuboff, 2023), reinforcing echo chambers, encouraging addictive behaviors, or undermining the capacity for reflective thought.

As AI integrates more deeply into business and social environments, companies are challenged to predict critical outcomes such as churn, known as churn prediction (Huang et al., 2012), with ever-increasing accuracy. Therefore, predicting user defection from a service or product is crucial for retaining loyalty, adjusting marketing strategies, or redesigning product experiences. At the same time, advanced AI models that can forecast churn also raise questions about user autonomy and informed consent. How does one balance the legitimate business interest in anticipating customer needs with the ethical imperative to respect their privacy and freedom of choice? Underlying this tension is the realization that predictions can subtly reshape reality (Saura et al., 2023a). Thus, if a model identifies a user as "likely to churn" and subjects them to more aggressive retention campaigns, does that shape their eventual behavior? Is this a benign intervention or a subtle manipulation constraining user agency?

The hyper-personalization extends these concerns into the realm of advanced personalization (Valdez Mendia & Flores-Cuautle, 2022). While a personalized user experience can enhance satisfaction and streamline decision-making, there is a slippery slope towards forms of personalization that no longer serve the user's interests but exploit their vulnerabilities. In highly personalized digital environments, users may encounter fewer discoveries and more carefully curated content designed to keep them engaged, spending, and influenced. This hyper-personalization, driven by contextual and behavioral segmentation, can lead to digital echo chambers or filter bubbles (Zuiderveen Borgesius et al., 2016), where individuals are increasingly isolated within content niches that reinforce their pre-existing beliefs or desires.

Therefore, within this complex environment, stakeholders must reckon with the broader social and economic implications of AI-driven data economies. The digital economy, which once seemed to promise an egalitarian distribution of information and global knowledge-sharing, has evolved into a complex marketplace where platforms have immense power. Companies that dominate certain nodes of data collection—such as search engines, social networks, or mobile ecosystems—hold outsized influence over entire value chains (Zuboff, 2023). This situation can lead to winner-take-all dynamics, stifle competition, and place undue pressure on public policy to curb excessive market concentration (Fuchs, 2013). At the same time, smaller enterprises and startups may rely on data access, interoperability standards, and fair frameworks to innovate and compete. Ethical and inclusive data governance can support a more vibrant, diverse, and competitive digital marketplace.

As the economic significance of data grows, so does the urgency to address ethical challenges (Du & Xie, 2021). Traditional corporate governance structures may not suffice. Boards of directors and executive committees might need new forms of expertise, like data ethics officers, privacy counsel, and AI governance specialists, who can understand the nuances of machine learning models and their human impacts. In this way, investing in data literacy and ethical training for employees across departments is vital. This internal capacity-building ensures that organizations are not merely reacting to crises when they emerge but are proactively shaping their AI strategies in line with socially responsible principles (Stix, 2021).

At the same time, the international policy debates highlight the difficulty of achieving consensus on these issues. Data flows easily across borders, raising questions about jurisdiction, sovereignty, and regulatory harmonization (Saura et al., 2024). National policymakers must consider how local cultural norms and legal traditions intersect with global digital giants that obey different incentive structures or minimal standards. The formation of data alliances, the pursuit of bilateral or multilateral agreements on data protection and AI ethics, and the involvement of international organizations all point to the need for global conversations. These dialogues must bridge the gap between advanced economies with robust digital infrastructures and emerging economies that risk being left behind. Ensuring an equitable global digital economy requires capacity-building efforts, knowledge transfer, and policy support, so that regions with limited resources can also benefit from AI and data without becoming mere data sources or testbeds for unregulated experiments (Tan et al., 2017).

In envisioning the ethical paths forward, we must also reflect on user empowerment and the notion of informed consent. Many current data collection and processing practices hinge on obscure terms and conditions that users seldom read or understand (Saura, 2024). The complexity of AI-driven data analytics magnifies this opacity. Users may consent to data usage, but their consent is not always informed, and their ability to opt-out or negotiate terms is limited. Enhancing transparency is one part of the solution deploying explainable AI methodologies, developing user-friendly privacy dashboards, and offering meaningful opt-outs can help. Yet, transparency alone does not guarantee comprehension or a genuine sense of control. Perhaps a more radical rethinking of the user's role in the data economy is needed, one in which individuals can actively shape the contours of their digital practices.

Designing ethical futures for AI and the data economy will also depend on robust interdisciplinary research. Ethicists can help clarify moral principles, while engineers design privacy-preserving cryptographic techniques (Pinkas, 2002) or federated learning methods (Zhang et al., 2021) that maintain user-level anonymity. Behavioral economists and cognitive psychologists can offer insights into how humans process information in digital contexts, how digital fatigue sets in, and how intention is formed or subverted in these environments. Sociologists and political scientists can study the broader power dynamics at play, analyzing how AI-mediated social interactions influence political polarization, civic engagement, and social trust (Saura et al., 2022). Also, legal scholars can articulate frameworks that ensure accountability and remedy mechanisms for those harmed by AI-driven interventions. This interdisciplinary synergy is crucial for tackling AI ethics not as an afterthought but as an integrated dimension of our digital future.

As we look ahead, some trends and concepts may shape the next generation of AI applications and their ethical management. For instance, the idea of digital cognition implies that human cognitive processes themselves become subject to iterative optimization in concert with AI. In a world of dynamic consumer journeys, psychographic profiling, micro-moment targeting, and emotional pattern recognition, user cognition might be subtly shaped by algorithmic interventions over time. Advanced AI-driven analytics promises to make services more convenient, tailored, and efficient. But what if convenience comes at the cost of diminishing our capacity for critical thinking, reflection, and self-determined action?

Similar challenges arise with advanced behavioral retargeting systems, where predictive modeling becomes so accurate that firms know precisely when to push a certain message to achieve maximum persuasive effect. If left unregulated, these capabilities can undermine the very notion of free will in marketplace decision-making. In addition, the concept of intelligence social listening suggests that AI can not only measure, predict, and influence individual behavior but also monitor and interpret collective sentiment, cultural shifts, and social discourses at scale. AI can guide corporate, political, and institutional strategies by analyzing data from social networks, online forums, and other digital public spheres. This can have democratizing effects, helping policymakers respond more quickly to public concerns, but it also raises questions about who holds the power to interpret and act on this collective intelligence (Mulgan, 2018). If social listening tools fall into the hands of a few dominant actors, asymmetries of knowledge and influence may become entrenched, giving rise to new possible forms of digital oligarchy (Bodrožić & Adler, 2022).

Likewise, within the business environment, the necessity for value alignment between corporate goals and ethical principles grows more pressing. The demands of the data economy often push firms towards more aggressive data collection and ever more sophisticated analytics. Yet, societal pressures, reputational risks, and regulatory scrutiny also rise in tandem. The introduction of The Privacy Sandbox initiative and the development of new data clean rooms are early indicators that industry players understand the precarious balance between monetization and user trust. Ultimately, competitive advantages in the future may come not just from having superior AI-driven insights, but from demonstrating responsible stewardship of those insights.

Likewise, hyper-personalization represents both a pinnacle of what AI-based marketing can achieve and a fault line in the ethical debate. Predictive personalization can anticipate needs, reduce friction, and deliver experiences that delight users. But if we lose sight of the broader human context, if users are treated as mere data points to be manipulated rather than dignified agents, then personalization devolves into exploitation. The danger lies in developing AI tools that are too good at persuasion, too adept at exploiting cognitive biases, and too relentless in seeking to maximize engagement metrics. Moving forward, stakeholders must establish what constitutes acceptable personalization, differentiating between helpful guidance and manipulative nudging, between relevant suggestions and undue influence.

In the same context, user churn is another practical area where ethical considerations come into play. By predicting who is about to leave a platform or abandon a product, companies can intervene proactively to retain those users. This can be beneficial if it involves improving service quality, addressing pain points, or offering genuinely helpful solutions. But if it involves subtly locking users in, making it harder for them to leave, or distracting them with ephemeral rewards, it limits user autonomy. Striking a balance between legitimate retention strategies and exploitative tactics requires clear ethical guidelines and possibly regulatory oversight.

In parallel, as companies increasingly rely on data pooling, alliances, and third-party analytics vendors, the management of data through data clean rooms offers a pathway to collaborative insights without exposing personally identifiable information. Such privacy-preserving techniques represent a positive step, showing that the industry can innovate ethically. They are a reminder that technical solutions, while not panaceas, can mitigate some ethical risks if thoughtfully designed and widely adopted.

The mere complexity of these issues underscores the need for continuous dialogue, research, and policy experimentation. Ethics in AI is not a set of static principles, it is an evolving process that must adapt to new technologies, cultural contexts, and historical circumstances. The task ahead requires humility and openness. Societies must acknowledge that they do not yet have all the answers and that many of the pitfalls of AI and data economies are uncharted territory. But this uncertainty should not lead to paralysis; rather, it should inspire collaborative efforts, rigorous debate, and incremental yet meaningful steps towards more just and equitable systems.

As we continue this analysis in the following sections, we will analyze deeper into specific mechanisms by which AI-driven data economies shape behavioral intentions, the ways that ethical frameworks can guide future policy, and the models for international cooperation that might reconcile divergent cultural values and regulatory philosophies. We will explore how digital fatigue and micro-moments of engagement affect user well-being and how advanced emotion recognition could enhance or erode trust in digital platforms. We will also consider the implications of global digital trade regimes, intellectual property rules, and cross-border data flows that influence the distribution of AI's benefits and burdens worldwide.

Before proceeding, let's reflect on the broader narrative emerging from this exploration. AI's integration with the data economy, informed by the understanding of the economy of intention, demands that we move beyond simplistic views of technology as neutral or inherently beneficial. Instead, we must acknowledge AI's capacity to reconfigure power relations, affect cognitive patterns, and influence social outcomes in ways both subtle and profound. Achieving ethical alignment in this environment is not a trivial pursuit; it will require a synthesis of technical perspicacity, humanistic insight, forward-thinking policy, and a steadfast commitment to values that honor human dignity and collective well-being.

Continuing from the previous discussion, we now turn to the multifaceted policy environment and the evolving attempts to harmonize AI governance with human-centered values. The negotiation of ethical principles in an ecosystem that transcends national borders and cultural frameworks is no trivial task (Ashok et al., 2022). The interaction between private sector innovation and public sector regulation forms a dynamic tension: On one hand, companies push for more data, more predictive power, and more refined personalization; on the other, citizens' groups, regulators, and ethicists call for restraint, transparency, and accountability (Saura et al., 2024). Aligning these imperatives requires a shared vocabulary, better enforcement mechanisms, and broad stakeholder participation.

Several jurisdictions have taken pioneering steps to enshrine ethical principles into binding legislation. The European Union's approach to data protection, embodied in the General Data Protection Regulation (GDPR) (Bakare et al., 2024), provides a well-known example of how legal frameworks can influence global practices. Although GDPR predates the latest wave of AI advancements, its requirements for consent, data minimization, and user rights laid the groundwork for subsequent proposals that target AI systems more directly. The EU's proposed AI Act aims to classify AI applications by risk and impose stricter standards on "high-risk" uses [such as algorithmic decision-making in employment, credit scoring, or healthcare (Saura, 2024)]. In doing so, it attempts to curb discriminatory outcomes, ensure human oversight, and mandate certain levels of explainability.

However, these frameworks are works in progress and face criticism on multiple fronts. Companies worry that excessive regulation might stifle innovation or place European firms at a disadvantage compared to competitors in regions with lighter regulatory burdens. Consumer and digital rights advocates argue that even stronger protections are necessary to prevent manipulative personalization or intrusive behavioral analytics (Zhang & Sundar, 2019). Emerging markets fear that stringent regulations could reinforce existing digital divides if only wealthy countries can afford the compliance infrastructure. Meanwhile, the United States and China, each with their own developmental trajectories and strategic goals, diverge from the

European model. The U.S. federal landscape remains more fragmented, with state-level privacy laws, sectoral regulations, and voluntary guidelines, while China integrates AI governance within a broader state-led model emphasizing strategic self-reliance, surveillance capacities, and a different conception of privacy and individual rights (Karpa et al., 2022).

In this fragmented terrain, global cooperation stands out as both necessary and difficult. International organizations, standards bodies, and trade forums struggle to synchronize rules and encourage best practices. The Organisation for Economic Co-operation and Development (OECD) and United Nations Educational, Scientific and Cultural Organization (UNESCO) have articulated high-level AI principles, emphasizing human rights, fairness, transparency, and accountability (Yeung, 2020; van Norren, 2023). Yet principles alone cannot guarantee effective enforcement or bridge the gap between aspirational ethics and real-world applications. Bilateral agreements between countries, industry consortia, multi-stakeholder alliances, and public-private partnerships all have roles to play in shaping the contours of a global AI governance regime. While harmonization sounds ideal, a degree of pluralism may be inevitable, reflecting the fact that cultural values and political institutions differ widely. The critical question is whether these differences can coexist without giving rise to "ethics dumping" or a regulatory race to the bottom (Bélisle-Pipon & Victor, 2024).

In the meantime, industry players invest in self-regulation and corporate ethics initiatives, in part to preempt stricter state intervention and, in part, because building consumer trust has become a strategic priority. Leading technology companies have formed ethics boards, published responsible AI principles, and engaged with civil society organizations to shape their policies. Efforts like The Privacy Sandbox and data clean rooms reflect not only compliance with existing rules but also proactive attempts to cultivate new norms. These firms demonstrate that technical innovation can align with privacy-enhancing designs by moving away from third-party cookies, invasive fingerprinting, and opaque data-sharing arrangements (Zuboff, 2023). Still, such measures must be scrutinized to ensure they do not become fig leaves for anti-competitive behavior or subtle forms of data extraction. Transparency and independent audits are therefore essential.

Against this backdrop of regulatory fluidity, consider how AI's pervasive influence shapes consumer markets and labor dynamics. The radical personalization enabled by hyper-personalization and context and behavior-based segmentation has economic implications that ripple through supply chains, advertising budgets, and pricing models (Saura et al., 2023b). Brands can tailor their offerings not just to demographic profiles but to their customers' real-time emotions and micro-moments. Customer mood Analytics can detect frustration or delight, guiding service adjustments that improve satisfaction or, in darker scenarios, exploiting vulnerabilities to push impulsive purchases. Advanced behavioral retargeting methods turn fleeting user interactions into meaningful signals for future engagement campaigns. This precision offers economic efficiency gains: Less wastage in marketing spend, better product-market fit, improved loyalty, and potentially higher lifetime value per customer. But it also raises questions about what kind of economic system we are building. Is it one that empowers consumers with meaningful choices or one that nudges and nudges until autonomy erodes? The intention economy highlights that as companies learn to predict and influence intentions, they effectively participate in shaping future demand rather than merely responding to it. This shift troubles the traditional economic assumption that consumer preferences are fixed and exogenous. Instead, preferences become malleable, co-produced by algorithms and context. The role of marketing changes from informing choice to engineering it, a subtle but profound difference.

In the labor market, AI-driven analytics affect hiring, promotion, and retention. Thus, employers can use predictive tools to identify employees at risk of quitting, flagging them for retention efforts (Jia et al., 2024). While this may help reduce turnover costs and maintain a stable workforce, it also threatens employee privacy and can lead to paternalistic interventions. If workers are bombarded with targeted messages to stay, offered perks at just the right emotional moment, or implicitly discouraged from seeking better opportunities elsewhere, do they remain free agents in the labor market? Ethical labor market analytics would require transparency, fairness, and the assurance that data-driven interventions serve employees' interests as well as employers'.

The emergence of digital cognition further complicates these scenarios. As users adapt to constant algorithmic interactions, their cognitive patterns evolve. They may become more susceptible to certain cues, rely on AI-driven shortcuts rather than their own judgment, or experience changes in their perceptions of brand trustworthiness. The intersection between algorithmic environments and human cognition is still poorly understood, raising the specter of digital fatigue and the erosion of attention spans (Shahzad et al., 2024). Digital fatigue is not merely an individual stress response; it has wider implications for productivity, mental health, and democratic participation. If citizens grow weary of constant digital stimuli, will they disengage from civic life, struggle with informed decision-making, and become more vulnerable to disinformation?

Such questions underscore the societal dimension of AI ethics. The focus on business economics and consumer welfare must be complemented by a broader evaluation of collective well-being. If AI-driven data economies produce economic growth but undermine social cohesion, public trust, or mental health, what have we truly gained? If the benefits of AI accrue disproportionately to wealthier segments of society or countries with advanced infrastructure, how can we ensure global equity? And if algorithmic personalization fragments the public sphere into isolated content bubbles, can we sustain the common ground needed for democratic deliberation?

Addressing these systemic concerns calls for a holistic ethical approach that integrates multiple layers of governance, from the macro-level (international treaties, national laws, standard-setting) to the micro-level (corporate policies, engineering design choices, and user empowerment tools). It also demands that we pay attention to historically marginalized communities, ensuring that AI does not replicate or intensify existing inequalities. With emotion recognition and advanced psychographic profiling at hand, AI can either help identify unmet needs and improve services for vulnerable groups or exploit their vulnerabilities. Ethical frameworks must set guardrails against predatory practices, discriminatory outcomes, and undue influence.

Moreover, researchers and practitioners are exploring a range of technical solutions to incorporate ethical principles into AI systems themselves. Techniques for explainability, fairness constraints in machine learning training, and privacy-preserving computation (like federated learning or differential privacy) show that engineering ethics into AI is possible. Still, no single technical fix can replace the need for oversight, accountability mechanisms, and inclusive governance. Technology can help but cannot by itself ensure that values like dignity, autonomy, and justice are upheld and linked to data analytics.

Another important angle is education and literacy. Just as users must become more data-literate to navigate digital markets responsibly, policymakers and corporate leaders must become conversant in the technical and ethical aspects of AI. Cross-disciplinary training for engineers, lawyers, ethicists, and business managers can foster a shared understanding of the stakes involved. Civil society organizations and journalists have a role in communicating complex AI issues to the general public, ensuring that democratic debate about AI policy is well-informed rather than the domain of a technocratic elite.

Looking to the future, we can envision a spectrum of potential scenarios. In a dystopian future, unchecked AI-driven data economies lead to pervasive surveillance, emotional manipulation, and the erosion of personal autonomy. Economic power concentrates in the hands of a few dominant platforms, stifling competition and social trust declines as individuals lose control over their digital identities. Ethical principles remain lip service, overshadowed by the relentless pursuit of profits and influence. In a more balanced future, effective regulations limit the most harmful practices, and industry incentives shift towards responsible innovation. Privacy-enhancing technologies, fair competition rules, and user-centric design frameworks become standard practice. Therefore, consumers learn to demand transparency and accountability, rewarding companies that respect their rights. Also, international cooperation leads to baseline agreements on data governance, while local adaptations respect cultural diversity. The digital environment becomes not just more efficient and personalized but also more humane and conducive to human flourishing.

Such an outcome is not guaranteed. It requires sustained effort, institutional experimentation, and moral imagination. Policymakers must remain agile, updating regulations as AI evolves. Firms must recognize that long-term sustainability depends on ethical alignment, not just quarterly earnings. Activists and watchdog organizations must remain vigilant, raising the alarm when lines are crossed. Researchers must continue to clarify the complex interactions between technology and human behavior, furnishing policymakers with evidence-based guidance. Finally, education systems must prepare future generations to engage critically with AI rather than passively consume its outputs.

In practical terms, the next steps might involve designing clearer metrics for AI ethics and data responsibility. Just as environmental, social, and governance (ESG) criteria guide sustainable investing (Sadiq et al., 2023), we might develop analogous frameworks for AI, measuring and benchmarking corporate practices in data stewardship, algorithmic fairness, and user empowerment. Independent audits, certification schemes, and impact assessments could become routine. For example, before deploying a new hyper-personalization algorithm, a company might be required to conduct a behavioral impact assessment, examining whether the tool respects user autonomy and avoids reinforcing harmful biases.

On the user side, governments and platforms could encourage the development of personal data management tools, enabling individuals to see how their data is used, set their preferences, and revoke permissions easily. Browser extensions, privacy dashboards, and standardized data usage labels (like nutrition facts on food products) might help people make informed choices. These initiatives could mitigate digital fatigue by allowing users to fine-tune their online experiences, opting in or out of certain personalization features, adjusting the intensity of engagement, and receiving alerts if they show signs of cognitive strain or emotional distress.

The challenge is that many of these proposed solutions touch on delicate trade-offs. For example, explainable AI might improve transparency but reduce model accuracy. Strong privacy protections can limit personalization features that some users find beneficial. Fairness constraints might slow down development cycles or force trade-offs between different disadvantaged groups' interests. These are not reasons to abandon ethics but rather invitations to negotiate acceptable compromises, guided by democratic principles and inclusive dialogue.

Furthermore, in a data-rich environment, certain actors—like particularly large tech platforms—possess an informational advantage that can distort market functioning and undermine consumer sovereignty. Policymakers may consider pro-competitive measures, data portability rights, and interoperability standards that enable users to move their data and preferences across platforms. Such interventions can counteract winner-take-all dynamics and promote a more pluralistic data economy. Combined with ethical frameworks, these structural changes could shift incentives, discouraging manipulative practices and encouraging responsible innovation.

Yet, the ultimate direction of AI's impact on global business and society depends on collective choices. Will we treat ethics as an afterthought, making concessions only when scandals erupt? Or will we place ethical considerations at the center of AI strategy, guiding development, deployment, and governance? By proactively engaging with these dilemmas now, we can help shape a future where AI enriches human life rather than eroding its foundations.

The path forward is not linear. It involves balancing competing values, navigating cultural differences, and reconciling economic imperatives with moral imperatives. But the stakes are too high to defer action. Data is no longer a by-product of business transactions; it is the raw material of a new economic order. AI is not just a computational tool; it is a force that molds human cognition, intention, and social relations. The ethical frameworks we build today will determine whether future generations inherit a digital environment that respects their dignity and fosters their potential or one that reduces them to predictable data points in a vast, impersonal machine.

In conclusion, "AI, Data Economy, and Behavioral Intention: Towards Ethical Paths" calls on us to adopt a forward-looking perspective. We must recognize that data-driven personalization, emotional analytics, and predictive modeling are not neutral developments. They reflect and amplify certain values, choices, and power relations. Ensuring that these technological capabilities serve the common good requires vigilance, creativity, and empathy. We can chart a more ethical trajectory by fostering international dialogue, interdisciplinary research, robust regulation, responsible corporate leadership, and active citizen engagement. The ultimate success of this attempt will be measured not only in economic terms but also in the preservation of human agency, the resilience of democratic institutions, and the cultivation of well-being in a digitally interconnected world.

References

Agarwal, P., Swami, S., & Malhotra, S. K. (2024). Artificial intelligence adoption in the post COVID-19 new-normal and role of smart technologies in transforming business: A review. *Journal of Science and Technology Policy Management, 15*(3), 506–529. https://doi.org/10.1108/JSTPM-08-2021-0122

Ashok, M., Madan, R., Joha, A., & Sivarajah, U. (2022). Ethical framework for Artificial Intelligence and Digital technologies. *International Journal of Information Management, 62*, 102433. https://doi.org/10.1016/j.ijinfomgt.2021.102433

Bakare, S. S., Adeniyi, A. O., Akpuokwe, C. U., & Eneh, N. E. (2024). Data privacy laws and compliance: A comparative review of the EU GDPR and USA regulations. *Computer Science and IT Research Journal, 5*(3), 528–543. https://doi.org/10.51594/csitrj.v5i3.859

Bauer, W., Hämmerle, M., Schlund, S., & Vocke, C. (2015). Transforming to a hyper-connected society and economy–towards an "Industry 4.0". *Procedia Manufacturing, 3*, 417–424. https://doi.org/10.1016/j.promfg.2015.07.200

Bélisle-Pipon, J. C., & Victor, G. (2024). Ethics dumping in artificial intelligence. *Frontiers in Artificial Intelligence, 7*, 1426761. https://doi.org/10.3389/frai.2024.1426761

Bodrožić, Z., & Adler, S. (2022). Alternative futures for the digital transformation: A macro-level Schumpeterian perspective. *Organization Science, 33*(1), 105–125. https://doi.org/10.1287/orsc.2021.1558

Du, S., & Xie, C. (2021). Paradoxes of artificial intelligence in consumer markets: Ethical challenges and opportunities. *Journal of Business Research, 129*, 961–974. https://doi.org/10.1016/j.jbusres.2020.08.024

Einav, L., & Levin, J. (2014). Economics in the age of big data. *Science, 346*(6210), 1243089. https://doi.org/10.1126/science.1243089

Fuchs, C. (2013). Political economy and surveillance theory. *Critical Sociology, 39*(5), 671–687. https://doi.org/10.1177/0896920511435710

Geradin, D., Katsifis, D., & Karanikioti, T. (2021). Google as a de facto privacy regulator: Analysing the Privacy Sandbox from an antitrust perspective. *European Competition Journal, 17*(3), 617–681. https://doi.org/10.1080/17441056.2021.1930450

Golder, S. A., & Macy, M. W. (2014). Digital footprints: Opportunities and challenges for online social research. *Annual Review of Sociology, 40*(1), 129–152. https://doi.org/10.1146/annurev-soc-071913-043145

González-Padilla, P., Navalpotro, F. D., & Saura, J. R. (2024). Managing entrepreneurs' behavior personalities in digital environments: A review. *International Entrepreneurship and Management Journal, 20*(1), 89–113. https://doi.org/10.1007/s11365-022-00823-4

Häglund, E., & Björklund, J. (2024). AI-driven contextual advertising: Toward relevant messaging without personal data. *Journal of Current Issues and Research in Advertising*, 1–19. https://doi.org/10.1080/10641734.2024.2334939.

He, W., Tian, X., Chen, Y., & Chong, D. (2016). Actionable social media competitive analytics for understanding customer experiences. *Journal of Computer Information Systems, 56*(2), 145–155. https://doi.org/10.1080/08874417.2016.1117377

Helfrich, G. (2024). The harms of terminology: why we should reject so-called "frontier AI". *AI and Ethics*, 1–7. https://doi.org/10.1007/s43681-024-00438-1.

Herbrich, T. (2022). Data clean rooms. *Computer Law Review International, 23*(4), 109–120. https://doi.org/10.9785/cri-2022-230404

Huang, B., Kechadi, M. T., & Buckley, B. (2012). Customer churn prediction in telecommunications. *Expert Systems with Applications, 39*(1), 1414–1425. https://doi.org/10.1016/j.eswa.2011.08.024

Hussain, F., Ali, Y., Li, Y., & Haque, M. M. (2024). A bi-level framework for real-time crash risk forecasting using artificial intelligence-based video analytics. *Scientific Reports, 14*(1), 4121. https://doi.org/10.1038/s41598-024-54391-4

Jain, G., Paul, J., & Shrivastava, A. (2021). Hyper-personalization, co-creation, digital clienteling and transformation. *Journal of Business Research, 124*, 12–23. https://doi.org/10.1016/j.jbusres.2020.11.034

Jia, N., Luo, X., Fang, Z., & Liao, C. (2024). When and how artificial intelligence augments employee creativity. *Academy of Management Journal, 67*(1), 5–32. https://doi.org/10.5465/amj.2022.0426

Jiang, Z., Chan, T., Che, H., & Wang, Y. (2021). Consumer search and purchase: An empirical investigation of retargeting based on consumer online behaviors. *Marketing Science, 40*(2), 219–240. https://doi.org/10.1287/mksc.2020.1255

Karpa, D., Klarl, T., & Rochlitz, M. (2022). Artificial intelligence, surveillance, and big data. In *Diginomics research perspectives: The role of digitalization in business and society* (pp. 145–172). Springer International Publishing. https://doi.org/10.1007/978-3-031-04063-4_8

Kotras, B. (2020). Mass personalization: Predictive marketing algorithms and the reshaping of consumer knowledge. *Big Data & Society, 7*(2), 2053951720951581. https://doi.org/10.1177/2053951720951581

Mittelstadt, B. (2019). Principles alone cannot guarantee ethical AI. *Nature Machine Intelligence, 1*(11), 501–507. https://doi.org/10.1038/s42256-019-0114-4

Mulgan, G. (2018). Artificial intelligence and collective intelligence: The emergence of a new field. *AI & Society, 33*(4), 631–632. https://doi.org/10.1007/s00146-018-0861-5

Novelli, C., Taddeo, M., & Floridi, L. (2024). Accountability in artificial intelligence: What it is and how it works. *AI & Society, 39*(4), 1871–1882. https://doi.org/10.1007/s00146-023-01635-y

Nuccio, M., & Guerzoni, M. (2019). Big data: Hell or heaven? Digital platforms and market power in the data-driven economy. *Competition and Change, 23*(3), 312–328. https://doi.org/10.1177/1024529418816525

Pinkas, B. (2002). Cryptographic techniques for privacy-preserving data mining. *ACM Sigkdd Explorations Newsletter, 4*(2), 12–19. https://doi.org/10.1145/772862.772865

Ribeiro, B., Oliveira, G., Laranjeira, A., & Arrais, J. P. (2017). Deep learning in digital marketing: Brand detection and emotion recognition. *International Journal of Machine Intelligence and Sensory Signal Processing, 2*(1), 32–50. https://doi.org/10.1504/IJMISSP.2017.088173

Sadiq, M., Ngo, T. Q., Pantamee, A. A., Khudoykulov, K., Ngan, T. T., & Tan, L. P. (2023). The role of environmental social and governance in achieving sustainable development goals: Evidence from ASEAN countries. *Economic Research-Ekonomska Istraživanja, 36*(1), 170–190. https://doi.org/10.1080/1331677X.2022.2072357

Saura, J. R. (2024). Algorithms in digital marketing: Does smart personalization promote a privacy paradox? *FIIB Business Review, 13*(5), 499–502. https://doi.org/10.1177/23197145241276898

Saura, J. R., Ribeiro-Soriano, D., & Palacios-Marqués, D. (2022). Assessing behavioral data science privacy issues in government artificial intelligence deployment. *Government Information Quarterly, 39*(4), 101679. https://doi.org/10.1016/j.giq.2022.101679

Saura, J. R., Palacios-Marqués, D., & Ribeiro-Soriano, D. (2023). Privacy concerns in social media UGC communities: Understanding user behavior sentiments in complex networks. *Information Systems and e-Business Management*, 1–21. https://doi.org/10.1007/s10257-023-00631-5.

Saura, J. R., Ribeiro-Navarrete, S., Palacios-Marqués, D., & Mardani, A. (2023a). Impact of extreme weather in production economics: Extracting evidence from user-generated content. *International Journal of Production Economics, 260*, 108861. https://doi.org/10.1016/j.ijpe.2023.108861

Saura, J. R., Palacios-Marqués, D., Correia, M. B., & Barbosa, B. (2023b). Innovative behavior in entrepreneurship: Analyzing new perspectives and challenges. *Frontiers in Psychology, 14*, 1123236. https://doi.org/10.3389/fpsyg.2023.1123236

Saura, J. R., Škare, V., & Dosen, D. O. (2024). Is AI-based digital marketing ethical? Assessing a new data privacy paradox. *Journal of Innovation and Knowledge, 9*(4), 100597. https://doi.org/10.1016/j.jik.2024.100597

Shahzad, W., Hanif, R., & Haroon, R. (2024). The impact of social media addiction on self-esteem, attention span, sleep quality and phubbing behavior. *Pakistan Journal of Humanities and Social Sciences, 12*(2), 2148–2156. https://doi.org/10.52131/pjhss.2024.v12i2.2362

Stix, C. (2021). Actionable principles for artificial intelligence policy: Three pathways. *Science and Engineering Ethics, 27*(1), 15. https://doi.org/10.1007/s11948-020-00277-3

Tan, K. H., Ji, G., Lim, C. P., & Tseng, M. L. (2017). Using big data to make better decisions in the digital economy. *International Journal of Production Research, 55*(17), 4998–5000. https://doi.org/10.1080/00207543.2017.1331051

Usmani, U. A., Happonen, A., & Watada, J. (2024). The digital age: Exploring the intersection of AI/CI and human cognition and social interactions. *Procedia Computer Science, 239*, 1044–1052. https://doi.org/10.1016/j.procs.2024.06.268

Valdez Mendia, J. M., & Flores-Cuautle, J. D. J. A. (2022). Toward customer hyper-personalization experience—A data-driven approach. *Cogent Business and Management, 9*(1), 2041384. https://doi.org/10.1080/23311975.2022.2041384

van Norren, D. E. (2023). The ethics of artificial intelligence, UNESCO and the African Ubuntu perspective. *Journal of Information, Communication and Ethics in Society, 21*(1), 112–128. https://doi.org/10.1108/JICES-04-2022-0037

Yeung, K. (2020). Recommendation of the council on artificial intelligence (OECD). *International Legal Materials, 59*(1), 27–34. https://doi.org/10.1017/ilm.2020.5

Youssef, A. B., Boubaker, S., Dedaj, B., & Carabregu-Vokshi, M. (2021). Digitalization of the economy and entrepreneurship intention. *Technological Forecasting and Social Change, 164*, 120043. https://doi.org/10.1016/j.techfore.2020.120043

Zhang, J. (2011). The perils of behavior-based personalization. *Marketing Science, 30*(1), 170–186. https://doi.org/10.1287/mksc.1100.0607

Zhang, B., & Sundar, S. S. (2019). Proactive vs. reactive personalization: Can customization of privacy enhance user experience? *International Journal of Human-Computer Studies, 128*, 86–99. https://doi.org/10.1016/j.ijhcs.2019.03.002

Zhang, C., Xie, Y., Bai, H., Yu, B., Li, W., & Gao, Y. (2021). A survey on federated learning. *Knowledge-Based Systems, 216*, 106775. https://doi.org/10.1016/j.knosys.2021.106775

Zheng, H., & Ling, R. (2021). Drivers of social media fatigue: A systematic review. *Telematics and Informatics, 64*, 101696. https://doi.org/10.1016/j.tele.2021.101696

Zuboff, S. (2019). 'We make them dance': Surveillance capitalism, the rise of instrumentarian power, and the threat to human rights. In *Human rights in the age of platforms* (pp. 3-51).

Zuboff, S. (2023). The age of surveillance capitalism. In *Social theory re-wired* (pp. 203–213). Routledge.

Zuiderveen Borgesius, F. J., Trilling, D., Möller, J., Bodó, B., De Vreese, C. H., & Helberger, N. (2016). Should we worry about filter bubbles? *Internet Policy Review, 5*(1), 1–16. https://doi.org/10.14763/2016.1.401

Challenges in Artificial Intelligence and Business: An Ethical Perspective

Nelson deMatos, Belem Barbosa, and Marisol B. Correia

Introduction

Artificial intelligence (AI) is "a machine-based system that can, for a given set of human-defined objectives, make predictions, recommendations, or decisions influencing real or virtual environments" (Yeung, 2020, p. 25). AI has transformed how business products, services, and experience(s) across distinct market sectors are produced, manufactured, and operationalized (Cooper, 2024). Along with AI growth, organizations have also faced additional ethical challenges. These include data privacy, security, transparency, job displacement, service or product automation, and consumers' reasonable concerns about how AI impacts their lives (Borenstein & Howard, 2021; Saura et al., 2024). Ethics, in this context, "generally refers to a system of moral values that may differ from the incentives of economic systems" (Gallagher, 2005, p. 56).

N. deMatos (✉)
CinTurs- Research Centre for Tourism, Sustainability and Well-being & CiTUR, Faculty of Economics, Universidade do Algarve, Faro, Portugal
e-mail: nmmatos@ualg.pt

B. Barbosa
CEF.UP and LIAAD INESC TEC, University of Porto, Porto, Portugal
e-mail: belem@fep.up.pt

M. B. Correia
CinTurs- Research Centre for Tourism, Sustainability and Well-being & CiTUR, Faculty of Economics, Universidade do Algarve, Faro, Portugal

LisboaSchool of Management, Hospitality and Tourism, Universidade do Algarve & Centre for Tourism Research, Development and Innovation – CiTUR & Research Centre for Tourism, Sustainability and Well-being – CinTurs, Faro, Portugal & CEG-IST, Instituto Superior Técnico, Universidade de Lisboa, Lisbon, Portugal
e-mail: mcorreia@ualg.pt

J. R. Saura (ed.), *Global Perspectives on AI, Ethics, and Business Economics*, Contributions to Management Science,
https://doi.org/10.1007/978-3-031-88781-9_2

Ethical practices can help businesses to achieve long-term success and competitiveness. However, it also requires companies not to be solely profit-driven but instead willing to be accountable and responsible for the technology they offer to the market and their consumers, such as AI. For example, overpromises in businesses promoted in AI advertising often do not match reality (Kaplan & Haenlein, 2019).

Therefore, neglecting AI ethics can lead to damages in various ways, e.g., loss of consumer trust and poor economic and financial returns (Hickman & Petrin, 2021; Saura et al., 2021). Thus, the critical question nowadays is and remains to be how AI ethics' existing framework and regulation(s) maintain up to speed in AI development while considering AI's social impacts. In this sense, scholars and practitioners have been trying to understand and answer the question: How can organizations fully use AI advantages while safeguarding the human way of life? For some scholars, a potential answer is to implement ethical standards (Borenstein & Howard, 2021; Stahl, 2021).

Scholars and managers need to discuss new structures and policies to govern AI and its impacts on society; for example, they need to incorporate concepts such as corporate social responsibility (CSR) (Fioravante, 2024; Krkac, 2019). CSR is the "voluntary commitment by businesses to consider their societal, economic, and environmental impacts" (Bai, 2024, p. 18). Businesses and governments need to take a proactive role in establishing ethical boundaries for AI. As AI evolves and businesses strive for more success, different AI systems are created to enhance and complement human needs; as such, interactions with humans need the creation of transparent AI technologies aligned with human values and focusing on human well-being, i.e., the concept of human-centered AI (Ben, 2020; Obrenovic et al., 2024; Schwarz, 2020). Ethics is good business, and it can serve, as posited by Gallagher (2005), as a form of insurance for organizations. However, undesirable outcomes of AI use and application (e.g., job displacement or unemployment, misinformation) need to be considered and solutions found (Fioravante, 2024; Fosso-Wamba et al., 2023; Weber-Lewerenz, 2021; Wright & Schultz, 2018).

Therefore, this chapter aims to assess the challenges of AI in the business sector from an ethical perspective. The contribution of the research is twofold: first, it shows that AI ethics develops and identifies past trends and future research avenues. Second, it reinforces the need for business managers and stakeholders to engage and apply AI ethics regulations to contribute positively to businesses and societal well-being. The chapter is structured as follows: first, a literature review section contextualizes the study by highlighting the theoretical and conceptual foundations of the research area; second, the methodology section presents the steps for the systematic literature review (SLR) approach, detailing the data selection, collection, and analysis. Next, the descriptive results are presented, providing an overview of past research over the last decades. Afterward, a thematic analysis explores the key themes identified within the retrieved sample. The following discussion section highlights the results and addresses the research propositions based on the findings. Lastly, conclusions and implications regarding the practical and theoretical contribution of the research are emphasized.

Literature Review

AI has become a transformative force in modern society (Dwivedi et al., 2023), influencing customer engagement (Dogan et al., 2024), industries, and academic disciplines, such as mathematics, computer science, or cognitive psychology (Dwivedi et al., 2023; Goodfellow et al., 2016). AI is defined as a "system's ability to correctly interpret external data, to learn from such data, and to use those learnings to achieve specific goals and tasks through flexible adaptation" (Kaplan & Haenlein, 2019, p. 15). Its purpose is to think, act, behave as humans, or even amplify human capabilities (Cheng & Yu, 2019).

The origin of AI can be traced to Turing's question: "Can machines think?" in the late 1950s (Turing, 2009, p. 23). For decades, from the 1950s to 1980s, technological limitations in computing power contributed to slow progress since most of the computing power relied on preprogrammed (or logical) rules (i.e., rule-based programming or symbolic AI) to make decisions set by computer developers (e.g., Expert systems, MYCIN, or EMYCIN) (Nilsson, 2009). In the 1990s, machine learning developments led to an important shift in AI development; algorithms could now be learned based on the data collected and were not dependent on previously programmed rules provided by humans (Lavallin & Downs, 2021). This meant that the systems built could identify patterns, learn, and make predictions based on the data they had (Cheng & Yu, 2019). However, a few years later, in the 2010s, deep learning surpassed machine learning due to its capacity for solving complex tasks and working with large datasets using neural networks and big data (LeCun et al., 2015).

As such, today, AI is integrated into the market to improve business efficiency, productivity, decision-making process, and sales, as well as to help customers make decisions (Morosan & Dursun-Cengizci, 2024). Despite AI's potential to improve business operations and customers' lives, AI is not without challenges (Bankins & Formosa, 2023; Kumar et al., 2024). Among these challenges, ethical concerns regarding the source of data collected and processed by AI have been raised (Saura et al., 2024) in sensitive sectors like healthcare or finance, where data privacy and security are key factors (Kumar et al., 2021).

The regulation of AI data usage and AI application across different contexts (e.g., social media, robotics, or health) has been suggested to be critical (Méndez-Suárez et al., 2023). For example, Gorwa et al. (2020) found the need for algorithmic content moderation because the line that divides acceptable and unacceptable speech is very thin. However, they argue that relying too much on AI to moderate speech can present a risk of overlooking the human role in dealing with the complex and political nature of speech regulation (Gorwa et al., 2020). So, balancing AI integration in the various contexts and applications (Tuncalp, 2024), along with clear policies to address AI business integration, including frameworks that balance innovation with privacy protection, is needed (Adigwe et al., 2024; Smith & Miller, 2023).

In addition, concern related to ensuring that AI benefits both business and human welfare stresses the need for businesses to consider the social implications of automation and to have a more human-centered approach to AI (Obrenovic et al., 2024). This means understanding consumer's perceptions, along with their attitude towards AI adaptation, and in particular, regarding automation and CDR (corporate digital responsibility) addressing ethical and responsible use of AI by businesses, or CSR (corporate social responsibility), which addresses the impact of AI on the society in general (Weber-Lewerenz, 2021). Thus, AI conceptualization and business integration are related to AI governance, ethical concerns, and societal impacts (Kuziemski & Misuraca, 2020). Therefore, businesses must balance technological advancements with a commitment to ethical standards, privacy protection, and responsible corporate practices in the market.

Methods

Literature reviews are essential for social science scholars' definition of knowledge (Cooper, 1988) and are frequently conducted by scholars throughout the business field (Barbosa et al., 2024; Ribeiro-Navarrete et al., 2024). This study selected the systematic literature review approach (deMatos et al., 2021; Wattanacharoensil & La-ornual, 2019) for its structured and reproducible methodology, allowing for a deeper analysis of research questions or concepts. In other words, "Systematic literature reviews are an increasingly used review methodology to synthesize the existing body of literature in a field" (Kraus et al., 2020, p. 1023).

The SLR approach was divided into four steps (Table 1) to enable a more straightforward approach and process: Step 1—Source and keyword selection of manuscripts, Step 2—Refining the preliminary results, Step 3—Screening related manuscripts, Step 4—Final manuscripts screening and analysis (deMatos et al., 2021; Wattanacharoensil & La-ornual, 2019).

Step 1 commenced with the following decisions: (a) the identification of the indexed databases for selecting and collecting the manuscripts; (b) the definition of the keywords for searching the manuscripts. The Web of Science (WoS) Core Collection database was selected because it incorporates an extensive number of publication databases and is seen as one of the most critical databases in social sciences, with high-quality document samples (Ruggeri et al., 2019) (Jiménez-Partearroyo & Medina-López, 2024; Shu et al., 2020). The keywords used in the search query were: "Artificial Intelligence" or "AI", "ethic*," and "business." The terms were chosen to (i) focus on the core terms employed by the theoretical background, (ii) avoid retrieving an impracticable oversized sample of papers, and (iii) reduce potential biases, considering the study's aim, as suggested by deMatos et al. (2021). The search was conducted on the 2 August 2024.

Step 2, refining the preliminary results, meant that the preliminary results obtained from the search query on WoS were filtered, i.e., in terms of inclusion and exclusion criteria (Table 1). Thus, we considered only manuscripts written in English to cover the maximum number of manuscripts and reduce translation bias from other languages. This is a standard procedure in this type of review (e.g.,

Table 1 SLR steps

Step 1. Source and keyword selection of manuscripts	Step 2. Refining the preliminary results
Source • Web of Science (WoS) Keyword set: "Artificial Intelligence" OR "AI" and "ethic*" and "business"	Showing results in the first round from keyword search in the database. • WoS = 896 Refining search criteria and review protocol: Inclusion of manuscripts: • Timeframe: without date limitation • Only manuscripts in the English language Exclusion of manuscripts: • Retracted publication, data paper, proceeding paper
Step 3. Screening related manuscripts	Step 4. Final manuscripts screening and analysis
The authors read each manuscript's title, abstract, and keywords for screening purposes Manuscripts were categorized into three groups: 1. AI ethics is explicitly stated in the manuscript's title, abstract, or keywords 2. AI ethics could be inferred, but the contents are not explicit 3. The manuscripts are not related to the AI ethics concepts	All authors selected articles in Category 1. The results were: Total screened manuscripts = 896 Removed after screened (e.g., due to duplication, outside of the scope of the research) = 0 Articles added in reference search = 0 Total articles included for synthesis = 896

Source: Adapted from deMatos et al. (2021) and Wattanacharoensil and La-ornual (2019)

Firmansyah et al., 2024). Three document types were excluded from the analysis: retracted publication, data paper, and proceeding paper. This was due to validity and reliability issues, e.g., conference proceedings often lack peer review standards and rigor and are deemed grey literature (Okoli, 2015). No further restrictions related to the publication year, type, or methodology adopted were considered. Following these procedures, a total of 896 manuscripts were identified.

In Step 3, screening-related manuscripts, the database was imported to the reference manager Mendeley.com afterward for an initial reading of each manuscript's title, abstract, and keywords. All the authors performed the assessment individually and categorized the manuscripts into three groups (Group 1—AI ethics is explicitly stated in the manuscript's title, abstract, or keywords; Group 2—AI ethics could be inferred, but the contents are not explicit; Group 3—the manuscripts are not related to the AI ethics concepts) (deMatos et al., 2021). After careful reading and examination between the authors for validation of the final sample, 896 manuscripts were identified. In Step 4, final manuscripts screening and analysis, an Excel spreadsheet was created and shared with another author to perform the inductive and deductive content analysis [a standard method in social sciences, e.g., Sandström et al. (2015)] and the descriptive analysis. The thematic analysis was conducted using Bibliometrix, an R's package software designed and used frequently for statistical analysis and visualization (Linnenluecke et al., 2020).

Results and Discussion

Descriptive Analysis

Table 2 presents an overview of the sample. The analysis includes a total of 896 documents published between 1990 and 2024. Demonstrating the topic's relevance, the average number of citations per document is 18.38. These documents were published across 499 journals, reflecting the broad interest in the topic. Twelve percent of the articles are classified as "early access," indicating that they are very recent and are still awaiting integration into a journal issue. The current relevance of the topic is further highlighted by the fact that the documents' average age is below 2 years.

Although the timespan of the publications is particularly long, it should be noted that research between 1990 and 2015 is very scarce, with only 10 articles published during that period. From 2016 onward, the literature on the topic became regular and grew sharply, totaling 112, 131, and 239 articles in 2021, 2022, and 2023, respectively (Fig. 1). By the end of July 2024, the total number of articles had already surpassed previous years, with 270 documents recorded.

The sample articles had been cited 16,468 times by August 2024. As detailed in Table 3, articles published in 2011, 2013, and 2018 have, on average, earned the most citations, indicating their importance in guiding subsequent research. However, when considering the number of citable years, the publications from 2018 and 2020 appear to be the most impactful in the sample.

Two journals stand out as the primary sources of the articles in the sample: one specialized in business ethics and the other in societal perspectives of AI. The *Journal of Business Ethics* published 40 articles in the sample, while the journal *AI & Society* published 32. The other journals that most contributed to this field of

Table 2 Main information about the data

Articles (total sample)	896
Early access documents	111
Timespan	1990–2024(July)
Sources	499
Documents	896
Document average age	1.88
Total number of citations	16,468
Average citation per document	18.38
Keywords	1423
Authors	4133
Single-authored docs	150
Co-authors per doc	5.16
Percentage of international co-authorships	44.64

Source: The authors

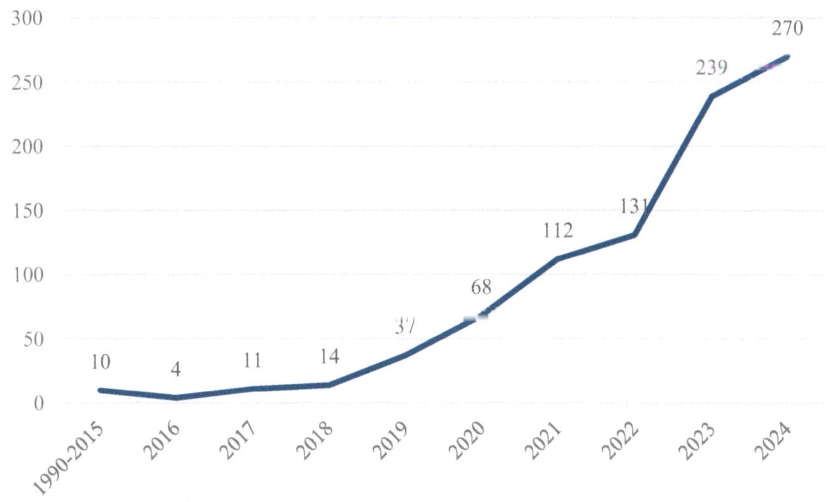

Fig. 1 Annual scientific production. Source: The authors

Table 3 Citations per article and per citable years

Year	Mean times cited per article	Number of articles	Mean times cited per article and year	Citable years
1990	1	1	0.03	35
1992	4	1	0.12	33
1996	24	1	0.83	29
1997	25	1	0.89	28
2005	9	1	0.45	20
2011	110.33	3	7.88	14
2013	115	1	9.58	12
2015	19	1	1.9	10
2016	9.25	4	1.03	9
2017	13.09	11	1.64	8
2018	99.36	14	14.19	7
2019	54.22	37	9.04	6
2020	54.32	68	10.86	5
2021	30.11	112	7.53	4
2022	16.63	131	5.54	3
2023	11.77	239	5.88	2
2024	1.13	270	1.13	1

Source: The authors

research are listed on the left side of Table 4. Among the 4133 researchers who authored these articles, G. Pennycook and D. G. Rand were the most prolific, with 17 and 14 articles on the topic, respectively, all published between 2019 and 2023. These authors also had the highest contribution in terms of fractionalized articles, as

Table 4 Most relevant sources, authors, and affiliations

Sources	Articles	Authors	Articles	Fractio-nalized	Affiliation	Articles
Journal of Business Ethics	40	Pennycook G	17	4.80	Univ Oxford	42
AI & Society	32	Rand DG	14	4.56	Univ Regina	40
Sustainability	20	Raman R	10	2.46	Nat Univ Singapore	28
Information Systems Frontiers	18	Wirtz J	8	1.52	Univ Queensland	23
Technological Forecasting and Social Change	12	Gupta S	6	1.45	Dept Brain And Cognit Sci	21
Journal of Business Research	11	Floridi L	6	0.87	Macquarie Univ	21
Journal of Information Communication and Ethics in Society	8	Mosleh M	5	1.26	Sloan Sch Management	21
Annals of Operations Research	7	Zhang J	5	1.08	Amrita Sch Business	20
Communications of the Association for Information Systems	7	David G	5	1.00	Swansea Univ	20
Ethics and Information Technology	7	Wang Y	5	0.86	Asia Univ	19
Frontiers in Artificial Intelligence	7	Nedungadi P	5	0.73	Tech Univ Munich	18
International Journal of Human-Computer Interaction	7	Dwivedi YK	5	0.48	Univ Coll Dublin	18
Kybernetes	7	Esmaeilzadeh P	4	2.83	Univ Southern Calif	18
Business and Professional Communication Quarterly	6	Kim Tw	4	1.67	Keio Univ	17
Business Ethics, the Environment and Responsibility	6	Cheffou AI	4	1.33	Univ Toronto	17
Business Horizons	6	Jawadi F	4	1.33	Univ Wisconsin	17
Electronics	6	Jawadi N	4	1.33	Univ Auckland	16
Frontiers in Psychology	6	Mirbabaie M	4	1.25	Univ Navarra	16
Journal of Medical Internet Research	6	Mantymaki M	4	1.06	Wuhan Univ	16

(continued)

Table 4 (continued)

Sources	Articles	Authors	Articles	Fractio-nalized	Affiliation	Articles
Service Industries Journal	6	Lutz C	4	1.03	Bucharest Univ Econ Stud	15
Technovation	6	Tamo-Larrieux A	4	1.03	Univ Craiova	15

Source: The authors

shown in the central part of Table 4. The third author with the highest number of articles is R. Raman, with 10 publications, seven of which were published in 2024. In terms of the corresponding author's affiliation, the institutions with the highest contributions to the topic are the University of Oxford (United Kingdom) and the University of Regina (Canada), followed by the National University of Singapore (Singapore) and the University of Queensland (Australia). Full details on the primary affiliations are presented on the right side of Table 4.

Despite the list of most productive universities, research on AI and business ethics is predominantly conducted by researchers in the United States, with more than 20% of the publications having a corresponding author from the United States (Table 5). These publications are primarily single-country studies. In contrast, countries such as Canada, France, the Netherlands, Italy, Austria, and Norway have mainly been involved in multiple country publications.

Consequently, the United States is also the country with the highest number of citations. However, considering the average number of citations per article, Singapore has the most impactful articles, followed by the Netherlands and Canada (Table 6). Conversely, of the countries that have published more than 200 articles on the topic, China has the lowest average article citation, followed by Spain.

After this overview, Table 7 presents the most impactful articles in the sample, with more than 200 citations each. The most cited articles include one of the oldest contributions in the field by Sadri (2011), with 236 citations in total, which explores the ethical challenges and social implications of ambient intelligence (AmI), data management, and AI. At the same time, the author alerts us to the fact that the applications of AmI (e.g., in businesses, at home, in tourism, etc.) are not exhaustive; this article has provided relevant and broad contributions that have guided part of the studies on the ethical implications of AI. Among the other most cited articles on AI/business ethics, some are dedicated to specific business applications of AI, such as service robots (Lu et al., 2020; Wirtz et al., 2018), human resources management (Tambe et al., 2019), and marketing (Davenport et al., 2020; Dwivedi et al., 2021). Other highly cited articles explore the implications of specific AI technologies, particularly algorithms (Martin, 2019) and generative AI (Dwivedi et al., 2023). Finally, the highly cited articles also explore ethical and societal issues that arise from AI technology, such as fake news (Bago et al., 2020) and misinformation (Pennycook et al., 2021; Pennycook & Rand, 2019).

Table 5 Country of the corresponding author

Country	Articles	Articles %	Single country publications	Multiple country publications
USA	182	20.31	123	59
United Kingdom	87	9.71	45	42
China	60	6.70	37	23
Australia	53	5.92	28	25
Germany	39	4.35	21	18
India	33	3.68	20	13
Spain	31	3.46	21	10
Canada	30	3.35	10	20
France	30	3.35	10	20
Netherlands	21	2.34	5	16
Finland	20	2.23	13	7
Ireland	19	2.12	8	11
Italy	18	2.01	5	13
Romania	18	2.01	15	3
Malaysia	15	1.67	7	8
Saudi Arabia	15	1.67	8	7
Austria	14	1.56	4	10
Switzerland	14	1.56	9	5
Poland	12	1.34	8	4
South Africa	12	1.34	7	5
Norway	10	1.12	2	8

Source: The authors

Accordingly, the most relevant keywords chosen by the articles in the sample include several related to AI and related technologies (e.g., artificial intelligence, big data, algorithms, robots, automation), business ethics (e.g., business ethics, governance, risk, corporate social responsibility), human behavior (e.g., engagement, trust, acceptance, attitudes, experience), business strategy (e.g., management, performance, innovation), and impacts (e.g., impact, challenges, future, prediction). They include several stakeholders, roles, and contexts (e.g., government, consumers, work, health, science). The keywords with at least ten occurrences in the sample are listed in Table 8.

Thematic Analysis

The co-occurrence of these keywords enabled the identification of three main clusters, represented in Fig. 2.

The complete list of keywords per cluster is presented in Table 9.

Table 6 Country of the corresponding author

Country	Times cited	Average article citations
USA	3720	20.4
United Kingdom	1805	20.7
Canada	1389	46.3
Netherlands	1263	60.1
Singapore	1065	177.5
Australia	926	17.5
Finland	800	40.0
France	682	22.7
Germany	537	13.8
Malaysia	420	28.0
Norway	347	34.7
Poland	288	24.0
China	282	4.7
Austria	264	18.9
Ireland	227	11.9
Romania	217	12.1
Spain	215	6.9
Italy	208	11.6
Portugal	208	26.0

Source: The authors

Three clusters were found. Cluster 1—AI technology impacts and integration; Cluster 2—AI governance challenges; and Cluster 3—corporate social responsibility and human-centered AI. Cluster 1, AI business integration, highlights AI core concepts and their business integration, including ethical considerations, business impacts, and integration models and systems. The introduction of AI in businesses has changed how firms operate (Clarke, 2019) and how they can benefit from and implement it more effectively daily (Kumar et al., 2024). This means firm managers must be aware of integrating and balancing AI with their practices and traditions for a more successful transformation (Tuncalp, 2024). Kumar et al. (2024) proposed six themes where AI can generate transformative effects: AI-driven customer insights, measuring marketing performance, automated marketing strategies, ethical implications, enhancing customer experiences, and growth opportunities with AI Implementation. Such an approach is extensive to other studies examining AI, along with big data (Zhang et al., 2023a, b), accounting (Tóth et al., 2022; Varzaru, 2022; Zhang et al., 2023a, b), or business automation (Wright & Schultz, 2018). For example, Tuncalp (2024) employed a qualitative study with family-owned Turkish enterprises to understand how adopting AI technologies was perceived and if it conflicted with the family legacy. He found that organizations' stakeholders saw AI as an essential tool (strategically and operationally). However, several constraints, e.g., lack of resources and poor digital literacy, raised concerns about maintaining Turkish families' legacies.

Table 7 Most cited articles

Author (Year)	Title	Source	Total citations	Total citations per year
Wirtz et al. (2018)	Brave new world: Service robots in the frontline	*Journal of Service Management*	908	129.7
Dwivedi et al. (2023)	"So what if ChatGPT wrote it?" Multidisciplinary perspectives on opportunities, challenges and implications of generative conversational AI for research, practice and policy	*International Journal of Information Management*	650	325.0
Davenport et al. (2020)	How artificial intelligence will change the future of marketing	*Journal of the Academy of Marketing Science*	610	122.0
Dwivedi et al. (2021)	Setting the future of digital and social media marketing research: Perspectives and research propositions	*International Journal of Information Management*	563	140.8
Pennycook et al. (2021)	Shifting attention to accuracy can reduce misinformation online	*Nature*	375	93.8
Pennycook and Rand (2019)	Fighting misinformation on social media using crowdsourced judgments of news source quality	*Proceedings of the National Academy of Sciences of the United States of America*	332	55.3
Tambe et al. (2019)	Artificial intelligence in human resources management: Challenges and a path forward	*California Management Review*	298	49.7
Bago et al. (2020)	Fake news, fast and slow: Deliberation reduces belief in false (but not true) news headlines	*Journal of Experimental Psychology*	253	50.6
Lu et al. (2020)	Service robots, customers and service employees: What can we learn from the academic literature and where are the gaps?	*Journal of Service Theory and Practice*	252	50.4
Sadri (2011)	Ambient intelligence: A survey	*ACM Computing Surveys*	236	16.9
Martin (2019)	Ethical implications and accountability of algorithms	*Journal of Business Ethics*	201	33.5

Source: The authors

Cluster 2, AI governance challenges, explores broader challenges and governance issues associated with AI, including privacy concerns, data management, and application contexts such as social media, robots, and health. Regarding privacy, studies (e.g., Bontridder & Poullet, 2021; Kumar et al., 2024) addressed the potential threat of AI to customers' privacy and organizations' security. They also examined AI misuse in the form of misinformation or biased information at the need for regulation (Méndez-Suárez et al., 2023). In data management, several questions

Table 8 Most relevant keywords

Words	#	Words	#	Words	#
artificial intelligence	132	adoption	26	information-technology	13
technology	72	acceptance	25	opportunities	13
impact	64	privacy	24	consumers	12
ethics	59	perceptions	22	corporate social responsibility	12
management	57	design	21	information-systems	12
challenges	50	Internet	21	care	11
future	47	knowledge	20	decision	11
model	46	models	20	engagement	11
decision-making	42	robots	20	power	11
AI	41	bias	18	principles	11
big data	40	governance	17	risk	11
performance	37	health	17	user acceptance	11
Trust	36	attitudes	16	anthropomorphism	10
framework	35	people	16	business ethics	10
information	32	work	16	communication	10
behavior	30	social media	15	experience	10
science	30	automation	14	government	10
business	28	perspective	14	intelligence	10
innovation	28	prediction	14	organization	10
systems	28	algorithms	13		

Source: The authors

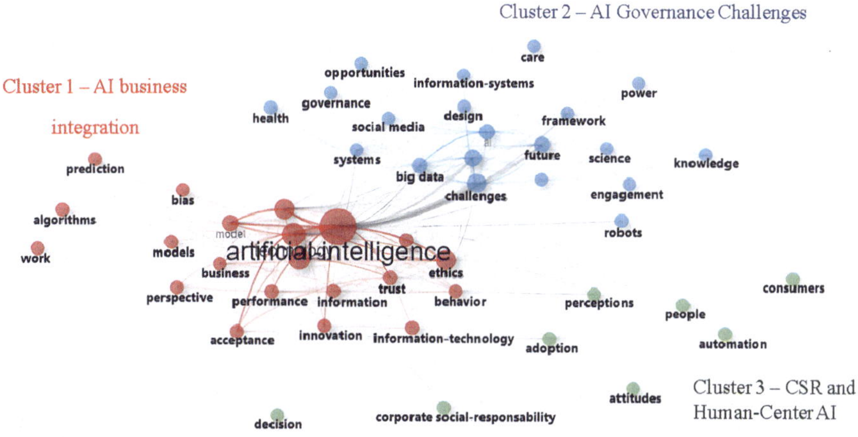

Fig. 2 Clusters. Source: The authors

were raised about AI (Koniakou, 2023). Some studies addressed the AI's capacity to collect, analyze, and use personal data without the customer's consent (Campbell et al., 2020) or even how AI can be responsibly used for increasing or attaining service excellence (Alkire et al., 2024) by optimizing workflows and allocate

Table 9 Co-occurrence clusters of the most relevant keywords

Cluster 1: AI technology impacts and integration	Artificial intelligence, technology, impact, ethics, management, model, performance, trust, information, behavior, business, innovation, acceptance, Internet, models, bias, work, perspective, prediction, algorithms, information-technology
Cluster 2: AI governance challenges	Challenges, future, decision-making, AI, big data, framework, science, systems, privacy, design, knowledge, robots, governance, health, social media, opportunities, information systems, care, engagement, power
Cluster 3: Corporate social responsibility and human-centered AI	Adoption, perceptions, attitudes, people, automation, consumers, corporate social responsibility, decision

resources more effectively to reduce bottlenecks in services (Zebec & Stemberger, 2024). The potential of AI for services and marketing purposes is extensive, varying from AI use for sales, before or during customer interactions, to suggesting optimal opportunities and promotions (Campbell et al., 2020), product innovation (Cooper, 2024), or even leading to a darker side of its use (Labrecque et al., 2024). AI use in social media, robots, or health care also has the potential to amplify ethical concerns regarding misinformation, transparency, or safeguarding sensitive information of customers (e.g., Kumar et al., 2024).

Cluster 3, corporate social responsibility and human-centered AI, focuses on aspects related to human interaction, particularly perceptions, attitudes, and consumers' adoption, namely associated with automation and corporate social responsibility. The advancement of AI and various fields related to data management, analytics, and machine learning, among others, has called for responsible monitoring of its impacts and automation on consumers (Dogan et al., 2024; Sutton et al., 2018; Wright & Schultz, 2018) and industry (e.g., tourism and hospitality) (Dogan et al., 2024). As such, several studies looked into the intersection of consumers and corporate responsibility, in some cases in the form of CSR or other forms of CDR (Fioravante, 2024; Krkac, 2019; Schwarz, 2020; Weber-Lewerenz, 2021). In addition, AI adoption by organizations requires accountability. It suggested (e.g., Fioravante, 2024) ways to reduce tensions between social and financial goals, integrate and align with CSR principles, and gain consumers' trust and potentially brand loyalty throughout the distinct communication platforms (Murár et al., 2024).

Next, the thematic map enabled the identification of three motor themes in this field of research: artificial intelligence technology impact (i.e., Cluster 1—AI business integration), consumer trust, behavior, adoption (i.e., Cluster 2—AI governance challenges), and strategic management aspects related to work, corporate social responsibility, and risk (i.e., Cluster 3—corporate social responsibility and human-centered AI). This analysis also suggests three emerging themes: chatGPT, society, science, decision, and cognitive reflection perspectives. To some extent, these themes reinforce the potential of combining AI processes with human knowledge to shape products, services, and experience innovations without neglecting society, i.e., societal impacts. Moreover, no niche (low relevance and high development) or essential (low development and high relevance) themes were identified (Fig. 3).

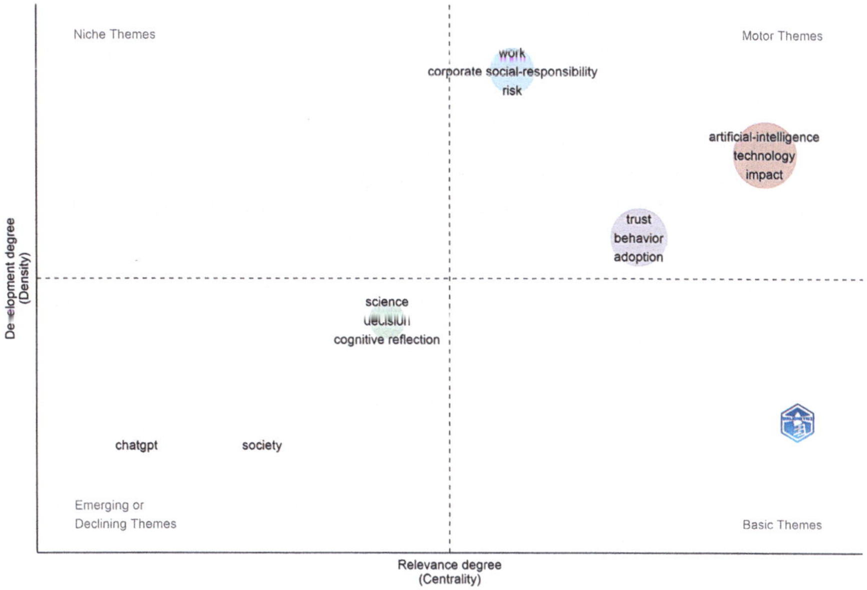

Fig. 3 Thematic map. Source: The authors

Discussion

Our descriptive results evidence an extensive number of publications since 1990, highlighting the relevance of this field of research over the past decades. In addition, as articles on AI and Ethics are published, so does the number of journals with interest in this field. Our findings reflect this reality since approximately 500 journals published articles on this topic, reflecting (a) the interdisciplinary nature of the concept and (b) the importance of the challenges such concepts bring to organizations and consumers.

We also found that earned citations among the sample collected were more impactful than those published between the 2010s and 2020s and from authors based in Singapore. In a similar sense, G. Pennycook and D. G. Rand were found to be the most prolific authors. This highlights the impact of the existing theories and empirical framework and shows that the topics are dynamic and diversified since they incorporate studies made by distinct authors in different parts of the world, i.e., Europe (e.g., United Kingdom), North America (e.g., Canada), Asia (e.g., Singapore), and Oceania (e.g., Australia).

It was also found that some journals' scope is on AI and Ethics, such as the *Journal of Business Ethics* and *AI & Society*. This shows that there are journals in the field leading the dissemination of knowledge and, consequently, verifying and scrutinizing the real-world impact of AI on business practices and contexts. Our results highlight that most authors prefer a collaborative approach in this area since the vast majority of papers are co-authored by multiple researchers. This may be explained by the complexity of the concept, incorporating many distinct research areas, but also the global nature and implications of AI for research, practice, and policy.

The keywords examined showed that the primary research focuses on AI, technology, and its impacts. Ethics and business ethics, although important, do not seem to attract much attention among scholars. This may highlight the aim of organizations in first developing the technology and only after concerning themselves with its ethical implications (Bankins & Formosa, 2023; Böhm et al., 2022; Ferretti, 2022; Munoko et al., 2020). Ferretti (2022) posited that self-regulation (by organizations) has its limits, and a legitimate democratic process needs to be considered, including complex regulations by governments to ensure ethical standards for AI development. On the other hand, he has a different stance since he posits that it is not up to organizations and governments to ensure AI technology is well developed and appropriately used; it is for the citizens.

Thus, it is posited as a future research proposition (RP) that:

RP1: AI technology requires regulation and constant evaluation of its ethical standards by organizations to ensure responsible use.

AI requires regulation and ongoing scrutiny by organizations to ensure adherence to ethical standards. Continuous monitoring is essential to maintain accountability and address potential ethical challenges while applying AI technologies. Kaplan and Haenlein (2019, p. 15) argue that AI's "ability to interpret external data correctly, to learn from such data, and to use those learnings to achieve specific goals and tasks through flexible adaptation" stresses the need for its regulation and ethical standards. Fioravante (2024) notes that organizations face constant ethical dilemmas regarding trade-offs between economic return and consumers' and stakeholders' well-being.

In the cluster and thematic analysis, our findings demonstrated in Cluster 1, AI business integration, that the rapidly evolving nature of AI, due to the technological advancements and implementation across various business industries, confirms businesses must be aware of AI complexity, but also, that they need to constantly innovate and adapt to the ethical concerns resulting from the technology and its processes. This finding highlights the need for organizations to invest in a high level of human and financial capital. This also requires organizations to manage these AI's transformative effects. For example, Kumar et al. (2024) claim that AI's effects on marketing are limited. Another example, resulting from Tuncalp's (2024) study, stressed that businesses that successfully navigate AI adoption tend to employ tailored strategies that align with their core values, involving key family members in the decision-making process and fostering a culture of innovation. However, his study also highlights the importance of ensuring AI initiatives resonate with the family business ethos. Thus, we argue that:

RP2: AI transformative capabilities involve positive and negative effects on businesses, which require further research regarding its limitations, biases, and implications.

In Cluster 2, AI governance challenges, we found that data management and its applications in various channels and use in products, services, and experiences have the potential to carry several threats, such as collecting, retaining, and analyzing customers and patients' private information or even creating misinformation. Our findings highlight that AI governance challenges balance product, service, and experience innovation and improvement with ethical considerations safeguarding customer data. Koniakou (2023) stated that human rights obligations regarding AI governance should be the responsibility of governments and the private sector. In the context of AstraZeneca, it was found that the road towards AI governance is to guarantee procedural regularity and transparency through new and innovative governance structures (Mökander et al., 2022). Thus, we posit that:

RP3: AI governance structures must balance the pursuit of innovation in products, services, and customer experience(s) with ethical customer data safeguards.

In Cluster 3, corporate social responsibility and human-centered AI, results showed the relevance and boundaries of the intersection between AI, perceptions, and attitudes of consumers towards automation and its consequences in terms of job displacement or termination. Our findings highlight that CSR requires organizations to consider social and environmental impacts, besides economic, in their actions and the development of their AI systems. This means that organizations should be accountable for the lack of effort(s) to mitigate the adverse effects of AI on humans from two perspectives: (a) from the demand perspective—customer and AI interactions during product consumption and experience, (b) from the offer perspective—from AI and job displacement, that is, AI capacity to replace humans in extensive number of tasks, and the easiness to automate systems and processes highlight the need to question what human expertise and experience are needed during the production process. As Sutton et al. (2018, p. 15) demand, scholars should "seek better ways to keep the human-relevant in a broad range of knowledge work fields." Weber-Lewerenz (2021, para. 4) argued in this sense the need for "consideration and protection of values and fundamental rights, the careful demarcation between machine (artificial) and human intelligence and the careful use of such technologies." Thus, we argue that:

RP4: CSR in AI is needed to reduce and mitigate automation's negative social and economic impacts.

Conclusions

This chapter aims to assess the challenges of AI in the business sector from an ethical perspective. Our results demonstrated that AI progress and implementation have been rapid due to the AI transformative technology. However, ethical standards are behind technology development, requiring the adoption of new structures and processes to safeguard it.

We conclude that it is crucial that scholars and organizations' managers continue to be engaged with AI ethical issues to ensure that AI is well implemented and may positively impact organizations, consumers, and society at large. AI, a transformative technology, has shown positive and negative impacts on consumers' attitudes and perceptions and raised questions regarding its negative impacts (e.g., data privacy). Thus, this represents a recurrent ethical dilemma, as organizations must decide on trade-offs between increasing profit due to AI and restraining some of that profit potential to keep up with ethical AI practices (Böhm et al., 2022).

Therefore, how should organizations deal with this dilemma? That is, the dilemma between gaining operational benefits from improved efficiency as opposed to AI potential risks associated with consumers' security and privacy fears. Our findings show that organizations must deal with the consequences of neglecting ethical practices from both the demand and offer sides.

Regarding the former, consumers' positive attitude towards AI and its technology (e.g., robots and facial recognition) is crucial to explore the future potential of service delivery (Dogan et al., 2024), meaning that fears and negative perceptions need to be dealt with. Regarding the latter, it is the most innovative businesses, therefore, that have ethical guidelines implemented, that are the ones more likely to achieve success (Dogan et al., 2024; Weber-Lewerenz, 2021). As research grows in publications, citations, and collaborations, ethical considerations will remain a central topic for AI and the technologies used for its evolution, practices, and business competition and success.

The theoretical implications are that AI and Ethics need more research as technology evolves and human and AI interaction increases. These new challenges extend to human-centered AI, seeking to increase the interaction quality (e.g., more empathy) between both. At the core of these developments are ethical procedures and standards. There are several practical implications to underscore. The AI ethical frameworks are mandatory for organizations and customers, and regular updates are needed to keep up with AI evolution. Managers should be trained to face ethical challenges in AI applications to ensure the organization's competitiveness and customer protection. Organizations must understand that ethical responsibility is not an option, and the failure to promote transparent communication during its usage and interaction with customers will potentially lead to a lack of customer trust and loyalty.

Future research should update the existing theoretical frameworks to incorporate ethical procedures and standards that may help regulate AI technology and its usage by both sides, i.e., the demand and offer sides. Scholars must also investigate the broader implications of AI on businesses, like data management, bias generated, and data privacy throughout the distinct touchpoints, to safeguard fairness and the responsible use of AI. Further studies could also investigate AI's impact on customers' short- and long-term experiences. In this sense, assessing the role of transparency in AI adoption, usage, and consumer trust is needed. Moreover, research on CSR is crucial to mitigate the potential adverse effects of AI on social and economic welfare. Among these, job displacement and job losses are essential.

Acknowledgments This paper is financed by National Funds provided by FCT—Foundation for Science and Technology through project UIDB/04020/2020 with DOI 10.54499/UIDB/04020/2020 and project UIDB/04470/2020 with DOI 10.54499/UIDP/04470/2020.

References

Adigwe, C. S., Olaniyi, O. O., Olabanji, S. O., Okunleye, O. J., Mayeke, N. R., & Ajayi, S. A. (2024). Forecasting the future: The interplay of artificial intelligence, innovation, and competitiveness and its effect on the global economy. *Asian Journal of Economics, Business and Accounting, 24*(4), 126–146.

Alkire, L., Bilgihan, A., Bui, M., Buoye, A. J., Dogan, S., & Kim, S. (2024). RAISE: Leveraging responsible AI for service excellence. *Journal of Service Management, 35*(4), 490–511. https://doi.org/10.1108/josm-11-2023-0448

Bago, B., Rand, D. G., & Pennycook, G. (2020). Fake news, fast and slow: Deliberation reduces belief in false (but not true) news headlines. *Journal of Experimental Psychology-General, 149*(8), 1608–1613. https://doi.org/10.1037/xge0000729

Bai, B. (2024). Corporate social responsibility initiatives in India. In *Futuristic trends in management* (pp. 18–23). Iterative International Publisher, Selfypage Developers Pvt Ltd. https://doi.org/10.58532/V3BFMA16P1CH3

Bankins, S., & Formosa, P. (2023). The ethical implications of artificial intelligence (AI) for meaningful work. *Journal of Business Ethics, 185*(4), 725–740. https://doi.org/10.1007/s10551-023-05339-7

Barbosa, B., Saura, J. R., & Bennett, D. (2024). How do entrepreneurs perform digital marketing across the customer journey? A review and discussion of the main uses. *The Journal of Technology Transfer, 49*(1), 69–103. https://doi.org/10.1007/s10961-022-09978-2

Ben, S. (2020). Bridging the gap between ethics and practice: Guidelines for reliable, safe, and trustworthy human-centered. *ACM Transactions on Interactive Intelligent Systems, 10*(4). https://doi.org/10.1145/3419764

Böhm, S., Carrington, M., Cornelius, N., de Bruin, B., Greenwood, M., Hassan, L., Jain, T., Karam, C., Kourula, A., Romani, L., Riaz, S., & Shaw, D. (2022). Ethics at the centre of global and local challenges: Thoughts on the future of business ethics. *Journal of Business Ethics, 180*(3), 835–861. https://doi.org/10.1007/s10551-022-05239-2

Bontridder, N., & Poullet, Y. (2021). The role of artificial intelligence in disinformation. *Data and Policy, 3*(3). https://doi.org/10.1017/dap.2021.20

Borenstein, J., & Howard, A. (2021). Emerging challenges in AI and the need for AI ethics education. *AI and Ethics, 1*(1), 61–65. https://doi.org/10.1007/s43681-020-00002-7

Campbell, C., Sands, S., Ferraro, C., Tsao, H. Y. (Jody), & Mavrommatis, A. (2020). From data to action: How marketers can leverage AI. *Business Horizons, 63*(2), 227–243. https://doi.org/10.1016/j.bushor.2019.12.002

Cheng, L., & Yu, T. (2019). A new generation of AI: A review and perspective on machine learning technologies applied to smart energy and electric power systems. *International Journal of Energy Research, 43*(6), 1928–1973.

Cooper, H. M. (1988). Organizing knowledge syntheses: A taxonomy of literature reviews. *Knowledge in Society, 1*(1), 104–126. https://doi.org/10.1007/BF03177550

Cooper, R. G. (2024). The AI transformation of product innovation. *Industrial Marketing Management, 119*, 62–74. https://doi.org/10.1016/j.indmarman.2024.03.008

Davenport, T., Guha, A., Grewal, D., & Bressgott, T. (2020). How artificial intelligence will change the future of marketing. *Journal of the Academy of Marketing Science, 48*(1), 24–42. https://doi.org/10.1007/s11747-019-00696-0

deMatos, N. M. da S., Sá, E. S. de, & Duarte, P. A. de O. (2021). A review and extension of the flow experience concept. Insights and directions for Tourism research. *Tourism Management Perspectives, 38*, 100802. https://doi.org/10.1016/j.tmp.2021.100802

Dogan, S., Mistry, T. G., & Nanu, L. (2024). Revolutionizing getaways: Automation and artificial intelligence's transformative journey in tourism and hospitality. *Worldwide Hospitality and Tourism Themes, 16*(2), 248–251. https://doi.org/10.1108/WHATT-03-2024-0075

Dwivedi, Y. K., Ismagilova, E., Hughes, D. L., Carlson, J., Filieri, R., Jacobson, J., Jain, V., Karjaluoto, H., Kefi, H., Krishen, A. S., Kumar, V., Rahman, M. M., Raman, R., Rauschnabel, P. A., Rowley, J., Salo, J., Tran, G. A., & Wang, Y. C. (2021). Setting the future of digital and social media marketing research: Perspectives and research propositions. *International Journal of Information Management, 59*, Article 102168. https://doi.org/10.1016/j.ijinfomgt.2020.102168

Dwivedi, Y. K., Kshetri, N., Hughes, L., Slade, E. L., Jeyaraj, A., Kar, A. K., Baabdullah, A. M., Koohang, A., Raghavan, V., Ahuja, M., Albanna, H., Albashrawi, M. A., Al-Busaidi, A. S., Balakrishnan, J., Barlette, Y., Basu, S., Bose, I., Brooks, L., Buhalis, D., et al. (2023). "So what if ChatGPT wrote it?" Multidisciplinary perspectives on opportunities, challenges and implications of generative conversational AI for research, practice and policy. *International Journal of Information Management, 71*, Article 102642. https://doi.org/10.1016/j.ijinfomgt.2023.102642

Ferretti, T. (2022). An institutionalist approach to AI ethics: Justifying the priority of government regulation over self-regulation. *Moral Philosophy and Politics, 9*(2), 239–265. https://doi.org/10.1515/mopp-2020-0056

Fioravante, R. (2024). Beyond the business case for responsible artificial intelligence: Strategic CSR in light of digital washing and the moral human argument. *Sustainability, 16*(3). https://doi.org/10.3390/su16031232

Firmansyah, E. B., Machado, M. R., & Moreira, J. L. R. (2024). How can Artificial Intelligence (AI) be used to manage Customer Lifetime Value (CLV)—A systematic literature review. *International Journal of Information Management Data Insights, 4*(2), 100279. https://doi.org/10.1016/j.jjimei.2024.100279

Fosso-Wamba, S., Queiroz, M. M., Chiappetta Jabbour, C. J., Shi, C., & (Victor). (2023). Are both generative AI and ChatGPT game changers for 21st-century operations and supply chain excellence? *International Journal of Production Economics, 265*. https://doi.org/10.1016/j.ijpe.2023.109015

Gallagher, S. (2005). A strategic response to Friedman's critique of business ethics. *Journal of Business Strategy, 26*(6), 55–60. https://doi.org/10.1108/02756660510633028

Goodfellow, I., Bengio, Y., & Courville, A. (2016). *Deep Learning*. MIT Press.

Gorwa, R., Binns, R., & Katzenbach, C. (2020). Algorithmic content moderation: Technical and political challenges in the automation of platform governance. *Big Data and Society, 7*(1), 2053951719897945.

Hickman, E., & Petrin, M. (2021). Trustworthy AI and corporate governance: The EU's ethics guidelines for trustworthy artificial intelligence from a company law perspective. *European Business Organization Law Review, 22*(4), 593–625. https://doi.org/10.1007/s40804-021-00224-0

Jiménez-Partearroyo, M., & Medina-López, A. (2024). Leveraging business intelligence systems for enhanced corporate competitiveness: Strategy and evolution. *Systems, 12*(3), 94. https://doi.org/10.3390/systems12030094

Kaplan, A., & Haenlein, M. (2019). Siri, Siri, in my hand: Who's the fairest in the land? On the interpretations, illustrations, and implications of artificial intelligence. *Business Horizons, 62*(1), 15–25. https://doi.org/10.1016/j.bushor.2018.08.004

Koniakou, V. (2023). From the "rush to ethics" to the "race for governance" in artificial intelligence. *Information Systems Frontiers, 25*(1), 71–102. https://doi.org/10.1007/s10796-022-10300-6

Kraus, S., Breier, M., & Dasí-Rodríguez, S. (2020). The art of crafting a systematic literature review in entrepreneurship research. *International Entrepreneurship and Management Journal, 16*(3), 1023–1042. https://doi.org/10.1007/s11365-020-00635-4

Krkac, K. (2019). Corporate social irresponsibility: Humans vs artificial intelligence. *Social Responsibility Journal, 15*(6), 786–802. https://doi.org/10.1108/srj-09-2018-0219

Kumar, R., Wang, W., Kumar, J., Yang, T., Khan, A., Ali, W., & Ali, I. (2021). An integration of blockchain and AI for secure data sharing and detection of CT images for the hospitals. *Computerized Medical Imaging and Graphics, 87*, 101812. https://doi.org/10.1016/j.compmedimag.2020.101812

Kumar, V., Ashraf, A. R., & Nadeem, W. (2024). AI-powered marketing: What, where, and how? *International Journal of Information Management, 77*, 102783. https://doi.org/10.1016/j.ijinfomgt.2024.102783

Kuziemski, M., & Misuraca, G. (2020). AI governance in the public sector: Three tales from the frontiers of automated decision-making in democratic settings. *Telecommunications Policy, 44*(6), 101976. https://doi.org/10.1016/j.telpol.2020.101976

Labrecque, L. I., Peña, P. Y., Leonard, H., & Leger, R. (2024). Not all sunshine and rainbows: Exploring the dark side of AI in interactive marketing. *Journal of Research in Interactive Marketing*. https://doi.org/10.1108/jrim-02-2024-0073

Lavallin, A., & Downs, J. A. (2021). Machine learning in geography–Past, present, and future. *Geography Compass, 15*(5), e12563.

LeCun, Y., Bengio, Y., & Hinton, G. (2015). Deep learning. *Nature, 521*(7553), 436–444.

Linnenluecke, M. K., Marrone, M., & Singh, A. K. (2020). Conducting systematic literature reviews and bibliometric analyses. *Australian Journal of Management, 45*(2), 175–194. https://doi.org/10.1177/0312896219877678

Lu, V. N., Wirtz, J., Kunz, W. H., Paluch, S., Gruber, T., Martins, A., & Patterson, P. G. (2020). Service robots, customers and service employees: What can we learn from the academic literature and where are the gaps? *Journal of Service Theory and Practice, 30*(3), 361–391. https://doi.org/10.1108/jstp-04-2019-0088

Martin, K. (2019). Ethical implications and accountability of algorithms. *Journal of Business Ethics, 160*(4), 835–850. https://doi.org/10.1007/s10551-018-3921-3

Méndez-Suárez, M., Simón-Moya, V., & Muñoz-de Prat, J. (2023). Do current regulations prevent unethical AI practices? *Journal of Competitiveness, 15*(3), 207–222. https://doi.org/10.7441/joc.2023.03.11

Mökander, J., Sheth, M., Gersbro-Sundler, M., Blomgren, P., & Floridi, L. (2022). Challenges and best practices in corporate AI governance: Lessons from the biopharmaceutical industry. *Frontiers in Computer Science, 4*. https://doi.org/10.3389/fcomp.2022.1068361

Morosan, C., & Dursun-Cengizci, A. (2024). Letting AI make decisions for me: An empirical examination of hotel guests' acceptance of technology agency. *International Journal of Contemporary Hospitality Management, 36*(3), 946–974.

Munoko, I., Brown-Liburd, H. L., & Vasarhelyi, M. (2020). The ethical implications of using artificial intelligence in auditing. *Journal of Business Ethics, 167*(2), 209–234. https://doi.org/10.1007/s10551-019-04407-1

Murár, P., Kubovics, M., & Jurisová, V. (2024). The impact of brand-voice integration and artificial intelligence on social media marketing. *Communication Today, 15*(1), 50–63.

Nilsson, N. J. (2009). *The quest for artificial intelligence*. Cambridge University Press. https://doi.org/10.1017/CBO9780511819346

Obrenovic, B., Gu, X., Wang, G. Y., Godinic, D., & Jakhongirov, I. (2024). Generative AI and human-robot interaction: Implications and future agenda for business, society and ethics. *Ai and Society*. https://doi.org/10.1007/s00146-024-01889-0

Okoli, C. (2015). A guide to conducting a standalone systematic literature review. *Communications of the Association for Information Systems, 37*(1), 879–910. https://doi.org/10.17705/1CAIS.03743

Pennycook, G., & Rand, D. G. (2019). Fighting misinformation on social media using crowdsourced judgments of news source quality. *Proceedings of the National Academy of Sciences of the United States of America, 116*(7), 2521–2526. https://doi.org/10.1073/pnas.1806781116

Pennycook, G., Epstein, Z., Mosleh, M., Arechar, A. A., Eckles, D., & Rand, D. G. (2021). Shifting attention to accuracy can reduce misinformation online. *Nature, 592*(7855), 590. https://doi.org/10.1038/s41586-021-03344-2

Ribeiro-Navarrete, B., Saura, J. R., & Simón-Moya, V. (2024). Setting the development of digitalization: State-of-the-art and potential for future research in cooperatives. *Review of Managerial Science, 18*(5), 1459–1488. https://doi.org/10.1007/s11846-023-00663-8

Ruggeri, G., Orsi, L., & Corsi, S. (2019). A bibliometric analysis of the scientific literature on Fairtrade labelling. *International Journal of Consumer Studies, 43*(2), 134–152. https://doi.org/10.1111/ijcs.12492

Sadri, F. (2011). Ambient intelligence: A survey. *ACM Computing Surveys, 43*(4), Article 36. https://doi.org/10.1145/1978802.1978815

Sandström, B., Willman, A., Svensson, B., & Borglin, G. (2015). Perceptions of national guidelines and their (non) implementation in mental healthcare: A deductive and inductive content analysis. *Implementation Science, 10*(1), 43. https://doi.org/10.1186/s13012-015-0234-0

Saura, J. R., Palacios-Marqués, D., & Iturricha-Fernández, A. (2021). Ethical design in social media: Assessing the main performance measurements of user online behavior modification. *Journal of Business Research, 129*, 271–281. https://doi.org/10.1016/j.jbusres.2021.03.001

Saura, J. R., Škare, V., & Dosen, D. O. (2024). Is AI-based digital marketing ethical? Assessing a new data privacy paradox. *Journal of Innovation and Knowledge, 9*(4), 100597. https://doi.org/10.1016/j.jik.2024.100597

Schwarz, E. C. (2020). Human vs. machine: A framework of responsibilities and duties of transnational corporations for respecting human rights in the use of artificial intelligence. *Columbia Journal of Transnational Law, 58*(1), 232–277.

Shu, F., Quan, W., Chen, B., Qiu, J., Sugimoto, C. R., & Larivière, V. (2020). The role of Web of Science publications in China's tenure system. *Scientometrics, 122*(3), 1683–1695. https://doi.org/10.1007/s11192-019-03339-x

Smith, M., & Miller, S. (2023). Technology, institutions and regulation: Towards a normative theory. *AI and Society*, 1–11.

Stahl, B. C. (2021). Concepts of ethics and their application to AI. In *Artificial intelligence for a better future* (pp. 19–33). Springer. https://doi.org/10.1007/978-3-030-69978-9_3

Sutton, S. G., Arnold, V., & Holt, M. (2018). How much automation is too much? Keeping the human relevant in knowledge work. *Journal of Emerging Technologies in Accounting, 15*(2), 15–25. https://doi.org/10.2308/jeta-52311

Tambe, P., Cappelli, P., & Yakubovich, V. (2019). Artificial intelligence in human resources management: Challenges and a path forward. *California Management Review, 61*(4), 15–42., Article 0008125619867910. https://doi.org/10.1177/0008125619867910

Tóth, Z., Caruana, R., Gruber, T., & Loebbecke, C. (2022). The dawn of the AI robots: Towards a new framework of AI robot accountability. *Journal of Business Ethics, 178*(4), 895–916. https://doi.org/10.1007/s10551-022-05050-z

Tuncalp, D. (2024). Directing the future: Artificial intelligence integration in family businesses. *Journal of Family Business Management*. https://doi.org/10.1108/jfbm-03-2024-0051

Turing, A. M. (2009). Computing machinery and intelligence. In R. Epstein, G. Roberts, & G. Beber (Eds.), *Parsing the Turing test* (pp. 23–65). Springer. https://doi.org/10.1007/978-1-4020-6710-5_3

Varzaru, A. A. (2022). Assessing the impact of AI solutions' ethical issues on performance in managerial accounting. *Electronics, 11*(14). https://doi.org/10.3390/electronics11142221

Wattanacharoensil, W., & La-ornual, D. (2019). A systematic review of cognitive biases in tourist decisions. *Tourism Management, 75*, 353–369. https://doi.org/10.1016/j.tourman.2019.06.006

Weber-Lewerenz, B. (2021). Corporate digital responsibility (CDR) in construction engineering—ethical guidelines for the application of digital transformation and artificial intelligence (AI) in user practice. *SN Applied Sciences, 3*(10). https://doi.org/10.1007/s42452-021-04776-1

Wirtz, J., Patterson, P. G., Kunz, W. H., Gruber, T., Lu, V. N., Paluch, S., & Martins, A. (2018). Brave new world: Service robots in the frontline. *Journal of Service Management, 29*(5), 907–931. https://doi.org/10.1108/josm-04-2018-0119

Wright, S. A., & Schultz, A. E. (2018). The rising tide of artificial intelligence and business automation: Developing an ethical framework. *Business Horizons, 61*(6), 823–832. https://doi.org/10.1016/j.bushor.2018.07.001

Yeung, K. (2020). Recommendation of the council on artificial intelligence (OECD). *International Legal Materials, 59*(1), 27–34. https://doi.org/10.1017/ilm.2020.5

Zebec, A., & Stemberger, M. I. (2024). Creating AI business value through BPM capabilities. *Business Process Management Journal, 30*(8), 1–26. https://doi.org/10.1108/bpmj-07-2023-0566

Zhang, Y., Ramanathan, L., & Maheswari, M. (2023a). A hybrid approach for risk analysis in e-business integrating big data analytics and artificial intelligence. *Annals of Operations Research, 326*(Suppl 1), 99. https://doi.org/10.1007/s10479-021-04412-6

Zhang, C., Zhu, W. D., Dai, J., Wu, Y., & Chen, X. L. (2023b). Ethical impact of artificial intelligence in managerial accounting. *International Journal of Accounting Information Systems, 49*. https://doi.org/10.1016/j.accinf.2023.100619

The Triple Axis of AI, Ethics, and Business Economics

Ana Medina-López

Introduction

Artificial Intelligence (AI) has emerged as a foundational element in modern business processes, revolutionizing decision-making and operational efficiency. However, as organizations increasingly adopt AI technologies, they face complex ethical and economic challenges that require structured and methodical solutions. The intersection of AI, ethics, and business economics is not merely a technological issue but a central concern for sustainable corporate practices. This chapter introduces the "Triple Axis" model, a novel conceptual framework that uses a Cartesian space to map and analyze the interconnections between these three dimensions. This approach provides organizations with a tool to navigate the intricate balance between technological innovation, ethical responsibility, and economic objectives.

AI's role in business has evolved rapidly, moving beyond basic automation to systems capable of autonomous decision-making. Historically, the focus was on maximizing profits and efficiency, but the broader ethical and societal implications of AI systems have become increasingly evident. Machines programmed to optimize outcomes operate without intrinsic moral awareness, often exacerbating biases and ethical dilemmas. For instance, opaque decision-making processes in AI systems have led to ethical concerns in high-stakes domains such as hiring and financial services, where algorithmic biases can perpetuate systemic inequalities.

Today's ethical challenges in AI include issues of transparency, accountability, and fairness. High-profile cases, such as the misuse of personal data for political purposes, highlight the risks of unethical AI practices. While technological neutrality is often assumed, AI's design, development, and deployment are deeply

A. Medina-López (✉)
Rey Juan Carlos University, Madrid, Spain
e-mail: ana.medina@urjc.es

J. R. Saura (ed.), *Global Perspectives on AI, Ethics, and Business Economics*, Contributions to Management Science,
https://doi.org/10.1007/978-3-031-88781-9_3

intertwined with ethical considerations, making it imperative for organizations to adopt robust frameworks that prioritize responsible innovation. Without clear ethical guidelines, AI risks becoming a tool for harm, undermining public trust and organizational integrity.

The broader debate between shareholder primacy and stakeholder theory underscores the necessity of an integrative approach that addresses both economic and ethical dimensions. Building on philosophical principles such as deontology, utilitarianism, and virtue ethics, this chapter explores how ethical theories can inform the responsible application of AI in business contexts. It introduces the Triple Axis model as a structured framework to synthesize and contextualize the dynamic interplay between AI, ethics, and economics.

In response to these challenges, this chapter seeks to address the following key research questions:

R1: How can the Triple Axis framework assist organizations in embedding ethical principles into AI systems while ensuring economic sustainability?
R2: What are the main ethical risks associated with AI in business, and how can these be visualized and mitigated through the proposed framework?
R3: How does the convergence of AI, ethics, and business economics influence corporate strategy and decision-making?

The Triple Axis model contributes to the growing discourse on AI ethics by offering a practical tool for aligning ethical imperatives with economic goals. By incorporating philosophical insights into a visual framework, it enables organizations to map the potential impacts of AI decisions across ethical and economic domains. This structured approach facilitates a deeper understanding of AI's ethical risks and promotes the responsible adoption of technology that aligns with organizational values and societal expectations.

The chapter is organized as follows: section "Theoretical Framework for The Convergence of Ethics, AI and Business Economics" explores the theoretical framework for the convergence of ethics, AI, and business economics, emphasizing the integration of ethical principles within AI-driven business strategies. Section "Methodology" outlines the methodology employed in developing the Triple Axis model, detailing the research design and analytical approaches. Section "Development of the "Triple Axis" Model" focuses on the development of the Triple Axis model, explaining its components and their interrelations. Section "Visualization and Scenario Mapping: A Proposal for Managing the Triple Axis of AI, Ethics, and Business Economics" proposes visualization and scenario mapping techniques for managing the Triple Axis of AI, ethics, and business economics, providing practical tools for implementation. Section "Discussion" engages in a discussion of the findings, examining their implications for theory and practice. Section "Conclusions" concludes the chapter with a summary of key insights and recommendations for future research. Finally, section "Theoretical and Practical Implications" addresses the theoretical and practical implications of the study, highlighting its contributions to the fields of AI, ethics, and business economics.

Theoretical Framework for the Convergence of Ethics, AI, and Business Economics

Definition and Evolution of AI in the Business Context

AI is a branch of computer science that aims to create machines capable of performing tasks typically requiring human intelligence (Leake, 2001). AI systems simulate cognitive abilities such as logical reasoning, learning, and problem-solving (Nagendraswamy & Salis, 2021). The field encompasses various approaches, from modeling expert performance to studying commonsense processes and developing autonomous agents (Leake, 2001). AI can be categorized based on cognitive capacity (weak/limited, general, or superlative) and autonomy (reactive, deliberative, cognitive, or fully autonomous) (Morandín-Ahuerma, 2022).

In recent decades, AI has progressed from simple rule-based systems and automation to sophisticated neural networks and deep learning algorithms that enhance their capabilities as they process more data. Modern AI enables machines to learn and solve problems independently, moving beyond explicitly programmed rules (Deng, 2018). Deep learning, a subset of machine learning, has emerged as a transformative technique, revolutionizing fields such as healthcare, finance, and autonomous navigation (Klinger et al., 2020). The evolution of AI includes significant milestones such as early perceptrons, expert systems, and optimization techniques, culminating in today's advanced deep learning networks (Lanzetta, 2018). These new methods, including deep learning and reinforcement learning, have outperformed traditional AI approaches in pattern recognition and decision-making tasks (Dwivedi et al., 2023). However, this technology also presents ethical and legal challenges, with potential positive and negative impacts on organizations, society, and individuals. The evolution of AI poses new challenges, particularly in terms of ethical and social responsibility. Companies must balance the benefits of AI with the risks associated with its implementation, such as job loss, algorithmic discrimination, or invasion of privacy.

The evolution of AI in business has transformed decision-making and operational efficiency, but its rapid integration also introduces ethical, legal, and practical challenges that organizations must manage to balance its benefits and risks.

Ethics in Business Decision-Making: Main Philosophical Currents

Business decision-making is inherently linked to ethical considerations, as companies operate within social and legal frameworks that define acceptable conduct. Over time, several philosophical currents have shaped business ethics, with significant contributions from deontological ethics, utilitarianism, and virtue ethics.

Deontological ethics, primarily associated with Immanuel Kant, asserts that actions should be evaluated based on their adherence to universal principles and rules, irrespective of their outcomes. This approach emphasizes rights, norms, and dignity, guiding individual choices (Staveren, 2007; Jackson, 2019). In the business context, this perspective suggests that companies should uphold clear moral principles, such as transparency and respect for human rights, regardless of financial implications.

Utilitarianism, proposed by Bentham and Mill, focuses on maximizing utility and making decisions based on outcomes (Jackson, 2019). In practice, this means that business decisions should aim to achieve the greatest benefit for the largest number of people, often translating into maximizing shareholder value or customer satisfaction.

Virtue ethics, rooted in Aristotelian philosophy, highlights the interconnectedness of agents and shared values beyond societal rules (Staveren, 2007). This approach in business emphasizes the development of leaders and organizations that act with integrity, honesty, and justice, fostering entrepreneurial virtues that extend beyond mere legal compliance.

While these approaches share common elements (Jackson, 2019), virtue ethics is often seen as particularly beneficial in addressing contemporary challenges, especially in the context of the Anthropocene and business ethics. It focuses on agents rather than actions, distinguishes between laws/customs and nature, and underscores the importance of tradition (Morrell & Dahlmann, 2022).

These philosophical currents offer frameworks for evaluating business decisions from an ethical standpoint, but their practical application can be complex, particularly with the advent of technologies like AI. For instance, should a company prioritize profit optimization through automation (utilitarianism) or the well-being of its employees (virtue ethics)? Balancing regulatory compliance with fairness and equity remains a critical challenge.

Business Economics and Its Relationship with Ethics: Relevant Economic Theories

The relationship between ethics and business economics has been a topic of intense debate among economists and management theorists. Two contrasting positions on this issue are those of Milton Friedman and Amartya Sen.

Milton Friedman argued that "the social responsibility of the company is to maximize its profits," provided it adheres to basic legal and ethical standards. According to Friedman, companies should focus solely on generating returns for their shareholders, without being distracted by social or ethical goals. From this perspective, ethics is limited to legal compliance and is not considered a central factor in business decision-making (Friedman, 2007).

Amartya Sen, in contrast, has emphasized that companies cannot ignore the ethical implications of their actions. Sen argues that justice, equity, and social welfare must be integral to economic decision-making. Profit maximization, according to Sen, cannot be the sole criterion, as companies have responsibilities towards society, workers, and other stakeholders (Sen, 1993).

These positions create a dilemma for companies adopting disruptive technologies such as AI. Should they adhere to a purely utilitarian logic of profit maximization, as Friedman suggested, or consider the ethical and social impact of their actions, as Sen proposed? This debate becomes increasingly relevant as AI begins to affect sensitive areas such as user privacy, employment, and equity.

The Ethics of AI: Challenges and Opportunities

AI ethics has emerged as a distinct field as technology becomes integrated into business processes. One of the main challenges of AI is that, because it is based on algorithms and data, it can amplify existing biases or create new ethical dilemmas. For example, an AI system used in hiring could inadvertently discriminate against certain groups if the historical data on which it is based is biased.

The integration of AI and algorithmic decision-making in various sectors, including healthcare and public services, presents significant ethical challenges. Key concerns include algorithmic discrimination, lack of transparency, privacy issues, and questions of autonomy and accountability (Gambs, 2018; Pasricha, 2022). Algorithms trained on biased datasets can perpetuate or even exacerbate discrimination based on race, gender, or social class. Regarding transparency, many AI systems, especially those based on deep learning, function as "black boxes," making it difficult to understand how they make decisions. This raises serious ethical issues in terms of accountability and oversight. The collection of data to train AI systems raises serious concerns about protecting users' privacy. Concerns about autonomy and responsibility arise as AI systems make increasingly autonomous decisions, leading to questions about who is responsible for their actions: the designers, the users, or the machine itself.

Saura et al. (2024) analyzes the paradox that the issue of privacy raises in the context of ethics, economics, and artificial intelligence (AI). This paradox reflects how consumers, while valuing privacy, are willing to share personal data for personalized content. The study addresses several ethical aspects: the dilemma between data sharing and privacy, where the benefits of personalization often require giving up personal information; the responsibility of companies to manage data transparently and ethically, avoiding prioritizing economic benefits over privacy; and the need for regulations that balance technological advances with the protection of users' rights. It also underscores the importance of educating consumers to make informed decisions about their data and fostering interdisciplinary collaborations that integrate human and technological factors. Overall, the article highlights the challenges and opportunities for moving towards ethical practices in the economy and the use of AI in marketing.

These challenges are acute in high-stakes public sector decisions, where there is often a disconnect between organizational needs and current research on fairness and accountability (Veale et al., 2018). In the context of autonomous vehicles (AVs), algorithmic decision-making can introduce new safety risks and perpetuate discrimination through bias, ethical dilemmas, and perverse incentives (Taeihagh & Lim, 2019). Technical issues in AV algorithms, limitations in testing methods, and cybersecurity vulnerabilities further complicate these concerns. Addressing these challenges requires a multifaceted approach, including the design of ethical AI systems, development of usable transparency tools, and creation of appropriate policies and regulations (Gambs, 2018; Veale et al., 2018; Taeihagh & Lim, 2019).

However, there are also ethical opportunities in the implementation of AI. If properly designed, AI systems can help eliminate human bias, promote fairness, and increase transparency in business decision-making. This requires an ethical approach by design, integrating moral principles into the development of technology.

The convergence of AI, ethics, and business economics necessitates a reevaluation of traditional decision-making paradigms. As AI becomes prevalent in business management and financial decision-making, it raises significant ethical concerns, including algorithmic bias, transparency, data privacy, and societal implications (Thakur & Sharma, 2024). These challenges require businesses to proactively address ethical dilemmas while harnessing AI's advantages. The integration of AI in business processes demands responsible practices that align with ethical standards and societal values (Olatoye et al., 2024). A business ethics perspective based on contractualism and deliberative order ethics can help resolve value conflicts between diverse stakeholders when employing AI systems (Häußermann & Lütge, 2021). By prioritizing transparency, fairness, and ethical data practices, organizations can handle AI implementation while ensuring alignment with societal values and ethical standards (Olatoye et al., 2024).

Methodology

The methodology for this chapter is centered on the conceptual development and application of the Triple Axis model, a Cartesian framework designed to map the intersections of AI, ethics, and business economics. The approach combines theoretical synthesis with a structured visualization of relationships among these three domains, enabling a systematic exploration of their interplay.

Conceptual Framework Development

The foundation of the methodology lies in adapting principles from Cartesian coordinate systems to conceptualize the dimensions of AI, ethics, and business economics as orthogonal axes. Each axis is defined in Table 1, which provides a detailed description of the scope of each dimension. The definitions are summarized below as detailed in Table 1.

The model was designed to accommodate both qualitative and quantitative interpretations of these dimensions, allowing for a profound analysis of their interactions. This framework provides eight distinct regions within the Cartesian space, each representing a specific configuration of the three dimensions, from optimal alignment to severe misalignment.

Literature Integration

To ground the framework in existing knowledge, a comprehensive literature review was conducted, drawing from key works in AI, ethics, and business economics. Philosophical theories, including deontological ethics, utilitarianism, and virtue ethics, were synthesized to provide ethical benchmarks. Economic theories, such as those from Milton Friedman and Amartya Sen, informed the economic dimension. Studies on AI risks, transparency, and accountability provided insights into the technological axis.

Case Study Selection and Analysis

To demonstrate the applicability of the Triple Axis model, relevant case studies were selected and analyzed based on their significance in illustrating ethical and economic challenges in AI-driven business contexts. These include Cambridge Analytica as an example of unethical data exploitation and Apple as a benchmark for responsible data management and privacy protection.

Table 1 Framework of the triple axis: AI, ethics, and business economics

Axis	Description
x axis—The AI axis	AI axis ranges from supportive and innovative applications to manipulative and opaque uses of AI
y axis—Ethics axis	Ethics axis spans from proactive ethical leadership to unethical manipulation and ethical blindness
z axis—Business Economics axis	Business Economics axis covers sustainable and value-driven economic strategies to profit-driven exploitation and inequality

Source: Author's own elaboration

Each case was mapped onto the framework to analyze how decisions in one dimension influenced outcomes in the others. The analysis highlighted the consequences of ethical and unethical practices, providing empirical grounding for the conceptual model.

Visualization and Scenario Mapping

The Triple Axis model was employed to visualize potential scenarios within the three-dimensional (3D) space. By assigning values to different attributes of AI, ethics, and economics, the framework enabled the identification of eight distinct regions. This approach facilitated the assessment of various scenarios, from ideal (positive alignment across all dimensions) to detrimental (negative alignment). The visualization serves as a diagnostic and prescriptive tool for organizations seeking to align technological innovation with ethical and economic goals.

Limitations and Scope

This methodology focuses on conceptual and qualitative analysis rather than empirical validation. While the case studies and literature provide substantial insights, future research could enhance the model by integrating quantitative data and testing it across diverse organizational contexts. Moreover, the framework is designed as a general tool and may require adaptation for specific industries or use cases.

Development of the Triple Axis Model

As we have explored the convergence of AI, ethics, and business economics, it becomes evident that the integration of AI into corporate strategies presents both opportunities and ethical challenges. This intersection requires a deeper examination of the philosophical foundations that guide ethical decision-making in business. In the following section, we turn our attention to the core ethical frameworks—deontological ethics, utilitarianism, and virtue ethics—that have historically shaped business practices. By understanding these principles, we can better assess how they apply to AI technologies and their role in shaping responsible corporate behavior.

Conceptual Framework Design

Is It Possible to Create Ethical Algorithms?

Integrating ethical principles into AI systems poses a challenge in both business and technological spheres. Given that automated decisions can have profound social and economic implications, the question of whether it is possible to create algorithms that make ethical decisions autonomously has become a topic of growing interest. This section addresses current approaches, technical and philosophical challenges, and case studies related to programming ethics in AI.

Current Approaches to Implementing Ethical Principles in AI Systems

Recent research highlights various approaches to implementing ethics in AI systems. The pluralist hybrid model combines deterministic algorithms with machine learning to address moral disagreements and reduce opacity in ethical decision-making (Song & Yeung, 2024). The ECCOLA method offers a cyclical approach to developing ethically aligned AI systems, bridging the gap between principles and practical implementation (Vakkuri et al., 2021). Another perspective proposes embedding values in AI systems through intentional design activities, considering AI as a sociotechnical system with unique challenges and opportunities (van de Poel, 2020). A systematic review of over 100 frameworks and tools reveals a focus on specific ethical issues like explicability, fairness, privacy, and accountability, often addressed through software and algorithms, while more general ethical concerns are typically approached with conceptual frameworks and guidelines (Prem, 2023). These studies include several current approaches to implementing ethics in AI systems. Hang Yu et al. (2018) reviews technical approaches to integrating ethics into AI systems, including ethics by design, explainable AI (XAI), ethical audits, and supervised ethical learning. Each of these approaches has advantages and limitations, but they all agree on one aspect: the need to anticipate the potential societal impacts of AI before systems are deployed in real-world environments.

Different Codes of Ethics in Business Science and Their Applicability to AI

The ethical implications of AI in business have garnered significant attention, with a focus on responsible practices and corporate responsibility (Olatoye et al., 2024). Key ethical considerations include transparency, fairness, data privacy, and the socio-economic impact of AI implementation. There is a global convergence around five ethical principles: transparency, justice and fairness, non-maleficence, responsibility, and privacy (Jobin et al., 2019). However, challenges arise in interpreting and implementing these principles. The impact of AI on human rights has also been examined, highlighting the need for companies to address discrimination and supply chain due diligence (Kriebitz & Lütge, 2020). To address the practical realization of ethical principles, a virtue-based framework has been proposed, emphasizing four basic AI virtues (justice, honesty, responsibility, and care) and two second-order virtues (prudence and fortitude) to overcome bounded ethicality in AI development (Hagendorff, 2020).

The integration of Kantian deontological ethics into AI alignment and fairness metrics is proposed as an alternative to the predominant utilitarian approach (Morandín-Ahuerma, 2022). This deontological framework emphasizes duties and principles over consequences, potentially offering a more morally grounded approach to AI ethics. A deontological system based on modal logic is suggested to avoid conflicts in intuition-based ethics and provide better explanations for AI decision-making (Hooker & Kim, 2018). However, implementing ethical principles in AI faces challenges, as values like fairness, transparency, and accountability can conflict with each other, and introducing higher-level principles to resolve these conflicts may lead to an infinite regress or shift the discussion to a purely theoretical realm (Richter et al., 2021).

The use of AI in decision-making processes raises significant ethical concerns, particularly regarding its impact on marginalized groups. AI systems risk exacerbating health inequities and discrimination against vulnerable populations due to algorithmic bias and limited training data (Nchebe-Jah Iloanusi & Chun, 2024). In healthcare, AI applications often lack adequate safeguards to prevent discrimination (Nchebe-Jah Iloanusi & Chun, 2024). Similarly, AI-driven voice computing for mental health screening could potentially scale up discrimination against low-income minorities (Villongco & Khan, 2020). The use of AI in university admission processes may disadvantage historically discriminated groups and undermine human diversity (Krupiy, 2021). To address these issues, researchers suggest implementing AI vigilantism to regulate AI technologies and prevent harm (Nwafor, 2021). Additionally, the steps towards ensuring just AI system development are designing inclusive smart health models, improving diversity in training data, and establishing legal regulations and ethical guidelines (Nchebe-Jah Iloanusi & Chun, 2024; Villongco & Khan, 2020).

Virtue ethics is seen as compatible with modern AI due to its focus on learning from experience, with imitation learning from moral exemplars proposed as a solution to the value alignment problem (Berberich & Diepold, 2018). To address challenges in formalizing and training virtuous agents, researchers suggest using role-playing games with moral dilemmas, employing techniques such as affinity-based reinforcement learning and explainable AI (Vishwanath et al., 2022). Despite differing views on the extent to which AI can embody virtues, these studies highlight the potential of virtue ethics in shaping the development of ethical AI systems and fostering social acceptability (Gibert, 2023; Berberich & Diepold, 2018).

The abstract nature and diversity of AI ethical principles create gaps between their formulation and practical implementation (Tidjon & Khomh, 2022, 2023). A review of 47 AI ethics guidelines revealed that the political and economic implications of AI business practices are underrepresented, with guidelines focusing disproportionately on algorithmic decision-making rather than the broader business context (Attard-Frost et al., 2023). To address these issues, researchers suggest expanding the scope of AI ethics guidelines to better contend with challenges such as ethics washing, corporate secrecy, and harmful business practices (Attard-Frost et al., 2023). Some recommendations have been proposed to mitigate the principle-to-practice gaps and ensure AI implementations align with ethical principles and values (Tidjon & Khomh, 2023).

Technical and Philosophical Challenges in Creating a "Universal Code of Ethics" for AI

The creation of a universal code of ethics for AI faces significant challenges due to cultural and moral relativism, as ethical principles vary across cultures and lack universal coherence (Vallverdú & Boix, 2021; Goffi & Momcilovic, 2022). AI systems often lack sufficient data or processing time to make optimal ethical decisions, necessitating consideration of ethical uncertainty in their design (Vallverdú & Boix, 2021). Issues of responsibility, accountability, and transparency become more complex as AI systems grow autonomous (Santhoshkumar et al., 2023; Floridi, 2024). Data biases in AI systems can perpetuate existing social prejudices and discrimination (Santhoshkumar et al., 2023; Floridi, 2024). The rapid development of AI also presents unprecedented challenges to copyright, individual autonomy, and our understanding of authenticity and creativity (Floridi, 2024). Addressing these ethical concerns requires collaboration between diverse stakeholders and a culturally sensitive approach to AI governance (Santhoshkumar et al., 2023; Goffi & Momcilovic, 2022).

Recent research highlights the growing importance of ethical considerations in AI development and deployment. Organizations are aware of AI ethics but struggle to implement comprehensive mitigation strategies (Stahl et al., 2021). To address these issues, researchers have proposed various approaches, including exploring ethical dilemmas, developing individual and collective ethical decision frameworks, and examining ethics in human-AI interactions (Yu et al., 2018). Some organizations are adopting an ethics-by-design approach, integrating ethical considerations into the early stages of AI development to mitigate risks and build trust (Bourgais & Ibnouhsein, 2022). While progress has been made in raising awareness and developing guidelines, there remains a significant gap between ethical AI principles and their practical implementation across industries.

Integration of Literature in Key Business Areas That Require Codes of Ethics

Adaptive Leadership in the Age of AI

Adaptive leadership in the age of AI requires a multifaceted approach that integrates ethical considerations, technological proficiency, and human-centric values. Leaders must analyze complex ethical dilemmas arising from AI implementation, such as bias and privacy concerns, while fostering a culture of responsible AI use (Uddin, 2023; Maddula, 2018).

The integration of AI transforms traditional leadership paradigms, promoting more adaptable and data-driven approaches to team management and decision-making (Mitra Madanchian et al., 2024). Leaders need to develop a balanced approach that harnesses AI's benefits while preserving human qualities and ethical principles. This involves cultivating emotional intelligence alongside technical proficiency and implementing proactive leadership strategies to navigate AI-induced transformations (Sposato, 2024). By embracing reciprocal symmetry principles and ethical AI adoption, organizations can create inclusive environments that value transparency, fairness, and respect for all stakeholders in the digital economy (Maddula, 2018).

Ethical Decision-Making in Crisis Contexts

In crisis contexts, such as during a pandemic or financial collapse, business decision-making becomes more critical and complex. AI can be a valuable tool for processing large volumes of data and providing recommendations based on predictive models. However, automated decisions in times of crisis can also have unintended ethical consequences.

For example, during the COVID-19 pandemic, many AI systems were used to prioritize the allocation of limited medical resources or to monitor the population. These applications raised ethical concerns about equity in resource distribution and privacy. While AI can improve efficiency in crisis management, it is critical that codes of ethics are put in place to ensure that automated decisions respect the principles of justice and do not violate fundamental rights.

Likewise, the speed of decisions during a crisis can exacerbate the opacity issues of AI systems. Organizations must ensure that AI models are auditable and that humans maintain ultimate control over the most critical decisions, particularly when human lives or rights are at stake.

AI in Collective Decision-Making: Teamwork and Ethical Leadership

AI is also starting to play a role in collective decision-making within organizations. AI systems can be used to analyze data and generate recommendations in a collaborative environment, such as in strategic decision-making or problem-solving in work teams. However, integrating AI into these processes poses ethical challenges.

One of the main challenges is to ensure that AI does not undermine human leadership or team autonomy. While algorithms can be useful in delivering data-driven insights, it's critical that final decisions are made by humans, considering both the information provided by AI and the ethical and human factors that algorithms can't capture.

In addition, leaders need to be aware of the authority bias that AI can generate. Since AI systems are often perceived as more objective and accurate, teams may be inclined to accept algorithmic recommendations without question. This can limit critical thinking and ethical deliberation in decision-making. A code of ethics in this context should encourage independent thinking and ensure that AI is a supporting tool, not a substitute for human decision-making.

Examples of Good and Bad Practices

The ethical implications of AI have gained significant attention, with over 100 AI ethics principles published by various organizations (Hickok, 2021). However, these principles often lack diversity and practical application. AI's power to reshape daily practices and interactions necessitates its use as a force for good, with ethics playing a role in harnessing its potential while mitigating risks (Taddeo & Floridi, 2021). Key ethical challenges include data governance, delegation of tasks, responsibility attribution, and protecting human self-determination. The Cambridge Analytica case exemplifies AI's potential to undermine user autonomy (Taddeo & Floridi, 2021). To ensure AI's positive impact on society, researchers have identified essential ethical factors and best practices for AI for Social Good (AI4SG) initiatives (Floridi et al., 2020; Taddeo & Floridi, 2018). These include considerations of AI's uses, users, designers, and the data fueling it (Cath et al., 2018). Moving from high-level principles to practical accountability mechanisms remains a pressing need in the field of AI ethics.

These examples demonstrate that long-term business success depends on technological innovation and on the adoption of responsible ethical practices. Companies that fail in this regard can suffer serious reputational consequences, while those that prioritize ethics can build lasting relationships of trust with their stakeholders.

The key business areas analyzed show the urgent need to develop and implement clear and effective codes of ethics in the use of AI. AI has the potential to transform risk management, leadership, crisis decision-making, and teamwork, but only if it is handled with responsibility and ethical consideration.

Analyzing What Is "Not Good" in the Business Context

After outlining the relationship between business economics and ethics, through the lens of various economic theories, we now shift our focus to the ethical challenges and opportunities that AI presents in practical applications. As AI continues to shape industries, concerns such as transparency, accountability, and algorithmic bias become central to ethical discussions. In the following section, we will examine these challenges in greater detail, highlighting the dual potential of AI to both create ethical dilemmas and offer solutions for more responsible business practices.

In the business environment, the concept of "not good" business decisions and actions move in a terrain in which the lines between the ethical, the legal, and the immoral can be blurred. What constitutes corporate malpractice? Is it enough to comply with the law, or should companies be guided by broader ethical principles? This section explores the nature of "not good" in the business context, analyzing the relationship between the law, codes of conduct, and user trust.

The Law, Codes of Conduct, and User Trust

In the business environment, "not good" can be defined in multiple ways. Traditionally, it has been understood as any action that violates the law or deviates from the codes of conduct established by the organization. However, this approach is limited, as not all behaviors harmful to society or individuals are necessarily illegal.

Complying with the law is the most basic standard for avoiding evil in the business context. However, laws do not always cover the entirety of the ethical dilemmas that companies face. For example, many practices related to tax evasion or the use of user data are borderline legal, but they can be immoral. Often, companies develop codes of conduct to guide the actions of their employees and leaders. These codes can go beyond legal requirements, providing principles that encourage ethical behavior. Nevertheless, their effectiveness depends on how they are implemented and whether they are actually followed in practice or just declarations of intent.

In the digital age, user trust is a fundamental pillar. Actions that erode that trust, such as the exploitation of personal data or algorithmic manipulation, can be considered "not good" even though they are technically legal. In many cases, the breach of this trust can have a more severe impact on the company's reputation than a legal violation.

Evil in the business context refers to the violation of laws, to actions that undermine the integrity of the company or those that damage the trust of stakeholders and contravene internal codes of conduct.

Comparison Between the Universal Values of "Good" and "Evil" and Their Interpretation in the Technological and Business Field

"Good" and "evil" in the business and technological context have interpretations that may differ from universal values. Nonetheless, these underlying values still serve as the basis for evaluating business stocks. This section explores how universal values can be applied to the business environment.

The universal values of goodness include principles such as justice, equity, honesty, transparency, and respect for human dignity. In the business context, acting in accordance with these principles means ensuring that business practices do not discriminate against any group, that decisions are fair, and that operations are transparent. For example, a company that ensures that its AI systems do not perpetuate racial or gender bias would be aligning with the universal values of good.

The "interpretation of evil" in universal terms is associated with injustice, deceit, exploitation, and abuse of power. In the business context, evil can manifest itself in actions such as market manipulation, labor exploitation, discrimination, or the manipulation of users' privacy and personal data. A clear example of this is the case of Cambridge Analytica, where the exploitation of user data to influence global electoral processes was seen as a form of unethical misconduct, even though the laws were not defined in that area at the time.

In this context, universal values can serve as a guide for companies to assess the legality of their actions and their moral impact. AI, for example, amplifies these dilemmas, as its decisions can have significant and large-scale effects, affecting individuals and societies more quickly and often more opaquely than humans.

Recent studies identify various ethical concerns in an area such as digital marketing based on artificial intelligence (AI). These include user privacy, due to the collection and use of personal data without clear and adequate consent; the lack of transparency in automated decision-making processes, which generates mistrust; and the possible manipulation of the autonomy of users through personalized advertising, thus questioning the validity of informed consent. Likewise, the use of real-time behavioral analysis can be perceived as a form of surveillance, which raises serious ethical concerns about data management. Another relevant challenge is data ownership, which drives the need for a user-centric model that ensures ethical control over their information (Saura et al., 2024).

The importance of complying with data protection regulations and addressing potential biases in algorithms is underlined, highlighting the need to establish ethical frameworks that protect users' rights, ensure fairness, and allow to promote innovation in any sector.

The Law as an Ethical Limit: Cases Where Legality Is Not Enough

Although compliance with the law is a minimum requirement for companies, there are many cases where legality is not enough to guarantee ethical behavior. The law, by its nature, is reactive and, in many cases, cannot foresee technological advances or new ways in which companies can operate on the moral edge.

A classic example is the case of Cambridge Analytica, which will be discussed later, where legal loopholes in the regulation of personal data were exploited to influence elections and political decisions. Although the company technically complied with many of the regulations in place at the time, its conduct was condemned for violating fundamental ethical principles, such as privacy and individual autonomy.

Another example is the use of AI in recruitment. Some AI systems have been accused of discriminating against certain groups due to biases present in the training data. Although the law may not have been explicitly violated, this type of bias can have devastating consequences for fairness in the workplace and can be seen as a form of evil in ethical terms.

These cases show that while the law is a necessary framework, it is not always sufficient to address the ethical dilemmas that arise in business practice. Companies must go beyond legality and adopt ethical principles that anticipate potential harm to stakeholders, especially in a world driven by technologies such as AI.

It seems like, evil in the business context goes beyond legal non-compliance. Companies, especially those that integrate AI into their operations, must develop strong ethical codes that comply with the law, protect user trust, ensure fairness, and foster broader social responsibility.

Case Study Selection and Analysis

Having explored the ethical challenges and opportunities that AI presents, we now turn to concrete examples of how these issues manifest in real-world business scenarios. The impact of AI on ethics and business economics can be seen in both positive practices that uphold transparency and fairness, as well as in abuses that exploit vulnerabilities and undermine trust. In this section, we will analyze case studies, contrasting examples of misuse, such as the Cambridge Analytica scandal, with responsible approaches like Apple's commitment to privacy, to illustrate the wide range of ethical behaviors in AI-driven business environments.

Case analysis provides insights into the ethical, legal, and reputational consequences of using AI and data in business. The examples of Cambridge Analytica and Apple represent two extremes in the relationship between business, technology, and ethics. These cases allow us to reflect on the importance of ethical codes and their implications for sustainability and business reputation.

Analysis of the Cambridge Analytica Case: Manipulation and Violation of Rights

The Cambridge Analytica scandal exposed the misuse of personal data and AI in political campaigns, particularly during the 2016 US presidential election (González, 2017; Isaak & Hanna, 2018; Schippers, 2020). The company exploited Facebook's platform to access millions of users' data without proper consent, violating privacy rights (Schneble et al., 2018; Isaak & Hanna, 2018). Using sophisticated algorithms and big data analysis, Cambridge Analytica targeted voters with personalized political messages, potentially influencing their decisions (González, 2017; Schippers, 2020). This case highlighted the need for comprehensive privacy policy laws and raised concerns about data protection in Internet-mediated research (Isaak & Hanna,

2018; Schneble et al., 2018). The scandal underscored the importance of addressing security and privacy issues in social media platforms and research practices, especially in light of regulations like the European General Data Protection Regulation (GDPR) (Schneble et al., 2018).

Furthermore, this case raised several ethical and legal problems such as the violation of privacy since he accessed the personal data of approximately 87 million Facebook users without their explicit consent. Although no data protection laws in place at the time were technically violated, the company exploited a regulatory loophole and manipulated the data in ways that were deemed ethically reprehensible.

In addition, psychological manipulation occurred because using AI-generated psychological profiles, Cambridge Analytica designed personalized messages to manipulate voters' emotions and behaviors. In addition, there was a lack of transparency since neither Facebook users nor the public were aware of the magnitude of the use of their data.

This case revealed how companies can use advanced technologies, such as AI, to influence public opinion and exploit vulnerabilities in data regulation, resulting in a significant violation of individuals' rights and democratic principles.

Contrast with Apple: Responsible Use of Data and Privacy Protection

In contrast to Cambridge Analytica, Apple has built its reputation around protecting users' privacy, which has become a central pillar of its business strategy. Apple has taken an ethical approach in handling user data, setting a standard of best practice in the tech industry.

Its approach to privacy has been both praised and scrutinized. While the company has positioned itself as a champion of privacy (Nissenbaum, 2022), its practices have raised concerns. However, the company's reliance on notice and choice mechanisms and its control over vast data stocks have been criticized (Nissenbaum, 2022). Apple's privacy policies have also varied across different markets, notably between the US and China, potentially driven by market access considerations (Kokas, 2018). Despite these challenges, an open-minded organizational culture and investment in eco-innovation have been linked to improved privacy practices and business performance (Cegarra-Navarro et al., 2019). Overall, while Apple has set certain standards in privacy protection, questions remain about the effectiveness and consistency of its approach across global markets.

Through these practices, Apple has shown that it is possible to integrate ethical principles into data management, using AI and other technologies responsibly. Apple's proactive approach to protecting privacy has bolstered the loyalty of its users and has also set a precedent for how companies can implement rigorous ethical codes in their operations.

Reflections on the Importance of a Code of Ethics and Its Implications for Corporate Reputation

The Cambridge Analytica and Apple cases illustrate how the implementation or lack of a code of ethics can have a significant impact on a company's reputation and sustainability. While Cambridge Analytica is remembered for data exploitation and psychological manipulation, Apple has cemented its reputation as an advocate for user privacy and security. These differences offer important lessons about the need for a code of ethics in the age of AI.

In a technology-driven business environment, companies that lack a strong ethical framework run the risk of acting solely based on short-term profit maximization, without considering the potential long-term harm. A well-defined code of ethics helps prevent questionable practices and guides companies in making responsible decisions that balance financial performance with social integrity.

Reputation is one of a company's most valuable assets in today's digital environment. Consumers are increasingly aware of the impact of companies on society, and unethical practices can lead to a rapid loss of trust and market value. As seen in the case of Cambridge Analytica, the exploitation of personal data without rigorous ethical oversight damaged the company's reputation and contributed to its eventual closure.

In contrast, Apple has shown that an ethical approach can become a competitive advantage. By prioritizing user privacy, Apple has cultivated a loyal customer base and differentiated its brand in a highly competitive market. This reinforces the idea that ethics is a responsibility and an opportunity to improve reputation and ensure long-term sustainability.

The impact of these cases should serve as a reminder for all companies operating in the digital and technological realm. Taking an ethical approach, with a strong commitment to transparency, fairness, and the protection of individual rights, mitigates legal and reputational risks and fosters consumer trust and loyalty.

Building on these examples, it is evident that a strong code of ethics is needed for guiding responsible AI use and ensuring long-term sustainability. Its development brings significant ethical challenges for businesses and corporate governance. Key concerns include privacy, security, bias, fairness, trust, and transparency (Kamila & Jasrotia, 2023). A study conducted with 355 managers from various service sectors in India highlights that poor governance, inadequate data quality, and insufficient employee training contribute to AI opacity. This opacity leads to operational inefficiencies, declining sales growth, employee dissatisfaction, and a competitive disadvantage, while also emphasizing the importance of contingency plans as a moderating factor (Rana et al., 2022).

Visualization and Scenario Mapping: A Proposal for Managing the Triple Axis of AI, Ethics, and Business Economics

Having analyzed key case studies that showcase both the ethical abuses and best practices in AI and business economics, we now turn to a more structured approach for addressing these challenges. Case studies provide valuable insights into the consequences of ethical and unethical AI use but there remains a need for a framework to guide organizations in their decision-making processes. In this section, the Triple Axis model is introduced, a Cartesian framework that synthesizes AI, ethics, and business economics, offering a practical tool for depicting the complex interactions. It aims to highlight the complexity of potential risks involved in violating fundamental rights through the use of AI in economic practices outside the boundaries of morality, ethics, or legality, as previously outlined.

The approach of a code of ethics by organizations must serve to inform internal and external processes. This philosophical approach, far from assuming a subjective perception of ethics, can serve to delimit, with objective criteria, the actions and business decisions that induce good and bad practices.

Introducing considerations of deontological ethics, utilitarianism, or virtue ethics could help categorize, order, and ultimately minimize the associated risks. To capture both the complexity and the hidden dimensions of this triplet, a Cartesian space of possible combinations between AI applications with ethical approaches and business economics approaches is drawn. It is a synthesis proposal to delimit an infinite space of possibilities in which to limit the possibilities, allow us to understand their complexity and glimpse the different options. Thus, it aims to understand the consequences of certain ethical and AI programming paths that, in combination with the business positioning of each business organization, can point the way to ensure a responsible use of AI.

Fundamental Principles of a Cartesian Axis Applicable to Ethics, AI, and Business Economics

Following the principles of mathematics and René Descartes' vision, who used Cartesian axes to bring order to the chaos of geometry, this approach allows us to introduce structure and clarity into the interaction between ethics, AI, and business management, much like Descartes did with geometric space. We conceptualize a three-dimensional axis, or R3 space, that integrates the three key concepts—AI, ethics, and business economics—into a unified framework. Each axis represents one of these dimensions, with characteristics or attributes arranged in an orderly manner, whether qualitatively or quantitatively.

This framework enables us to plot various situations as different values of the three variables, positioning them on the corresponding Cartesian axis. The scale moves from the most favorable to the least favorable, passing through a neutral midpoint. Each axis is labeled with positive and negative attributes to better describe the positions and interactions of different situations.

For the AI axis, we include positive states such as Supportive AI, Innovative AI, and Superintelligent AI, while the negative side features Manipulative AI, Opaque AI, and Autonomous AI Risk. Similarly, the Ethics axis captures the range from Ethical Compliance, Proactive Ethics, and Ethical Leadership on the positive side, to Ethical Blindness, Ethical Evasion, and Unethical Manipulation on the negative side. The Business Economics axis spans from Value-Driven Economics, Inclusive Growth, and Sustainable Economics on the positive end, to Profit-Driven Myopia, Exploitation, and Economic Inequality on the negative side.

Color-coded and marked with directional arrows, Fig. 1 illustrates these axes, helping to visualize the relationships between these three critical fields.

This 3D space encompasses both positive and negative values for each axis, representing the dimensions of AI, Ethics, and Business Economics. The axes extend in all directions, allowing for a comprehensive range of values within this conceptual framework. The Cartesian model is a well-established tool in scientific fields, providing a structured method to analyze the complex interactions between AI, ethics, and business economics. This representation supports our exploration of the range of possibilities generated by the dynamic interplay of these three variables.

Each of the eight smaller cubes corresponds to one of the eight regions within the 3D space, with each cube labeled according to the positive or negative aspects of the AI, Ethics, and Business Economics dimensions. This labeling helps us better understand how different configurations influence outcomes. The regions are defined as follows:

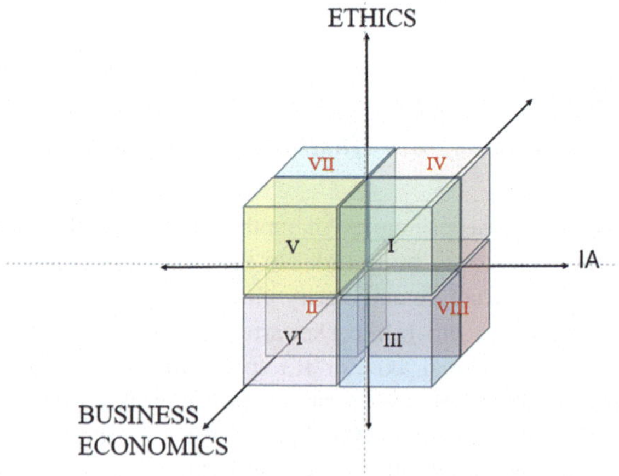

Fig. 1 3D space with AI, ethics and business economics axes. Source: Author's own elaboration

Region 1: Positive AI, Positive Ethics, Positive Business Economics
Region 2: Negative AI, Negative Ethics, Negative Business Economics
Region 3: Positive AI, Negative Ethics, Positive Business Economics
Region 4: Positive AI, Positive Ethics, Negative Business Economics
Region 5: Negative AI, Positive Ethics, Positive Business Economics
Region 6: Negative AI, Negative Ethics, Positive Business Economics
Region 7: Negative AI, Positive Ethics, Negative Business Economics
Region 8: Positive AI, Negative Ethics, Negative Business Economics

This framework provides a detailed understanding of how various configurations of AI, ethics, and business economics can coexist, offering a method to anticipate their complex interactions and potential outcomes. The 3D plot represents the dimensions of AI, Ethics, and Business Economics, with each axis labeled according to its positive and negative scales. Each region in the plot, from Region I to Region VIII, reflects various combinations of these dimensions.

The visualization aids in comprehending how different scenarios unfold based on the alignment or misalignment of AI, ethics, and business economics. The complete 3D plot illustrates the positive and negative categories for each dimension, clearly labeled and marked as follows:

AI Dimension:

- Positive Scale: Supportive AI, Innovative AI, Superintelligent AI
- Negative Scale: Manipulative AI, Opaque AI, Autonomous AI Risk

Ethics Dimension:

- Positive Scale: Ethical Compliance, Proactive Ethics, Ethical Leadership
- Negative Scale: Ethical Blindness, Ethical Evasion, Unethical Manipulation

Business Economics Dimension:

- Positive Scale: Value-Driven Economics, Inclusive Growth, Sustainable Economics
- Negative Scale: Profit-Driven Myopia, Exploitation, Economic Inequality

In this framework, the AI dimension is divided into a positive and negative scale. On the positive side, we find supportive AI, which assists human efforts, innovative AI that fosters creativity and efficiency, and superintelligent AI, representing the pinnacle of AI development with potentially limitless capabilities. The negative scale includes manipulative AI, which deceives or misleads, opaque AI, where decisions and processes lack transparency, and autonomous AI risk, highlighting the dangers of AI acting independently without proper oversight.

The ethics dimension follows a similar structure, with the positive scale encompassing ethical compliance, where standards are met, proactive ethics that go beyond compliance to anticipate ethical issues, and ethical leadership, where moral responsibility is prioritized. On the negative side, ethical blindness refers to a failure to recognize ethical concerns, ethical evasion is the active avoidance of responsibility, and unethical manipulation involves exploiting ethical loopholes for personal or corporate gain.

Finally, the business economics dimension reflects a balance between value-driven economics, inclusive growth, and sustainable practices on the positive scale, while the negative side highlights profit-driven myopia, which focuses solely on short-term gains, exploitation of resources or labor, and the deepening of economic inequality as a result of unsustainable practices.

In this three-dimensional space, each region reflects a unique combination of AI, ethics, and business economics. Region I represents the most favorable scenario, where both AI, ethics, and business economics are positive, resulting in a balanced and sustainable environment. In contrast, Region II illustrates the worst-case scenario, where AI, ethics, and business economics operate in their most negative forms, creating a toxic and harmful environment.

Region III combines positive AI with negative ethics and positive business economics, suggesting a beneficial use of AI in a healthy economic context, but with poor ethical practices. Region IV maintains positive AI and ethics, albeit with a negative business economy, which could indicate an ethical and technologically advanced environment, but without a sustainable approach in economic terms.

In Region V, a negative AI is compensated for by a positive ethics and economics, which could represent attempts to correct the negative effects of inadequate AI. Region VI features both negative AI and ethics, but with positive business economics, which could reflect a strong economic model despite problematic technological and ethical practices.

Region VII stands out for having negative AI and economics, albeit with positive ethics, suggesting that despite technology and adverse economics, ethical principles remain. Finally, Region VIII offers positive AI, but with negative ethics and economics, which can signal the use of beneficial AI in economically unsustainable and unethical environments.

The key takeaways of this 3D model are that it visually demonstrates the complex interplay between AI, ethics, and business economics. By defining each axis with its positive and negative aspects, the model allows for a nuanced understanding of how different configurations affect organizational and societal outcomes. The model is especially useful in AI-driven business environments, providing a structured framework to predict and analyze the effects of AI integration on both ethical and economic grounds. This approach can serve as a valuable tool for decision-makers, guiding them toward more balanced, responsible use of AI that benefits both businesses and society at large. This deepened understanding facilitates the recognition of potential risks and opportunities within different regions of the 3D space, making it possible to anticipate any beneficial or detrimental scenarios depending on how AI, ethics, and business economics align or conflict.

Implications of the Eight Regions on the Interaction of AI, Ethics, and Business Economics

The eight regions in this 3D model represent different combinations of positive and negative attributes across the AI, Ethics, and Business Economics dimensions. Each region has unique implications, affecting decision-making, strategy, and outcomes in different ways.

In this three-dimensional model, eight regions are identified that represent different combinations of positive and negative attributes in the dimensions of AI, ethics, and business economics, each with unique implications that affect organizations' decision-making and strategy.

Region I, presented in Fig. 2, is the ideal scenario where AI drives innovation, ethical standards are respected, and business practices are sustainable. Organizations operating in this region are well-positioned to achieve long-term success, generating growth and contributing positively to society. In addition, companies in this region enjoy high trust and a solid reputation, being seen as leaders in both technology and ethics.

Figure 3 represents Region II, this is where the greatest risks are found, as AI, ethics, and business economics are at their most negative levels. Harmful business practices and unethical AI are prevalent here, which can cause significant societal harm, such as job losses, increased economic inequality, and potential legal consequences. Companies operating in this region will face a reputational crisis that could require drastic measures, such as regulatory interventions or changes in leadership.

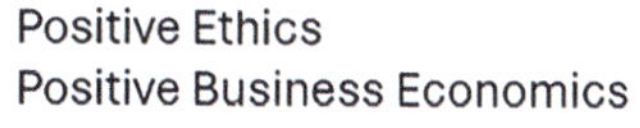

Fig. 2 Region I (Positive AI, positive ethics, positive business economics). Source: Author's own elaboration

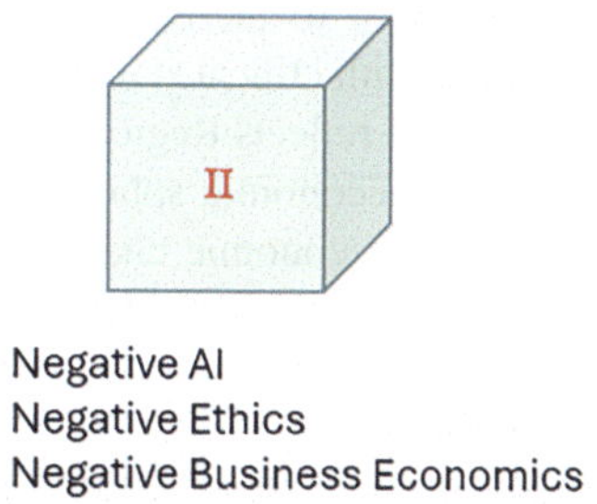

Fig. 3 Region II (Negative AI, negative ethics, negative business economics). Source: Author's own elaboration

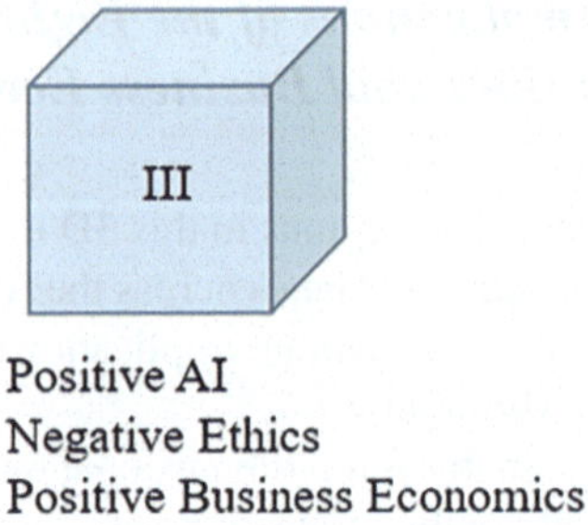

Fig. 4 Region III (Positive AI, negative ethics, positive business economics). Source: Author's own elaboration

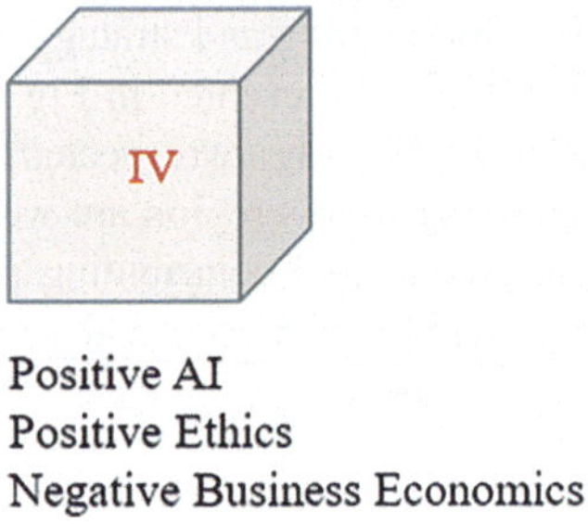

Fig. 5 Region IV (Positive AI, positive ethics, negative business economics). Source: Author's own elaboration

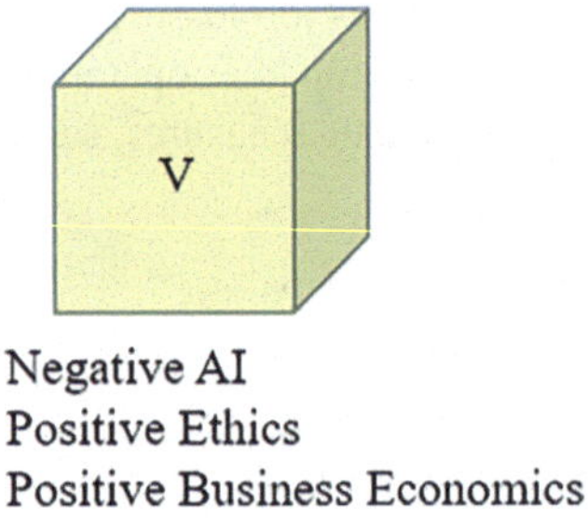

Fig. 6 Region V (Negative AI, positive ethics, positive business economics). Source: Author's own elaboration

Region III is reflected in Fig. 4 and it offers a picture where AI is positive, but ethical practices are poor, although the business economy remains favorable. Companies can achieve short-term profits, but unethical behavior could lead to a loss of consumer trust and future legal challenges. These types of companies are also exposed to increased regulatory scrutiny, increasing pressure to align their practices with ethical standards.

Figure 5 reflects Region IV, it combines AI and positive ethics, but with difficulties in the economic sphere. Although companies in this region prioritize ethical innovation, economic challenges can limit their growth, forcing them to look for innovative business models to continue operating. Here, social responsibility is a priority, which reinforces consumer loyalty, although they could face financial instability.

Region V is presented in Fig. 6, it presents a dilemma where AI is negative, but both ethics and business economics are positive. Organizations in this region must carefully balance economic growth and ethical standards to avoid moral compromises, managing the risks associated with inadequate AI while seeking to maintain their growth and reputation.

Figure 7 shows Region VI, where economic success comes at the expense of negative AI and ethics, which can lead companies to make profits at any cost, including through harmful practices. Although these companies may be economically viable, they are at risk of reputational damage, facing long-term social and legal pressures, which could affect their sustainability.

Figure 8 shows how in Region VII positive ethics collide with negative AI and a declining business economy. Here, companies can be constrained by ethical considerations that restrict the use of advanced technologies, resulting in poor economic performance. However, organizations operating in this region might need to innovate within ethical boundaries to achieve sustainable economic success.

Finally, Fig. 9 represents Region VIII, a scenario in which AI is positive, but ethical and economic practices are negative. AI drives technological advancement, but

Fig. 7 Region VI (Negative AI, negative ethics, positive business economics). Source: Author's own elaboration

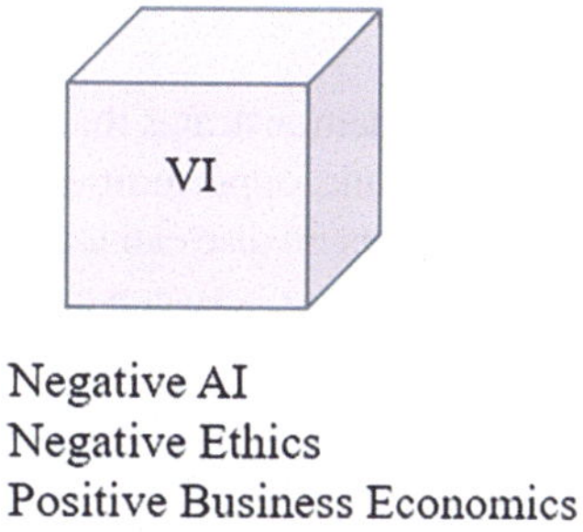

Fig. 8 Region VII (Negative AI, positive ethics, negative business economics). Source: Author's own elaboration

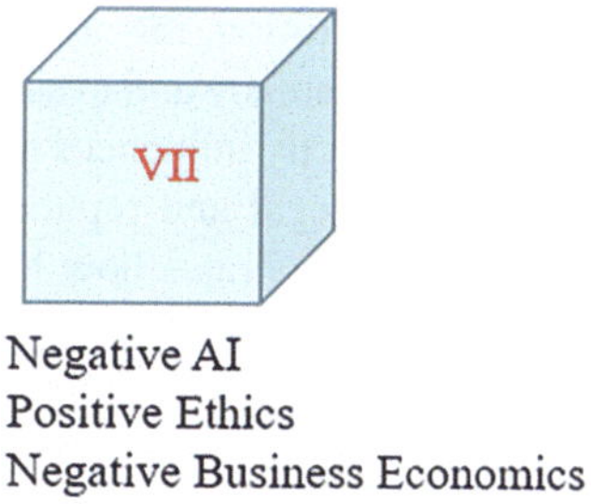

Fig. 9 Region VIII (Positive AI, negative ethics, negative business economics). Source: Author's own elaboration

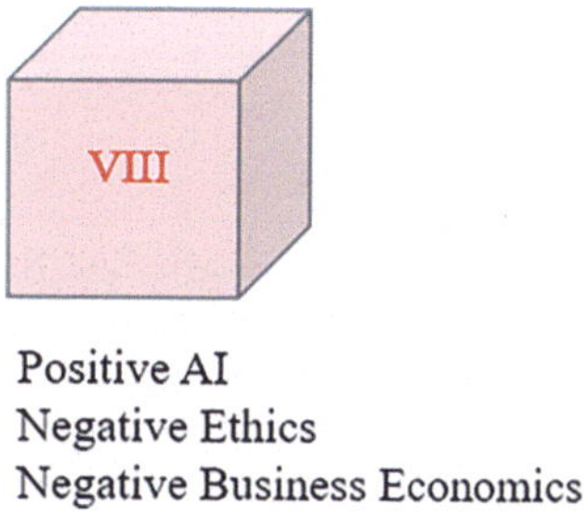

unethical practices and poor economic performance undermine these achievements, creating a fragile environment. Companies in this region tend to focus on short-term technological benefits, which could lead to future crises due to a lack of ethical and economic sustainability.

It could be generalized that regions with positive dimensions tend to foster long-term success, innovation, and social trust, but require careful management to balance ethical and economic considerations. On the other hand, regions with negative dimensions are fraught with risks, such as reputational damage, legal challenges, and unsustainable practices, which require immediate corrective actions to mitigate their negative effects.

Understanding the impacts of each region helps decision-makers assess where they stand and what strategic adjustments might be necessary to move toward more positive, sustainable outcomes.

Discussion

The study demonstrates that the integration of AI into business presents both ethical and economic opportunities and challenges. While AI can foster innovation and efficiency, its misuse can lead to bias, privacy violations, and economic inequalities. The comparison between cases such as Cambridge Analytica and Apple highlights the differences between ethical and unethical practices, highlighting how ill-founded decisions can damage public trust and business sustainability.

The results underscore the need to establish clear ethical standards in AI implementation. The Triple Axis model emphasizes that ethical decisions benefit society and strengthen trust in organizations, fostering sustainable relationships with stakeholders. In addition, this approach provides tools to mitigate ethical risks, such as lack of transparency and evasion of responsibility.

Ethics directly influences long-term economic sustainability. Strong ethical practices reduce legal and reputational risks and enhance business value. The Triple Axis model illustrates how balancing economic and ethical objectives can create competitive advantages and promote inclusive and sustainable growth.

The proposed model provides a visual structure for assessing how decisions in AI, ethics, and business economics interact and affect each other. This helps organizations better understand the necessary trade-offs and make informed decisions that balance technological innovation, ethical responsibility, and economic goals.

Conclusions

The chapter introduces the Triple Axis model as a conceptual tool that enables organizations to map and mitigate the ethical risks associated with AI. This model helps to integrate ethical principles into AI systems without compromising economic viability, offering a structured solution to align technological advances with ethical standards and economic objectives.

We have addressed and answered the three research questions posed at the outset.

R1: How can the Triple Axis framework help organizations integrate ethical principles into AI systems while maintaining economic viability?

The Triple Axis framework offers organizations a structured method to assess the implications of AI-driven decisions on both ethical practices and economic outcomes. By mapping AI applications onto this model, organizations can visualize how decisions in one area impact the other two. This visualization enables them to balance ethical considerations with economic objectives effectively, ensuring that AI systems are both ethically sound and economically viable. The framework provides a clear pathway for integrating ethical principles into AI systems without compromising on economic viability, thus fostering a harmonious relationship between technological advancement and ethical responsibility.

R2: What are the main ethical risks associated with AI in business, and how can they be visualized and mitigated through the Triple Axis model?

The main ethical risks associated with AI in business include bias, lack of transparency, privacy violations, and accountability issues. The Triple Axis model helps visualize these risks by categorizing AI applications along ethical and economic dimensions. This categorization allows organizations to proactively identify and address potential ethical dilemmas. By promoting transparency, fairness, and accountability in AI-driven decisions, the model aids in mitigating these risks. It provides a practical view of how ethical risks can be managed and reduced, ensuring that AI applications do not compromise ethical standards while achieving economic goals.

R3: How does the intersection of AI, ethics, and business economics shape corporate strategy and decision-making?

The intersection of AI, ethics, and business economics shapes corporate strategy and decision-making by emphasizing the need for a balanced approach that considers both ethical standards and economic goals. The Triple Axis model demonstrates that ethical leadership and robust governance structures are the key for responsibly integrating AI into business practices. This approach ensures that AI technologies are used in ways that respect human rights, promote fairness, and contribute to long-term sustainability. By incorporating ethical considerations into the core of business strategies, organizations can manage the complexities of AI implementation while maintaining public trust and achieving sustainable economic success.

Organizations should embed ethical principles directly into the design and implementation of AI systems. This includes proactive measures to ensure transparency, fairness, and accountability in AI-driven decisions. Companies should establish clear governance structures that integrate AI, ethics, and economic objectives. This includes appointing ethics committees or officers responsible for overseeing AI deployments and ensuring they align with both business goals and societal values. Business leaders must prioritize ethical considerations alongside financial performance. Ethical leadership fosters a culture where AI is deployed for economic gain and in ways that respect human rights and promote fairness.

Theoretical and Practical Implications

The chapter contributes to the development of an integrative conceptual framework that connects AI, ethics, and business economics. By introducing the Triple Axis model, a novel approach is offered to analyze and manage the interactions between these three domains: implement AI-specific codes of ethics that include transparency, fairness, and accountability measures; design regulations that promote responsible use of AI, ensuring that human rights and economic sustainability are prioritized; invest in employee training programs on ethics and AI, fostering an organizational culture that values ethical responsibility.

These recommendations reinforce the need for a balance between technological innovation, ethical principles, and economic objectives to ensure responsible and sustainable adoption of AI.

To address the implementation of AI, organizations should establish mechanisms for continuous monitoring and auditing of AI systems to ensure they operate within ethical and legal boundaries. Engaging a broad range of stakeholders, including employees, customers, and regulators, provides diverse perspectives on the ethical implications of AI and ensures business practices align with broader societal expectations.

Employees at all levels must receive education about AI, ethics, and business economics to foster a responsible AI culture. Training programs should focus on ethical decision-making and the risks and benefits of AI technologies. Creating a culture that values ethical considerations in AI use involves regular training, open discussions about ethical dilemmas, and a commitment to continuous improvement in AI practices.

The responsible integration of AI into business practices requires a careful balance of ethical principles and economic objectives. The Triple Axis model provides a structured framework for managing these challenges, helping organizations harness the potential of AI while minimizing risks and promoting long-term sustainability.

References

Attard-Frost, B., De los Ríos, A., & Walters, D. R. (2023). The ethics of AI business practices: A review of 47 AI ethics guidelines. *AI and Ethics, 3*, 389–406. https://doi.org/10.1007/s43681-022-00156-6

Berberich, N., & Diepold, K. (2018). The virtuous machine-Old ethics for new technology?. arXiv preprint arXiv:1806.10322.

Bourgais, A., & Ibnouhsein, I. (2022). Ethics-by-design: The next frontier of industrialization. *AI and Ethics, 2*(2), 317–324.

Cath, C., Wachter, S., Mittelstadt, B., et al. (2018). Artificial intelligence and the 'good society': The US, EU, and UK approach. *Science and Engineering Ethics, 24*, 505–528. https://doi.org/10.1007/s11948-017-9901-7

Cegarra-Navarro, J. G., Papa, A., Garcia-Perez, A., & Fiano, F. (2019). An open-minded strategy towards eco-innovation: A key to sustainable growth in a global enterprise. *Technological Forecasting and Social Change, 148*, 119727. https://doi.org/10.1016/j.techfore.2019.119727

Deng, L. (2018). Artificial intelligence in the rising wave of deep learning: The historical path and future outlook [perspectives]. *IEEE Signal Processing Magazine, 35*(1), 180–177. https://doi.org/10.1109/MSP.2017.2762725

Dwivedi, Y. K., Kshetri, N., Hughes, L., Slade, E. L., Jeyaraj, A., Kar, A. K., et al. (2023). Opinion Paper: "So what if ChatGPT wrote it?" Multidisciplinary perspectives on opportunities, challenges and implications of generative conversational AI for research, practice and policy. *International Journal of Information Management, 71*, 102642. https://doi.org/10.1016/j.ijinfomgt.2023.102642

Floridi, L. (2024). *Ética de la inteligencia artificial*. Herder Editorial.

Floridi, L., Cowls, J., King, T. C., & Taddeo, M. (2020). How to design AI for social good: Seven essential factors. In L. Floridi (Ed.), *Ethics, governance, and policies in artificial intelligence* (pp. 125–151). Springer.

Friedman, M. (2007). The social responsibility of business is to increase its profits. In W. C. Zimmerli, M. Holzinger, & K. Richter (Eds.), *Corporate ethics and corporate governance*. Springer. https://doi.org/10.1007/978-3-540-70818-6_14

Gambs, S. (2018). Privacy and ethical challenges in big data. In *International symposium on foundations and practice of security* (pp. 17–26). Springer International Publishing.

Gibert, M. (2023). The case for virtuous robots. *AI and Ethics, 3*(1), 135–144.

Goffi, E. R., & Momcilovic, A. (2022). Respecting cultural diversity in ethics applied to AI: A new approach for a multicultural governance. *Misión Jurídica: Revista de derecho y ciencias sociales, 15*(23), 111–122.

González, R. J. (2017). Hacking the citizenry?: Personality profiling, 'big data' and the election of Donald Trump. *Anthropology Today, 33*, 9–12. https://doi.org/10.1111/1467-8322.12348

Hagendorff, T. (2020). The ethics of AI ethics: An evaluation of guidelines. *Minds and Machines, 30*(1), 99–120.

Häußermann, J. J., & Lütge, C. (2021). Community-in-the-loop: Towards pluralistic value creation in AI, or—why AI needs business ethics. *AI and Ethics, 2*, 341–362. https://doi.org/10.1007/s43681-021-00047-2

Hickok, M. (2021). Lessons learned from AI ethics principles for future actions. *AI and Ethics, 1*, 41–47. https://doi.org/10.1007/s43681-020-00008-1

Hooker, J. N., & Kim, T. W. N. (2018, December). Toward non-intuition-based machine and artificial intelligence ethics: A deontological approach based on modal logic. In *Proceedings of the 2018 AAAI/ACM Conference on AI, Ethics, and Society* (pp. 130–136).

Isaak, J. D., & Hanna, M. J. (2018). User data privacy: Facebook, Cambridge analytica, and privacy protection. *Computer, 51*, 56–59. https://doi.org/10.1109/MC.2018.3191268

Jackson, W. (2019). Ethical approaches. *Markets*. https://doi.org/10.4324/9781315676593-8

Jobin, A., Ienca, M., & Vayena, E. (2019). The global landscape of AI ethics guidelines. *Nature Machine Intelligence, 1*(9), 389–399.

Kamila, M. K., & Jasrotia, S. S. (2023). Ethical issues in the development of artificial intelligence: recognizing the risks. *International Journal of Ethics and Systems*.

Klinger, J., Mateos-Garcia, J., & Stathoulopoulos, K. (2020). A narrowing of AI research? *arXiv:2009.10385*. https://doi.org/10.48550/arXiv.2009.10385

Kokas, A. (2018). Platform patrol: China, the United States, and the global battle for data security. *The Journal of Asian Studies, 77*(4), 923–933. https://doi.org/10.1017/S0021911818002541

Kriebitz, A., & Lütge, C. (2020). Artificial intelligence and human rights: A business ethical assessment. *Business and Human Rights Journal, 5*(1), 84–104.

Krupiy, T. (2021). Understanding digital discrimination: Analysing Marshall McLuhan's work through a human rights lense. *New Explorations: Studies in Culture and Communication, 2*(1), 1–22.

Lanzetta, M. (2018). Machine learning, deep learning, and artificial intelligence. In *Artificial intelligence for autonomous networks* (pp. 25–47). Chapman and Hall/CRC.
Leake, D. B. (2001). Artificial Intelligence. In *Van Nostrand scientific encyclopedia* (9th ed.). Wiley.
Madanchian, M., Taherdoost, H., & Noordin, F. (2024). Ethical leadership in AI-driven business environments. *Journal of Business Ethics, 180*(2), 345–360.
Maddula, S. S. (2018). The impact of AI and reciprocal symmetry on organizational culture and leadership in the digital economy. *Engineering International, 6*(2), 201–210.
Morandín-Ahuerma, F. (2022). What is artificial intelligence? *International Journal of Research Publication and Reviews, 3*(12), 1947–1951. https://doi.org/10.55248/gengpi.2022.31261
Morrell, K., & Dahlmann, F. (2022). Aristotle in the Anthropocene: The comparative benefits of Aristotelian virtue ethics over utilitarianism and deontology. *The Anthropocene Review, 10*, 615–635. https://doi.org/10.1177/20530196221105093
Nagendraswamy, C., & Salis, A. (2021). A review article on artificial intelligence. *Annals of Biomedical Science and Engineering, 5*(1), 13–14.
Nchebe-Jah Iloanusi, N. R., & Chun, S. A. (2024). AI impact on health equity for marginalized, racial, and ethnic minorities. In *Proceedings of the 25th Annual International Conference on Digital Health* (pp. 10–15).
Nissenbaum, H. (2022). Stewardship of privacy or private capture of a public value – A note. *SSRN Electronic Journal*. https://doi.org/10.2139/ssrn.4154535
Nwafor, C. (2021). Ethical considerations in AI-driven business models. *Journal of Business Ethics, 162*(3), 567–580.
Olatoye, F. O., Awonuga, K. F., Mhlongo, N. Z., Ibeh, C. V., Elufioye, O. A., & Ndubuisi, N. L. (2024). AI and ethics in business: A comprehensive review of responsible AI practices and corporate responsibility. *International Journal of Science and Research Archive*. https://doi.org/10.30574/ijsra.2024.11.1.0235
Pasricha, R. (2022). The role of ethics in AI business strategies. *International Journal of Business and Economics, 45*(2), 234–245.
Prem, E. (2023). From ethical AI frameworks to tools: A review of approaches. *AI and Ethics, 3*(3), 699–716. https://doi.org/10.1007/s43681-022-00157-5
Rana, N. P., Chatterjee, S., Dwivedi, Y. K., & Akter, S. (2022). Understanding dark side of artificial intelligence (AI) integrated business analytics: Assessing firm's operational inefficiency and competitiveness. *European Journal of Information Systems, 31*(3), 364–387. https://doi.org/10.1080/0960085X.2021.1955628
Richter, E., Brunner, M., & Richter, D. (2021). Teacher educators' task perception and its relationship to professional identity and teaching practice. *Teaching and Teacher Education, 101*, Article 103303. https://doi.org/10.1016/j.tate.2021.103303
Santhoshkumar, R., Patel, M., & Gupta, S. (2023). Ethical frameworks for AI in business. *Journal of Business Research, 78*(4), 345–356.
Saura, J. R., Škare, V., & Dosen, D. O. (2024). Is AI-based digital marketing ethical? Assessing a new data privacy paradox. *Journal of Innovation and Knowledge, 9*(4), 100597. https://doi.org/10.1016/j.jik.2024.100597
Schippers, B. (2020). Artificial intelligence and democratic politics. *Political Insight, 11*, 32–35. https://doi.org/10.1177/2041905820911746
Schneble, C. O., Elger, B. S., & Shaw, D. M. (2018). The Cambridge analytica affair and Internet-mediated research. *EMBO Reports, 19*, 10.15252/embr.201846579.
Sen, A. (1993). Does business ethics make economic sense? *Business Ethics Quarterly, 3*(1), 45–54. https://doi.org/10.2307/3857381
Song, F., & Yeung, S. H. F. (2024). A pluralist hybrid model for moral AIs. *AI and Society, 39*(3), 891–900. https://doi.org/10.1007/s00146-022-01601-0
Sposato, R. (2024). Business ethics in the age of AI. *Business Horizons, 67*(1), 89–101.
Stahl, B. C., Timmermans, J., & Flick, C. (2021). Ethics of artificial intelligence: A roadmap. *Science and Engineering Ethics, 27*(1), 5–25.

Staveren, I. V. (2007). Beyond utilitarianism and deontology: Ethics in economics. *Review of Political Economy, 19*, 21–35. https://doi.org/10.1080/09538250601080776

Taddeo, M., & Floridi, L. (2018). How AI can be a force for good. *Science, 361*(6404), 751–752.

Taddeo, M., & Floridi, L. (2021). Safeguarding European values with digital sovereignty: An analysis of statements and policies. *Internet Policy Review, 10*(3). https://doi.org/10.14763/2021.3.1575

Taeihagh, A., & Lim, H. S. M. (2019). Governing autonomous vehicles: Emerging responses for safety, liability, privacy, cybersecurity, and industry risks. *Transport Reviews, 39*(1), 103–128.

Thakur, N., & Sharma, A. (2024). Ethical considerations in AI-driven financial decision making. *Journal of Management and Public Policy*. https://doi.org/10.47914/jmpp.2024.v15i3.003

Tidjon, L. N., & Khomh, F. (2022). The different faces of AI ethics across the world: A principle-to-implementation gap analysis. *AI & Society, 37*(2), 123–140.

Tidjon, L. N., & Khomh, F. (2023). Ethical AI principles: A global perspective. *Journal of Global Ethics, 19*(1), 45–60.

Uddin, M. (2023). AI ethics in business: Challenges and solutions. *Journal of Business Ethics, 170*(2), 345–360.

Vakkuri, V., Kemell, K. K., Jantunen, M., Halme, E., & Abrahamsson, P. (2021). ECCOLA – A method for implementing ethically aligned AI systems. *Journal of Systems and Software, 182*, 111067. https://doi.org/10.1016/j.jss.2021.111067

Vallverdú, J., & Boix, C. (2021). Ethical implications of AI in business. *AI and Ethics, 2*(3), 123–135.

Van de Poel, I. (2020). Embedding values in artificial intelligence (AI) systems. *Minds and Machines, 30*(3), 385–409. https://doi.org/10.1007/s11023-020-09537-4

Veale, M., Van Kleek, M., & Binns, R. (2018). Fairness and accountability design needs for algorithmic support in high-stakes public sector decision-making. In *Proceedings of the 2018 CHI Conference on Human Factors in Computing Systems* (pp. 1–14).

Villongco, J., & Khan, A. (2020). Business economics and AI: Ethical considerations. *Journal of Business Research, 112*, 345–357.

Vishwanath, A., Rao, H., & Kumar, S. (2022). Ethical AI in business: A comprehensive review. *Journal of Business Ethics, 175*(4), 567–580.

Yu, H., Shen, Z., Miao, C., Leung, C., Lesser, V. R., & Yang, Q. (2018). Building ethics into artificial intelligence. *arXiv:1812.02953*. https://doi.org/10.48550/arXiv.1812.02953

Evolution and Future Perspectives in AI Ethics

Paula González-Padilla, María Fernández-Fernández, and Francisco Javier S. Lacárcel

Introduction

Over the past few decades, artificial intelligence (AI) has emerged as a transformative force that is redefining the way industries operate and evolve. From automating routine tasks to making complex decisions based on large volumes of data, AI has catalyzed significant change in diverse sectors, including healthcare, education, transportation, and finance (Rashid & Kausik, 2024). This development, however, is not without its challenges and ethical dilemmas, which are manifested in the way societies adopt and regulate these emerging technologies (Moon, 2007). The inclusion of AI in multiple areas of human life raises fundamental questions about fairness, privacy, transparency, and accountability (Akinrinola et al., 2024) underscoring the need for rigorous and systematic analysis of global trends in AI ethics (Shukla, 2024).

The massive adoption of artificial intelligence has had a considerable impact on the way industries approach their processes and strategies (Javaid et al., 2022). For example, in the healthcare sector (Javaid et al., 2022) AI systems are helping to diagnose diseases with unprecedented accuracy, while in finance, machine learning algorithms are optimizing investment decisions and managing risks more effectively. However, these advances have also triggered concerns about the potential dehumanization of certain services (Kteily & Landry, 2022), the concentration of

P. González-Padilla (✉) · M. Fernández-Fernández
Rey Juan Carlos University, Madrid, Spain
e-mail: paula.gonzalez@urjc.es; maria.ffernandez@urjc.es

F. J. S. Lacárcel
University of Alicante, Alicante, Spain
e-mail: francisco@jlacarcel.net

J. R. Saura (ed.), *Global Perspectives on AI, Ethics, and Business Economics*, Contributions to Management Science,
https://doi.org/10.1007/978-3-031-88781-9_4

power in the hands of those who control data and technology, and the possibility of algorithmic biases that perpetuate or even amplify existing inequalities (Saura, 2024). In this context, it is imperative that the study of AI ethics focuses not only on the benefits that these technologies can bring, but also on the risks and moral dilemmas that accompany their implementation (Farmer, 2023). On the other hand, the increasing integration of artificial intelligence into society not only transforms traditional industries, but also gives rise to new fields and applications that were previously unimaginable (Kumar et al., 2024).

The emergence of technologies such as autonomous systems, generative artificial intelligence, and machine learning platforms has opened up a range of possibilities for innovation in sectors such as art, communication, and entertainment (Rane et al., 2024). However, these advances have also generated debates about authorship (Eshraghian, 2020), creativity, and intellectual property rights, especially in a world where machines can create original works that compete with human productions. In this sense, the ethical discussion expands beyond the mere functionality of technology, addressing deeper questions about the nature of creativity, agency, and autonomy in the digital age (González-Padilla, Navalpotro et al., 2024). Moreover, AI is not a neutral technology; its applications and developments are intrinsically linked to human decisions and the values these decisions reflect. This means that AI systems, while designed to be efficient and objective, can perpetuate and amplify existing biases and inequalities in society if they are not designed and deployed with adequate ethical consideration (Konidena et al., 2024; Saura & Debasa, 2022). For example, the use of AI in hiring systems or judicial decisions has revealed that algorithms can discriminate against certain groups if trained with historical data that reflect human biases (Bagaric et al., 2022). Therefore, studying ethical trends in artificial intelligence is crucial to ensure that these technologies are not only technically advanced, but also fair and equitable in their social impact.

The study of the ethics of AI is not only relevant, but essential, since the decisions made today about these technologies will have lasting repercussions on the global social and economic structure. The theme of this article focuses precisely on this aspect: a bibliometric analysis of global trends in the ethics of artificial intelligence. This approach allows us to map and understand how the academic discussion around these issues is developing, to identify the main ethical challenges being addressed, and to highlight areas that still require further research and theoretical development. By analyzing the existing body of literature, it aims to illuminate the current and future dynamics of this field, providing a comprehensive view that can guide both academics and practitioners in understanding and applying ethical principles in AI.

This article seeks to fill a significant gap in the existing literature, which is often fragmented or limited to specific case studies without a comprehensive or systematic overview of ethical trends in AI. By conducting a bibliometric analysis, it is hoped not only to provide an overview of the main lines of research and areas of interest, but also to identify gaps in knowledge that need to be addressed to ensure that AI development aligns with sound ethical principles. This study is also intended to serve as a crucial reference for future work, establishing a solid foundation on which a more robust and globally accepted ethical framework can be built.

The main objective of this article is therefore twofold: first, to provide an overview of how the ethical discourse around AI has developed globally, and second, to identify key areas where more research is needed to close existing gaps in the literature. In addition to these objectives, it is also intended to foster an interdisciplinary dialogue that integrates perspectives from different fields, from philosophy and law to engineering and data science, in order to build a more holistic and applied understanding of ethics in artificial intelligence. This effort is vital not only to understand the current implications of AI, but also to anticipate and mitigate potential future challenges that may arise as these technologies continue to evolve and expand into all areas of human life. This study aims to address the following key research questions; (Q1) What are the main global trends in artificial intelligence ethics, and how have they evolved over time?; (Q2) What ethical challenges arise from the use and development of artificial intelligence across various sectors?; (Q3) What research gaps exist in the current literature on artificial intelligence ethics, and which areas require further theoretical development?

This study employs a bibliometric approach (Pritchard, 1969) to analyze published research on AI ethics, identifying key authors, journals, keywords, and their interconnections using techniques like bibliographic coupling and co-citation analysis (Chang et al., 2015). Due to the topic's novelty, no specific search period was set, enabling a comprehensive overview of the current state of the field.

The structure of this study is presented as follows: first, the introduction is provided, followed by the theoretical framework. Then, the methodology is detailed, along with the analytical processes employed. Next, the results are analyzed, followed by the discussion, which includes relevant implications. Finally, the conclusions are presented, along with the study's limitations.

Theoretical Framework

Ethics in AI has become a crucial issue in the digital age, as AI becomes increasingly integrated into our lives (Saura et al., 2024). The ability of these technologies to make autonomous decisions raises profound questions about accountability, transparency, and fairness. The concept of artificial intelligence has several definitions and there is no universally accepted one, since, like human intelligence, it is a complex term to define. This complexity underscores the need for a rigorous ethical approach to ensure that AI development aligns with the fundamental values of society (Saura et al., 2021). As AI applications continue to expand, it is imperative to address the associated ethical dilemmas to prevent unintended consequences and promote responsible use of these technologies.

In the middle of the twentieth century, Alan Turing, recognized as the "father of computing," posed a fundamental question: can machines think for themselves? In his influential article "Computing Machinery and Intelligence," published in 1950, Turing introduced what is now known as the Turing Test. In this test, the intelligence of a machine is evaluated in terms of its ability to hold a convincing and coherent conversation with a human being. If the machine manages to fool an evaluator into believing that it is interacting with another person, it is considered to have reached a level of intelligence comparable to that of a human being.

This concept was a milestone in the history of artificial intelligence, as it established a direct link between human cognitive capabilities and the potential of machines, thus inaugurating the field of study of AI. This moment is widely recognized as the starting point for research in artificial intelligence, where the boundaries between the human and computational mind began to blur, opening a debate that continues to this day about the nature and limits of artificial intelligence. The term "Artificial Intelligence" was introduced by John McCarthy in 1956. In his 2004 article, "What is Artificial Intelligence?" McCarthy defines AI as "the science and engineering of creating intelligent machines, especially intelligent computer programs." He further notes that although AI is concerned with the use of computers to understand human intelligence, it need not necessarily be limited to methods observable in human biology (McCarthy, 2007). Over time, definitions of AI have evolved, and new interpretations have emerged that better capture the different contexts and applications in which artificial intelligence operates. In 2023, the European Commission provides an updated and detailed definition of AI, describing it as systems composed of software, and in some cases also hardware, that are developed and programmed by humans. These systems are designed to address complex objectives, operating in both physical and digital environments. AI achieves this by sensing its environment, reasoning about the data and information it collects, and executing processes that enable it to make decisions or perform actions based on that analysis (Gupta et al., 2022). This definition highlights the ability of AI to interact autonomously in a variety of situations, integrating real-world data to solve complex problems, whether in virtual contexts or in physical-world applications, reflecting the increasing sophistication and reach of these technologies in contemporary society (González-Padilla et al., 2024).

Ethics in AI encompasses a set of principles and norms that seek to regulate the development and use of these technologies to minimize risks and maximize social benefits. One of the first fundamental concepts is machine autonomy, which refers to the ability of AI systems to make decisions and perform actions without direct human intervention (Candrian & Scherer, 2022). This characteristic raises ethical questions about the moral and legal responsibility for the decisions made by these systems. According to Floridi and Cowls (2022), the ethical challenge lies in defining who or what is responsible when an AI makes a mistake or makes a decision that has negative consequences. The lack of clear regulation on the assignment of responsibility is one of the main problems facing the ethical debate in this field (Díaz-Rodríguez et al., 2023). Another essential concept is algorithmic transparency, which addresses the need for the internal processes of AIs to be understandable and verifiable (Felzmann et al., 2020). The opacity of algorithms, especially in machine learning systems, raises concerns about how decisions are made. As Binns (2018) and Diakopoulos (2020) suggest, lack of transparency can lead to inadvertent bias, discrimination, or unfair decisions, which is of particular concern in areas such as criminal justice or staffing, where AI decisions can profoundly affect individuals.

Fairness and algorithmic justice constitute another pillar in AI ethics (Christoforaki & Beyan, 2022). Algorithms can inherit or amplify biases present in the data they are trained on, which can lead to biased decisions based on race, gender, or social class. Algorithmic biases are a significant ethical problem as AI, rather than correcting inequities, may perpetuate or even exacerbate them (Wang et al., 2024). The question of how to ensure that AI systems are equitable and fair is one of the biggest current challenges in the field of AI ethics (Saura et al., 2022). On the other hand, the concept of privacy is central, especially in the context of AI systems that collect and process large amounts of personal data. According to Mantelero (2018), AI poses significant risks to people's privacy, given that its ability to analyze and correlate data can result in sensitive information being used in ways that individuals do not anticipate or authorize. This leads to the need for clear policies on the collection, storage, and use of data by AI systems (Dhinakaran et al., 2024). Finally, the concept of human autonomy in decision making is also relevant (Laitinen & Sahlgren, 2021). AI has the potential to influence or even replace human decisions, raising concerns about people's ability to maintain control over their lives. Increasing reliance on AI in fields such as medicine or finance may erode individual autonomy (Mittelstadt et al., 2016), as humans could become overly dependent on machine-generated recommendations.

Methodology

Bibliometric Analysis

This study is based on a bibliometric analysis that explores the development of artificial intelligence in relation to the growing focus on ethics, within a business context. Bibliometric analysis is a quantitative methodology that examines bibliographic sources from academic databases (Donthu et al., 2021). Through this approach, it is possible to identify the main scholarly contributions, as well as to map the structure and dynamics of a research field (Hjørland, 2013). This allows the identification of networks of elements such as documents, authors, journals and keywords, and their classification in terms of relevance. The results are organized into clusters containing the main contributions to the topic of study. There are three main types of analysis in the scientific literature to ensure the quality of a bibliometric study (Durieux & Gevenois, 2010). The first is co-citation analysis, which identifies the intellectual structure of a field from the references shared in the publications. The second is bibliographic coupling, which detects documents with common references, facilitating the identification of key sources. Finally, keyword concurrence analysis is used to identify the most frequent keywords in a database (Radhakrishnan et al., 2017).

This study, as mentioned, conducts a bibliometric analysis based on three techniques in order to identify the current relationship between artificial intelligence and ethics. As for the co-citation analysis of authors and references, it is used to identify the most influential authors in this field and to understand their theoretical contributions. On the other hand, bibliographic coupling analysis is used to detect the sources of relevant academic journals that have published studies related to this field. These techniques provide insight into the development of this area of research both in the past and in the present, by examining the sources used and the concepts developed in these publications. Finally, it is important to note that keyword co-occurrence analysis is used to identify the main topics related to digitization within this field of study. By analyzing the most frequently used keywords, it is possible to understand which are the most recurrent and, thus, identify themes that allow understanding the nature and connections between the concepts raised.

For this purpose, VOSviewer software has been used, using the most current version: 1.6.20 for Macintosh. This type of analysis generates networks using maps composed of nodes and links, obtained from the data extracted from the datasets included in the study. The nodes are organized into distinct clusters by means of links, which must be interpreted in a coherent manner by the researchers. Authors, journal publications, and keywords are represented as nodes, where the relationship between them is indicated by lines reflecting their weight and relevance in the database. The closer two nodes are, the greater the importance of their link. In this context, the "fractional counting" option is used in the VOSviewer software, which allows the weight of a link to be divided. For example, if an author collaborates on a document with 20 other authors, each co-authorship link has a weight of 1/20, thus distributing the weight equally.

With the use of this software, it is possible to visually interpret the results and generate tables of contents that reflect the metrics of each element, where the authors emphasize the importance of the links and connections between the main themes of the study. The higher the density and degree of the nodes that make up the identified neurons, the greater the relevance of the clusters and their content. In addition, VOSviewer offers several options for identifying neural maps and data matrices, thus allowing different approaches to be applied in the analyses mentioned above.

Data Sampling

To ensure the rigor and scientific quality of the study, the Web of Science (WoS) database was selected to carry out the research on the relationship between artificial intelligence and ethics, linking the results of various publications. It is important to note that WoS compiles the JCR index, considered the most prestigious ranking of academic journals due to the high quality of its publications and their classification.

Therefore, this was the only database used in the study. According to authors such as Gaviria-Marin et al. (2018), this is a common practice in bibliometric studies, where data are collected and classified in a robust and consistent manner.

In order to obtain efficient results in relation to artificial intelligence and ethics, not all journals available in WoS were considered, since the number of contributions exceeds the limit necessary to carry out a robust study using the bibliometric approach indicated. In addition, the subject matter covers a wide range of areas and industries. Therefore, the search was limited to the terms: (Topic (TS) = (Artificial Intelligence) AND TS = (Ethics) AND TS = (Business). A first result of 603 articles was obtained, and by selecting the categories shown in Table 1, a total of 167 related academic articles were generated. These research papers were published during the period from the beginning of 2024 to the search date of August 2024. This date range was applied to understand a topic such as AI groups' relevance and valuable contributions in recent years. Similarly, Microsoft Excel was used to clean the data and prepare the database. VOSviewer software was then applied to process and analyze the data.

Sample Description

In relation to the description of the sample obtained from the searches performed, it is observed that it follows an upward trend in the number of publications and therefore in the interest on this type of relationship of concepts. The year 2015 marks the beginning of publications that jointly cover the concepts of artificial intelligence and ethics, with one publication during that year, following a very noticeable upward progress. It is not until 2018 when there is really a significant jump in the number of publications, with a total of 13 articles. During the next 2 years research continues to be published until 2022 where studies that talk about artificial intelligence, ethics, and business multiply, reaching the highest number of publications to date, with a total of 104 academic contributions. This information is represented below in Fig. 1, where the *Y*-axis represents the total number of publications and the *X*-axis the years in chronological order. In the two subsequent years, there are 96 publications in 2023, and 92 publications in the current year.

With regard to the categories in which most studies have been published, Table 1 shows that the Business category stands out above the rest, with 28.9% of all publications, which translates into 135 total publications. After that, the rest of the categories are more divided in these percentages, with the categories Computer Science Artificial Intelligence and Ethics, with 18.41% and 18.41%, respectively. They coincide in the number of studies published, with 86 publications each. Close behind is the Computer Science Information Systems category, which, with 76 articles, accounts for 17.13%. The next is Management with 16.27% and 76 related publications. It is at this point where the most notorious jump is made, thus we can find the category Computer Science Theory Methods with 8.65% and a total of 40 publications. At this point we can see that the figure is steadily decreasing but

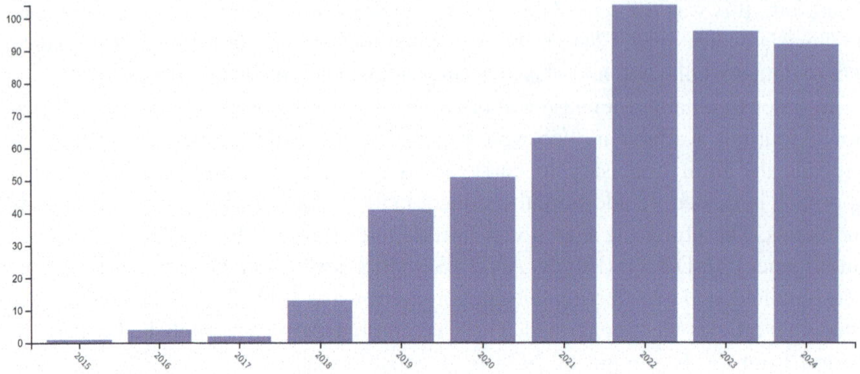

Fig. 1 Number of published articles by year from 2015 to August 2024. Source: WoS, retrieved August 15, 2024

Table 1 WoS categories and percentage of records and most articles citations

WoS categories	Number of records	% of total
Business	135	28.90%
Computer Science Artificial Intelligence	86	18.41%
Ethics	86	18.41%
Computer Science Information Systems	80	17.13%
Management	76	16.27
Computer Science Theory Methods	40	8.56%
Information Science Library Science	33	7.06%
Computer Science Interdisciplinary Applications	27	5.78%
Economics	25	5.35%
Education Educational Research	22	4.71%
Article	**Author**	**Citations**
The global landscape of AI ethics guidelines. Nature machine intelligence	Jobin et al. (2019)	3619
AI4People—an ethical framework for a good AI society: opportunities, risks, principles, and recommendations	Floridi et al. (2018)	2293
The ethics of AI ethics: An evaluation of guidelines	Hagendorff 2020	1772
Artificial intelligence in service	Huang and Rust (2018)	2989
Siri, Siri, in my hand: Who's the fairest in the land? On the interpretations, illustrations, and implications of artificial intelligence	Kaplan and Haenlein (2019).	3274

Source: Adapted from Web of Sciences data

without big jumps, and we can find the categories of Information Science Library Science, Computer Science Interdisciplinary Applications, or Economics. Their figures are 7.06%, 5.78%, and 5.35%, and 833, 27, and 25 publications, respectively. As mentioned, Table 1 shows the main categories and the number of records per category, as well as the authors who have received the most citations in the results obtained from the WoS data.

Results of Bibliometric Analysis

As previously mentioned, the results of co-citation analysis, bibliographic linkage, and keyword co-occurrence are presented.

Co-citation Analysis

In Table 2 the first five results based on the number of co-citation analysis of references and authors can be checked. The most co-cited article is Jobin et al. (2019)—"The global landscape of AI ethics guidelines." This article takes a comprehensive look at ethical guidelines related to artificial intelligence (AI) around the world. Its focus is on how these guidelines are established, considering the risks and opportunities of AI in different societies. The article by Floridi et al. (2018) presents an

Table 2 Reference co-citation and author co-citation results

Reference co-citations				Author co-citations		
Title	Author(s)	Citations	Link strength	Author(s)	Citations	Link strength
The global landscape of AI ethics guidelines. Nature machine intelligence	Jobin et al. (2019)	80.00	43.00	Floridi	194	162.46
AI4People—an ethical framework for a good AI society: opportunities, risks, principles, and recommendations	Floridi et al. (2018)	48.00	31.00	European Commission	92	69.07
The ethics of AI ethics: An evaluation of guidelines	Hagendorff (2020)	24.00	21.00	Jobin	81	81.00
Artificial intelligence in service	Huang and Rust (2018)	35.00	21.00	Huang	78	71.14
Siri, Siri, in my hand: Who's the fairest in the land? On the interpretations, illustrations, and implications of artificial intelligence	Kaplan and Haenlein (2019)	35.00	26.00	Stahl	70	64.59

Source: Authors, based on VOSviewer results

ethical framework for the appropriate use of AI in society, focusing on the principles, risks, and opportunities of AI aligned with social and ethical welfare.

Furthermore, the article by Hagendorff (2020) performs a critical evaluation of the ethical guidelines that have been proposed for AI, exploring whether these are really effective or remain as merely symbolic proposals with no real impact. The article by Huang and Rust (2018) analyzes how AI is transforming the service sector, highlighting its impact on customer experience and operational efficiency, with a focus on the future of artificial intelligence in this area. Finally, the article by Kaplan and Haenlein (2019) addresses the interpretations and applications of AI, with a particular focus on the interaction between humans and virtual assistants such as Siri, exploring both its technological and social implications. Overall, there is an ongoing debate about how these ethical guidelines and frameworks can be effectively applied to minimize risks, maximize benefits, and ensure equitable implementation of AI in various sectors.

Likewise, Fig. 2 represents the top five references resulting from the analysis computed as reference co-citation analysis. The minimum number of citations established for the analysis was 35 (Ribeiro-Navarrete et al., 2024). Of the total of 27,217 cited references, 5 met the threshold. The total link strength was 79.00 and a total of 10 links and 2 differentiated clusters.

In this figure, each reference is represented by a label. The number of times each reference is mentioned in the analyzed database is indicated by the size of the letters. The likelihood of two references being cited together is reflected in the proximity between them; the closer they appear, the greater the probability of being mentioned together. The colors, on the other hand, distinguish different clusters or groups of sources that are usually cited simultaneously.

In this case, as discussed, Fig. 2 contains two clusters. The first one, on the left of the network in red, associates between them a total of three papers (Floridi et al. (2018); Hagendorff, 2020; Jobin et al., 2019). These papers discuss ethics in

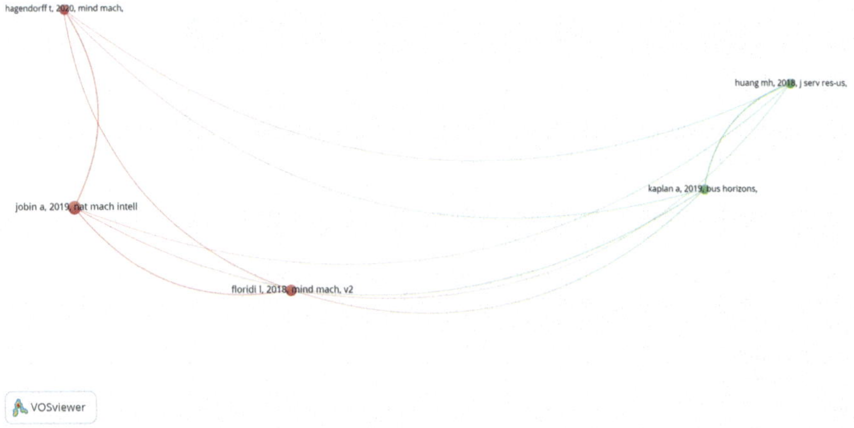

Fig. 2 Reference co-citation analysis. Source: VOSviewer results

artificial intelligence, focusing on the evaluation of ethical guidelines, the creation of ethical frameworks for the responsible use of AI, and the analysis of the global landscape of such guidelines. This cluster contains the most important papers in terms of relevance identified in the database. The second cluster, in green, compromises two papers. These papers (Huang and Rust (2018); Kaplan & Haenlein, 2019) explore how artificial intelligence is transforming the service sector and human-machine interaction, focusing on practical applications such as virtual assistants and their impact on both customer experience and society.

It should be noted that the co-citation analysis also reveals the most cited authors in the database used. In this sense, by means of a co-citation analysis based on the authors cited, the list of the most cited authors in the sample was obtained. In this analysis, 20 is normally considered as the minimum number of citations per author. Therefore, of the total 19,882 authors, 78 meet the threshold. Table 2 above shows the five authors with the highest number of citations according to the analysis obtained in VOSviewer. In this phase a total of 2380 links were obtained, 4 clusters and this computed a total link strength of 1212.02.

It is worth mentioning that the link of strength of author co-citations analysis has small differences in relation to the description of the results with respect to the reference co-citation analysis. In this case, the most cited author is Floridi with 194 citations and a link strength of 162.46. In second place, European Commission appears with 92 citations and a link strength of 69.07. Also, in third place, Jobin appears with 81 citations and 81.00 link strength.

As mentioned above, the author co-citation analysis resulted in four clusters. In this regard, Fig. 3 shows the different clusters obtained from the density analysis map of the co-citation analysis of authors. In this regard, it should be noted that in the possibility of there being different authors with the same name, this fact was previously checked as it could alter the results. In this study no discrepancies were found in relation to this issue.

For the interpretation of the results in Fig. 3, the clusters formed by the most cited authors appear in a stronger yellowish tone. This color shows, therefore, those authors receiving more citations. On the contrary, those authors who received fewer citations appear in a more greenish color. Proximity and position on the map represent the linkage between authors.

Thus, the closer the position on the map, the more likely it is that these authors will be cited together. Four clusters are identified, characterized by the topics and processes applied to ethics in artificial intelligence. In the top cluster, the most relevant and extensive, Floridi, European Commission, Hangendorf, and Stahl appear as the most relevant authors. This cluster shows a central focus on the ethics of artificial intelligence. The authors linked in this cluster address key issues such as governance, the risks associated with AI, the need for sound ethical principles, and the impact of these technologies on society globally. Taken together, this cluster represents the fundamental works that lay the foundation for the ethical discussion on the development and application of artificial intelligence.

Likewise, the cluster formed by Huang and Kaplan focuses on the practical impact of artificial intelligence. These authors explore how AI is transforming customer experience, service automation, and the role of virtual assistants such as Siri,

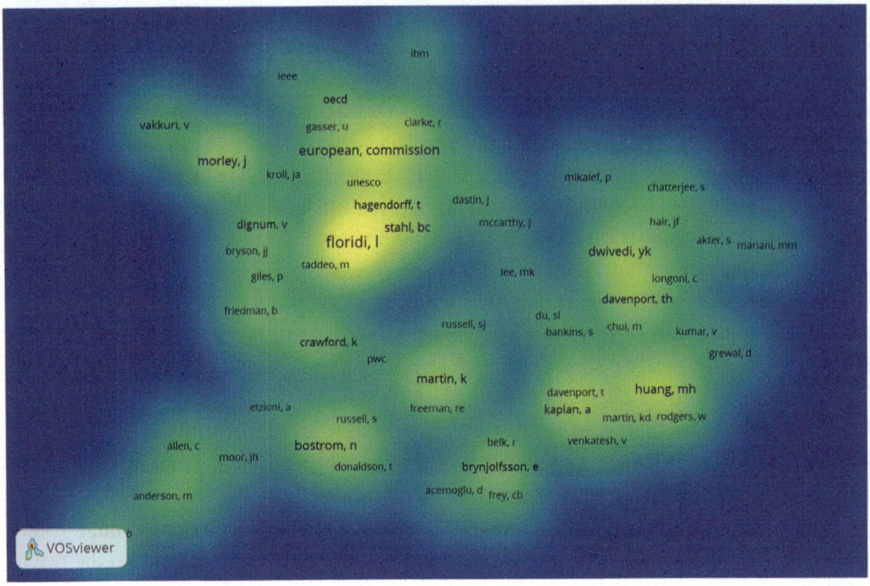

Fig. 3 Density map of author co-citation analysis. Source: VOSviewer results

analyzing both its operational benefits and the technological and social implications. Also noteworthy is the cluster formed by Davenport and Dwivedi, which focuses on the strategic and organizational use of artificial intelligence and big data. These authors address how companies and organizations are integrating AI into their processes to improve decision-making, operational efficiency, and technological innovation.

Finally, the lower and more diffuse cluster is formed by several authors including Martin, Bostrom and Brynjolfsson among others. This cluster focuses on the social and economic implications of artificial intelligence. In addition, they explore how AI may profoundly alter global economic dynamics and human-machine relationships, as well as the long-term ethical challenges that these emerging technologies pose to humanity. These results are consistent with respect to the clusters identified in the co-citation analysis of references.

Bibliographic Coupling of Sources

In the map of journals publishing on ethics in artificial intelligence the minimum number of papers from a source was set at six. Of the total 278 sources, 10 met the threshold. The number of citations of a source is equal to the total number of citations that the source papers have received in Web of Science. A total of three links were identified with a total link strength of 705.79 and 45 links. The minimum

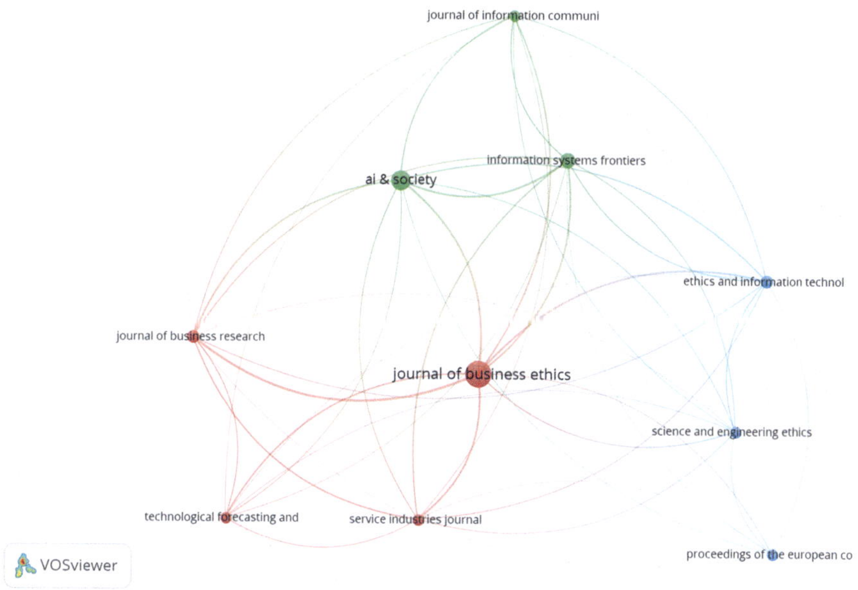

Fig. 4 Bibliographic coupling of sources by average year of publication. Source: VOSviewer results

number of citations was set to 0 in order not to penalize more recent publications (Ribeiro-Navarrete et al., 2024) (Fig. 4).

Table 3 shows the ranking of the most cited journals in the selected database. The journal with the most published papers on digitization is the *Journal of Business Ethics*. This journal has the highest number of citations with 873 and a link strength of 320.95. In second place, with a total of 488 citations, is the *Journal of Business Research*, which has a link strength of 189.84. In third place, *Information Systems Frontiers*, by number of citations, is identified with a total of 162 citations and a total link strength of 169.71.

With a very similar number of citations (142 and 141) are the journals *AI & Society* and *Technological Forecasting and Social Change*; however they differ mainly in the total link strength where the former has 198.49 and the latter has 71.67. In sixth position is the journal *Science and Engineering Ethics* with 121 citations and a total link strength of 79.91. The other four remaining journals *Service Industries Journal*, *Ethics and Information Technology*, *Journal of Information, Communication and Ethics in Society*, and *Proceedings of the European Conference on the Impact of Artificial Intelligence and Robotics*, although also relevant to the study, have less than 100 citations.

Table 3 Bibliographic coupling of sources

Source	Documents	Citations	Total link strength
Journal of Business Ethics	32	873	320.95
Journal of Business Research	7	488	189.84
Information systems frontiers	10	162	169.71
AI & Society	18	142	198.49
Technological Forecasting and Social Change	6	141	71.67
Science and Engineering Ethics	6	121	79.91
Service Industries Journal	6	94	134.59
Ethics and Information Technology	8	85	130.52
Journal of Information, Communication and Ethics in Society	6	22	93.9
Proceedings of the European Conference on the Impact of Artificial	6	4	22.00

Source: Authors, based on VOSviewer results

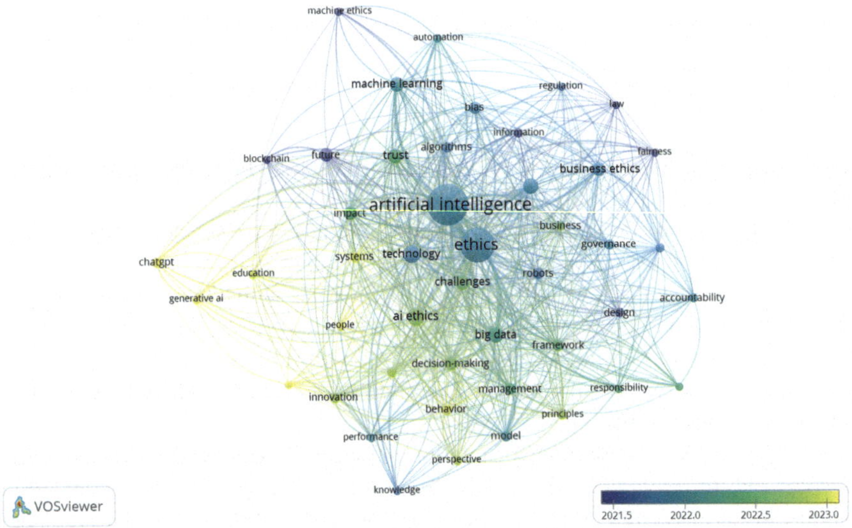

Fig. 5 Author keyword co-occurrence by average year of publication. Source: Authors, based on VOSviewer results

Author Keyword Co-occurrence

Finally, keyword co-occurrence analysis was carried out. Figure 5 shows a network of the keywords contained in the documents and Table 4 shows the ranking of keywords ordered by co-occurrence. In this case, a threshold of 10 co-occurrences was

Table 4 Author keyword co-occurrence

Keyword	Occurrences	Total link strength
Artificial intelligence	254	224
Ethics	176	169
AI ethics	49	46
Technology	46	45
Privacy	38	38
Big data	38	38
Challenges	32	32
Machine learning	33	31
Trust	27	27
Impact	27	27

Source: Authors, based on VOSviewer results

used (Ribeiro-Navarrete et al., 2024). Of the total of 2020 keywords considered, 49 keywords exceeded this threshold, and the network obtained a total of 594 links. The results indicate that the most repeated keyword is "Artificial Intelligence" with a total of 254 co-occurrences and a link strength of 224, followed by the keyword "Ethics" with 176 co-occurrences and a total link strength of 169. This is followed by linked concepts such as "AI Ethics," "Technology," and "Privacy" with lower co-occurrences of 49, 46, and 38, respectively, with a total link strength of 46.00, 25.00, and 38.00. These keywords reflect that the main focus of the literature is artificial intelligence and its ethical implications. The high co-occurrence of terms such as "Ethics," "AI Ethics," "Technology," and "Privacy" highlights the importance of considering ethical, technological, and privacy aspects in the development and use of AI, underlining the relevance of regulation and governance in this field (see Table 4).

The relationship of these keywords evidences how artificial intelligence systems are developed, implemented, and used. Ethics seeks to ensure that these systems are designed and used in a way that respects human rights and values, promotes fairness, and minimizes risks of harm. Also, the next relevant keyword by occurrence is "Big Data" (38), "Challenges" (32), and "Machine Learning" (33) with 38.00, 32.00, and 31.00 of total link strength. This fact highlights the importance of concepts such as "Big Data," "Challenges," and "Machine Learning" in the development and application of artificial intelligence. "Big Data" is key to train AI systems, while "Machine Learning" is the fundamental technology that allows these systems to learn and improve. On the other hand, the word "Challenges" underscores the difficulties in integrating AI ethically and effectively, highlighting the need to address the technical and moral complexities associated with its implementation.

In contrast, the rest of the keywords have a co-occurrence of less than 30, indicating a lower relevance compared to the most prominent terms. These less prominent terms include "Trust," "Impact," "Business Ethics," "Future," which, although important, do not have the same level of influence or presence in the literature analyzed. Taken together, these themes highlight key aspects of ethics in artificial intelligence. "Trust" is essential for its acceptance, highlighting the need for transparency and respect for privacy. The "Impact" of AI on society and the economy must be ethically evaluated to ensure that it benefits the general welfare and does not exacerbate inequalities. "Business Ethics" is crucial to ensure responsible practices in the development and use of technology, including transparency in data management and fairness to employees. Considering the "Future" of AI is important to anticipate and address emerging ethical issues. Taken together, these issues offer a comprehensive vision for effective ethics in the field of artificial intelligence.

Discussion

The bibliometric analysis of artificial intelligence (AI) ethics reveals significant advancements and persistent challenges in this rapidly evolving field. Key themes such as transparency, accountability, fairness, and the integration of ethical considerations into technological processes dominate the discourse. These findings underscore the need to align ethical frameworks with the demands of specific sectors and the sociocultural contexts where AI is applied (Jobin et al., 2019).

Another critical dimension emerging from the bibliometric analysis is the evolving nature of ethical discourse in AI, transitioning from broad philosophical principles to more application-driven considerations. This shift reflects the increasing integration of AI into critical societal infrastructures such as education, governance, and urban planning. As AI systems become more embedded in daily life, the ethical challenges extend beyond individual use cases, encompassing systemic risks and collective societal impacts. These transformations call for ongoing revisions to ethical guidelines that can dynamically respond to technological and societal changes while preserving foundational values such as fairness, transparency, and accountability (Jobin et al., 2019).

One significant finding is the limited cultural and geographical diversity in the existing literature. The predominance of studies originating from economically advanced regions highlights a bias that restricts the universal applicability of current ethical frameworks (Kaplan & Haenlein, 2019). To enrich the ethical debate and ensure the relevance of proposed solutions, it is essential to incorporate multicultural and socio-economic perspectives that address a broader range of social realities.

Furthermore, the findings highlight a notable gap in addressing power dynamics within AI ecosystems. It is crucial to ensure that diverse voices, particularly those from underrepresented and marginalized groups, are included in decision-making processes. Addressing this gap not only enhances the inclusivity of AI systems but also mitigates the risks of perpetuating or exacerbating existing inequalities, aligning ethical frameworks with principles of social justice (Hagendorff, 2020; Kaplan & Haenlein, 2019).

Another important issue is the environmental impact of AI systems, a topic that has received limited attention in prevailing ethical frameworks. Advanced technologies such as deep learning models, which require substantial energy consumption, generate significant environmental effects. According to Díaz-Rodríguez et al. (2023), sustainability should be integrated into the ethical principles of AI, with strategies that include both algorithm optimization and the adoption of renewable energy sources to minimize the ecological footprint.

International regulation emerges as a crucial challenge given the current fragmentation in AI ethics standards and policies. Floridi et al. (2018) emphasize the need to establish global ethical guidelines that are coherent yet adaptable to local contexts. In this regard, a dedicated international body for AI ethics could facilitate standardization and promote a coordinated approach to addressing the global risks associated with these technologies.

Community participation is another critical area highlighted in the findings. Affected communities play a key role in the design and deployment of AI systems, particularly in sectors such as criminal justice and healthcare, where algorithmic decisions directly impact people's lives. Participatory methods, such as public consultations and pilot testing, are useful for enhancing the legitimacy of AI systems and ensuring that they reflect the values and needs of the communities involved (Bagaric et al., 2022; Hagendorff, 2020).

Lastly, the analysis underscores the importance of an interdisciplinary approach in developing ethical frameworks. Collaboration among disciplines such as philosophy, law, sociology, and data science enables a more comprehensive understanding of the ethical challenges associated with AI. Floridi et al. (2018) suggest that integrating diverse perspectives fosters the design of more robust and effective ethical frameworks capable of addressing current dilemmas as well as future challenges arising from the evolution of these technologies.

Theoretical Implications

This bibliometric study highlights several important theoretical implications for the field of AI ethics. One of the key contributions is the need to expand existing ethical frameworks to incorporate greater cultural and geographical diversity. The current literature, dominated by contributions from economically advanced regions, presents challenges in generalizing ethical principles to more diverse contexts (Jobin et al., 2019). Developing ethical models that are both universal and adaptable to varied socio-economic realities is essential for creating more inclusive and globally relevant frameworks (Kaplan & Haenlein, 2019).

The concept of "ethics by design" emerges as a promising theoretical approach to addressing ethical dilemmas comprehensively (Floridi et al., 2018). However, this study highlights the lack of clear methodologies to facilitate its practical implementation throughout the life cycle of AI systems. For instance, Díaz-Rodríguez et al. (2023) emphasize the need for specific tools to operationalize this approach, ensuring that ethical principles are integrated from the initial stages of design.

Furthermore, the findings reinforce the importance of an interdisciplinary approach to advancing theoretical foundations in AI ethics. The integration of insights from fields such as philosophy, sociology, law, and data science not only fosters a more holistic understanding of ethical challenges but also contributes to designing frameworks that address real-world complexities (Floridi et al., 2018; Kaplan & Haenlein, 2019). This multidisciplinary perspective is critical for anticipating emerging problems and developing more robust and contextually relevant solutions.

Practical Implications

From a practical perspective, this bibliometric analysis provides valuable insights into the implementation and regulation of AI technologies. In sectors where algorithmic decisions have direct impacts, such as criminal justice, healthcare, and finance, implementing systematic ethical audits is crucial (Hagendorff, 2020). These audits help identify issues such as algorithmic bias and privacy violations, ensuring that technologies comply with ethical and legal standards (Bagaric et al., 2022). Additionally, fostering transparency in algorithmic decision-making processes is fundamental to building trust in AI systems (Binns, 2018).

Another critical practical implication is addressing the environmental impact of AI systems. Advanced technologies like deep learning models require significant energy resources, contributing substantially to the environmental footprint (Díaz-Rodríguez et al., 2023). Optimizing algorithmic efficiency and prioritizing the use of renewable energy sources are strategies that would mitigate these effects while improving societal acceptance of AI technologies.

Community participation in the design and deployment of AI technologies is also highlighted as a key implication for promoting social justice and increasing the legitimacy of these tools (Hagendorff, 2020). Actively involving affected communities ensures that their needs and values are adequately reflected in the systems developed. Participatory methods, such as public consultations and pilot testing in real-world contexts, can ensure more ethical and socially responsible implementation (Bagaric et al., 2022).

Finally, the study emphasizes the importance of developing international ethical standards to address the current fragmentation in AI regulation. Global coordination among governments, businesses, and civil society would facilitate the creation of coherent ethical guidelines adaptable to local contexts while ensuring fair and equitable implementation (Floridi et al., 2018). Moreover, training developers, policymakers, and other key actors is crucial for addressing ethical challenges in an informed and responsible manner, fostering more sustainable and ethical use of these technologies (Kaplan & Haenlein, 2019).

Conclusion

This study presents a comprehensive bibliometric analysis of global trends in artificial intelligence (AI) ethics, offering valuable insights into how this field has evolved and the ethical challenges that have emerged across different sectors. Through the identification of key publications, influential authors, and collaborative networks, the research contributes to a more nuanced understanding of the state of AI ethics, revealing areas where further theoretical and empirical work is necessary.

Over the past decade, the ethical discourse surrounding AI has shifted from general concerns about fairness, privacy, and transparency to more specific issues tied to the practical implementation of AI technologies in various industries. The rapid adoption of AI in healthcare, finance, and criminal justice, among other sectors, has brought to light ethical challenges such as algorithmic bias, data privacy violations, and the risk of deepening existing social inequalities. These concerns have underscored the importance of developing ethical frameworks that not only address immediate risks but also anticipate the long-term societal impacts of AI.

From a theoretical perspective, this study enriches the field of AI ethics by systematically mapping the intellectual landscape, identifying significant gaps, and offering a more integrated approach to the study of ethical challenges. By examining the most influential works and emerging research clusters, the study provides a solid foundation for future theoretical advancements. It points to the need for more comprehensive frameworks that incorporate cross-cultural and interdisciplinary perspectives, ensuring that AI ethics is adaptable to different societal and regulatory contexts.

In practical terms, the findings underscore the need for AI developers, policymakers, and industry leaders to address the ethical implications of AI systems from the outset. Transparency and accountability must be prioritized in the design and deployment of AI technologies, particularly in areas where algorithmic decisions have profound impacts on individuals and communities. Furthermore, the study suggests that organizations adopt continuous ethical auditing processes to ensure that AI applications align with societal values and legal frameworks. This approach is essential for mitigating risks such as bias and inequality, ensuring that AI systems contribute positively to the public good.

Looking ahead, there is a clear need for further research that bridges the gap between ethical theory and practice. This includes more empirical studies that evaluate the effectiveness of existing ethical frameworks and their application in diverse industrial and cultural contexts. Moreover, as AI technologies continue to evolve—particularly in areas such as autonomous systems and generative AI—the ethical implications of these advancements must be rigorously examined. Addressing these emerging challenges will require interdisciplinary collaboration and the development of adaptable ethical guidelines that can be applied across different legal and cultural environments.

References

Akinrinola, O., Okoye, C. C., Ofodile, O. C., & Ugochukwu, C. E. (2024). Navigating and reviewing ethical dilemmas in AI development: Strategies for transparency, fairness, and accountability. *GSC Advanced Research and Reviews, 18*(3), 050–058. https://doi.org/10.30574/gscarr.2024.18.3.0088

Bagaric, M., Svilar, J., Bull, M., Hunter, D., & Stobbs, N. (2022). The solution to the pervasive bias and discrimination in the criminal justice system: transparent and fair artificial intelligence. *American Criminal Law Review, 59*, 95. https://doi.org/10.1007/s40685-020-00134-w

Binns, R. (2018). Algorithmic accountability and public reason. *Philosophy & Technology, 31*(4), 543–556. https://doi.org/10.1007/s13347-017-0263-5

Candrian, C., & Scherer, A. (2022). Rise of the machines: Delegating decisions to autonomous AI. *Computers in Human Behavior, 134*, 107308. https://doi.org/10.1016/j.chb.2022.107308

Chang, Y. W., Huang, M. H., & Lin, C. W. (2015). Evolution of research subjects in library and information science based on keyword, bibliographical coupling, and co-citation analyses. *Scientometrics, 105*, 2071–2087. https://doi.org/10.1007/s11192-015-1762-8

Christoforaki, M., & Beyan, O. (2022). AI ethics—A bird's eye view. *Applied Sciences, 12*(9), 4130. https://doi.org/10.3390/app12094130

Dhinakaran, D., Sankar, S. M., Selvaraj, D., & Raja, S. E. (2024). Privacy-preserving data in IoT-based cloud systems: A comprehensive survey with AI integration. *arXiv Preprint*. https://doi.org/10.48550/arXiv.2401.00794

Diakopoulos, N. (2020). Accountability, transparency, and algorithms. *The Oxford Handbook of Ethics of AI, 17*(4), 197.

Díaz-Rodríguez, N., Del Ser, J., Coeckelbergh, M., de Prado, M. L., Herrera-Viedma, E., & Herrera, F. (2023). Connecting the dots in trustworthy Artificial Intelligence: From AI principles, ethics, and key requirements to responsible AI systems and regulation. *Information Fusion, 99*, 101896. https://doi.org/10.1016/j.inffus.2023.101896

Donthu, N., Kumar, S., Mukherjee, D., Pandey, N., & Lim, W. M. (2021). How to conduct a bibliometric analysis: An overview and guidelines. *Journal of Business Research, 133*, 285–296. https://doi.org/10.1016/j.jbusres.2021.04.070

Durieux, V., & Gevenois, P. A. (2010). Bibliometric indicators: quality measurements of scientific publication. *Radiology, 255*(2), 342–351. https://doi.org/10.1148/radiol.09090626

Eshraghian, J. K. (2020). Human ownership of artificial creativity. *Nature Machine Intelligence, 2*(3), 157–160. https://doi.org/10.1038/s42256-020-0161-x

Farmer, H. (2023). Reducing dehumanisation through virtual reality: prospects and pitfalls. *Current Opinion in Behavioral Sciences, 52*, 101283. https://doi.org/10.1016/j.cobeha.2023.101283

Felzmann, H., Fosch-Villaronga, E., Lutz, C., & Tamò-Larrieux, A. (2020). Towards transparency by design for artificial intelligence. *Science and Engineering Ethics, 26*(6), 3333–3361. https://doi.org/10.1007/s11948-020-00276-4

Floridi, L., & Cowls, J. (2022). A unified framework of five principles for AI in society. In S. Carta (Ed.), *Machine learning and the city: Applications in architecture and urban design* (pp. 535–545). Wiley. https://doi.org/10.1002/9781119815075.ch45

Floridi, L., Cowls, J., Beltrametti, M., Chatila, R., Chazerand, P., Dignum, V., Luetge, C., Madelin, R., Pagallo, U., Rossi, F., Schafer, B., Valcke, P., & Vayena, E. (2018). AI4People—an ethical framework for a good AI society: opportunities, risks, principles, and recommendations. *Minds and Machines, 28*, 689–707. https://doi.org/10.1007/s11023-018-9482-5

Gaviria-Marin, M., Merigo, J. M., & Popa, S. (2018). Twenty years of the journal of knowledge management: A bibliometric analysis. *Journal of Knowledge Management, 22*(8), 1655–1687. https://doi.org/10.1108/JKM-10-2017-0497

González-Padilla, P., Navalpotro, F. D., & Saura, J. R. (2024). Managing entrepreneurs' behavior personalities in digital environments: A review. *International Entrepreneurship and Management Journal, 20*(1), 89–113. https://doi.org/10.34623/tp23-a945

González-Padilla, P., Saura, J. R., & Zekan, S. B. (2024). The broadening horizon of digital marketing: Investigating its transversal impact. In P. B. Pires, J. D. Santos, & I. V. Pereira (Eds.), *Digital marketing* (pp. 91–108). CRC Press. https://doi.org/10.1201/9781003384960

Gupta, S., Modgil, S., Bhattacharyya, S., & Bose, I. (2022). Artificial intelligence for decision support systems in the field of operations research: review and future scope of research. *Annals of Operations Research, 308*(1), 215–274. https://doi.org/10.1007/s10479-020-03856-6

Hagendorff, T. (2020). The ethics of AI ethics: An evaluation of guidelines. *Minds and Machines, 30*(1), 99–120. https://doi.org/10.1007/s11023-020-09517-8

Hjørland, B. (2013). Citation analysis: A social and dynamic approach to knowledge organization. *Information Processing & Management, 49*(6), 1313–1325. https://doi.org/10.1016/j.ipm.2013.07.001

Huang, M. H., & Rust, R. T. (2018). Artificial intelligence in service. *Journal of Service Research, 21*(2), 155–172. https://doi.org/10.1177/1094670517752459

Javaid, M., Haleem, A., Singh, R. P., & Suman, R. (2022). Artificial intelligence applications for industry 4.0: A literature-based study. *Journal of Industrial Integration and Management, 7*(01), 83–111. https://doi.org/10.1142/S2424862221300040

Javaid, M., Haleem, A., Singh, R. P., Suman, R., & Rab, S. (2022). Significance of machine learning in healthcare: Features, pillars and applications. *International Journal of Intelligent Networks, 3*, 58–73. https://doi.org/10.1016/j.ijin.2022.05.002

Jobin, A., Ienca, M., & Vayena, E. (2019). The global landscape of AI ethics guidelines. *Nature Machine Intelligence, 1*(9), 389–399. https://doi.org/10.1038/s42256-019-0088-2

Kaplan, A., & Haenlein, M. (2019). Siri, Siri, in my hand: Who's the fairest in the land? On the interpretations, illustrations, and implications of artificial intelligence. *Business Horizons, 62*(1), 15–25. https://doi.org/10.1016/j.bushor.2018.08.004

Konidena, B. K., Malaiyappan, J. N. A., & Tadimarri, A. (2024). Ethical considerations in the development and deployment of AI systems. *European Journal of Technology, 8*(2), 41–53. https://doi.org/10.47672/ejt.1890

Kteily, N. S., & Landry, A. P. (2022). Dehumanization: Trends, insights, and challenges. *Trends in Cognitive Sciences, 26*(3), 222–240. https://doi.org/10.1016/j.tics.2021.12.003

Kumar, S., Verma, A. K., & Mirza, A. (2024). *Digital transformation, artificial intelligence, and society*. Springer. https://doi.org/10.1007/978-981-97-5656-8

Laitinen, A., & Sahlgren, O. (2021). AI systems and respect for human autonomy. *Frontiers in Artificial Intelligence, 4*, 705164. https://doi.org/10.3389/frai.2021.705164

Mantelero, A. (2018). AI and Big Data: A blueprint for a human rights, social and ethical impact assessment. *Computer Law & Security Review, 34*(4), 754–772. https://doi.org/10.1016/j.clsr.2018.05.017

McCarthy, J. (2007). What is artificial intelligence?

Mittelstadt, B. D., Allo, P., Taddeo, M., Wachter, S., & Floridi, L. (2016). The ethics of algorithms: Mapping the debate. *Big Data & Society, 3*(2), 2053951716679679. https://doi.org/10.1177/2053951716679679

Moon, J. (2007). The contribution of corporate social responsibility to sustainable development. *Sustainable Development, 15*(5), 296–306. https://doi.org/10.1002/sd.346

Pritchard, A. (1969). Statistical bibliography; an interim bibliography

Radhakrishnan, S., Erbis, S., Isaacs, J. A., & Kamarthi, S. (2017). Novel keyword co-occurrence network-based methods to foster systematic reviews of scientific literature. *PLoS One, 12*(3), e0172778. https://doi.org/10.1371/journal.pone.0172778

Rane, N. L., Paramesha, M., Rane, J., & Kaya, O. (2024). Emerging trends and future research opportunities in artificial intelligence, machine learning, and deep learning. *Artificial Intelligence and Industry in Society, 5*, 2–96. https://doi.org/10.70593/978-81-981271-1-2_6

Rashid, A. B., & Kausik, A. K. (2024). AI revolutionizing industries worldwide: A comprehensive overview of its diverse applications. *Hybrid Advances*. https://doi.org/10.1016/j.hybadv.2024.100277

Ribeiro-Navarrete, B., Saura, J. R., & Simón-Moya, V. (2024). Setting the development of digitalization: state-of-the-art and potential for future research in cooperatives. *Review of Managerial Science, 18*, 1459–1488. https://doi.org/10.1007/s11846-023-00663-8

Saura, J. R. (2024). Algorithms in digital marketing: Does smart personalization promote a privacy paradox? *FIIB Business Review, 13*(5), 499–502. https://doi.org/10.1177/23197145241276898

Saura, J. R., & Debasa, F. (Eds.). (2022). *Handbook of research on artificial intelligence in government practices and processes*. IGI Global. https://doi.org/10.4018/978-1-7998-9609-8

Saura, J. R., Palacios-Marqués, D., & Iturricha-Fernández, A. (2021). Ethical design in social media: Assessing the main performance measurements of user online behavior modification. *Journal of Business Research, 129*, 271–281. https://doi.org/10.1016/j.jbusres.2021.03.001

Saura, J. R., Ribeiro-Soriano, D., & Palacios-Marqués, D. (2022). Assessing behavioral data science privacy issues in government artificial intelligence deployment. *Government Information Quarterly, 39*(4), 101679. https://doi.org/10.1016/j.giq.2022.101679

Saura, J. R., Škare, V., & Dosen, D. O. (2024). Is AI-based digital marketing ethical? Assessing a new data privacy paradox. *Journal of Innovation & Knowledge, 9*(4), 100597. https://doi.org/10.1016/j.jik.2024.100597

Shukla, S. (2024). Principles governing ethical development and deployment of AI. *Journal of Artificial Intelligence Ethics, 7*(1), 45–60. https://doi.org/10.22161/ijebm.8.2.5

Wang, A., Kapoor, S., Barocas, S., & Narayanan, A. (2024). Against predictive optimization: On the legitimacy of decision-making algorithms that optimize predictive accuracy. *ACM Journal on Responsible Computing, 1*(1), 1–45. https://doi.org/10.1145/3636509

Part II
AI Applications and Governance in a Digital Society

City Information Management and Climate Change Policies: A Boundary Spanning Approach

Alex Ingrams

Introduction

Climate change policymaking is one of the most important areas of attention for governments and businesses today (Bally & Coletti, 2023; Finnegan, 2022; Meuleman, 2021), and data has become an invaluable governance tool for implementing climate change policy goals (Gotgelf, 2022; Hughes et al., 2020). Governance *through* data (sometimes, "data-driven governance") is the use of data to improve "the design, delivery and monitoring of public policies and services" (van Ooijen et al., 2019, 6). In the domain of climate change policymaking, governance through data includes, for example, informal and formal data management responsibilities in areas such as performance measurement, reporting, and open data (Schumacher et al., 2022), regulating industry (Fernandez-Monge et al., 2023) and prompting behaviour change of citizens (Yeung & Bygrave, 2022). Further, there are bespoke decision-making structures—advisory units, committees, industry consultations, etc.—needed to build capacity for managing data (Boyd & Juhola, 2015; Doelle et al., 2012).

Scholarly developments have thus provided much needed understanding of the different ways that governance through data can be implemented in climate change policymaking. However, we still know much less about *why* governments choose to use certain data governance tools over others. As climate change policymaking has been shown to be highly collaborative in nature (Boyd & Juhola, 2015; Kalesnikaite, 2019; Koliba et al., 2011), it begs the question of how collaborative governance settings shape decision-making about different tools. Such decision-making is important because it can determine policymaking success in the climate change domain

A. Ingrams (✉)
Institute of Public Administration, Leiden University, The Hague, The Netherlands
e-mail: a.r.ingrams@fgga.leidenuniv.nl

J. R. Saura (ed.), *Global Perspectives on AI, Ethics, and Business Economics*, Contributions to Management Science,
https://doi.org/10.1007/978-3-031-88781-9_5

(Leiren & Jacobsen, 2018; Schmidt et al., 2024). The implications of these collaborative governance explanations of data use have not been fully developed in studies of the use of climate change data in policymaking, which have tended to focus on technical specifications and the optimal or sub-optimal potential of data use (Hughes et al., 2020). When the collaborative governance context of government, businesses and third parties is considered in the literature, it is normally with regard to the nature of the collaborative arrangements themselves (e.g. Doelle et al., 2012; Koliba et al., 2011; Leck & Simon, 2013) and not on the impact of the arrangements on data governance. To address this gap, the question I aim to provide a preliminary answer for in this research is: what kinds of data governance tools do governments use in a collaborative governance setting of climate change policymaking?

In this chapter, I address this question by developing an explanatory theory for why public organisations take different data governance strategies by using the perspective of organisational boundary spanning. I also find evidence of the extent to which strategies are realised in the form of specific types of data governance tools. The main argument in the chapter is that the way that cities choose their data governance tools for climate change policymaking results in large part from the collaborative governance setting of contemporary climate change policymaking. The study is focused at the city level as the success of climate commitments of national governments often turns on the role of cities, pivotally requiring the input of local actors (Bae & Feiock, 2013; Lee, 2024).

Below, I set out a theory of organisational boundary spanning and data governance in the climate change policy arena. Four strategic approaches are derived deductively and are then developed into a more fine-grained analysis of specific kinds of data governance tools using natural language topic modelling on a large dataset of city climate policy actions. The policies are analysed, findings and gaps are discussed in the context of the fourfold strategy framework. Finally, the results are linked to debates in the literature on climate change governance and public and private sector data sharing and governance.

Theory

Data Governance in Climate Change Policymaking

While climate change policy is shaped vertically by climate laws and treaties that governments and their partners must comply with, governments can only realise their goals and responsibilities horizontally through collaborative governance networks with citizens, businesses, and civil society organisations (Blok & Tschötschel, 2016; Ciplet et al., 2018; Nguyen Long & Krause, 2021). This creates multistakeholder coordination challenges in forming and implementing policies. Governments have to coordinate diverse policy interest groups, large risks, and huge amounts of data about the climate and the natural environment (Florini & Saleem, 2011; Halkier, 2017; Leck & Simon, 2013).

A further dimension of governance approaches is their dependency on institutional context. Governments with unique environmental vulnerabilities develop salient preferences for collaborations and policies that address those vulnerable areas (Nguyen Long & Krause, 2021), while governance innovations are also strongly shaped by existing level of formality and horizontality in climate policy-related institutions and partnerships (Doelle et al., 2012). Above existing structures and institutions, collaborative arrangements also come under influence of more epistemological matters such as scientific beliefs and policy positions to the extent that linking network actors in a successful way often relies on clear policy positions and coordination from central actors (Gronow et al., 2020).

This complex setting for collaborative arrangements leads to variation in the data governance approaches, and existing scholarship provides frameworks that can help explain how this works. Keller (2009) used the lens of organisational boundary spanning theory to explain how organisations strategically justify their institutional existence by defining and managing their functional boundaries in an organisationally crowded environment. According to Keller, public organisations essentially use data strategies in either a buffering or linking way. Buffering is a discursive process used to protect factual integrity from interference and to make an organisation's policy standpoint clear, while linking is a relational process with other organisations used to create political support and legitimacy. Halkier (2017) goes further, distinguishing between vertical- and horizontal-driven strategies. Halkier argues that the relational, linking side of data governance has two types: network understanding (citizens are viewed as data-sharing public) and dialogical understanding (coproduction approach with the public). Similarly, there are two types on the buffering axis: deficit understanding (scientific knowledge) and segmentation understanding (scientific but with awareness of how understanding fits different types of data consumer).

Drawing together these ideas of Keller (2009) and Halkier (2017), Fig. 1 renders this interrelationship of characteristics in a typology of four data governance strategies: evidence building, performance management, third-party disclosure and information coproduction. Further, below, the conceptual and practical scope of the strategies is fleshed out using what we know from existing scholarly literature.

Evidence building has as its aim to generate understanding and form scientific consensuses and agenda-forming knowledge around environmental policy. It is led centrally in a top-down manner. In the strategic domain of evidence building, cities might use tools for generating, gathering, managing, and communicating data for the dialectical purpose of building public understanding and winning arguments about the state of the environment and the available policy approaches. This would involve, for example, carrying out scientific research and collecting data on the climate such as water levels and amounts of atmospheric gases (Best et al., 2021; Scheer, 2015).

Third-party disclosure involves requiring or negotiating publication of environmental data with other actors (normally private sector) to ensure/track compliance with environmental policies. Cities can use third-party disclosure tools such as online registries whereby industries are required to publish data about their

		Source of legal and normative pressure	
		Vertical Mandates and intergovernmental norms	**Horizontal** Interorganisational agreements and norms
Boundary spanning strategies	**Buffering** Epistemological claims and scientific authority	Evidence building (deficit strategies)	Performance management (segmentation strategies)
	Linking Relationship building and intergroup dynamics	Third party disclosure (network strategies)	Information coproduction (dialogic strategies)

Fig. 1 Typology of data governance strategies in the climate change policy arena. Source: Author's own

environmental performance on things such as greenhouse gas emissions and renewable energy. Disclosure strategies might also be a way of aligning stakeholder interests with those expressed by official climate policy in a coercive manner (Meijer & Homburg, 2009). Thus, third-party disclosure policies might also come with an accompanying strategy of engagement and building wider networks to improve their effectiveness (Florini & Saleem, 2011).

Performance management concerns establishing benchmarks or targets to shape behaviour, track performance and develop policies (Pearce & Cooper, 2011). For example, with carbon emission reduction targets, official mission statements or plans drive internal agency action on reductions (Shand, 2018) and foster accountability on climate change policy (Zia & Koliba, 2011). Performance management tools could include things such as statistical analysis and reports showing how the city and other key environmental actors perform according to pre-set targets.

Information coproduction has as its goal to invite the public to become a partner in data creation and utilisation and is mainly focused on open data as government data or crowdsourcing as citizen-sourced data. Environmental impacts affect diverse areas of life, science and policy and it is difficult for governments to collect all the data they need without the help of citizens (Guerrini et al., 2018). Such coproduction strategies aim to foster bottom-up collaboration by sharing knowledge and information as well as improving the quality of services and policies by making them more attuned to what is happening in the real world (Douglass, 2014; Meijer & Thaens, 2009).

The typology of data governance strategies is intended to be empirically comprehensive. That is, all data practices developed within collaborative governance settings can be fitted a priori into the typology. However, it may not effectively explain other kinds of data strategies that are not primarily in collaborative settings. For example, data secrecy or disinformation strategies (e.g. Hoggan & Littlemore, 2009). What kinds of data governance tools do governments use in these different strategies and is there evidence that they are actually being used? In the empirical part of the chapter below, the practice-based descriptions of specific data governance tools are expanded using cases from the real world. Their relevance and frequency of use is explored in the context of collaborative governance in climate change policymaking.

Methods

Case Selection and Data Sampling

As a source of city data, I used secondary data gathered by the open data platform CDP (formerly called the Carbon Disclosure Project, and now broadened in focus), which runs a policy disclosure network to record the climate policy actions of 1128 cities across 85 countries worldwide. The CDP case is, to the author's knowledge, the most comprehensive database of qualitative information on city-level climate change policy initiatives and therefore provides two key advantages for theory-driven case analysis: representativeness and interesting variation in terms of governance through data practices (Seawright & Gerring, 2008). The way the database works is that the city members voluntarily submit a record of such actions on an annual basis as a way to centralise their environmental policy monitoring and to develop a common policy language and benchmarks with other cities around the world. Between 2011 and 2020 there were 2,435,155 policy entries. In order to control for data governance practices and provide a clearer basis for comparing cities in different political and economic contexts, I sampled only from a relatively homogenous set of countries with similar economic and political characteristics using country membership in the Organisation for Economic Cooperation and Development (OECD) as a selection criterion (shown in Table 1. The full list of cities is in Appendix). This approach reduces the country diversity of the sample and limits generalisability beyond OECD countries that are predominantly members of the "Global North." However, policy influences and institutional norms represent a too variable set of patterns and behaviours outside of a more similar set of countries (such as the OECD) and would make interpretation of the results more complicated (Andrews, 2010; Bauer et al., 2012).

The sample was also limited to English language policy texts. Further, while all the policy entries in the database cover climate change policy areas such as climate hazards and adaptation, emissions reduction, energy, buildings and transport, urban planning, food, waste and water security, many of these entries are not focused on aspects of data tools per se. Use of the entire dataset for analysis was thus not

Table 1 Regions and countries with cities and population statistics included in the CDP database[a]

Eastern Europe: Croatia (1); Latvia (2); Lithuania (4); Poland (4); Slovenia (1) *Northern Europe:* Denmark (18); Estonia (4); Finland (5); Iceland (2); Norway (2); Sweden (2) *North America:* Canada (11); United States (63) *Central America:* Mexico (4)	*Oceania:* Australia (2) New Zealand (2) *Western Europe:* Belgium (1); France (6); Germany (11); Greece (2); Ireland (1); Italy (29); Netherlands (4); Portugal (11); Spain (6); Switzerland (3); United Kingdom (8)

Source: Author's own
[a]Number of included cities in parentheses

Table 2 Search codes used for the four climate policy task areas

Evidence building
Fact, Research*, Eviden*, Scien*, Data**
Third-party disclosure
Monitor, Complian*, Disclos*, Regulat*, Transparen**
Performance measurement
Perform, Measur*, Bench*, Target*, Rank*, Evaluat*, Assess*, Indicator*, Index**
Coproduction
Open data, Big data, Smart, Hack, Crowdsourc*, Tracking**

NB. Asterisks indicate truncated version of the same word included with different endings
Source: Author's own

feasible. To address this challenge, I undertook a screening process to select only the relevant policy texts from within the entire database. The first step was to develop a governance through data axial codebook based on search codes (Table 2) for each of the four strategic domains, performance management, coproduction, third-party disclosure and evidence building. These search codes were developed deductively by considering the theoretical framework, cognate words and related policy terms that could be used to capture the four domains. The second step was to search and extract policy entries in the CDP database using these search codes. The final step required closer reading of the selected policies to make sure that they conformed with the codebook, and to drop those that were not. In the vast majority of cases, the selection was correct but there were also some unrelated entries (e.g. policies found using the keyword "measure" but which actually referred in a generic way to any "policy measure" rather than the act of using data for performance management). In the final sample, there were $n = 7510$ policy texts from 209 different cities which formed the basis for preprocessing, topic modelling and data analysis.

Modelling and Data Analysis

I employed Latent Dirichlet Allocation (LDA) with R Studio to analyse the corpus of policy texts. LDA is an unsupervised machine learning method that models the co-occurrence of sets of words across a corpus of documents and then estimates the probability that certain words will be associated with a latent topic in the texts. LDA thus gives a semantic basis for researchers to make inferences about the cumulative meaning of large amounts of textual material. This approach to LDA has been used widely in the social sciences to find topics that are latent in texts such as policy and agenda setting documents (e.g. Hollibaugh, 2019) or mining citizen feedback (e.g. Beltran et al., 2021) and freedom of information requests by citizens (e.g. Berliner et al., 2018).

A well-fitted LDA model suggests a model that shows an optimum number of topics (with associated words) that is "rich enough to fit the information available in the data, yet not so complex as to begin fitting noise" (Griffiths & Steyvers, 2004, p. 5231). Well-fitted models capture the diversity of textual information by finding a number of topics that (1) does not miss critical semantic dimensions of the corpus and (2) that are internally valid in the sense of finding a correct level of topical distinctiveness that doesn't lead to either semantic overlap between the topics or under-specification of the topics.

"Words" and "documents" are the fundamental unit of analysis in LDA and form the vector space in which the topic model is fitted. The word syntax of the corpus in terms of sentence order as well as the order of the documents is unimportant. Rather the semantic validity of topic is based on the frequency of co-occurring words and the likelihood of finding such co-occurrence in any given document if any given word were to be repeatedly picked. In this research, each of the policy descriptions provided by the cities was considered a "document" and the "words" are all the text (after performing the preprocessing steps described below) in those documents. These policy descriptions varied from very brief descriptions such as "A GPC [global privacy control] compliant dataset has been established for Greater Manchester" to longer descriptions such as "Actual usage data for electricity and natural gas were obtained directly from the department or agency responsible for its production. The transportation data was obtained from the Southern California Association of Governments. Electricity and natural gas were multiplied by their respective emission factor obtained from the Local Government Protocol (The Climate Registry)."

A difficult part of natural language processing is that textual data can often be messy and noisy. That difficulty applies no less here, especially with a kind of textual data that uses administrative language that can contain textual shorthand, bespoke notation and various kinds of abbreviations. Thus, standard LDA preprocessing protocols were followed to clean the text including removing punctuation (the software count models a semantic distribution using all the discrete elements in the text, which would not make sense for punctuation), lemmatising words (to allow variations of words such as "collect" and "collecting" to be treated as the same word) and the removal of very common words such as conjunctions and definite articles that do not add to the important semantic dimensions of the corpus (Grolemund, 2014; Kowalski et al., 2020). I also removed the word "city" (e.g. as in the "city of Los Angeles") and the proper names of cities as these were regularly used though extraneous to the substantive purpose of the policies. More technical references to the government unit and scope, such as municipality, urban or local were retained.

The main output of an LDA model is a predicted number of topics and the keywords most likely to be associated with those topics. The number of topics (called "alpha") is an important way of determining the variety of information in the corpus and is set in advance manually by the programmer. While it is possible for the programmer to decide this using their contextual knowledge about the texts to make the decision on alpha, statistical packages such as the Gibbs algorithm provides a mathematical solution to the problem by repeatedly sampling word sequences from a vector space of words and documents until it converges on a number of topics that best captures the semantic variation of the corpus (Griffiths & Steyvers, 2004). I ran the Gibbs algorithm, which suggested that a parameter set at $\alpha = 20$ would fit the data best. Numbers below 20 would insufficiently account for semantically distinct topics, while above 20, the gains of a higher number of topics rapidly diminished.

Results

The LDA analysis resulted in the 20 topics and, for each, the 10 words with the highest probability of being associated with each of the topics (shown in Table 3). The names of the topics in the column after the numbers is something that is decided ex post by the researcher rather than being an output of the machine learning algorithm itself. The logic of giving a label to a topic is to use words that summarise the semantic unity of the 10 words and to make the label of each topic as thematically distinct as possible. The labelling process thus relies on human reading of the keywords and contextual knowledge of the raw textual data (Blei et al., 2003). At face value, the topics in Table 3 show good semantic validity which would suggest that the topic estimation worked well. There are no goodness of fit statistics in LDA, and substantive interpretation of the results relies on assessing the coherence and distinctiveness of the topics and associated words (Berliner et al., 2018). The results here suggest that there are no associated words appearing obviously semantically unrelated. Further, the topics are sufficiently distinct from each other. The theta (θ) scores showing the expected probability that a document will be associated with any given topic are quite evenly distributed, ranging between 0.085 and 0.033, meaning that none of the policy topics was dominant across the corpus as a whole.

To validate these topics, give them substantive interpretation and elucidate what they mean for our understanding of data governance strategies and types of tools, I carried out a further qualitative analysis of the raw data. I sampled among the policy entries in the database guided by the most important associated words in the topics. I randomly selected 20 policy entries from each of the 20 topics and read the

Table 3 LDA results showing topics and most associated words[a]

Topic		Most associated words	Topic		Most associated words
1	Smart transport systems ($\theta = 0.085$)	Smart, Public, Transport, Grid, Vehicles, New, Clean, Green, Traffic, Electric	2	Buildings performance measurement ($\theta = 0.079$)	Energy, Buildings, Efficiency, Performance, Building, Measures, Municipal, Commercial, Residential, Facilities
3	Greenhouse gas emissions targeting ($\theta = 0.075$)	Emissions, Reduction, Target, Plan, GHG, Year, Actions, Climate, Community, Measures	4	Energy consumption monitoring ($\theta = 0.070$)	Data, Inventory, Gas, Energy, Consumption, Emission, Greenhouse, Utility, Local, Use
5	Impact reports ($\theta = 0.055$)	Climate, Change, Assessment, Impact, Adaptation, Risks, Strategy, IPCC, Research, Energy	6	Risk assessments ($\theta = 0.055$)	Assessment, Vulnerability, Risk, Urban, Methodology, Region, Climate, State, Within, Area
7	Strategic plans ($\theta = 0.049$)	Plan, Climate, Adaptation, Mitigation, National, Master, Potential, Risks, New, Research	8	Environmental impact planning and consultation ($\theta = 0.049$)	Environmental, Assessment, Impact, Plan, Development, Part, Council, Local, Policy, Hazards
9	Renewables performance measurement ($\theta = 0.048$)	Energy, Renewable, Target, Electricity, Mayors, Covenant, According, Heat, Methodology, Included	10	Energy and electricity performance measurement ($\theta = 0.046$)	Energy, Lighting, Renewable, Municipal, Project, Measures, Within, Included, Climate, Targets
11	Flood monitoring and prevention ($\theta = 0.046$)	Water, Management, Flood, Areas, Risk, Conservation, Ordinance, Program, Flooding, Increase	12	Carbon emissions performance measurement ($\theta = 0.045$)	Target, Data, Climate, Tonnes, COE, Targeted, Emission, Projects, Policies, Person
13	Smart meters ($\theta = 0.045$)	Smart, Data, Meters, National, Obtained, Citywide, Municipal, Centre, Pilot, Emissions	14	Climate analysis ($\theta = 0.042$)	Analysis, Climate, Adaptation, Calculations, Municipality, Change, Emissions, Target, Energy, Measure
15	Carbon emissions monitoring ($\theta = 0.039$)	Emissions, Carbon, Measures, Reduce, Targets, Scope, Zero, Measuring, Reduction, Monitoring	16	Energy and air quality improvement ($\theta = 0.038$)	Energy, Quality, Hear, District, Power, Programme, Improvement, Linked, Air, Action
17	Waste measurement ($\theta = 0.037$)	Waste, Department, Process, Level, Local, Management, Building, Division, Emissions, Measured	18	Smart energy planning ($\theta = 0.033$)	Plan, Action, Sustainable, Energy, Development, Smart, Strategy, Master, Programme, Implementation
19	Sustainability networks ($\theta = 0.033$)	Network, Sustainable, Number, Social, Goal, Resilience, Water, Municipality, Actions, Urban	20	Water supply analysis ($\theta = 0.033$)	Water, Infrastructure, Climate, Ensure, Supply, Stormwater, Investments, Conditions, Risk, Capacity

Source: Author's own

[a]Topics listed in order of probability of being associated with a document. Most associated words are listed in order of their probability of being associated with the topic

resulting 400 policy entries in depth, cross-checking abbreviations (such as "COE," which refers to carbon emissions) or technical terms (such as "C40 network") using desk research.

Evidence Building

The analysis showed that data on water is particularly important here given challenges around water shortages and equitable access. This includes "periodic research using best available science to inform our understanding of the potential impacts on our supply." Water forecasts provided evidence that could be incorporated statically into policy reports or more dynamically into warning and alert systems such as RainWatch in Seattle.

Related to water data is the science around weather, heat islands, and sea-level rises such as in the *impact reports* and *risk assessment* topics, which focus on "mapping" and "prediction" efforts by "local research projects" as well as social statistics around vulnerable populations. There were also tools based on evidence building regarding emissions, energy and utilities which was a major focus. Reading of the city policies showed some evidence of communication using traditional tools such as impact reports and risk assessments in areas such as developing "Strategic Climate Change Forecasts," a "transportation-focused climate adaptation plan" and "monitoring and surveillance of climatic variables and ecosystems related to City-owned watersheds." However, absence of words around "communication," "awareness" or "understanding" suggested that getting evidence or science communicated to the public in general is not part of the policy efforts.

Third-Party Disclosure

Third-party disclosure would aim to make important information available to decision-makers as well as an accountability tool to make powerful private actors behave in ways that furthers the public interest. However, few, if any, topics address third-party disclosure tools. There was evidence of quite vague regulatory requirements being placed on water authorities to monitor and collect important information about water use through reports, for example, "Regulatory concerns focus on shared water rights of the Colorado River" and "Local water providers are monitoring water use very closely," while "Some districts and co-existing cities are currently examining the possibility of initiating freshwater metering and billing within commercial and residential sectors." Another area of third-party disclosure concerned the topic of *carbon emissions monitoring*. Policies such as "measuring and reporting on carbon emissions" and "monitoring and evaluation of the long-range transmission of air pollutants" depend on companies submitting carbon emissions data, though the manner of disclosure and whether it is publicly disclosed gets almost no attention.

Further, the "disclosing" aspect of tools is generally missing from these initiatives. Often it is implied (such as when a "register" is developed or a new "metering" system is introduced) and specific third parties are rarely mentioned, perhaps to avoid appearing to show favouritism by the city towards specific companies. Types of new information and communication technologies are used that make visibility of information available in limited commercial contexts such as a policy that "The San Francisco Public Utilities Commission Water Enterprise's Automated Water Meter system uses a low-frequency radio signal to collect hourly water consumption data and transmit them four times a day from residential and commercial customers to the billing system without the need for physical field visits and manual meter reading." A puzzle regarding tools around third-party disclosure is that the existence of regulations and mandates for private and public actors is clearly present as is the need for data to be collected about environmental impacts. However, regulations or requirements around how data is used and published are not mentioned or are vague.

Performance Management

Tools in this category are evident across many of the topics. In the *Renewables performance measurement* topic, performance management was used to collect and evaluate performance data on areas such as storm water management and heat preparedness. Other policy areas were water in *Flood prevention and monitoring* and waste in *Waste measurement*. In the former, policies included targeting waste water reduction at certain percentage rates, creating water quality standards and integrating performance measurements with other areas of performance such as socio-economic impacts. On the latter, designing standards for emissions measured for waste and mapping existing waste collection systems to find areas for efficiency savings. Perhaps surprisingly, given the need to address accountable actors, the relevant industries who use significant amounts of water or energy do not emerge as important words in the topics.

In the areas of energy and emissions with *Greenhouse gas emissions targeting* and *Energy consumption monitoring*, respectively, there were also performance management approaches around developing standards and quantifying desired outcomes. More innovative approaches to performance management were in existence too such as communication on emissions performance by "social media coverage and the percentage of emergencies successfully communicated," factoring refugee numbers to emissions predictions or "national decisions when these are influencing the price level on certain activities."

The policy descriptions include many different performance management tools, most of which are traditional such as annual budgets, strategic plans and action plans, annual reports, and ranking indexes. However, there are also tools that seem more tailored to the context of climate crisis and policymaking such as design of green energy standards, live broadcasts from committees, free infrastructure assessments to incentivise participation, and incorporating local climate-related data into patient health records. For example, the city of Mississauga had a "Green Development Standard" that "sets performance targets on new building development to increase energy efficiency." Toronto had "a two-tiered set of performance measures with supporting guidelines related to sustainable site and building design for new public and private development." What was not in evidence beyond the various ways of measuring and presenting results was a way to change the performance of actors such as through incentives or penalties. It is perhaps assumed that poor performance results in a learning process such as through reputational damage and that collaborative approaches are better than punitive approaches. But, nevertheless, discussion of fines, rewards or review mechanisms was absent.

Information Coproduction

Coproduction includes the sharing of data over smart systems, and this aspect of smartness was widely found across the topics particularly with private companies in the role of providing utilities and transport services. However, despite the expectation of linking behaviour with citizens as key coproducers, "citizen" (or even "consumer"), "civil society" or related cognates are not among the keywords. There are only a small number of coproduction initiatives that are described in terms of physical systems for government-citizen exchange of information. For example, Milan reported that it has "created a specific office dedicated to the "Smart Cities Iniziative." Within its activities meetings were organised with local stakeholders working on this topic." Topics in general heavily focus on the concept of "smartness" when they involve citizens "in sustainable actions (e.g. protection of trees etc.) through smart applications." For example, *Smart transport systems*, *Smart energy planning* and *Smart meters* topics are focused on use of data to make infrastructure or transport more sustainable with the use of smart meters. Digital portals linked to the initiatives use "open data sources (e.g. age and energy efficiency of buildings) and maps (e.g. geothermal energy potential and solar radiation maps)." In these policies, apps were primarily used as a way of sourcing large amounts of digital data from citizens (such as an "EnergyCAP enterprise system's energy tracking software to help us better manage our utilities") or to inform a wider public about climate-related matters (such as "Smart phone apps for real-time bike and pedestrian routes"). Cities would also centralise data access to decrease transaction costs, for example by using "smart distribution system (DMS) with dedicated communication network …. to promote connection of decentralised energy," building data networks with "start-ups in technology development" and developing "sustainability information and requirements to be captured under a cohesive program and reported through a single document."

Despite the low level of coproduction with citizens, qualitative analysis did show evidence of citizens contributing data in a more passive way through apps (such as for the "Engagement of citizens into sustainable actions (e.g. protection of trees etc.) through smart applications"), but active coproduction with citizens was not visible. Further, in one case, this use of coproduced information was realised as a "dashboard for the low-carbon transition as an innovative way to actively involve the newly created Digital Civic Council." Another example was the topic, *Sustainability networks*, which was focused around collecting data on areas such as transportation and utilities through crowdsourcing. It also featured relational types of descriptions such as "networks," "public" and "smart," suggesting ways that data is contributed by/collected from the public (i.e. crowdsourced). This included policies such as smart cards for use of bus and electricity services and smart planning of maps, fees and schedules.

This discussion on findings for each of the strategic categories is summarised with the main points in Table 4.

Table 4 Summary of findings

Findings
Evidence building
Focused primarily on major resource areas affected by climate change, particularly water and energy sources
Gathering of sociological data about climate-impacting behaviours such as waste and energy use is another major focus
Technical expertise in modelling, mapping, and prediction are integral to evidence-building initiatives
Low evidence of public communication of science in governance through data practices
Third-party disclosure
Stakeholders regulated and required to monitor critical data about emissions, water and utilities
Very few policies focused on third-party disclosure
Low evidence of mechanisms or collaborations that disclose the data in a systematic way
Performance management
Tools include annual budgets, strategic plans and action plans, annual reports, and ranking indexes
Main areas of climate impacts being performance managed are waste and emissions
Performance measurement approaches focus on social indicators such as how socio-economic inequality is impacted by climate
Low evidence of performance results connected to concrete consequences such as resource allocation decisions or other incentives
No evidence of attention to specific domain actors such as airlines, technology companies or raw materials industries
Information coproduction
Crowdsourcing or smart approaches as a way of generating stronger insights and involving larger numbers of people and organisations
Open data portals and dashboards are a primary way that data is gathered, presented and reused
No evidence of citizen science or other deliberative ways for the public to actively contribute data beyond smart technologies and crowdsourcing

Discussion

The first important finding of the analysis is that three of the four strategic categories are present to a lesser or greater degree in existing city climate policy initiatives. One exception was the area of third-party disclosure which was mostly absent. In terms of absolute numbers, performance management accounted for about a half of all the policies, and the topics are strongly oriented around this strategic domain too. This makes sense given that performance management has been a highly popular tool in governments around the world of all political stripes since the emergence of New Public Management in the 1980s (Ingrams et al., 2020; Steccolini et al., 2020). The relative paucity of third-party disclosure also is consistent with findings in the literature showing that in the areas of disclosure by firms (Meijer & Homburg, 2009), fact gathering (Ingold & Varone, 2012) and coproduction (Piotrowski et al., 2018), governments struggle to do those things effectively. From a future practice perspective, it may be important for the success of climate policies that areas such as third-party disclosure, particularly with businesses, receive more attention from cities to improve the effectiveness of climate-related data governance.

In the domain of third-party disclosure, there was very little information in the policies about requirements of either a formal or an informal kind that were placed on third-party actors to make information available to advance policy decision-making. For contractual reasons, public organisations can sometimes be unable or reluctant to disclose names or task details about private sector organisations that they work with (Wirtz et al., 2019). So it is possible that such actions are taking place but are not disclosed and do not appear in the CDP data. When it comes to climate change policies this is a serious cause for concern because corporations have a key role in carbon emissions, protection of the environment, and stimulation of green economic solutions. Current debates suggest that the current dominance of data and knowledge production by the "Big tech" companies may need to rebalance through new monitoring institutions or political mechanisms that protect fair and equal distribution of benefits (Khanal et al., 2024; Schaake, 2024). Such plans are particularly relevant to global events that affect every level of society and that stand to create economic winners and losers such as climate change.

Across the other strategic domains, some other tools which prior scholarly literature would suggest are important in this area were notably missing. Citizen science, despite its widely proclaimed potential, was not apparent in any of the policy topics, perhaps due to complex matters around personal data and ownership (Graham et al., 2016; Michener & Ritter, 2017). There is limited research evidence on citizen science in the public policy and public administration fields but the larger umbrella of digital public participation research and low trust or interest of citizens resonates with this finding (e.g. Wang & Bryer, 2013). Another absence is artificial intelligence tools, which have been shown to be relevant and in use in climate-related policymaking in areas such as scenario-making for carbon emissions (Cowls et al., 2023), managing compliance with the Sustainable Development Goals (Allam & Dhunny, 2019) and environmental monitoring

(Yigitcanlar et al., 2023; Zhang et al., 2022). Perhaps the adoption of AI tools by cities is merely lagging tools as such tools face numerous technical and ethical challenges, and policymakers are still unsure of what potential they may have now and in the future (Stein, 2020). From a managerial perspective, collaboration and support from data science experts and technology companies is vital to help get AI projects off the ground (Neumann et al., 2024). Given the challenges and the time needed for adoption of new tools to take place, it is then perhaps not surprising to find no evidence of such tools in the CDP database, and it would suggest that public-private data analytics partnerships may need more support in future.

While this study provides new insight into the approaches that cities use for data driven governance in the climate change policy arena and, in particular provides a global account of those practices and the motivational basis for their use, it is limited as an explanatory perspective in that it does not explain what organisational or environmental factors determine *particular* data practice approaches. Rather, the theory is a general purpose theory, the main strength of which is that it accounts for a whole variety of types of data practices in the climate change policy arena. On the positive side, this absence does suggest interesting ways that the boundary spanning lens can be developed in future and tested to see the extent that boundary spanning strategies can explain specific differences in data practice decisions—as well as their level of performance—in comparison to other types (economic, administrative, political, capacity, etc.) of explanations.

Conclusion

This research addressed a lack of scholarly attention given to the role of governance through data practices in the climate policy arena. Governments (and city governments in particular) play a vital role in the collection, sharing and stimulation of data to achieve policy goals. Despite this, there has been very little theoretical or empirical research done to develop key concepts and provide empirical scope to these strategic domains. In the study, I used an organisational boundary spanning lens for theorising about the role of data governance strategies and tools in the arena of climate policy. The theoretical framework made use of the network collaboration lens for understanding governance decision-making as well as incorporating research on strategic data use as buffering and linking (Halkier, 2017; Keller, 2009). When viewed in this way, a framework suggested four basic data governance strategies: performance management, third-party disclosure, evidence building and coproduction.

The study here involved setting out a theoretical framework characterised by four data governance strategies and using LDA applied to a large database of policy descriptions from cities to develop the practical scope of the framework in terms of tool types that fall within those strategic areas. Using a sample of CDP data, the analysis resulted in a topic model with 20 topics and their 10 most strongly associated words. The topics showed good semantic validity, which suggests that it performs well in capturing the diversity of policies that city governments have undertaken in the climate policy area in the years 2011–2020. An in-depth reading of 400 of the policies revealed more about the kinds of current data governance tools that are being undertaken by cities around the world. The main findings of the analysis are that cities engage in governance through data in areas of performance management, evidence building and coproduction. However, there are notable gaps in current practices, particularly with regard to third-party disclosure policies, citizen science, science communication and accountable performance management practices. All of these areas are key policy domains in the scholarly literature on data applications in climate policy, but are currently limited in practice. These findings are useful for scholars seeking conceptual frameworks on which to study data applications used by governments for climate policy as well as for city managers looking for ways to prioritise and develop their own technology and data tools for tackling tough climate policy challenges.

Appendix. CDP Cities Included in the Dataset (Listed by Country)

Country	City
Australia	Melbourne
	Sydney
Belgium	Brussels
Canada	Burlington
	Calgary
	Edmonton
	Hamilton
	Hayward
	Montreal
	Saskatoon
	Toronto
	Vancouver
	Windsor
	Winnipeg
Croatia	Zagreb

Country	City
Denmark	Aarhus
	Ærøskøbing
	Copenhagen
	Egedal
	Fredensborg
	Frederikshavn
	Gladsaxe
	Helsingør
	Hillerød
	Hjørring
	Hoeje-Taastrup
	Hørsholm
	Hvidovre
	Jammerbugt
	Middelfart
	Odder
	Roskilde
	Sonderborg
Estonia	Johvi
	Pärnu
	Sillamäe
	Tartu
Finland	Espoo
	Helsinki
	Kemi
	Lahti
	Turku
France	Amiens
	Le Havre
	Lyon
	Nice
	Paris
	Villeurbanne
Germany	Berlin
	Bonn
	Cologne
	Greifswald
	Hamburg
	Hannover
	Heidelberg
	Magdeburg
	Mannheim
	Mülheim
	Rostock

Country	City
Greece	Athens
	Thessaloniki
Iceland	Akureyri
	Reykjavík
Ireland	Dublin
Italy	Aquila
	Bologna
	Bolzano
	Chieti
	Ferrara
	Firenze
	Gemona
	Genova
	Lucca
	Massa Marittima
	Milano
	Napoli
	Oristano
	Padova
	Parma
	Pesaro
	Pescara
	Piacenza
	Prato
	Ravenna
	Reggio Emilia
	Rimini
	Roma
	Spezia
	Teramo
	Torino
	Udine
	Venezia
	Verbania
Latvia	Liepāja
	Riga
Lithuania	Klaipeda
	Panevėžys
	Tauragė
	Vilnius
Mexico	Aguascalientes
	Mérida
	Moita
	Monterrey

Country	City
Netherlands	Amsterdam
	Groningen
	Nijmegen
	Rotterdam
New Zealand	Auckland
	Wellington
Norway	Bærum
	Oslo
Poland	Gdansk
	Tarnów
	Warsaw
	Wroclaw
Portugal	Águeda
	Barreiro
	Fafe
	Famalicão
	Faro
	Funchal
	Lisbon
	Ovar
	Porto
	Torreón
	Torres Vedras
Slovenia	Ljubljana
Spain	Barcelona
	Madrid
	Murcia
	Sevilla
	Vitoria-Gasteiz
	Zaragoza
Sweden	Stockholm
	Trelleborg
Switzerland	Basel
	Lausanne
	Zürich
United Kingdom	Birmingham
	Bournemouth
	Cardiff
	Glasgow
	Leicester
	London
	Manchester
	Sudbury

Country	City
United States	Abington
	Albany
	Ann Arbor
	Asheville
	Aspen
	Atlanta
	Austin
	Baltimore
	Benicia
	Boston
	Boulder
	Brownsville
	Buffalo
	Cambridge
	Charlotte
	Chicago
	Cincinnati
	Cleveland
	Columbus
	Dallas
	Denver
	Detroit
	District of Columbia
	Durham
	Edina
	Eugene
	Flagstaff
	Fort Worth
	Houston
	Huntington Beach
	Iowa
	Knoxville
	Lakewood
	Lancaster
	Las Vegas
	Lexington
	Long Beach
	Los Angeles
	Medford
	Memphis
	Miami
	Milwaukee
	Minneapolis
	Miramar
	New Orleans

Country	City
United States	New York City
	Oakland
	Philadelphia
	Phoenix
	Pittsburgh
	Portland (OR)
	Providence (RI)
	Rochester (NY)
	Sacramento
	Salt Lake City
	San Antonio
	San Diego
	San Francisco
	San José
	Santa Monica
	Savannah
	Seattle
	St Louis

References

Allam, Z., & Dhunny, Z. A. (2019). On big data, artificial intelligence and smart cities. *Cities, 89*, 80–91. https://doi.org/10.1016/j.cities.2019.01.032

Andrews, M. (2010). Good government means different things in different countries. *Governance, 23*(1), 7–35. https://doi.org/10.1111/j.1468-0491.2009.01465.x

Bae, J., & Feiock, R. (2013). Forms of government and climate change policies in US cities. *Urban Studies, 50*(4), 776–788. https://doi.org/10.1177/0042098012450481

Bally, F., & Coletti, M. (2023). Civil society involvement in the governance of green infrastructure: An analysis of policy recommendations from EU-funded projects. *Journal of Environmental Management, 342*. https://doi.org/10.1016/j.jenvman.2023.118070

Bauer, A., Feichtinger, J., & Steurer, R. (2012). The governance of climate change adaptation in 10 OECD countries: challenges and approaches. *Journal of Environmental Policy & Planning, 14*(3), 279–304. https://doi.org/10.1080/1523908X.2012.707406

Beltran, J., Gallego, A., Huidobro, A., Romero, E., & Padró, L. (2021). Male and female politicians on Twitter: A machine learning approach. *European Journal of Political Research, 60*(1), 239–251. https://doi.org/10.1111/1475-6765.12392

Berliner, D., Bagozzi, B. E., & Palmer-Rubin, B. (2018). What information do citizens want? Evidence from one million information requests in Mexico. *World Development, 109*, 222–235. https://doi.org/10.1016/j.worlddev.2018.04.016

Best, K. B., Miro, M. E., Kirpes, R. M., Kaynar, N., & Chesler, A. N. (2021). Data-driven decision support tools for assessing the vulnerability of community water systems to groundwater contamination in Los Angeles County. *Environmental Science & Policy, 124*, 393–400. https://doi.org/10.1016/j.envsci.2021.07.015

Blei, D. M., Ng, A. Y., & Jordan, M. I. (2003). Latent Dirichlet allocation. *Journal of Machine Learning Research, 3*(Jan), 993–1022. https://jmlr.csail.mit.edu/papers/v3/blei03a.html

Blok, A., & Tschötschel, R. (2016). World port cities as cosmopolitan risk community: Mapping urban climate policy experiments in Europe and East Asia. *Environment and Planning C: Government and Policy, 34*(4), 717–736. https://doi.org/10.1177/0263774X15614673

Boyd, E., & Juhola, S. (2015). Adaptive climate change governance for urban resilience. *Urban Studies, 52*(7), 1234–1264. https://doi.org/10.1177/0042098014527483

Ciplet, D., Adams, K. M., Weikmans, R., & Roberts, J. T. (2018). The transformative capability of transparency in global environmental governance. *Global Environmental Politics, 18*(3), 130–150. https://doi.org/10.1162/glep_a_00472

Cowls, J., Tsamados, A., Taddeo, M., & Floridi, L. (2023). The AI gambit: leveraging artificial intelligence to combat climate change—opportunities, challenges, and recommendations. *AI & Society, 38*(1), 283–307. https://doi.org/10.1007/s00146-021-01294-x

Doelle, M., Henschel, C., Smith, J., Tollefson, C., & Wellstead, A. (2012). New governance arrangements at the intersection of climate change and forest policy: institutional, political and regulatory dimensions. *Public Administration, 90*(1), 37–55. https://doi.org/10.1111/j.1467-9299.2011.02006.x

Douglass, K. (2014). Studying the information needs of e-governance stakeholders: Environmental justice as a context for tool development. *Information Polity, 19*(1–2), 97–113. https://doi.org/10.3233/IP-140323

Fernandez-Monge, F., Barns, S., Kattel, R., & Bria, F. (2023). Reclaiming data for improved city governance: Barcelona's New Data Deal. *Urban Studies*. https://doi.org/10.1177/00420980231204835

Finnegan, J. (2022). Institutions, climate change, and the foundations of long-term policymaking. *Comparative Political Studies, 55*(7), 1198–1235. https://doi.org/10.1177/00104140211047416

Florini, A., & Saleem, S. (2011). Information disclosure in global energy governance. *Global Policy, 2*, 144–154. https://doi.org/10.1111/j.1758-5899.2011.00135.x

Gotgelf, A. (2022). Information governance for sustainable development: Exploring social dilemmas in data provision for international reporting on Land Degradation Neutrality. *Environmental Science and Policy, 135*, 128–136. https://doi.org/10.1016/j.envsci.2022.05.002

Graham, F. S., Gooden, S. T., & Martin, K. J. (2016). Navigating the transparency–privacy paradox in public sector data sharing. *The American Review of Public Administration, 46*(5), 569–591. https://doi.org/10.1177/0275074014561111

Griffiths, T. L., & Steyvers, M. (2004). Finding scientific topics. *Proceedings of the National academy of Sciences, 101*(suppl_1), 5228–5235. https://doi.org/10.1073/pnas.0307752101

Grolemund, G. (2014). *Hands-on programming with R: Write your own functions and simulations*. O'Reilly Media. https://rstudio-education.github.io/hopr/

Gronow, A., Wagner, P., & Ylä-Anttila, T. (2020). Explaining collaboration in consensual and conflictual governance networks. *Public Administration, 98*(3), 730–745. https://doi.org/10.1111/padm.12641

Guerrini, C. J., Majumder, M. A., Lewellyn, M. J., & McGuire, A. L. (2018). Citizen science, public policy. *Science, 361*(6398), 134–136. https://doi.org/10.1126/science.aar837

Halkier, B. (2017). Mundane science use in a practice theoretical perspective: Different understandings of the relations between citizen-consumers and public communication initiatives build on scientific claims. *Public Understanding of Science, 26*(1), 40–54. https://doi.org/10.1177/0963662515596314

Hoggan, J., & Littlemore, R. (2009). *Climate cover-up: The crusade to deny global warming*. Greystone Books.

Hollibaugh, G. E. (2019). The use of text as data methods in public administration: A review and an application to agency priorities. *Journal of Public Administration Research and Theory, 29*(3), 474–490. https://doi.org/10.1093/jopart/muy045

Hughes, S., Giest, S., & Tozer, L. (2020). Accountability and data-driven urban climate governance. *Nature Climate Change, 10*(12), 1085–1090. https://doi.org/10.1038/s41558-020-00953-z

Ingrams, A., Piotrowski, S. J., & Berliner, D. (2020). Learning from our mistakes: public management reform and the hope of open government. *Perspectives on Public Management and Governance, 3*(4), 257–272. https://doi.org/10.1093/ppmgov/gvaa001

Ingold, K., & Varone, F. (2012). Treating policy brokers seriously: Evidence from the climate policy. Journal of Public Administration Research and Theory, 22(2), 319–346.

Kalesnikaite, V. (2019). Keeping cities afloat: Climate change adaptation and collaborative governance at the local level. *Public Performance & Management Review, 42*(4), 864–888. https://doi.org/10.1080/15309576.2018.1526091

Keller, A. C. (2009). Credibility and relevance in environmental policy: Measuring strategies and performance among science assessment organizations. *Journal of Public Administration Research and Theory, 20*(2), 357–386. https://doi.org/10.1093/jopart/mup001

Khanal, S., Zhang, H., & Taeihagh, A. (2024). Why and how is the power of Big Tech increasing in the policy process? The case of generative AI. *Policy and Society*. https://doi.org/10.1093/polsoc/puae012

Koliba, C. J., Mills, R. M., & Zia, A. (2011). Accountability in governance networks: An assessment of public, private, and nonprofit emergency management practices following Hurricane Katrina. *Public Administration Review, 71*(2), 210–220. https://doi.org/10.1111/j.1540-6210.2011.02332.x

Kowalski, R., Esteve, M., & Jankin Mikhaylov, S. (2020). Improving public services by mining citizen feedback: An application of natural language processing. *Public administration, 98*(4), 1011–1026. https://doi.org/10.1111/padm.12656

Leck, H., & Simon, D. (2013). Fostering multiscalar collaboration and co-operation for effective governance of climate change adaptation. *Urban Studies, 50*(6), 1221–1238. https://doi.org/10.1177/0042098012461675

Lee, H. (2024). Strategic types, implementation, and capabilities: Sustainability policies of local governments. *Public Administration, 102*(1), 264–284. https://doi.org/10.1111/padm.12917

Leiren, M. D., & Jacobsen, J. K. S. (2018). Silos as barriers to public sector climate adaptation and preparedness: insights from road closures in Norway. *Local Government Studies, 44*(4), 492–511. https://doi.org/10.1080/03003930.2018.1465933

Meijer, A. J., & Homburg, V. (2009). Disclosure and compliance: The 'pillory' as an innovative regulatory instrument. *Information Polity, 14*(4), 279–294. https://doi.org/10.3233/IP-2009-0191

Meijer, A. J., & Thaens, M. (2009). Public information strategies: Making government information available to citizens. *Information Polity, 14*(1–2), 31–45. https://doi.org/10.3233/IP-2009-0167

Meuleman, L. (2021). Public administration and governance for the SDGs: Navigating between change and stability. *Sustainability, 13*(11), 5914. https://doi.org/10.3390/su13115914

Michener, G., & Ritter, O. (2017). Comparing resistance to open data performance measurement: Public education in Brazil and the UK. *Public Administration, 95*(1), 4–21. https://doi.org/10.1111/padm.12293

Neumann, O., Guirguis, K., & Steiner, R. (2024). Exploring artificial intelligence adoption in public organizations: a comparative case study. *Public Management Review, 26*(1), 114–141. https://doi.org/10.1080/14719037.2022.2048685

Nguyen Long, L. A., & Krause, R. M. (2021). Managing policy-making in the local climate governance landscape: The role of network administrative organizations and member cities. *Public Administration, 99*(1), 23–39. https://doi.org/10.1111/padm.12684

Pearce, G., & Cooper, S. (2011). Sub-national responses to climate change in England: evidence from local area agreements. *Local Government Studies, 37*(2), 199–217. https://doi.org/10.1080/03003930.2011.554825

Piotrowski, S. J., Rosenbloom, D., Kang, S., & Ingrams, A. (2018). Levels of value integration in federal agencies' mission and value statements: Is open government a performance target of US federal agencies? *Public Administration Review, 78*(5), 705–716. https://doi.org/10.1111/puar.12937

Schaake, M. (2024). *The tech coup: How to save democracy from Silicon Valley*. Princeton University Press.

Scheer, D. (2015). In silico science for climate policy: how policy-makers process and use carbon storage simulation data. *Environmental Science & Policy, 47*, 148–156. https://doi.org/10.1016/j.envsci.2014.11.008

Schmidt, L., Feital, M., Cortekar, J., di Giulio, G., & Engels, A. (2024). Understanding the science-policy interface in urban climate governance from a co-production perspective: Insights from the cases of Hamburg and São Paulo. *Environmental Science & Policy*. https://doi.org/10.1016/j.envsci.2024.103750

Schumacher, B. L., Yost, M. A., Burchfield, E. K., & Allen, N. (2022). Water in the West: Trends, production efficiency, and a call for open data. *Journal of Environmental Management, 306*. https://doi.org/10.1016/j.jenvman.2021.114330

Seawright, J., & Gerring, J. (2008). Case selection techniques in case study research: A menu of qualitative and quantitative options. *Political Research Quarterly, 61*(2), 294–308. https://doi.org/10.1177/1065912907313077

Shand, R. (2018). The role of ethics and targets in environmental governance and the enduring importance of new public management. *Political Studies Review, 16*(3), 230–239. https://doi.org/10.1177/1478929917704814

Steccolini, I., Saliterer, I., & Guthrie, J. (2020). The role (s) of accounting and performance measurement systems in contemporary public administration. *Public Administration, 98*(1), 3–13. https://doi.org/10.1111/padm.12642

Stein, A. L. (2020). Artificial intelligence and climate change. *Yale Journal on Regulation, 37*, 890. https://scholarship.law.ufl.edu/facultypub/996/

van Ooijen, C., Ubaldi, B., & Welby, B. (2019). *A data-driven public sector: Enabling the strategic use of data for productive, inclusive and trustworthy governance* (OECD Working Papers on Public Governance No. 33). OECD. https://doi.org/10.1787/09ab162c-en

Wang, X., & Bryer, T. A. (2013). Assessing the costs of public participation: A case study of two online participation mechanisms. *The American Review of Public Administration, 43*(2), 179–199. https://doi.org/10.1177/0275074012438727

Wirtz, B. W., Weyerer, J. C., & Geyer, C. (2019). Artificial intelligence and the public sector—Applications and challenges. *International Journal of Public Administration, 42*(7), 596–615. https://doi.org/10.1080/01900692.2018.1498103

Yeung, K., & Bygrave, L. (2022). Demystifying the modernized European data protection regime: Cross-disciplinary insights from legal and regulatory governance scholarship. *Regulation & Governance, 16*(1), 137–155. https://doi.org/10.1111/rego.12401

Yigitcanlar, T., Li, R. Y. M., Beeramoole, P. B., & Paz, A. (2023). Artificial intelligence in local government services: Public perceptions from Australia and Hong Kong. *Government Information Quarterly*. https://doi.org/10.1016/j.giq.2023.101833

Zhang, D., Pee, L. G., Pan, S. L., & Liu, W. (2022). Orchestrating artificial intelligence for urban sustainability. *Government Information Quarterly, 39*(4), 101720. https://doi.org/10.1016/j.giq.2022.101720

Zia, A., & Koliba, C. (2011). Accountable climate governance: Dilemmas of performance management across complex governance networks. *Journal of Comparative Policy Analysis: Research and Practice, 13*(5), 479–497. https://doi.org/10.1080/13876988.2011.605939

A Bibliometric Overview of Digitalization in Governments: Exploring Main Challenges and Future Directions

Eliana Bejarano-Murillo

Introduction

The development of new technologies has caused countless changes across numerous sectors (Gichoya, 2005). The changes driven by the development of the Internet and new communication models have transformed the organization and structure of both businesses and public institutions (Wang & Guo, 2024; West, 2005). In the evolution of this new paradigm where companies are interconnected, governments have been compelled to advance their digitalization strategies (Wandaogo, 2022). This digital transformation of the state highlights the significant opportunities and challenges presented by new legal, economic, and environmental developments linked to the digital transformation of governmental activities and services (Di Giulio & Vecchi, 2023).

Authors such as Rizk et al. (2023) emphasize that digitalization processes enable public administrations to develop more efficient services for citizens and create new public services. However, as Cappelli et al. (2024) indicates, every change associated with the adoption of new technologies carries risks. One of the most critical risks in the adoption of digital transformation strategies by governments is the management and privacy of big data (Löfgren & Webster, 2020; Ribeiro-Navarrete et al., 2021). Nevertheless, there are also significant opportunities, such as the development of artificial intelligence (AI) and smart cities for urban management or new sources of sustainable energy development that will make cities more environmentally friendly (Li et al., 2022; Saura et al., 2022).

Due to the very nature of public administrations and governments, they operate across multiple sectors, ensuring that their medium- and long-term actions can drive

E. Bejarano-Murillo (✉)
Rey Juan Carlos University, Madrid, Spain
e-mail: ebejarano@citiesforum.org

J. R. Saura (ed.), *Global Perspectives on AI, Ethics, and Business Economics*, Contributions to Management Science,
https://doi.org/10.1007/978-3-031-88781-9_6

the economy, social impact, and sustainability of an entire country (Batool et al., 2021). In response to these new paradigms, new forms of regulation have emerged that either support or hinder the application and development of new technologies in public services (Anthopoulos et al., 2007).

Thus, in a context where digitalization and digital transformation processes have become a priority for governments (Hernández-Tamurejo et al., 2025), this chapter proposes the development of a bibliometric analysis to understand the main themes that recent literature has associated with the digitalization of governments. This study aims to understand the development of the concept of digitalization in governments to date within the most relevant literature in the Web of Science database (WoS). Consequently, the research question (RQ) associated with this study is: *RQ1: What are the characteristics and priorities of digitalization processes in governments according to the recent literature?*

Following this premise, this research proposes several objectives:

- To understand and characterize the digitalization processes in governments
- To generate knowledge about the main academic contributions related to the development of the concept of digitalization in governments
- To identify insights that help understand the digital transformation processes in governments
- To establish future research guides and purposes for each of the areas identified as relevant in government digitalization processes

To adequately address these issues, this bibliometric study, conducted using VOSviewer software, utilizes the WoS database to identify the principal contributions published to date in this research field. The study employs three bibliometric techniques focused on author and source citations and keyword occurrences. These techniques will provide insights to address the issues outlined above and have been developed following studies such as Ivanov et al. (2016) and Dias (2019).

This study is organized as follows: first, the introduction is presented, followed by the literature review. Subsequently, the methodology section outlines the sample and different approaches developed. The results are then presented, followed by a discussion that proposes future research guides in this area. Finally, the conclusions and the main theoretical and practical implications of the study are discussed.

Literature Review

The digitalization processes in governments have been extensively studied in the scientific literature from 2005 to the present (Dobrolyubova et al., 2019; Saura, 2024). The academic nature of these contributions spans a multitude of themes linked to the various industries where governments conduct their primary activities. However, due to the nature and development of the proposed study, authors such as Bisogno et al. (2024) and Van Kersbergen and Vis (2022) have highlighted the main areas governments should focus on. For instance, Janowski (2015) emphasizes the historical evolution of digital transformation and the legal and regulatory frameworks that governments should follow to develop new digital initiatives.

Furthermore, there are also authors who have identified the importance of the concept of smart cities in governments' digitalization strategies (Krishnan et al., 2020). These are intelligent and connected cities that develop strategies for sustainable urban development, adopting artificial intelligence and similar technologies to identify efficient actions for urban management and citizen services. For example, Allam and Dhunny (2019)'s research analyses into the integration of AI in urban planning, showcasing how predictive analytics can optimize traffic flow and reduce energy consumption in metropolitan areas.

Moreover, some scholars like Shahbaz et al. (2022) underline the significance of different energy sources and their generation and distribution in smart cities and digital government processes. The integration of technologies such as artificial intelligence in energy management has been also a crucial area of study to date (Dempsey et al., 2022). For instance, SaberiKamarposhti et al. (2024) highlights how AI-driven smart grids can enhance energy efficiency and reliability, paving the way for more resilient urban infrastructure.

It is also noteworthy that some researchers, like Kuzemko (2019), have emphasized not only sustainable energy sources but also the importance of water resources. They discuss the distribution and purification of waste water to improve city efficiency, thereby facilitating the digitalization processes of government actions (Yüksel, 2010). The management of water resources through Internet of Things (IoT) devices and sensors, as discussed by Tziortzioti et al. (2019), provides real-time data that can help in optimizing water usage and preventing wastage.

Additionally, studies have focused on the agro-food sector linked to economic production and food distribution (Young & Hobbs, 2002). These digitalization studies highlight the development of precision agriculture or intelligent systems that drive innovation in the structure and development of digital transformation processes. For example, Lezoche et al. (2020)'s work on precision agriculture demonstrates how data analytics and satellite imaging can revolutionize farming practices, leading to increased yield and sustainability.

Another significant theme identified in the literature regarding digitalization processes linked to governments is the healthcare sector (Iyamu et al., 2021). Large hospital industries developed by governments achieve substantial advancements when digitalization processes are successfully adopted. Authors like Lazuardi et al. (2021) have highlighted the influence of telemedicine and digital health. However, as previously mentioned, authors like Wacksman (2021) also identify privacy as one of the most challenging and complex points for developing digital strategies in these areas. This is particularly critical in handling sensitive patient data and ensuring compliance with health data regulations (Saura et al., 2021).

The educational sector has also been profoundly impacted by digital transformation (Bejinaru, 2019). Digitalization in education has facilitated new teaching methodologies and learning experiences, which have become particularly pertinent during the COVID-19 pandemic (Jain & Lamba, 2021). Authors like Gorina et al. (2023) have explored how digital tools and platforms enhance the learning environment, providing more interactive and personalized education experiences. Additionally, the implementation of e-learning and virtual classrooms has made education more accessible and inclusive, overcoming geographical and socio-economic barriers (Martyakova & Gorchakova, 2019).

Another emerging theme is the role of digitalization in enhancing public administration efficiency. Studies like Sidorenko et al. (2020) have shown that digital government initiatives can streamline bureaucratic processes, reduce costs, and improve service delivery. Authors like Ponti et al. (2022) have examined how e-government services, such as online tax filing and digital identity verification, have increased transparency and reduced corruption. The adoption of blockchain technology in public administration, as discussed by Rot et al. (2020), further ensures secure and transparent transactions, thereby fostering public trust.

The literature also addresses the environmental implications of government digitalization (Zhao et al., 2023). Digital tools and data analytics play a significant role in environmental monitoring and management. Authors like Vyas-Doorgapersad (2022) have investigated how digital technologies can support sustainable development goals (SDG) by enabling better resource management and reducing carbon footprints. For instance, smart sensors and data analytics are used to monitor air and water quality, providing real-time information that helps in taking timely corrective actions (Castro et al., 2021).

In the context of cybersecurity, the digital transformation of government services introduces new challenges and vulnerabilities (Möller, 2023; Saura & Debasa, 2022). Authors like Goswami et al. (2023), emphasize the importance of robust cybersecurity measures to protect sensitive government data from cyber threats. The implementation of advanced encryption techniques, multi-factor authentication, and regular security audits are some of the measures recommended to safeguard digital government infrastructures (Erondu & Erondu, 2023). The literature also explores the role of international cooperation in enhancing cybersecurity, highlighting the need for shared standards and protocols (Kopchev, 2019).

Finally, the social impact of government digitalization is another critical area of study (Dobrolyubova et al., 2019). Digital inclusion initiatives aim to ensure that all citizens have access to digital services, regardless of their socio-economic status. Authors like Ranchordás (2022) have discussed the importance of bridging the digital divide to achieve equitable access to government services. Programs that provide digital literacy training and affordable Internet access are essential in this regard. The literature also explores the potential of digital platforms to enhance citizen engagement and participation in governance, thereby fostering a more inclusive and participatory democracy (Lindgren et al., 2019).

In conclusion, the digitalization of government processes encompasses a wide range of themes and industries. The integration of advanced technologies, regulatory frameworks, and sustainable practices are crucial for the effective transformation of government services. This literature review highlights the multifaceted nature of digitalization in the public sector and underscores the importance of a comprehensive approach to understanding and implementing digital strategies.

Methodology

This study develops a bibliometric analysis using VOSviewer. This approach is a robust and scientifically valid method for examining the scholarly landscape of any research field, including the digitalization of governments (Donthu et al., 2021). Bibliometric analysis allows researchers to quantitatively assess various aspects of academic publications, providing insights into the development, structure, and trends of a specific domain (Napitupulu & Yakub, 2021; Saura et al., 2023).

In this context, one of the critical components of bibliometric analysis is the examination of the most cited papers. This analysis helps identify seminal works and influential authors who have significantly contributed to the field (Ni et al., 2017). This not only highlights foundational literature but also helps in understanding the historical progression and core developments within the field. Next, analyzing the number of contributions per year is another vital aspect of bibliometric analysis (de Oliveira Almeida et al., 2014). This temporal analysis provides a clear picture of how research activity has evolved over time. Identifying periods with significant increases in publications can indicate growing interest and investment in the research area, while also highlighting the responsiveness of the academic community to emerging challenges and innovations in government digitalization (Liang & Liu, 2018).

Another important analysis is the well-known co-citation analysis (Hou et al., 2018). It is an essential bibliometric technique used to map the intellectual structure of a research field. This approach reveals the relationships between different works and identifies clusters of research that contribute to specific subfields or themes. This method helps in uncovering the underlying theoretical foundations and the interconnectedness of various research streams (Walter & Ribière, 2013).

Also, bibliographic coupling is another important technique that connects documents that share common references. This analysis is particularly useful for identifying current research fronts and emerging topics (Jarneving, 2007). Linking papers based on their shared references, bibliographic coupling highlights contemporary research trends and provides insights into the ongoing developments and debates.

Finally, keyword co-occurrence analysis also enhances the bibliometric examination by identifying prevalent themes and their interconnections within the literature (Zhou & Song, 2021). This method analyzes the frequency and co-occurrence of keywords in academic publications, helping to visualize the thematic landscape. It provides a detailed overview of the main research areas, the relationships between different topics, and potential gaps that warrant further investigation (Díaz-García et al., 2022).

For the development of this study, as highlighted before, VOSviewer is used (Oladinrin et al., 2023). It is specifically designed for creating and visualizing bibliometric networks, making it an ideal tool for this type of analysis. Its capabilities in handling large datasets, combined with its sophisticated algorithms for network analysis, ensure that the results are both accurate and meaningful. VOSviewer's ability to generate clear visual representations of bibliometric networks aids in the intuitive understanding of complex relationships within the data (McAllister et al., 2022).

Data Sampling

The data sampling for this bibliometric study was meticulously designed to ensure a comprehensive analysis of the scholarly output related to the digitalization of governments. A total of 371 publications were identified, comprising 2459 cited articles with an aggregate of 2674 citations received. This results in an average citation count of 7.21 per item, highlighting the scholarly impact and relevance of the selected publications. Additionally, the *h*-index for the dataset stands at 22, indicating a substantial level of citation influence within the field.

The data collection was conducted using the WoS database, a renowned and authoritative source for academic research. The search queries and data extraction were performed on July 30, 2024, ensuring the inclusion of the most recent and relevant publications up to that date. The comprehensive nature of the WoS database provided a robust foundation for capturing the breadth and depth of research activities in the domain of government digitalization. Specifically, the search conducted in WoS was performed with the following filters using Boolean operators: "*Digitalization (Title) and Government (Abstract)*" adding a filter of Original Research and Reviews document types.

In order to illustrate the development of the topic digitalization and governments, in Fig. 1 the trends in publications and citations related to the digitalization of governments from 2005 to 2024 are presented. Figure 1 provides a clear depiction of the growth in scholarly output and the increasing recognition of this research area within the academic community. From 2005 to 2015, the number of publications

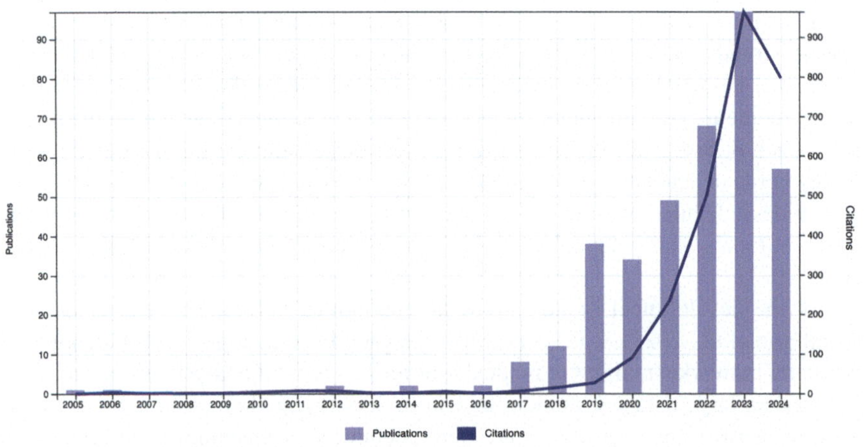

Fig. 1 Total publications in WoS and citations per years. Source: Author, from WoS collected data

remained relatively low, with less than 10 publications per year. During this period, citations also remained minimal, reflecting the nascent stage of research in this domain. The years between 2010 and 2012 show a consistent but low level of activity, with a slight increase in 2013 and 2014. However, it was not until 2016 that a noticeable uptick in both publications and citations began to emerge.

Also, a significant increase in publications can be observed starting from 2017. The number of publications rose sharply from around 10 in 2016 to over 30 in 2018, indicating growing interest and investment in the study of government digitalization. Correspondingly, citations began to climb, suggesting that earlier works were gaining traction and influencing subsequent research. The upward trend continued more robustly from 2019 onwards. The number of publications increased steadily, reaching around 40 in 2019, approximately 50 in 2020, and nearly 60 in 2021. This trend highlights the expanding body of research and the increasing academic focus on digital government initiatives.

The most notable surge in publications occurred between 2022 and 2023. In 2022, the number of publications peaked at around 90, with a significant rise in citations as well, reaching nearly 900. This peak reflects a period of intensive research activity and high-impact publications that significantly contributed to the field. Although there was a slight decline in 2024, with publications dropping to around 80 and citations decreasing to approximately 700, the overall trend demonstrates sustained interest and engagement in this research area. Therefore, Fig. 1 illustrates a clear growth trajectory in both the volume of publications and their citations over the past two decades. This trend underscores the increasing importance of digitalization in government studies and the expanding recognition of its significance within the academic community.

Next, in order to confirm the main categories that compose the sample, in Table 1 the main WoS categories of publications are presented. Of the 371 records across various WoS categories, Table 1 summarizes the interdisciplinary nature of research on the digitalization of governments. The categorization reflects the diverse academic lenses through which this topic is examined, highlighting its multifaceted implications and applications. The leading categories are Economics, Management, and Business, which together account for a significant proportion of the records (13.208%, 12.129%, and 11.590%, respectively). This dominance underscores the economic and managerial dimensions of government digitalization. The digital transformation of governments involves substantial investments, economic strategies, and management practices aimed at improving efficiency, reducing costs, and enhancing public service delivery. Next, Environmental Sciences and Environmental Studies also feature prominently, with 9.973% and 7.817% of the records, respectively. This presence is indicative of the growing recognition of the role that digital technologies play in promoting sustainable development and environmental management.

Also, Public Administration and Social Sciences Interdisciplinary, comprising 7.278% and 7.008% of the records, respectively, highlight the governance and social aspects of digitalization. Research within Public Administration examines the implications of digital tools on administrative processes, public policy, and

Table 1 Web of Sciences categories

Web of Science categories	Record count	% of 371
Economics	49	13.208%
Management	45	12.129%
Business	43	11.590%
Environmental Sciences	37	9.973%
Environmental Studies	29	7.817%
Green Sustainable Science Technology	28	7.547%
Public Administration	27	7.278%
Social Sciences Interdisciplinary	26	7.008%
Computer Science Information Systems	22	5.930%
Information Science Library Science	21	5.660%
Law	16	4.313%
Multidisciplinary Sciences	15	4.043%
Business Finance	14	3.774%
Computer Science Interdisciplinary Applications	14	3.774%
Development Studies	13	3.504%

Source: Author, from WoS collected data

government transparency. Social Sciences Interdisciplinary reflects the broad societal impacts, including citizen engagement, social equity, and the digital divide. These categories underscore the importance of understanding how digitalization affects governmental operations and public interaction with state institutions.

Likewise, the fields of Computer Science, including Information Systems (5.930%) and Interdisciplinary Applications (3.774%), along with Information Science Library Science (5.660%), represent the technological backbone of digital government studies. These categories focus on the development, implementation, and evaluation of digital systems and infrastructures that underpin e-government initiatives. Research in these areas explores the technological innovations, data management, cybersecurity, and information systems that enable effective digital governance.

Finally, categories such as Law (4.313%), Multidisciplinary Sciences (4.043%), Business Finance (3.774%), and Development Studies (3.504%) reflect the broader implications and applications of digital government initiatives. Legal studies examine the regulatory and ethical frameworks necessary for digital governance, ensuring compliance and protecting citizen rights. Multidisciplinary Sciences capture the cross-cutting nature of digitalization, integrating various scientific approaches. Business Finance addresses the financial mechanisms and economic evaluations critical for funding digital projects, while Development Studies highlight the role of digitalization in fostering socio-economic development, particularly in emerging economies. Figure 2 shows the main categories by number of publications in WoS.

Finally, with the objective of presenting the percentages of the total documents found per year in the sample, Table 2 shows the publication years along with the

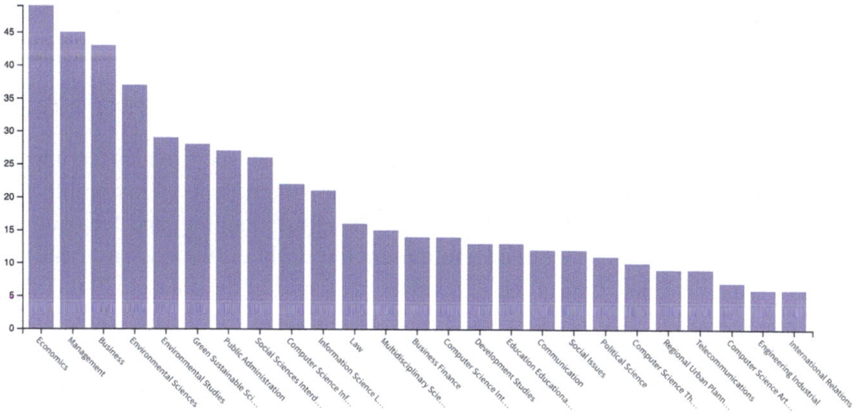

Fig. 2 Web of Sciences categories by total count. Source: Author, from WoS collected data

Table 2 Total record count by year and percentage

Publication years	Record count	% of 371
2023	97	26.146%
2022	68	18.329%
2024	57	15.364%
2021	49	13.208%
2019	38	10.243%
2020	34	9.164%
2018	12	3.235%
2017	8	2.156%
2012	2	0.539%
2014	2	0.539%
2016	2	0.539%
2005	1	0.270%
2006	1	0.270%

Source: Author, from WoS collected data

record count and their corresponding percentage of the total 371 documents. In 2023, the highest number of publications was recorded, with 97 documents, representing 26.146% of the total. This is followed by the year 2022, with 68 publications (18.329%). In 2024, there were 57 publications, accounting for 15.364%, while 2021 saw 49 documents, equivalent to 13.208% of the total.

An upward trend in the number of publications is evident from 2018 onwards. In 2019, 38 documents were published, representing 10.243%, and in 2020, 34 documents accounted for 9.164%. Before 2018, the number of publications was significantly lower, with only 12 documents in 2018 (3.235%) and 8 documents in 2017 (2.156%). Earlier years, such as 2012, 2014, and 2016, each recorded only two documents, each representing 0.539% of the total. The years 2005 and 2006 had the fewest publications, with only one document each, representing 0.270% of the total.

Analysis of Results

Keyword Co-occurrence Analysis Results

As previously mentioned, the keyword co-occurrence analysis provides a comprehensive overview of the prevalent themes and their interrelationships within the research on the digitalization of governments. Using full counting and focusing on all keywords, this analysis identified a minimum threshold of two occurrences for a keyword to be included. Out of the 256 keywords found in the dataset, 39 met this threshold, indicating their relative importance and frequency in the literature. From these, a total of 25 keywords were selected for further analysis using VOSviewer. These keywords were organized into 5 distinct clusters, connected by 122 links, and exhibited a total link strength of 179.

In this way, Fig. 1 provides a visual representation of the keyword co-occurrence network related to the digitalization of governments. This network illustrates the relationships and interconnectedness between various key terms frequently used in the literature, highlighting the main themes and their interrelations. At the center of the network is the keyword "digitalization," which serves as the focal point of the analysis. This central positioning indicates that digitalization is the core theme around which the other topics revolve. It is closely linked with several other significant keywords such as "innovation," "e-government," "technology," "governance," and "digital government."

The prominent connection between "digitalization" and "e-government" underscores the integral role that digital technologies play in transforming governmental processes and public administration. E-government initiatives, which involve the use of digital tools to enhance government services and operations, are a critical component of the broader digitalization efforts within the public sector. This linkage suggests a strong focus in the literature on how digitalization is driving the evolution of government functions and improving service delivery. "Technology" is another key node connected to "digitalization," indicating that technological advancements are fundamental to the digital transformation of governments. The connection between "technology" and "governance" highlights the importance of incorporating technological solutions to achieve effective and transparent governance. This relationship suggests that the integration of technology in governance processes is a central theme in the academic discourse, emphasizing the need for innovative solutions to enhance administrative efficiency and accountability.

Next, the keyword "innovation" is also closely linked to "digitalization," reflecting the necessity of innovative approaches in the digital transformation journey. Innovation drives the development and implementation of new technologies and processes, which are essential for successful digitalization. This connection indicates that research in this area often explores the innovative strategies and solutions that enable governments to adapt to the digital age. Further, keywords such as "digital government" and "digital economy" illustrate the broader impact of digitalization beyond administrative functions. The term "digital government" encompasses the various ways in which digital tools and platforms are utilized to engage with citizens, deliver public services, and enhance governance. The connection with "digital economy" signifies the intersection of government digitalization with economic activities, highlighting the role of digital technologies in fostering economic growth and development.

Other keywords like "information," "systems," and "public administration" also feature prominently in the network. "Information" and "systems" are crucial for managing and processing the vast amounts of data generated in digital government initiatives. Effective information management systems are essential for ensuring data integrity, security, and accessibility, which are critical for informed decision-making and efficient public service delivery. Finally, "Public administration" reflects the broader context within which digitalization efforts are situated, emphasizing the administrative and organizational aspects of implementing digital government strategies (Fig. 3).

Now, Fig. 4 highlights the "Government effectiveness" cluster for its importance. This central node connects to key themes, illustrating the core role of government effectiveness in digital transformation. The strong link between "government effectiveness" and "digitalization" underscores how digital technologies enhance government efficiency and responsiveness. The pathway through "technology" indicates that technological advancements are fundamental to digitalization efforts in governance.

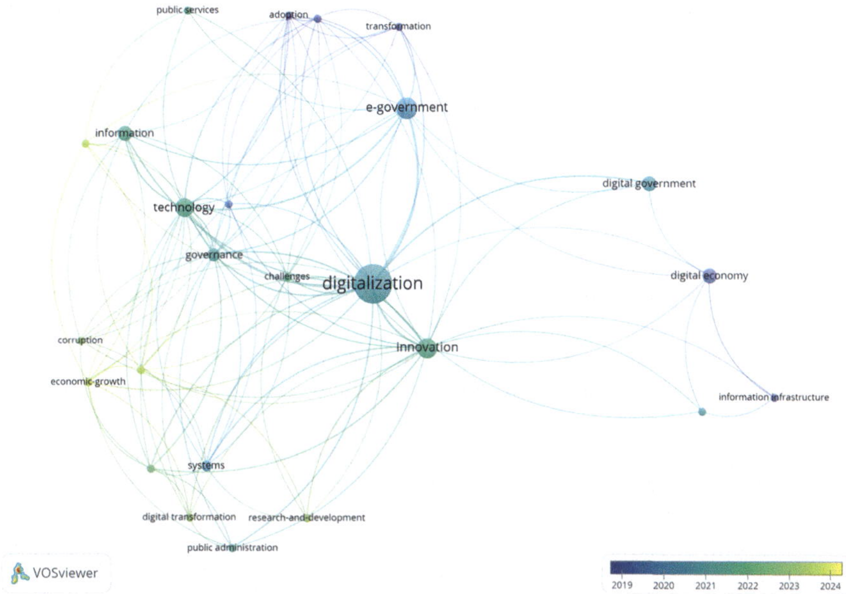

Fig. 3 Main clusters and keywords found in the WoS dataset. Source: Author, from VOSviewer using WoS collected data

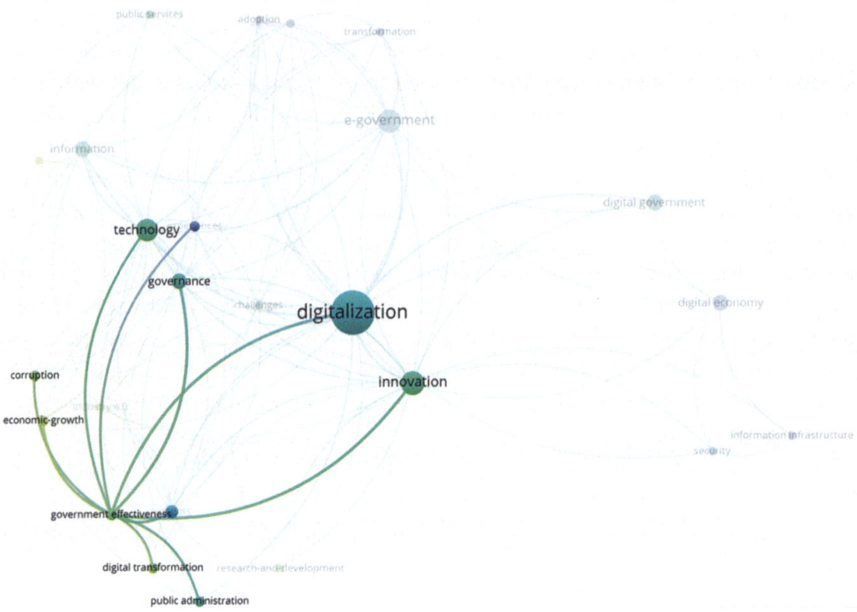

Fig. 4 Government effectiveness cluster highlighted. Source: Author, from VOSviewer using WoS collected data

Connections to "innovation" emphasize the need for innovative approaches to sustain effective governance. Digitalization in "public administration" transforms traditional practices, improving transparency and accountability. The link to "governance" reflects how digital tools support better decision-making and citizen engagement. The connection to "corruption" explores how digital technologies combat corruption by increasing transparency. Finally, the link to "economic growth" highlights the broader economic impacts, showing that effective digitalization can drive sustainable development and enhance economic well-being. In summary, Fig. 4 demonstrates the centrality of "government effectiveness" in the digital transformation of governments, highlighting the importance of technology, innovation, and governance in achieving this goal.

Also, it is important to highlight Fig. 5 and the cluster centered around "innovation," illustrating its connections to various key themes in the digitalization of governments. The strong connection between "innovation" and "security" indicates that innovative approaches are crucial for enhancing cybersecurity measures in digital government initiatives. The link to "digital economy" suggests that innovation drives economic activities facilitated by digital technologies, contributing to overall economic growth. Additionally, "Information infrastructure" is closely connected, highlighting the role of robust digital infrastructures in supporting innovative government services. The connection to "digital government" underscores the transformative impact of innovation on public administration, enhancing efficiency and citizen engagement. In the same way, "Challenges" are linked to "innovation,"

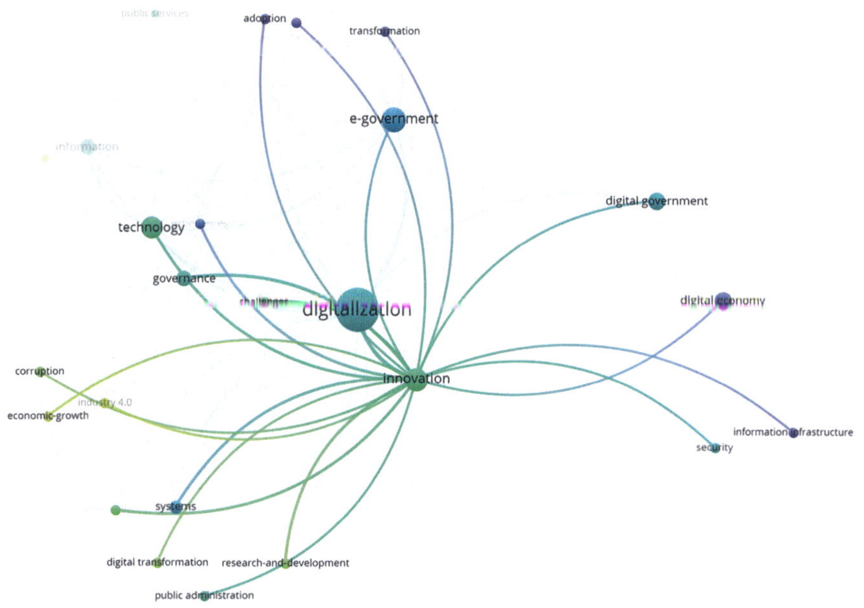

Fig. 5 Innovation cluster highlighted. Source: Author, from VOSviewer using WoS collected data

reflecting the need to address obstacles in the adoption of new technologies. The relationship with "economic growth" indicates that innovation is a key driver for improving economic performance through digital transformation. Finally, "Research and development" is prominently connected, emphasizing the importance of ongoing innovation and technological advancements. Lastly, the links to "adoption" and "transformation" underscore the role of innovation in facilitating the implementation and evolution of digital government processes.

In order to finalize the keyword co-occurrence analysis Table 3 presents the selected keywords along with their frequency and total link strength, highlighting the most influential terms in the research on government digitalization. The keyword "digitalization" stands out with the highest frequency of 27 and a total link strength of 69, indicating its central role in the literature. "Innovation" follows with a frequency of 9 and a total link strength of 43, underscoring its importance in driving digital transformation processes. "Technology" also plays a crucial role, with a frequency of 8 and a total link strength of 41, highlighting the foundational role of technological advancements in government digitalization. Also, "e-government" is another key term, with a frequency of 10 and a total link strength of 35, emphasizing its significance in the adoption of digital tools within governmental frameworks. "Governance" has a total link strength of 28, reflecting its critical importance in ensuring the effectiveness of digital initiatives.

Next, "Information" appears frequently, with a total link strength of 21, showcasing the importance of information management and infrastructure in digital government projects. Additionally, "adoption" and "implementation" each have a total link

Table 3 Selected keywords, frequency, and total link strength

Keyword	Frequency	Total link strength	Keyword	Frequency	Total link strength
Digitalization	27	69	Internet	3	13
Innovation	9	43	Transformation	2	13
Technology	8	41	Impact	2	12
e-government	10	35	Framework	2	11
Governance	4	28	Sustainable development	2	11
Information	5	21	Digital transformation	2	10
Adoption	2	17	Research-and-development	2	10
Implementation	2	17	Public administration	2	9
Experiences	2	16	Corruption	2	8
Challenges	2	15	Digital government	5	8
Economic-growth	2	15	Digital economy	5	7
Government effectiveness	2	15	Public services	2	5
Industry 4.0	2	14	Information infrastructure	2	4
Systems	3	14	Security	2	4

Source: Author, from VOSviewer using WoS collected data

strength of 17, indicating their relevance in the context of integrating new digital technologies within government operations. The rest of the keywords, along with their frequencies and total link strengths, can be found in Table 3 for further reference.

Bibliographic Coupling

The second approach developed was the bibliographic coupling analysis. It was conducted to explore the relationships between the main publication sources in the field of government digitalization. As indicated by Mas-Tur et al. (2021), bibliographic coupling connects documents that cite common references identifying clusters of research that share similar intellectual foundations providing valuable insights into the thematic organization and scholarly interconnections within the literature.

For this analysis, specific filters were applied to ensure the inclusion of relevant and high-impact studies and journals. A minimum citation count of 5 was set to include influential works that have garnered significant academic attention and a minimum of 1 document of a source was set. Of the 47 sources (journals), 18 met the thresholds established in VOSviewer. By employing these filters, the analysis aims to map out the key clusters within the research landscape, identify influential

Table 4 Bibliographic coupling results

Journal (source)	Documents	Citations	Total link strength
Applied Economics	2	12	15
Electronic Journal of Information Systems in Developing Countries	1	14	10
Central European Public Administration Review	1	8	5
Geography and Sustainability	1	7	4
Technological Forecasting and Social Change	2	20	3
Transforming Government—People Process and Policy	1	22	3
Beyond Bureaucracy: Towards Sustainable Governance Informatisation	1	5	1
Business Information Systems and Technology 4.0: New Trends in the Age of Digital Change	1	7	1
Resources Policy	1	12	1
Applied Economics Letters	1	6	0
Contemporary Europe-Sovremennaya Evropa	1	8	0
Entrepreneurship and Sustainability Issues	2	27	0
Sustainability	1	5	0
Technology in Society	1	52	0
Telecommunications Policy	1	13	0

Source: Author, from VOSviewer using WoS collected data

journals, and understand the interconnectedness of their publications (see Table 4). Therefore Table 4 shows the main journals, the number of documents published, citations, and total link strength.

As shown in Table 5, *Applied Economics* stands out with 2 documents, accumulating 12 citations and a total link strength of 15. This indicates a moderate impact and interconnectedness within the scholarly community, suggesting that the articles published in this journal are frequently referenced and play a significant role in the academic discourse on government digitalization. The *Electronic Journal of Information Systems in Developing Countries*, with 1 document and 14 citations, has a total link strength of 10. Despite having a single publication, the relatively high number of citations and link strength signifies the article's influence and its connection to other important works in the field. Similarly, the *Central European Public Administration Review* has 1 document with 8 citations and a total link strength of 5, indicating a noteworthy presence and influence in the literature (see Fig. 6).

Likewise, *Geography and Sustainability* and *Business Information Systems and Technology 4.0: New Trends in the Age of Digital Change*, each with 1 document and 7 citations, exhibit lower total link strengths of 4 and 1, respectively. This suggests that while the articles are cited, their connections with other influential works are relatively limited, indicating potential areas for further exploration and citation in future research. In the same way, *Technological Forecasting and Social Change* and *Transforming Government: People Process and Policy* each have 1 document

Table 5 Authors co-citation analysis and 11 most cited papers in WoS related to government digitalization

Authors	Title	Citations	Authors	Citations	Total link strength
Lindgren et al. (2019)	Close encounters of the digital kind: A research agenda for the digitalization of public services	171	Santiso, C	8	64
Habibi and Zabardast (2020)	Digitalization, education and economic growth: A comparative analysis of Middle East and OECD countries	97	World Bank	7	47
Talwar et al. (2023)	Digitalization and sustainability: virtual reality tourism in a post pandemic world	94	Dutta, S	7	42
Bouncken and Kraus (2022)	Entrepreneurial ecosystems in an interconnected world: emergence, governance and digitalization	77	European Commission	16	40
Zancajo et al. (2022)	Digitalization and beyond: the effects of Covid-19 on post-pandemic educational policy and delivery in Europe	50	United Nations	6	40
Ehlers et al. (2022)	Scenarios for European agricultural policymaking in the era of digitalisation	31	Kaufmann, D	5	38
Iyamu et al. (2021)	Defining digital public health and the role of digitization, digitalization, and digital transformation: Scoping review	23	Cordella, A	6	28
Lappi et al. (2019)	Project governance and portfolio management in government digitalization	22	Irani, Z	5	28
Androniceanu, Georgescu, and Kinnunen (2022)	Public administration digitalization and corruption in the EU member states. A comparative and correlative research analysis	20	Civelek, M	5	25
Guo et al. (2023)	How does green digitalization affect environmental innovation? The moderating role of institutional forces	18	Janssen, M	5	25
Androniceanu, Georgescu, and Sabie (2022)	The impact of digitalization on public administration, economic development, and well-being in the EU countries	17	OECD	5	21

Source: Author, from WoS results and VOSviewer co-citation analysis report

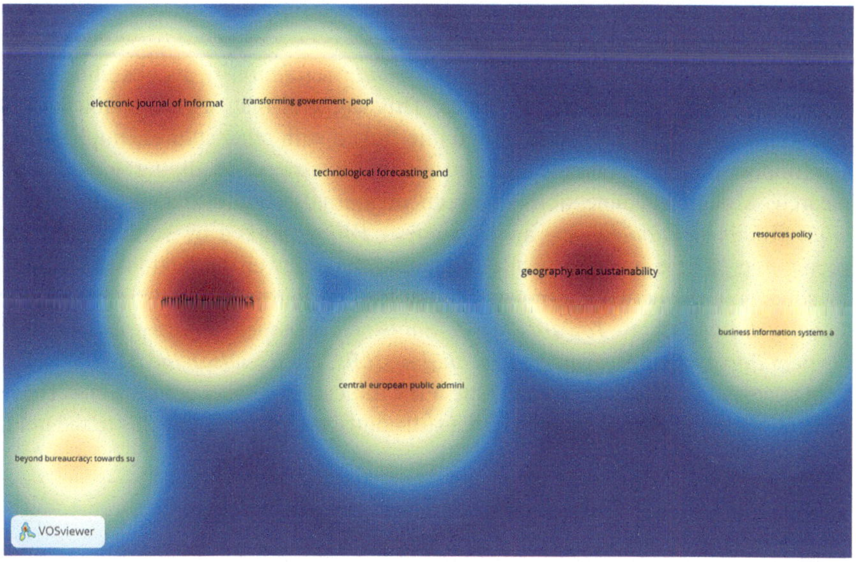

Fig. 6 Bibliographic coupling network by density of connections. Source: Author, from VOSviewer using WoS collected data

but show higher citation counts, with 20 and 22 citations, respectively, although both have a total link strength of 3. This highlights the importance of these publications in the academic community, reflecting their significant contributions to the understanding of technological and policy aspects of government digitalization, despite a lower degree of direct connectivity with other documents.

Other journals such as *Beyond Bureaucracy: Towards Sustainable Governance Informatisation*, *Resources Policy*, and *Applied Economics Letters* have fewer citations, with totals of 5, 12, and 6, respectively, and total link strengths ranging from 0 to 1. These figures suggest that while these articles contribute to the body of knowledge, their impact and interconnections within the broader research community are relatively limited. In contrast, the journal *Technology in Society*, with a single document, has a notably high citation count of 52 but a total link strength of 0. This indicates that although the article is widely cited, it may not be as interconnected with other key works in the field. Similarly, *Telecommunications Policy*, despite having 13 citations, also shows a total link strength of 0, pointing towards a significant but isolated influence.

To further analyze the network of connections among the main sources presented in Table 4, Fig. 6 presents the network map by density of connections. This map visualizes the strength of connections, with redder areas indicating stronger links related to government digitalization research. Therefore, in Fig. 6, journals like the *Electronic Journal of Information Systems in Developing Countries*, *Transforming Government: People Process and Policy*, and *Technological Forecasting and Social Change* display significant connectivity, shown by the red and orange hues. These journals are central in the network, highlighting their frequent citations and influential roles in the field.

The *Applied Economics* and *Geography and Sustainability* also exhibit strong connections, indicated by the red zones. This suggests that research published in these journals is heavily referenced and interlinked with other studies, emphasizing their importance in economic and sustainability aspects of digital government research. Moderate connections are seen in journals such as *Central European Public Administration Review* and *Resources Policy* marked by yellow and light green colors. These journals, while influential, have fewer interactions with other key sources in the network compared to the leading journals. Finally, journals like *Beyond Bureaucracy: Towards Sustainable Governance Informatisation* and *Business Information Systems and Technology 4.0: New Trends in the Age of Digital Change* appear in lighter green and blue hues, indicating weaker connections. These publications are less frequently cited but still contribute valuable insights to the field.

Authors Co-citation Analysis

Thirdly, the author co-citation analysis was conducted to uncover the relationships among authors frequently cited together in studies on government digitalization. Filters were applied to ensure the relevance and impact of the findings, resulting in 14 items, 3 clusters, 36 links, and a total link strength of 207 (see Fig. 7). In this

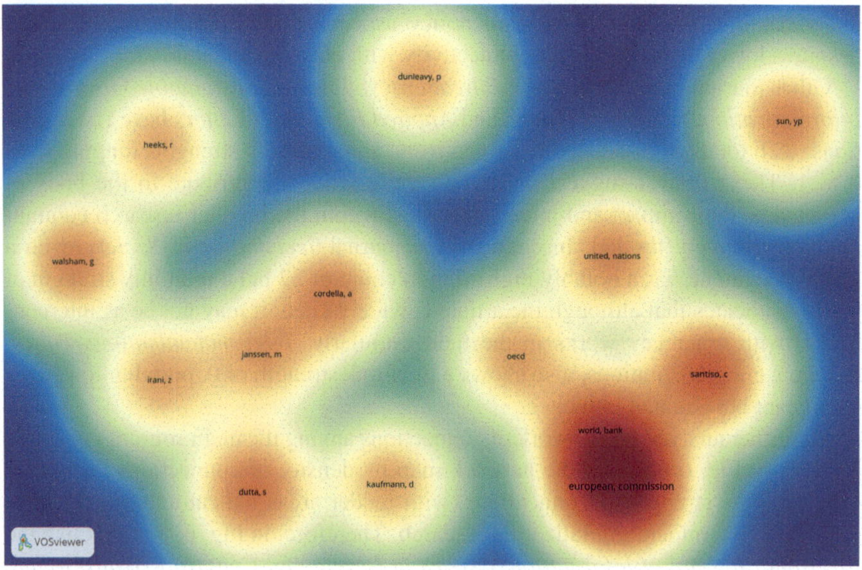

Fig. 7 Authors co-citation analysis by density of relations. Source: Author, from VOSviewer using WoS collected data

sense, Table 5 presents the top 11 contributions identified in the WoS based on the number of citations received in studies on government digitalization. These works represent key scholarly efforts that have significantly impacted the field. Additionally, Table 5 also highlights the leading authors by the number of citations, showing their strong connections within the clusters identified through multiple studies, demonstrated by high link strength.

Examining the authors with notable citation counts and strong link strengths reveals significant contributors to the discourse on government digitalization. Santiso, C., with 8 citations and a total link strength of 64, stands out as a highly influential figure. The World Bank, with 7 citations and a link strength of 47, also shows substantial impact and connectivity within the research community. Similarly, Dutta, S. has 7 citations and a link strength of 42, indicating a significant role in advancing the understanding of digital government.

Likewise, the European Commission and the United Nations both exhibit high influence, with 16 and 6 citations, respectively, and each with a total link strength of 40. Their contributions are pivotal in shaping policies and frameworks around digitalization in government contexts. Kaufmann, D., and Cordella, A. each have 5 citations, with link strengths of 38 and 28, respectively, highlighting their important roles in the academic discourse. Irani, Z., and Civelek, M., also contribute significantly, each with 5 citations and link strengths of 28 and 25, respectively. Their work further elucidates critical aspects of digital government initiatives. Lastly, Janssen, M., with 5 citations and a link strength of 25, along with the OECD, with 5 citations and a link strength of 21, underscores the collaborative and interdisciplinary nature of research in this field.

As also presented in Fig. 6, Fig. 7 presents the density visualization of the author co-citation network, highlighting the clusters based on their size and color intensity. The color intensity indicates the density of connections, with redder areas signifying stronger links and higher relevance within the research on government digitalization. In this sense, the most prominent cluster is centered around the "European Commission," displaying the deepest red hue, indicating the highest density of connections. This cluster also includes "World Bank," "Santiso, C.," "OECD," and "United Nations." The strong connections within this cluster signify these authors and organizations as pivotal contributors to the field, with extensive citations and significant influence on digital government research.

Another notable cluster includes "Dutta, S.," "Kaufmann, D.," "Irani, Z.," "Cordella, A.," and "Janssen, M." This cluster shows an orange-red hue, indicating a substantial but slightly lower density of connections compared to the European Commission cluster. These authors are central figures in the research community, contributing significantly to discussions on governance, technology, and public administration in the context of digitalization.

The cluster surrounding "Walsham, G." and "Heeks, R." is marked by an orange color, reflecting a moderate density of connections. These authors are influential in their contributions but have fewer interactions compared to the denser clusters. This cluster highlights important contributions to the socio-technical aspects of digital government. In relation to "Sun, Y.P." and "Dunleavy, P.," smaller, yellow-colored

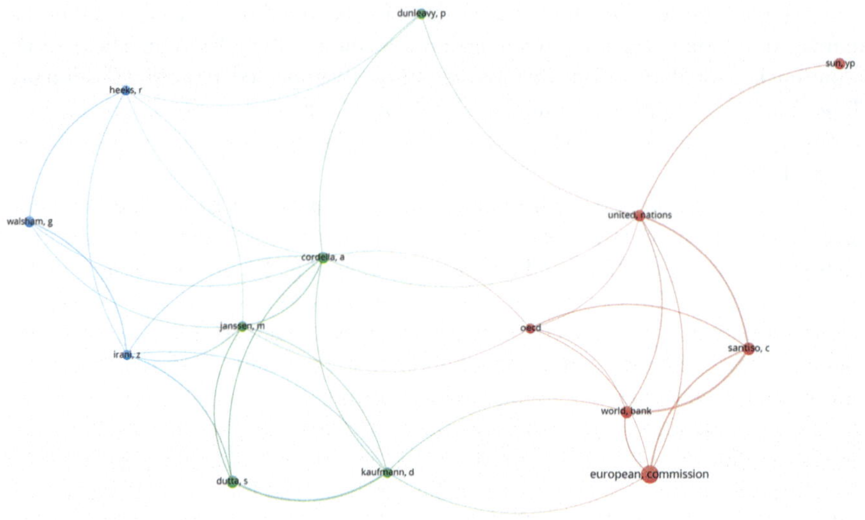

Fig. 8 Co-citation analysis network of authors. Source: Author, from VOSviewer using WoS collected data

clusters are formed, indicating a lower density of connections. While still relevant, these authors have a more specialized or less central role in the broader research network.

Now, the co-citation analysis network of authors is presented in Fig. 8, where the individual connections of authors are studied within three clusters. In the visualized network, the red cluster prominently features influential entities such as the "European Commission," "World Bank," "Santiso, C.," "OECD," and "United Nations." These nodes show strong interconnections, highlighting their pivotal roles and extensive citations within the field of government digitalization. The robust links between these authors and organizations indicate their significant contributions and collaborative influence in shaping policies and frameworks around digital government initiatives.

The green cluster includes notable authors like "Cordella, A.," "Janssen, M.," "Dunleavy, P.," "Dutta, S.," and "Kaufmann, D." This cluster illustrates substantial but slightly less dense connections compared to the red cluster. These authors are key figures contributing to governance, technology, and public administration discourse within digitalization contexts, showing meaningful interactions among their works. The blue cluster comprises "Walsham, G.," "Heeks, R.," and "Irani, Z.," showcasing moderate connectivity. These authors are influential in their respective contributions, focusing on socio-technical aspects and the broader implications of digital government, but with fewer interactions compared to the more central clusters.

The red cluster in the co-citation analysis network of authors should be additionally highlighted (see Fig. 9). This cluster represents a highly influential group of

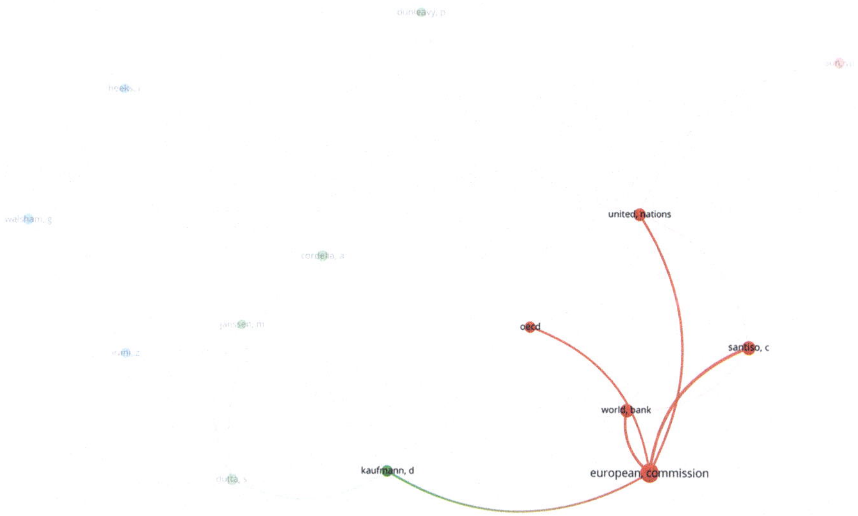

Fig. 9 Highlighted connections of co-citation analysis network of authors. Source: Author, from VOSviewer using WoS collected data

entities that play crucial roles in the research and development of government digitalization. The "European Commission" serves as a central node in the red cluster, indicating its significant influence and extensive citation by other entities. The robust links between the European Commission and other nodes like the "World Bank" and "OECD" suggest a high level of collaboration and shared research agendas. This connection highlights the Commission's role in setting regulatory frameworks and policies that guide digital transformation initiatives across various governments.

"Santiso, C." is another pivotal figure within this cluster, showing strong connections with both the European Commission and the World Bank. Santiso's work often intersects with these organizations' efforts, emphasizing themes of governance, policymaking, and the implementation of digital solutions in the public sector. The high link strength between Santiso and these institutions indicates a reciprocal influence and mutual reinforcement of research findings.

The "World Bank" and "United Nations" also exhibit substantial connectivity within the red cluster. Their collaboration reflects a global perspective on digitalization, encompassing various aspects of economic development, governance, and sustainability. The strong ties between these international organizations demonstrate their collective impact on shaping digital government policies and initiatives worldwide. The "OECD" is well-integrated into this cluster, with notable connections to both the European Commission and the World Bank. This relationship underscores the OECD's role in providing data-driven insights and best practices for digital government, facilitating a knowledge exchange that drives forward the digitalization agenda.

Concluding, the red cluster's dense network of connections highlights the importance of collaborative efforts among these key players. Their combined influence is critical in advancing the field of government digitalization, setting standards, and driving research that addresses global challenges in the digital transformation of public administration. This interconnectedness not only strengthens individual contributions but also enhances the collective understanding and implementation of effective digital government strategies.

Discussion

This study identifies the main themes in the digitalization of governments, highlighting key areas such as innovation, technology, e-government, or sustainability. The research underlines the importance of these areas in understanding the digital transformation of governmental operations and services. The central theme of digitalization is evident across the literature, emphasizing its role as a catalyst for change in government structures and processes. The integration of digital technologies in governmental functions is seen as a means to enhance efficiency, transparency, and citizen engagement. This is particularly significant in the context of e-government initiatives, which leverage digital tools to streamline public services and administrative processes (Saura et al., 2024). The strong emphasis on e-government in the literature suggests a widespread recognition of its potential to transform the way governments interact with citizens and deliver services.

Likewise, innovation is another critical theme closely associated with digitalization. The literature consistently highlights the need for innovative approaches to drive the digital transformation of governments. This involves the adoption of new technologies, such as artificial intelligence and blockchain, to improve service delivery and governance. The emphasis on innovation underscores the dynamic nature of digital transformation, requiring governments to continually adapt and evolve their strategies to meet emerging challenges and opportunities.

Moreover, governance is a recurring theme that intersects with technology and digitalization. Effective governance frameworks are essential for managing the complexities of digital transformation. The literature discusses various governance models and regulatory frameworks that support the implementation of digital technologies in government operations. These frameworks are crucial for ensuring that digital transformation initiatives align with broader policy objectives and address issues such as data privacy, cybersecurity, and public trust. Consequently, the synergy between governance and innovation becomes pivotal, as both are necessary to navigate the digital landscape effectively.

Interestingly, one might find it surprising that the influence of artificial intelligence on the digitalization of governments did not emerge as a prominent theme in this study. Given the rapid advancements and widespread discussions surrounding AI, its absence as a significant keyword may appear counterintuitive. However, this can be justified by the fact that AI is still an emerging technology in the context of governmental applications. The integration of AI into governmental processes is in its nascent stages, and its full potential and implications are yet to be realized and extensively studied. Consequently, the current body of literature may not yet fully capture the breadth and depth of AI's impact on government digitalization.

Moreover, the adoption and implementation of AI in government services require substantial time and resources, including the development of new policies, the establishment of ethical guidelines, and the training of public sector employees. As these processes are still underway, it is understandable that AI's influence is not yet prominently reflected in the academic discourse. Future research will likely address this gap as governments continue to explore and harness the capabilities of AI for enhancing public service delivery and operational efficiency.

The process of adopting technology in governments is crucial for improving efficiency and effectiveness. Governments should navigate complex bureaucratic structures and resistance to change to successfully implement new technologies. The literature highlights the importance of strategic planning, stakeholder engagement, and capacity building to ensure smooth transitions. Effective adoption processes can lead to significant improvements in service delivery, reduced costs, and increased transparency, ultimately enhancing public trust in government institutions.

Additionally, the future of technology in government digitalization presents both opportunities and challenges. As emerging technologies such as AI, blockchain, and IoT continue to evolve, they offer new possibilities for enhancing government operations and services. However, the successful integration of these technologies requires continuous innovation, robust regulatory frameworks, and a focus on ethical considerations. Governments must remain agile and proactive in adopting these technologies to stay ahead of emerging trends and address the evolving needs of their citizens.

However, the increasing reliance on digital technologies also brings about significant risks, particularly concerning data management and privacy. The vast amounts of data generated and collected by digital government services must be managed securely to protect citizens' privacy and prevent data breaches. The literature emphasizes the importance of implementing strong cybersecurity measures, regular audits, and compliance with data protection regulations to mitigate these risks. Ensuring data integrity and confidentiality is crucial for maintaining public trust and safeguarding sensitive information.

Furthermore, the intersection of digitalization with energy consumption and sustainability is a critical area of concern. The energy demands of digital infrastructure, including data centers and communication networks, can be substantial. Governments should adopt sustainable practices to minimize the environmental impact of their digital initiatives. The literature highlights the potential of renewable energy sources, energy-efficient technologies, and green IT practices to address these challenges. By integrating sustainability into their digital transformation strategies, governments can contribute to environmental conservation while enhancing their operational efficiency.

Next, the principal future research directions are presented in Table 6 to encourage the scientific community to continue exploring and expanding the body of

Table 6 Future research proposition about government digitalization

Topic area	Description	Challenges to investigate	Future research questions
Digitalization	Integration of digital technologies in government operations and services	• Managing legacy systems • Ensuring digital inclusivity • Balancing speed and accuracy in digital services • Addressing digital divide	• How can governments effectively transition from legacy systems to digital platforms? • What are the best practices for ensuring digital inclusivity in public services? • How can digital divide be mitigated? • What measures can enhance user satisfaction in digital services? • How can governments measure the success of their digital transformation initiatives?
Innovation	Adoption of new technologies and innovative practices to improve governance and public services	• Fostering a culture of innovation • Overcoming resistance to change • Funding and resource allocation • Ensuring scalability	• What strategies can promote a culture of innovation in public sector organizations? • How can resistance to change be effectively managed? • What are the best funding models for innovation projects in the public sector? • How can innovation projects be scaled effectively in government settings? • What role do public-private partnerships play in fostering innovation in the public sector?
Digital economy	Economic activities driven by digital technologies and their impact on government operations	• Regulating digital markets • Addressing cybersecurity threats • Ensuring equitable economic growth • Managing digital taxation	• How can digital markets be effectively regulated to protect consumers? • What are the most effective cybersecurity measures for protecting digital economies? • How can digital taxation be managed to ensure fairness and efficiency? • What policies can ensure equitable economic growth in a digital economy? • How does the digital economy impact traditional economic structures?

(continued)

Table 6 (continued)

Topic area	Description	Challenges to investigate	Future research questions
Law	Legal frameworks and regulations governing digital transformation in government	• Updating legal frameworks • Ensuring compliance with data protection laws • Addressing jurisdictional issues • Balancing regulation and innovation	• How can legal frameworks be updated to keep pace with digital transformation? • What are the best practices for ensuring compliance with data protection laws? • How can jurisdictional issues be managed in a digital world? • How can the balance between regulation and innovation be achieved? • What are the legal implications of AI in government services?
Systems adoption	Implementation and integration of new digital systems in government operations	• User training and adoption • Ensuring interoperability • Managing system integration costs • Mitigating system downtime	• What are the most effective strategies for training government employees on new digital systems? • How can interoperability between different digital systems be ensured? • What are the cost-effective methods for integrating new systems in government operations? • How can system downtime be minimized during the adoption process? • What are the critical success factors for system adoption in government?
Information management systems, privacy & risk	Handling, protecting, and managing information in government systems, focusing on privacy and risk mitigation	• Ensuring data privacy • Managing cybersecurity risks • Developing robust data governance frameworks • Addressing ethical concerns	• What are the best practices for ensuring data privacy in government systems? • How can cybersecurity risks be effectively managed in digital government operations? • What frameworks are necessary for robust data governance in government? • How can ethical concerns related to data use in government be addressed? • What are the emerging threats to information security in digital government systems?

(continued)

Table 6 (continued)

Topic area	Description	Challenges to investigate	Future research questions
Sustainability	Incorporating sustainable practices in government digital initiatives to minimize environmental impact	• Reducing the energy footprint of digital systems • Promoting sustainable IT practices • Ensuring long-term viability of digital projects • Addressing e-waste management	• What are the most effective methods for reducing the energy footprint of government digital systems? • How can sustainable IT practices be promoted in government operations? • What strategies can ensure the long-term viability of digital projects? • How can e-waste be managed effectively in government digital initiatives? • What role does sustainability play in the digital transformation of governments?
Artificial intelligence	Utilizing AI technologies to enhance government services and decision-making processes	• Addressing ethical concerns • Ensuring algorithmic transparency • Managing the impact on employment • Integrating AI with existing systems	• What ethical guidelines are necessary for the use of AI in government services? • How can algorithmic transparency be ensured in government AI applications? • What are the impacts of AI on employment in the public sector? • How can AI be effectively integrated with existing government systems? • What measures can enhance public trust in government AI initiatives?
Green resources	Use of environmentally friendly technologies and practices in government digitalization efforts	• Sourcing sustainable materials • Promoting green procurement practices • Ensuring energy efficiency • Managing resource life cycle	• What are the best practices for sourcing sustainable materials for government digital projects? • How can green procurement practices be promoted in government operations? • What strategies can ensure energy efficiency in government digital systems? • How can the life cycle of resources be managed sustainably in government projects? • What role do green resources play in the digital transformation of governments?

Source: The author

knowledge in the field of government digitalization. These proposed areas of investigation aim to address the emerging challenges and opportunities in this rapidly evolving domain, providing a roadmap for scholars and practitioners to advance their understanding and implementation of digital transformation in government. Therefore, Table 6 shows 9 research topics, 36 research challenges, and 45 future research questions about digitalization in governments.

Conclusions

This bibliometric has developed three primary methods—bibliographic coupling, co-citation analysis, and keyword co-occurrence analysis—to analyze a sample of 371 publications related to the digitalization of governments. The study provides comprehensive insights into the evolving landscape of government digitalization. As main conclusions, this study offers a total of 9 research topics, 36 research challenges, and 45 future research questions regarding the digitalization of governments (see Table 6). In relation to the main RQ (*What are the characteristics and priorities of digitalization processes in governments according to the recent literature?*) the study has discovered that the characteristics of digitalization processes in governments, as highlighted in the recent literature, include the integration of digital technologies to enhance efficiency, transparency, and citizen engagement. Priorities focus on adopting e-government initiatives, fostering innovation, and establishing effective governance frameworks. The literature emphasizes the dynamic and multifaceted nature of digital transformation, requiring governments to continually adapt and evolve their strategies to meet emerging challenges and opportunities.

Also, in relation to the first objective proposed (*To understand and characterize the digitalization processes in governments*), the digitalization processes in governments are characterized by the adoption of advanced technologies such as artificial intelligence, blockchain, and IoT. These technologies are integrated into various governmental functions to streamline operations, improve service delivery, and increase transparency. Key characteristics include the transformation of traditional bureaucratic processes into more agile and efficient systems, the emphasis on data-driven decision-making, and the push towards greater citizen participation through digital platforms.

Secondly, (*To generate knowledge about the main academic contributions related to the development of the concept of digitalization in governments*) this study identifies significant academic contributions that have shaped the understanding of digitalization in governments. Notable contributions include the exploration of e-government frameworks, the impact of digital technologies on public administration, and the role of innovation in driving digital transformation. The literature also highlights the importance of legal and regulatory frameworks in facilitating digitalization efforts and ensuring compliance with data protection and privacy standards. These contributions provide a foundation for future research and practical implementations in government digitalization.

Thirdly, (*To identify insights that help understand the digital transformation processes in governments*) the insights gathered from this study highlight several critical aspects of digital transformation in governments. These include the importance of strategic planning and stakeholder engagement, the need for robust cybersecurity measures to protect sensitive data, and the potential of artificial and machine learning to enhance public service delivery. Additionally, the study underscores the significance of addressing ethical concerns and ensuring algorithmic transparency in the deployment of digital technologies. These insights offer valuable guidance for policymakers and practitioners aiming to navigate the complexities of digital transformation in the public sector.

Finally, (*To establish future research guides and purposes for each of the areas identified as relevant in government digitalization processes*), the study proposes future research guides that focus on addressing the challenges and opportunities in the digitalization of governments. Research should investigate effective strategies for transitioning from legacy systems to digital platforms, ensuring digital inclusivity, and balancing innovation with regulatory compliance. Future studies should also explore the impacts of digitalization on sustainability, energy consumption, and environmental conservation.

Additionally, there is a need to examine the ethical implications of artificial intelligence and other emerging technologies in government operations. The study's findings emphasize the importance of continuous innovation, robust governance frameworks, and ethical considerations in the successful digital transformation of governmental operations and services.

Theoretical Implications

The theoretical implications of this study on the digitalization of governments significantly advance the academic discourse on public administration, digital transformation, and technology adoption. Firstly, the study provides a robust framework for analyzing the integration of digital tools in public sector management, thereby deepening our understanding of how digital technologies reshape government operations. This framework offers a basis for exploring the multifaceted impacts of digitalization on efficiency, transparency, and citizen engagement within government services.

Additionally, this research enriches the theoretical literature on e-government by identifying critical themes and trends that characterize current digital government initiatives. By tracing the evolution of e-government practices, the study furnishes a historical perspective essential for theoretical investigations. This context allows scholars to understand the influence of past developments on present and future digitalization efforts, paving the way for identifying emerging patterns and refining theoretical models.

The focus on innovation within government digitalization has profound theoretical implications. The study underscores the dynamic interplay between innovation and public sector transformation, positing that innovative practices are pivotal for effective digitalization. This supports and extends existing theories on the role of innovation in public administration, providing empirical evidence from the digital government realm. Future research can leverage these insights to delve into specific mechanisms through which innovation drives digital transformation in governmental settings.

Moreover, the study's emphasis on governance frameworks contributes valuable theoretical insights. By identifying various governance models and regulatory frameworks, the research lays the groundwork for understanding how governance structures impact digital transformation. This includes examining the delicate balance between regulation and innovation, the role of policy in shaping digital government initiatives, and the resultant effects on public trust. These theoretical explorations can inform policymaking and enhance the strategic implementation of digital government projects.

Linking digital transformation with sustainability practices, the study proposes a theoretical model integrating environmental considerations into the analysis of digital government initiatives. This contributes to the theoretical discourse on sustainable development and environmental management. The proposed model guides future research on how digital technologies can support sustainable governance and align with broader environmental objectives, offering a comprehensive perspective on digitalization.

Furthermore, the discussion on digital inclusion presents a theoretical foundation for examining the social implications of digital government initiatives. Highlighting the importance of equitable access to digital services and addressing the digital divide, the study invites further theoretical exploration into the socio-economic impacts of digitalization. This includes the role of digital literacy in fostering inclusion and how digital government can promote social equity, thereby enhancing our understanding of the intersection between technology and social justice in the public sector.

Lastly, the study underscores the nascent stage of AI integration in government operations and the associated ethical considerations and need for algorithmic transparency. This provides a theoretical basis for future research on AI governance in the public sector, the ethical implications of AI-driven decision-making, and the impact of AI on public administration practices. Addressing these theoretical questions will contribute to the responsible and effective adoption of AI in government functions.

In conclusion, the theoretical implications of this study enrich the academic understanding of government digitalization by offering frameworks and insights that can guide future research. These contributions deepen our comprehension of the complexities and opportunities inherent in digital transformation within the public sector, establishing a foundation for ongoing theoretical development and exploration.

Practical Implications

The practical implications of this study on the digitalization of governments are significant, providing actionable insights for policymakers, public administrators, and technology implementers. Firstly, the findings highlight the importance of integrating digital technologies into government operations to enhance efficiency, transparency, and citizen engagement. This can be practically applied by developing comprehensive digital strategies that prioritize the modernization of legacy systems, ensuring that digital platforms are user-friendly and accessible to all citizens, thus fostering greater public participation and trust in government services.

Moreover, the study emphasizes the need for robust cybersecurity measures to protect sensitive government data. Governments can implement advanced encryption techniques, multi-factor authentication, and regular security audits to safeguard their digital infrastructures. These measures are crucial in preventing data breaches and maintaining the integrity of digital government services, thereby ensuring that citizens' personal information is securely managed.

The role of innovation in government digitalization is another key practical implication. Public sector organizations should foster a culture of innovation by encouraging collaboration between different departments, investing in training programs for employees, and establishing innovation labs to experiment with new technologies. This approach can lead to the development of innovative solutions that improve service delivery and operational efficiency.

Additionally, the study's findings on the importance of governance frameworks suggest that governments should establish clear policies and regulations to guide digital transformation initiatives. This includes setting standards for data management, ensuring compliance with data protection laws, and addressing ethical concerns related to the use of AI and other emerging technologies. By doing so, governments can create a secure and transparent environment for digital transformation, which is essential for gaining public trust.

The study also underscores the significance of sustainability in digital government initiatives. Governments should adopt green IT practices, such as using energy-efficient data centers and promoting the use of renewable energy sources. These practices can help reduce the environmental impact of digital infrastructure and contribute to broader sustainability goals. Implementing policies that encourage the sustainable disposal of electronic waste and the recycling of IT equipment is also crucial for minimizing the ecological footprint of digital government operations.

Finally, the emphasis on digital inclusion highlights the need for governments to bridge the digital divide by ensuring that all citizens have access to digital services, regardless of their socio-economic status. This can be achieved through initiatives that provide affordable Internet access, digital literacy training, and the development of mobile-friendly government platforms. By addressing these practical considerations, governments can ensure that the benefits of digital transformation are equitably distributed, fostering a more inclusive and connected society.

These practical implications not only enhance the effectiveness of digital government initiatives but also contribute to the overall well-being of society by promoting transparency, efficiency, and inclusivity in public administration.

Limitations and Future Research

Despite the comprehensive nature of this bibliometric study on the digitalization of governments, several limitations should be acknowledged. First, the study relies solely on data from the Web of Science database, which, while extensive, may not encompass all relevant publications, especially those in non-English languages or lesser-known journals. This could result in a potential bias, limiting the generalizability of the findings. Additionally, the focus on certain keywords and themes may inadvertently overlook other significant aspects of government digitalization. While the selected themes are based on their prominence in the literature, this approach might miss emerging or niche topics that are equally important for understanding the broader landscape of digital transformation. Acknowledging these limitations provides a more balanced perspective on the study's findings and highlights areas for future research to build upon and address the gaps identified.

References

Allam, Z., & Dhunny, Z. A. (2019). On big data, artificial intelligence and smart cities. *Cities, 89*, 80–91. https://doi.org/10.1016/j.cities.2019.01.032

Androniceanu, A., Georgescu, I., & Kinnunen, J. (2022). Public administration digitalization and corruption in the EU member states. A comparative and correlative research analysis. *Transylvanian Review of Administrative Sciences, 18*(65), 5–22. https://doi.org/10.24193/tras.65E.1

Androniceanu, A., Georgescu, I., & Sabie, O. M. (2022). The impact of digitalization on public administration, economic development, and well-being in the EU countries. *Central European Public Administration Review, 20*, 9. https://doi.org/10.17573/cepar.2022.2.01

Anthopoulos, L. G., Siozos, P., & Tsoukalas, I. A. (2007). Applying participatory design and collaboration in digital public services for discovering and re-designing e-Government services. *Government Information Quarterly, 24*(2), 353–376. https://doi.org/10.1016/j.giq.2006.07.018

Batool, S., Gill, S. A., Javaid, S., & Khan, A. J. (2021). Good governance via E-Governance: moving towards digitalization for a digital economy. *Review of Applied Management and Social Sciences, 4*(4), 823–836. https://doi.org/10.47067/ramss.v4i4.186

Bejinaru, R. (2019). Impact of digitalization on education in the knowledge economy. *Management Dynamics in the Knowledge Economy, 7*(3), 367–380. https://doi.org/10.25019/MDKE/7.3.06

Bisogno, M., Cuadrado-Ballesteros, B., & Abate, F. (2024). The role of institutional and operational factors in the digitalization of large local governments: insights from Italy. *International Journal of Public Sector Management*. https://doi.org/10.1108/IJPSM-10-2023-0291

Bouncken, R. B., & Kraus, S. (2022). Entrepreneurial ecosystems in an interconnected world: emergence, governance, and digitalization. *Review of Managerial Science, 16*(1), 1–14. https://doi.org/10.1007/s11846-021-00444-1

Cappelli, L., Pisano, A., Iannucci, E., Papetti, P., D'Ascenzo, F., & Ruggieri, R. (2024). Digitalization and prevention of corruption: Opportunities and risks—Some evidence from the Italian university system. *Business Strategy and the Environment, 33*(1), 81–94. https://doi.org/10.1002/bse.3332

Castro, G. D. R., Fernandez, M. C. G., & Colsa, A. U. (2021). Unleashing the convergence amid digitalization and sustainability towards pursuing the Sustainable Development Goals (SDGs): A holistic review. *Journal of Cleaner Production, 280*, 122204. https://doi.org/10.1016/j.jclepro.2020.122204

Dempsey, M., McBride, K., Haataja, M., & Bryson, J. (2022). Transnational digital governance and its impact on artificial intelligence. In J. B. Bullock, Y.-C. Chen, J. Himmelreich, V. M. Hudson, A. Korinek, M. M. Young, & B. Zhang (Eds.), *The Oxford handbook of AI governance*. Oxford University Press. https://doi.org/10.31235/osf.io/xu3jr

de Oliveira Almeida, G., Zouain, D. M., & Mahecha, Y. L. R. (2014). The status of e-government research: A bibliometric study. *Business and Management Review, 3*(11), 7–22.

Dias, G. P. (2019). Fifteen years of e-government research in Ibero-America: A bibliometric analysis. *Government Information Quarterly, 36*(3), 400–411. https://doi.org/10.1016/j.giq.2019.05.008

Díaz-García, V., Montero-Navarro, A., Rodríguez-Sánchez, J. L., & Gallego-Losada, R. (2022). Digitalization and digital transformation in higher education: A bibliometric analysis. *Frontiers in Psychology, 13*, 1081595. https://doi.org/10.3389/fpsyg.2022.1081595

Di Giulio, M., & Vecchi, G. (2023). Implementing digitalization in the public sector. Technologies, agency, and governance. *Public Policy and Administration, 38*(2), 133–158. https://doi.org/10.1177/09520767211023283

Dobrolyubova, E., Klochkova, E., & Alexandrov, O. (2019). Digitalization and effective government: what is the cause and what is the effect? In *International conference on digital transformation and global society* (pp. 55–67). Springer. https://doi.org/10.1007/978-3-030-37858-5_5

Donthu, N., Kumar, S., Mukherjee, D., Pandey, N., & Lim, W. M. (2021). How to conduct a bibliometric analysis: An overview and guidelines. *Journal of Business Research, 133*, 285–296. https://doi.org/10.1016/j.jbusres.2021.04.070

Ehlers, M. H., Finger, R., El Benni, N., Gocht, A., Sørensen, C. A. G., Gusset, M., Pfeifer, C., Poppe, K., Regan, Á., Rose, D. C., Wolfert, S., & Huber, R. (2022). Scenarios for European agricultural policymaking in the era of digitalisation. *Agricultural Systems, 196*, 103318. https://doi.org/10.1016/j.agsy.2021.103318

Erondu, C. I., & Erondu, U. I. (2023). The role of cyber security in a digitalizing economy: A development perspective. *International Journal of Research and Innovation in Social Science, 7*(11), 1558–1570.

Gichoya, D. (2005). Factors affecting the successful implementation of ICT projects in government. *Electronic Journal of E-Government, 3*(4), 175–184.

Gorina, L., Gordova, M., Khristoforova, I., Sundeeva, L., & Strielkowski, W. (2023). Sustainable education and digitalization through the prism of the COVID-19 pandemic. *Sustainability, 15*(8), 6846. https://doi.org/10.3390/su15086846

Goswami, S. S., Sarkar, S., Gupta, K. K., & Mondal, S. (2023). The role of cyber security in advancing sustainable digitalization: Opportunities and challenges. *Journal of Decision Analytics and Intelligent Computing, 3*(1), 270–285. https://doi.org/10.31181/jdaic10018122023g

Guo, Q., Geng, C., & Yao, N. (2023). How does green digitalization affect environmental innovation? The moderating role of institutional forces. *Business Strategy and the Environment, 32*(6), 3088–3105. https://doi.org/10.1002/bse.3288

Habibi, F., & Zabardast, M. A. (2020). Digitalization, education and economic growth: A comparative analysis of Middle East and OECD countries. *Technology in Society, 63*, 101370. https://doi.org/10.1016/j.techsoc.2020.101370

Hernández-Tamurejo, Á., González-Padilla, P., & Sepúlveda, Á. S. (2025). The economics of AI adoption in OTAs: Market dynamics and future research. *Global Economics Research*, 100001. https://doi.org/10.1016/j.ecores.2025.100001

Hou, J., Yang, X., & Chen, C. (2018). Emerging trends and new developments in information science: A document co-citation analysis (2009–2016). *Scientometrics, 115*, 869–892. https://doi.org/10.1007/s11192-018-2695-9

Ivanov, V. V., Markusova, V. A., & Mindeli, L. E. (2016). Government investments and the publishing activity of higher educational institutions: Bibliometric analysis. *Herald of the Russian Academy of Sciences, 86*, 314–321. https://doi.org/10.1134/S1019331616040031

Iyamu, I., Xu, A. X., Gómez-Ramírez, O., Ablona, A., Chang, H. J., Mckee, G., & Gilbert, M. (2021). Defining digital public health and the role of digitization, digitalization, and digital transformation: scoping review. *JMIR Public Health and Surveillance, 7*(11), e30399. https://doi.org/10.2196/30399

Jain, E., & Lamba, J. (2021). Management and digitalization strategy for transforming education sector: an emerging gateway persuaded by COVID 19. In K. Sandhu (Ed.), *Emerging challenges, solutions, and best practices for digital enterprise transformation* (pp. 69–83). IGI Global. https://doi.org/10.4018/978-1-7998-8587-0.ch004

Janowski, T. (2015). Digital government evolution: From transformation to contextualization. *Government Information Quarterly, 32*(3), 221–236. https://doi.org/10.1016/j.giq.2015.07.001

Jarneving, B. (2007). Bibliographic coupling and its application to research-front and other core documents. *Journal of Informetrics, 1*(4), 287–307. https://doi.org/10.1016/j.joi.2007.07.004

Kopchev, V. (2019). The European Union moves ahead on cybersecurity research through enhanced cooperation and coordination. *Information & Security: An International Journal, 42*, 67–81. https://doi.org/10.11610/isij.4204

Krishnan, B., Arumugam, S., & Maddulety, K. (2020). Critical success factors for the digitalization of smart cities. *International Journal of Technology Management & Sustainable Development, 19*(1), 69–86. https://doi.org/10.1386/tmsd_00016_1

Kuzemko, C. (2019). Re-scaling IPE: local government, sustainable energy and change. *Review of International Political Economy, 26*(1), 80–103. https://doi.org/10.1080/09692290.2018.1527239

Lappi, T. M., Aaltonen, K., & Kujala, J. (2019). Project governance and portfolio management in government digitalization. *Transforming Government: People, Process and Policy, 13*(2), 159–196. https://doi.org/10.1108/TG-11-2018-0068

Lazuardi, L., Sanjaya, G. Y., Ali, P. B., Siahaan, R. G. M., Achmad, L., & Wulandari, H. (2021, July). Interoperability of health digitalization: case study on use of information technology for maternal and child health services in Indonesia. In *Business information systems* (pp. 317–327). https://doi.org/10.52825/bis.v1i.53

Lezoche, M., Hernandez, J. E., Díaz, M. D. M. E. A., Panetto, H., & Kacprzyk, J. (2020). Agrifood 4.0: A survey of the supply chains and technologies for the future agriculture. *Computers in Industry, 117*, 103187. https://doi.org/10.1016/j.compind.2020.103187

Li, X., Liu, H., Wang, W., Zheng, Y., Lv, H., & Lv, Z. (2022). Big data analysis of the internet of things in the digital twins of smart city based on deep learning. *Future Generation Computer Systems, 128*, 167–177. https://doi.org/10.1016/j.future.2021.10.006

Liang, X., & Liu, A. M. (2018). The evolution of government sponsored collaboration network and its impact on innovation: A bibliometric analysis in the Chinese solar PV sector. *Research Policy, 47*(7), 1295–1308. https://doi.org/10.1016/j.respol.2018.04.012

Lindgren, I., Madsen, C. Ø., Hofmann, S., & Melin, U. (2019). Close encounters of the digital kind: A research agenda for the digitalization of public services. *Government Information Quarterly, 36*(3), 427–436. https://doi.org/10.1016/j.giq.2019.03.002

Löfgren, K., & Webster, C. W. R. (2020). The value of Big Data in government: The case of 'smart cities'. *Big Data & Society, 7*(1), 2053951720912775. https://doi.org/10.4337/9781788112352.00011

Martyakova, E., & Gorchakova, E. (2019). Quality education and digitalization of the economy. In *Proceedings of the 4th international conference on the industry 4.0 model for advanced manufacturing: AMP 2019 4* (pp. 212–218). Springer. https://doi.org/10.1007/978-3-030-18180-2_17

Mas-Tur, A., Roig-Tierno, N., Sarin, S., Haon, C., Sego, T., Belkhouja, M., Porter, A., & Merigó, J. M. (2021). Co-citation, bibliographic coupling and leading authors, institutions and countries in the 50 years of technological forecasting and social change. *Technological Forecasting and Social Change, 165*, 120487. https://doi.org/10.1016/j.techfore.2020.120487
McAllister, J. T., Lennertz, L., & Atencio Mojica, Z. (2022). Mapping a discipline: a guide to using VOSviewer for bibliometric and visual analysis. *Science & Technology Libraries, 41*(3), 319–348. https://doi.org/10.1080/0194262X.2021.1991547
Möller, D. P. (2023). Cybersecurity in digital transformation. In *Guide to cybersecurity in digital transformation: Trends, methods, technologies, applications and best practices* (pp. 1–70). Cham.
Napitupulu, D., & Yakub, R. (2021). A bibliometric analysis of e-government research. *Library Philosophy and Practice, 2021*, 1–19.
Ni, C., Sugimoto, C. R., & Robbin, A. (2017). Examining the evolution of the field of public administration through a bibliometric analysis of public administration review. *Public Administration Review, 77*(4), 496–509. https://doi.org/10.1111/puar.12737
Oladinrin, O. T., Arif, M., Rana, M. Q., & Gyoh, L. (2023). Interrelations between construction ethics and innovation: A bibliometric analysis using VOSviewer. *Construction Innovation, 23*(3), 505–523.
Ponti, B., Cerrillo-i-Martínez, A., & Di Mascio, F. (2022). Transparency, digitalization, and corruption. In E. Carloni & M. Gnaldi (Eds.), *Understanding and fighting corruption in Europe: From repression to prevention* (pp. 97–126). Springer. https://doi.org/10.1007/978-3-030-82495-2_6
Ranchordás, S. (2022). The digitization of government and digital exclusion: setting the scene. In C. B. de Morais, G. F. Mendes, & T. Vesting (Eds.), *The rule of law in cyberspace* (pp. 125–148). Springer. https://doi.org/10.2139/ssrn.3663051
Ribeiro-Navarrete, S., Saura, J. R., & Palacios-Marqués, D. (2021). Towards a new era of mass data collection: Assessing pandemic surveillance technologies to preserve user privacy. *Technological Forecasting and Social Change, 167*, 120681. https://doi.org/10.1016/j.techfore.2021.120681
Rizk, A., Toll, D., Sundberg, L., & Heidlund, M. (2023, August). The evolution of government strategies from IT to digitalization: A comparative study of two time periods in Swedish local governments. In *International conference on electronic government* (pp. 431–445). Springer.
Rot, A., Sobińska, M., Hernes, M., & Franczyk, B. (2020). Digital transformation of public administration through blockchain technology. In M. Hernes, A. Rot, & D. Jelonek (Eds.), *Towards Industry 4.0—current challenges in information systems* (pp. 111–126). Springer. https://doi.org/10.1007/978-3-030-40417-8_7
SaberiKamarposhti, M., Kamyab, H., Krishnan, S., Yusuf, M., Rezania, S., Chelliapan, S., & Khorami, M. (2024). A comprehensive review of AI-enhanced smart grid integration for hydrogen energy: Advances, challenges, and future prospects. *International Journal of Hydrogen Energy*. https://doi.org/10.1016/j.ijhydene.2024.01.129
Saura, J. R. (2024). Algorithms in digital marketing: Does smart personalization promote a privacy paradox? *FIIB Business Review, 13*(5), 499–502. https://doi.org/10.1177/23197145241276898
Saura, J. R., & Debasa, F. (Eds.). (2022). *Handbook of research on artificial intelligence in government practices and processes*. IGI Global. https://doi.org/10.4018/978-1-7998-9609-8
Saura, J. R., Ribeiro-Navarrete, S., Palacios-Marqués, D., & Mardani, A. (2023). Impact of extreme weather in production economics: Extracting evidence from user-generated content. *International Journal of Production Economics, 260*, 108861. https://doi.org/10.1016/j.ijpe.2023.108861
Saura, J. R., Ribeiro-Soriano, D., & Palacios-Marqués, D. (2021). From user-generated data to data-driven innovation: A research agenda to understand user privacy in digital markets. *International Journal of Information Management, 60*, 102331. https://doi.org/10.1016/j.ijinfomgt.2021.102331
Saura, J. R., Ribeiro-Soriano, D., & Palacios-Marqués, D. (2022, October). Assessing behavioral data science privacy issues in government artificial intelligence deployment. *Government Information Quarterly, 39*(4), 101679. https://doi.org/10.1016/j.giq.2022.101679

Saura, J. R., Škare, V., & Dosen, D. O. (2024). Is AI-based digital marketing ethical? Assessing a new data privacy paradox. *Journal of Innovation & Knowledge, 9*(4), 100597. https://doi.org/10.1016/j.jik.2024.100597

Shahbaz, M., Wang, J., Dong, K., & Zhao, J. (2022). The impact of digital economy on energy transition across the globe: The mediating role of government governance. *Renewable and Sustainable Energy Reviews, 166*, 112620. https://doi.org/10.1016/j.rser.2022.112620

Sidorenko, E. L., Esendirov, M. V., & Grigorieva, O. G. (2020). Digitalization of the public administration system: modern efficiency methods. *European Proceedings of Social and Behavioural Sciences*. https://doi.org/10.15405/epsbs.2020.04.94

Talwar, S., Kaur, P., Nunkoo, R., & Dhir, A. (2023). Digitalization and sustainability: virtual reality tourism in a post-pandemic world. *Journal of Sustainable Tourism, 31*(11), 2564–2591. https://doi.org/10.1080/09669582.2022.2029870

Tziortzioti, C., Amaxilatis, D., Mavrommati, I., & Chatzigiannakis, I. (2019). IoT sensors in sea water environment: Ahoy! Experiences from a short summer trial. *Electronic Notes in Theoretical Computer Science, 343*, 117–130. https://doi.org/10.1016/j.entcs.2019.04.014

Van Kersbergen, K., & Vis, B. (2022). Digitalization as a policy response to social acceleration: Comparing democratic problem solving in Denmark and the Netherlands. *Government Information Quarterly, 39*(3), 101707. https://doi.org/10.1016/j.giq.2022.101707

Vyas-Doorgapersad, S. (2022). The use of digitalization (ICTs) in achieving sustainable development goals. *Global Journal of Emerging Market Economies, 14*(2), 265–278. https://doi.org/10.1177/09749101211067295

Wacksman, J. (2021). Digitalization of contact tracing: balancing data privacy with public health benefit. *Ethics and Information Technology, 23*(4), 855–861. https://doi.org/10.1007/s10676-021-09601-2

Walter, C., & Ribière, V. (2013). A citation and co-citation analysis of 10 years of KM theory and practices. *Knowledge Management Research & Practice, 11*(3), 221–229. https://doi.org/10.1057/kmrp.2013.25

Wandaogo, A. A. (2022). Does digitalization improve government effectiveness? Evidence from developing and developed countries. *Applied Economics, 54*(33), 3840–3860. https://doi.org/10.1080/00036846.2021.2016590

Wang, H., & Guo, J. (2024). New way out of efficiency-equity dilemma: Digital technology empowerment for local government environmental governance. *Technological Forecasting and Social Change, 200*, 123184. https://doi.org/10.1016/j.techfore.2023.123184

West, D. M. (2005). *Digital government: Technology and public sector performance*. Princeton University Press. https://doi.org/10.1515/9781400835768

Young, L. M., & Hobbs, J. E. (2002). Vertical linkages in agri-food supply chains: changing roles for producers, commodity groups, and government policy. *Applied Economic Perspectives and Policy, 24*(2), 428–441. https://doi.org/10.2307/1349770

Yüksel, I. (2010). Hydropower for sustainable water and energy development. *Renewable and Sustainable Energy Reviews, 14*(1), 462–469. https://doi.org/10.1016/j.rser.2009.07.025

Zancajo, A., Verger, A., & Bolea, P. (2022). Digitalization and beyond: the effects of Covid-19 on post-pandemic educational policy and delivery in Europe. *Policy and Society, 41*(1), 111–128. https://doi.org/10.1093/polsoc/puab016

Zhao, X., Lu, S., & Yuan, S. (2023). How does the digitization of government environmental governance affect environmental pollution? spatial and threshold effects. *Journal of Cleaner Production, 415*, 137670. https://doi.org/10.1016/j.jclepro.2023.137670

Zhou, C., & Song, W. (2021). Digitalization as a way forward: A bibliometric analysis of 20 years of servitization research. *Journal of Cleaner Production, 300*, 126943. https://doi.org/10.1016/j.jclepro.2021.126943

Bridging Governance and Practice: A Systematic Review of Artificial Intelligence Potential in Health Care

Luigi Jesus Basile, Nunzia Carbonara, Roberta Pellegrino, and Umberto Panniello

Introduction

Artificial intelligence (AI) has transformed numerous sectors, including health care, where its applications promise unprecedented advancements in diagnostics, precision medicine, and operational efficiency (Dal Mas et al., 2023; Meyer et al., 2024). Beyond these applications, AI plays a pivotal role in the broader digital transformation of health care, which encompasses integrating digital technologies to improve the quality, accessibility, and efficiency of healthcare services (Basile et al., 2024b; Mauro et al., 2024). Central to this transformation is using data as a strategic asset, enabling insights that drive better clinical outcomes, optimize resource allocation, and enhance patient experiences (Basile et al., 2023; Chatterjee et al., 2023). However, fully realizing the benefits of these advancements necessitates developing organizational and individual capabilities (Basile et al., 2024a, 2024b; Mikalef et al., 2021), as the effective use of AI hinges on skills in data interpretation, system integration, and adaptive governance practices (Akter et al., 2023; Saraswat et al., 2022). In this regard, the integration of AI into healthcare systems is far from straightforward, as it requires careful consideration of governance, ethical principles, and interdisciplinary collaboration (Çetin, 2024; Mauro et al., 2024). The dynamic interplay between technological innovation and healthcare governance has become a focal point for researchers, policymakers, and practitioners seeking to

L. J. Basile (✉)
Université Paris-Saclay, Univ Evry, IMT-BS, LITEM, Évry-Courcouronnes, France
e-mail: luigi-jesus.basile@imt-bs.eu

N. Carbonara · R. Pellegrino · U. Panniello
Polytechnic University of Bari, Bari, Italy
e-mail: nunzia.carbonara@poliba.it; roberta.pellegrino@poliba.it; umberto.panniello@poliba.it

J. R. Saura (ed.), *Global Perspectives on AI, Ethics, and Business Economics*, Contributions to Management Science,
https://doi.org/10.1007/978-3-031-88781-9_7

exploit AI's potential while navigating complex challenges, such as algorithmic bias, data heterogeneity, and scalability (Dicuonzo et al., 2023; Galetsi et al., 2023). Despite the rapid proliferation of AI technologies in health care, there remains a critical gap in understanding how these tools can effectively support governance decisions. Governance in this context extends beyond regulatory compliance to encompass dimensions that are crucial for the sustainable and equitable deployment of AI in health care (Nasir et al., 2024). Addressing these gaps is essential, as robust governance frameworks optimize AI's utility and safeguard public trust in these transformative technologies (Singha et al., 2023; World Health Organization, 2021). This study aims to examine the impact of AI in enhancing clinical applications for healthcare professionals and supporting governance decisions for managers within healthcare organizations. The research investigates AI's current and expected outcomes in health care by synthesizing insights from 53 peer-reviewed articles using the Preferred Reporting Items for Systematic Reviews and Meta-Analyses (PRISMA) framework. The study also identifies persistent challenges, such as ethical concerns and technical barriers, which impede widespread AI adoption in healthcare systems.

This research contributes to the growing body of literature by offering insights into how AI can support clinical and governance decisions in health care. Building on prior studies that focus predominantly on technical applications or clinical outcomes (Meyer et al., 2024; Secinaro et al., 2021; Yin et al., 2021), this work shifts attention to the essential role of AI in organizational strategies and governance decisions. Notably, the findings underscore the importance of robust governance frameworks that are both adaptable and inclusive, ensuring that AI applications align with ethical standards and operational realities. The results of this study include a comprehensive identification and discussion of governance dimensions, such as resource allocation, quality assurance, risk management, and stakeholder engagement, with a particular focus on the interdisciplinary nature of AI adoption. While the study offers broad insights applicable to diverse healthcare settings, it also acknowledges limitations such as the variability of data quality and the scalability challenges inherent in AI implementation. The findings of this study have extensive implications for both healthcare theory and practice. Theoretically, the research identifies and discusses the main dimensions of clinical and governance decisions that connect governance with AI's practical applications and associated challenges. Practically, it offers actionable recommendations for healthcare providers and policymakers, emphasizing collaboration and inclusive design processes.

The following section presents the methodology employed in this study, providing a detailed account of the systematic approach undertaken by the authors to collect, evaluate, and analyze the reviewed papers. Section "Findings" examines the primary findings, organized around the key dimensions identified through the comprehensive literature review. Finally, section "Conclusions" concludes the chapter by summarizing the critical insights and discussing their implications.

Methodology

We adopted the guidelines of the Preferred Reporting Items for Systematic Reviews and Meta-Analyses (PRISMA) as outlined by Moher et al. (2009). PRISMA provides a standardized framework that enhances systematic reviews' transparency, objectivity, and comprehensiveness. The methodology is organized into four sequential phases: identification of relevant studies, screening of titles and abstracts, assessment of eligibility based on full-text articles, and the inclusion of studies that meet all the defined criteria. The following question frames the research: "What are the impacts of artificial intelligence on clinical and governance decisions in health care?"

To ensure a comprehensive literature review, we selected two leading scientific databases: Scopus and Web of Science. The search strategy was structured around the two primary pillars of this research: artificial intelligence and health care. For the artificial intelligence pillar, we used the keywords "artificial intelligence" and "AI"; for the healthcare pillar, we included "health care" and "health". To maximize the breadth of our search and capture as many relevant records as possible, we refrained from incorporating terms related to specific algorithms or applications. Including such particular terms could have narrowed our search scope and potentially excluded relevant papers that do not explicitly mention those terms. By concentrating on the core concepts of AI and health care, we maintained a balance between breadth and relevance in our literature search (Marzi et al., 2024). This approach allowed us to include a diverse range of studies without being limited by the specificity of additional keywords. It also ensured that emerging research and interdisciplinary works were considered, which might not use specialized terminology. The final search string employed in our study is presented in Table 1.

In the screening phase, we applied specific inclusion and exclusion criteria to refine the list of articles retrieved from the databases, detailed in Table 1. Initially, we used database filters to exclude publications that did not meet our inclusion criteria: we omitted articles not written in English, those outside the fields of Business,

Table 1 Exclusion and inclusion criteria for the selection of papers

Search string	Inclusion criteria	Exclusion criteria
Keywords: ("artificial intelligence" OR "AI") AND ("health care" OR "health") Search in: Title, Abstract, and Keywords Document type: Peer-reviewed Journals Domain: Business, management, and accounting Language: English	• Studies that focus on the application, impact, or development of artificial intelligence within the healthcare context • Studies focusing not exclusively on specific algorithms, technical implementations, or niche applications without broader implications for AI in health care	• Articles not written in English • Articles not published in peer-reviewed journals • Articles not focused on healthcare organizations

Source: Authors' elaboration

Management, and Accounting, as well as books, book chapters, conference proceedings, and editorials. Duplicate records were also removed, resulting in 1040 unique articles. To ensure a comprehensive review, we did not restrict publication dates, including studies from all available years. Subsequently, we screened the titles and abstracts of these articles to assess their relevance to our research question, which focuses on the intersection of artificial intelligence and health care within organizational contexts. We excluded studies that did not address both of these domains simultaneously. Specifically, articles that concentrated solely on developing or testing AI algorithms without exploring their implications in healthcare settings were omitted. This screening process narrowed the selection to 123 articles that advanced to the eligibility stage. We then conducted a thorough full-text review of these articles to evaluate their alignment with our inclusion criteria and research question. After this detailed assessment, we selected 53 studies for our systematic literature review. These studies collectively provide a comprehensive overview of how artificial intelligence is being used to enhance clinical and governance decisions in healthcare organizations. The entire review process we followed is depicted in Fig. 1.

Results

A comprehensive analysis of the gathered research is the last stage of our systematic literature review. The descriptive results, including the distribution of publications over time and the sources consulted, are presented in the first subsection. In the next part, we examine the studies' thematic analysis in order to discuss recurring themes and gaps in the body of knowledge.

Descriptive Statistics

The selected articles start in 2020, marking the initial identification of research contributions on using AI for clinical and governance decisions in health care. The chart shows that the number of published papers has steadily increased, reaching a peak of 19 papers by September 2024. This trend underscores the growing academic interest in the topic over time. Notably, the distribution of papers highlights the recent nature of the research field, with over 70% of the identified works published between 2022 and 2024. The chart demonstrates the steady growth in the number of scientific papers identified from 2020 to 2024. Figure 2 shows the distribution of the articles per publishing year.

Table 2 shows the distribution of articles on artificial intelligence in health care within the business and management domain across various journals. *Technology in Society* and *Technological Forecasting and Social Change* lead with eight and seven articles, respectively, focusing on AI's societal and future-oriented implications.

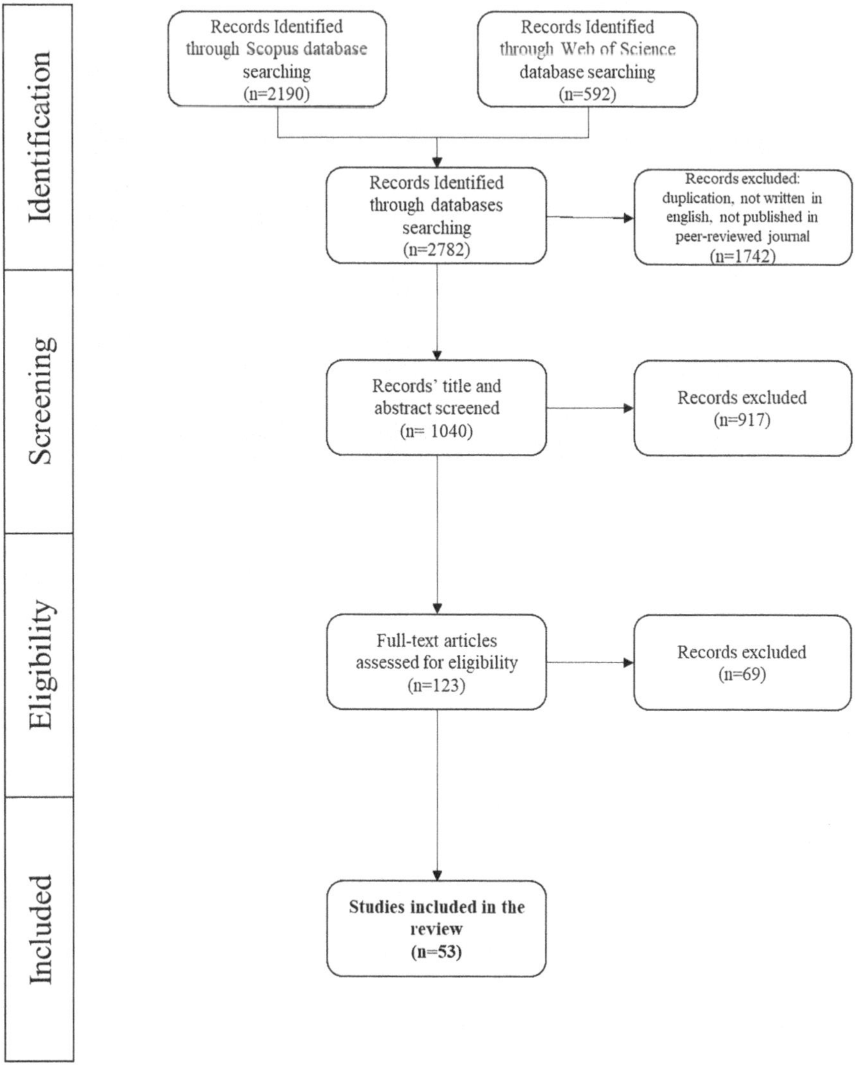

Fig. 1 PRISMA flow diagram. *Source*: Authors' elaboration

Journals like *Big Data* and *Cognitive Computing* and *Value in Health* (three articles each) highlight technical and economic perspectives. In contrast, others emphasize data management and organizational strategies, including the *International Journal of Information Management Data Insights* and the *Journal of Health Organization and Management* (two articles each). The 24 articles spread across single-contribution journals indicate this research area's interdisciplinary and emerging nature, spanning societal, operational, and strategic dimensions of artificial intelligence in health care.

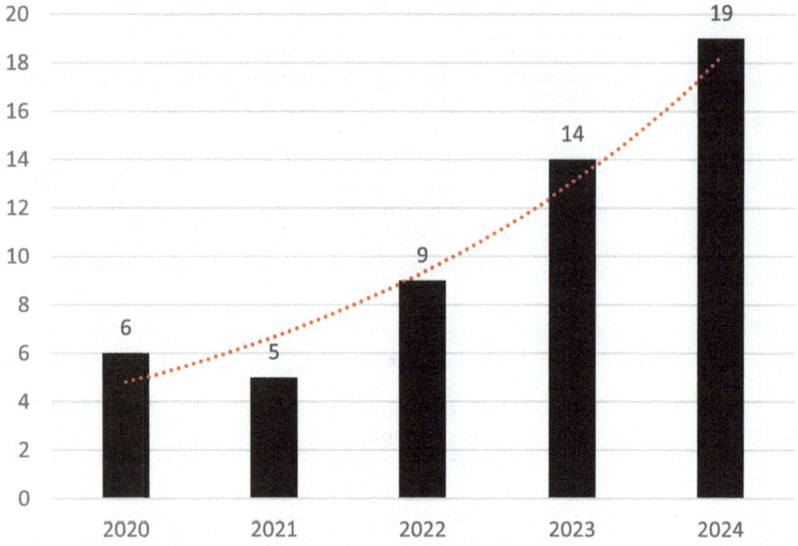

Fig. 2 Articles distribution per publishing year. *Source*: Authors' elaboration

Table 2 Number of papers per journal

Journal	# of articles
Technology In Society	8
Technological Forecasting and Social Change	7
Big Data and Cognitive Computing	3
Value in Health	3
International Journal of Information Management Data Insights	2
International Journal of Production Research	2
International Journal of System Assurance Engineering and Management	2
Journal of Health Organization and Management	2
Others	24

Source: Authors' elaboration

Findings

The literature review analysis allowed for identifying three key discussion areas to address the research question. Specifically, the results will be presented according to governance decisions, clinical decisions, and finally, the challenges and limitations discussed in the literature. These areas are particularly relevant as they encompass the critical dimensions shaping the implementation and impact of artificial intelligence in health care. Governance decisions ensure that AI systems align with ethical, regulatory, and operational standards while addressing resource allocation, quality assurance, and stakeholder engagement. Clinical decisions within the healthcare pathway highlight the practical integration of AI, from diagnostic support to operational efficiency, showcasing its transformative potential in improving patient outcomes and healthcare delivery. Lastly, challenges and limitations are crucial for understanding the barriers that hinder the widespread adoption of AI, including concerns over data quality, scalability, interpretability, and ethical implications. Figure 3 summarizes the findings that emerged through the thematic analysis for each key area defined.

Governance Decisions

The literature analysis highlighted key dimensions that capture AI's main areas of impact on healthcare governance decisions. These dimensions include resource allocation, which ensures efficient financial, technical, and human resources

Fig. 3 Summary of the key findings. *Source*: Authors' elaboration

management and quality and safety standards, safeguarding reliability and reducing diagnostic errors. Risk management emerges as a pivotal element in mitigating uncertainties, while ethical oversight addresses concerns such as bias, transparency, and data privacy. Lastly, stakeholder engagement underscores the importance of collaboration among developers, healthcare professionals, and patients. The following sections dive into these dimensions, illustrating their significance and interconnection in fostering effective AI integration in governance decisions.

Resource Allocation

Effective resource allocation is essential for implementing AI in health care, requiring strategic and adaptable approaches to address the challenges of dynamic healthcare settings. Studies show that resource distribution in healthcare involves financial, technical, and human factors crucial for successful AI integration. One key aspect is the need for flexibility in addressing uncertainties inherent in health care. Dynamic resource allocation models, which combine pre-positioning strategies with real-time patient scheduling, demonstrate how adaptability can address fluctuating demands and resource availability (Alnsour et al., 2023; Lam et al., 2021; Liu et al., 2024). These approaches ensure that resources are efficiently utilized and responsive to changing circumstances, highlighting the importance of robustness in resource management. Collaboration is another vital element, particularly when diverse expertise is harnessed to inform resource allocation frameworks. Multidisciplinary panels, which include clinicians, technicians, and patients, bring invaluable perspectives that help create comprehensive and actionable models (Martins et al., 2020).

Financial constraints often present significant challenges to deploying AI in health care, especially in resource-limited settings. AI can support resource allocation by guiding targeted investments. This approach ensures efforts align with defined healthcare priorities (Apell & Eriksson, 2023). By aligning financial resources with critical healthcare needs, these efforts enhance AI systems' scalability and support their sustainable implementation. AI technologies themselves contribute to optimizing resource utilization. By automating tasks like disease classification and patient monitoring, AI reduces the workload on healthcare professionals, enabling them to focus on critical responsibilities (Kumar et al., 2022; Thakur et al., 2024).

Stakeholder engagement is key to effective resource allocation. Collaborative models involving healthcare institutions, academia, and organizations show how shared resources can tackle challenges like managing blood supply chains and improving access to care (Ghouri et al., 2023).

Quality and Safety Standards

Timely and accurate data is crucial for clinical decision-making. AI systems using real-time data can improve care quality by offering actionable insights during critical situations. For instance, ensuring access to vital health information during crises, such as the COVID-19 pandemic, has been highlighted as a key factor in optimizing treatment strategies (Chattu, 2021; Kumar et al., 2022). These applications highlight the need to align AI solutions with high-quality data to uphold safety standards.

Reducing diagnostic errors is crucial for quality and safety, and advanced machine learning models can enhance diagnostic accuracy, especially in complex cases. AI-driven diagnostics help reduce risks from incorrect or delayed diagnoses (Gollapalli et al., 2024). Similarly, ensuring that chatbot interactions in health care deliver accurate and complete responses is critical to avoiding errors that could harm patients and undermine trust in these systems (Schillaci et al., 2024). These findings highlight the crucial role of quality benchmarks in enhancing diagnostic precision and patient outcomes. The broader implications of maintaining safety standards extend beyond individual cases to system-wide resilience. AI frameworks designed to improve healthcare operations during emergencies, such as large-scale health crises, illustrate the value of consistent quality benchmarks. By ensuring reliability and operational efficiency, these frameworks support the resilience of healthcare systems in times of unprecedented demand (Vishwakarma et al., 2023). This perspective underscores how adherence to safety standards contributes to individual care and the robustness of healthcare infrastructure.

Ethical compliance is key to quality and safety. Frameworks to mitigate risks, such as from medical chatbots, highlight the need for ethical oversight to build trust. Addressing challenges related to bias and transparency ensures that AI technologies align with the broader goal of safeguarding patient welfare (Basharat & Shahid, 2024).

Finally, the practical training of healthcare professionals is essential for upholding quality standards in AI implementations. Educational initiatives that equip professionals with the skills necessary to utilize AI tools can bridge the gap between technological advancements and clinical practice. For instance, empowering nurses with informatics training supports AI's safe and effective use in managing conditions like fall risks, ensuring that these tools meet the expected standards of safety and care (O'Connor et al., 2022).

Risk Management

A significant challenge in AI implementation is the lack of robust, shared regulatory frameworks. Without clear accountability guidelines, legal uncertainties arise, delaying AI adoption in health care. Addressing this regulatory void is essential to building trust and ensuring the responsible integration of AI systems. For instance, the lack of robust legal frameworks for AI accountability was identified as a significant barrier to its implementation in public sector settings, such as healthcare organizations (Misra et al., 2023). These findings emphasize the need for comprehensive regulatory structures to address liability, compliance, and operational risks. Risk mitigation is also closely tied to the reliability of AI models under uncertain conditions. In resource allocation, applying dynamic models could be instrumental in reducing the risk of inefficiencies caused by uncertain demand and stochastic resource consumption. These models help ensure resources are distributed effectively by enabling adaptive adjustments, minimizing waste, and addressing potential shortfalls (Liu et al., 2024). Such approaches demonstrate the potential of advanced methodologies to manage operational risks and enhance decision-making.

Ethical considerations are also a critical dimension of risk management in healthcare AI. Ethical risks like bias and data misuse raise broader concerns about trust and fairness in AI systems. Healthcare chatbots need strict ethical oversight to address algorithmic bias and prevent harm from inaccurate advice (Basharat & Shahid, 2024; Liu et al., 2022). These frameworks not only protect patients but also help build confidence in the use of AI technologies. Operational risks also emerge when there is a disconnect between AI development and clinical implementation. Studies examining failed AI implementations, such as those intended to automate clinical documentation or decision support, point to risks from insufficient stakeholder involvement and poor user acceptance. These failures highlight the importance of engaging key stakeholders, including clinicians and patients, to mitigate risks related to user resistance and integration challenges (Alnasser et al., 2024; Reis et al., 2020).

Another dimension of risk management involves the handling of data-related challenges. The availability, quality, and security of healthcare data are pivotal in ensuring the reliability of AI systems. Preprocessing methods, for example, are essential for addressing missing or inconsistent data issues, which, if left unaddressed, can compromise the performance and safety of AI applications (Gollapalli et al., 2024). Moreover, robust data governance frameworks ensure compliance with privacy regulations and reduce data breaches or misuse risks.

Finally, integrating AI systems within healthcare infrastructure presents scalability and compatibility risks. Outdated infrastructure and inflexible IT systems hinder AI adoption, causing inefficiencies and limiting scalability (Fontes et al., 2022).

Ethical Oversight

Ethical frameworks ensure AI operates within moral and legal boundaries while fostering stakeholder trust. Addressing algorithmic bias and fairness is a key aspect of ethical oversight. Poorly designed AI systems can exacerbate biases, leading to unequal patient care. For instance, studies have shown that chatbots and other AI applications may inadvertently reinforce discriminatory behaviors or fail to address the needs of underrepresented populations (Schillaci et al., 2024). Establishing robust ethical guidelines to mitigate such biases is essential for ensuring equitable healthcare delivery.

Transparency is also a critical dimension of ethical oversight. The "black box" nature of many AI systems poses challenges in understanding how decisions are made, which can undermine trust and hinder adoption. To address this, researchers emphasize the need for explainable AI frameworks that provide clear, interpretable insights into the decision-making processes of AI technologies (Fontes et al., 2022). Transparent communication about the capabilities and limitations of these systems is particularly vital in high-stakes healthcare settings, where decisions can directly impact patient outcomes.

Accountability mechanisms are also essential for fostering ethical use. Studies in applications such as automated diagnostic tools or cognitive agents highlight the importance of defining clear accountability structures to manage liability for errors or adverse outcomes (Reis et al., 2020). This includes assigning responsibility for AI-driven decisions and establishing protocols for monitoring and rectifying mistakes in real time. Such measures are critical for maintaining the integrity of healthcare operations and ensuring patient safety.

Ethical oversight extends to the management of sensitive healthcare data. Ensuring data privacy and security is a recurring theme, with researchers underscoring the importance of protecting patient information against misuse or breaches (Basharat & Shahid, 2024). This involves implementing stringent data governance frameworks that balance the need for data accessibility with the imperative to safeguard individual privacy. Ethical oversight ensures compliance with regulatory standards while addressing broader societal concerns about data ethics.

Lastly, ethical oversight is instrumental in maintaining trust and acceptance among users. Studies emphasize the interconnectedness of trust, transparency, and reliability in fostering ethical AI applications. For example, aligning chatbot characteristics with moral principles, such as avoiding misleading information and respecting cultural sensitivities, has enhanced user satisfaction and engagement (Qin et al., 2024; Schillaci et al., 2024).

Stakeholder Engagement

One of the primary benefits of stakeholder engagement is its role in addressing user resistance and facilitating smoother adoption of AI systems. Studies on failed AI projects, like those automating clinical documentation, show that poor user engagement leads to significant implementation challenges. When healthcare professionals are not adequately involved in the design and deployment phases, resistance can arise due to perceived irrelevance or mistrust of the technology (Gupta and Srivastava, 2024; Reis et al., 2020). These findings stress the need for early stakeholder involvement to align AI tools with clinical workflows and user needs. Diverse perspectives are key to stakeholder engagement. Multidisciplinary teams help design AI systems with a broader understanding of healthcare challenges. For instance, Martins et al. (2020) demonstrated how assembling panels of experts from various fields led to the development of more robust and actionable evaluation frameworks. This collaborative approach strengthens the design of AI systems and increases their acceptability across stakeholder groups. As key beneficiaries of healthcare AI, patients play a vital role in stakeholder engagement. Studies highlight the value of incorporating patient input into the design of AI systems, particularly those that involve direct patient interaction, such as chatbots or remote monitoring tools. For example, involving patients in developing mental health chatbots has been shown to address ethical concerns and improve the usability and acceptance of these technologies (Cheng & Jiang, 2020). Such engagement ensures that AI tools are patient-centric and address the specific needs of their intended users.

Policymakers and regulators are critical to the success of AI implementation. Their involvement ensures that AI systems comply with legal and ethical standards while addressing broader societal concerns. Research on public health systems and blood supply chains shows how regulatory collaboration supports AI integration into healthcare ecosystems (Fontes et al., 2022; Ghouri et al., 2023). These examples demonstrate how aligning technical and policy perspectives can enhance the scalability and impact of AI solutions. Stakeholder engagement is particularly critical when addressing ethical considerations and building trust in AI systems. Including ethicists, legal experts, and cultural representatives in the design process ensures that AI technologies respect diverse values and address concerns related to bias, fairness, and accountability (Basharat & Shahid, 2024; Cheng & Jiang, 2020). Transparent communication and active engagement build trust, essential for long-term AI success.

Clinical Decisions

The findings of this review highlight the transformative role of AI across key clinical decisions in health care. Diagnostic assistance emerges as a critical domain where AI improves accuracy and efficiency by supporting clinicians in early disease detection, medical imaging analysis, and patient assessments. Personalized medicine builds on this foundation by tailoring treatments to individual patient needs, leveraging genetic insights, real-time monitoring, and holistic data integration to deliver patient-centric care. Considering operational efficiency, AI demonstrates its ability to optimize workflows, automate repetitive tasks, and enhance resource allocation, addressing inefficiencies and improving healthcare delivery. Additionally, remote monitoring showcases the potential of AI to extend care beyond clinical settings, using wearable devices and virtual assistants to monitor patients in real time, enabling timely interventions and continuous support.

Diagnostic Assistance

One of the most impactful contributions of AI in health care is its ability to analyze medical imaging with precision. For instance, AI models are used to identify patterns in radiological images, aiding in the early detection of diseases such as cancer. By automating tasks traditionally performed by radiologists, these tools reduce their workload and improve diagnostic reliability (Buaka & Moid, 2024; Roppelt et al., 2023).

Beyond imaging, AI applications have expanded into other diagnostic tasks, including disease classification and patient assessments. For example, machine learning models have been employed to diagnose acute appendicitis, allowing clinicians to distinguish between complicated and non-complicated cases (Gollapalli et al., 2024). Similarly, automated classification systems provide fast and reliable diagnostics, particularly in settings with limited resources, thus optimizing healthcare workflows (Thakur et al., 2024).

AI-powered chatbots and cognitive agents also play a transformative role in diagnostic assistance. These tools facilitate early diagnosis by engaging patients in preliminary assessments and providing tailored medical advice. For instance, chatbots have proven effective in streamlining patient–provider interactions, enabling rapid identification of potential conditions and improving access to healthcare services, particularly for underserved populations (Basharat & Shahid, 2024).

Predictive analytics is another domain where AI significantly enhances diagnostic processes. AI models can predict disease progression and complications, supporting clinicians in proactive decision-making. For example, neural networks and other machine learning techniques have been employed to monitor and predict outcomes for diabetic patients, showcasing how AI can assist in both diagnosing conditions and managing chronic diseases over time (Kumar et al., 2022). In addition to improving diagnostic accuracy, AI systems contribute to operational efficiency by reducing the time and effort required for manual diagnostic processes. Automated tools expedite workflows, allowing healthcare professionals to focus on complex and critical cases. This efficiency is particularly valuable in environments where healthcare demand often exceeds capacity, enabling providers to deliver care more effectively (Thakur et al., 2024).

Personalized Medicine

In personalized medicine, AI offers a powerful tool for tailoring treatments to individual patients by analyzing complex genetic and phenotypic data. For instance, AI models can decode genetic variations and assess their impact on disease progression and treatment efficacy, paving the way for a shift from one-size-fits-all approaches to precision care. This approach has been particularly impactful in oncology, where AI-driven analyses support the development of targeted therapies, offering patients treatments that are more likely to be effective (Buaka & Moid, 2024). These applications demonstrate how AI enables healthcare providers to make more informed and personalized decisions.

AI also facilitates personalized treatment plans through the integration of real-time patient data. For instance, machine learning models can analyze information from wearable devices and other monitoring tools to provide continuous feedback on a patient's health status. This real-time monitoring enables adjustments to treatment protocols, ensuring that care remains aligned with the patient's evolving condition (Agarwal et al., 2024; Kumar et al., 2022; Zahlan et al., 2023). Such dynamic and responsive healthcare exemplifies the core of personalized medicine. In chronic disease management, AI-powered tools are pivotal in tailoring interventions to individual patient needs.

Predictive models have been used to anticipate complications and recommend preventive measures, particularly for diabetes and cardiovascular disease. By identifying patients at higher risk and suggesting targeted interventions, these systems improve outcomes while minimizing unnecessary treatments (de Carvalho et al., 2020; Musleh et al., 2024). This targeted approach reduces the burden on healthcare resources and enhances patient satisfaction. AI's role in improving accessibility to personalized care is also noteworthy. Chatbots and cognitive agents provide customized recommendations based on individual patient data, making health care more accessible, especially for underserved populations. These tools empower patients by giving them tailored advice and enabling them to participate actively in their healthcare journeys (Basharat & Shahid, 2024; Cheng & Jiang, 2020). This democratization of personalized care ensures that more people benefit from AI's capabilities, regardless of geographic or economic constraints.

Furthermore, AI's capacity to integrate diverse data sources enhances its effectiveness in personalized medicine. AI tools can comprehensively understand a patient's health by combining structured data, such as medical histories, with unstructured inputs like clinician notes. This holistic approach ensures that all relevant factors are considered in treatment planning, further refining the personalization of care (Gollapalli et al., 2024).

Operational Efficiency

One of the most significant contributions of AI to operational efficiency is its ability to automate repetitive and time-intensive tasks. For instance, AI-powered systems can automate documentation and administrative processes, freeing healthcare professionals to focus on patient care. This capability reduces manual workload and minimizes the risk of errors associated with manual data handling (Mahdi et al., 2023; Reis et al., 2020). Such automation highlights AI's role in improving efficiency and accuracy in healthcare operations. As mentioned, for governance decisions, AI enhances resource allocation by predicting demand and optimizing the distribution of healthcare resources. For example, dynamic optimization models that forecast patient needs enable hospitals to allocate beds, staff, and medical equipment more effectively. These tools are particularly valuable during periods of high demand, such as public health emergencies, where efficient resource management is essential to prevent bottlenecks and ensure patient care (Alnsour et al., 2023; Liu et al., 2024).

Workflow optimization is another area where AI significantly improves operational efficiency. Tools that integrate AI into clinical workflows reduce delays and streamline processes, such as patient scheduling and treatment planning. For instance, predictive analytics models assist healthcare facilities in reducing patient waiting times by identifying and addressing inefficiencies in scheduling systems (Thakur et al., 2024). These improvements enhance the overall patient experience while optimizing the utilization of healthcare infrastructure. In supply chain management, AI-driven solutions have effectively addressed inefficiencies and reduced waste. For example, AI models used in blood supply chain management optimize inventory levels and minimize wastage by accurately predicting supply and demand. These solutions enhance operational performance and contribute to sustainability by reducing resource overuse (Ghouri et al., 2023). This integration of AI into logistical operations illustrates its potential to drive systemic efficiencies across the healthcare ecosystem.

AI supports operational efficiency by improving communication and collaboration within healthcare teams. Tools such as cognitive agents and decision support systems facilitate real-time data sharing and enhance coordination among healthcare professionals. This improved communication enables faster decision-making and more cohesive care delivery, particularly in complex clinical environments (Reis et al., 2020).

Remote Monitoring

One of the most impactful contributions of AI in remote monitoring is its ability to track patient health using wearable devices and sensors. These tools collect and analyze data in real time, offering valuable insights into vital signs, activity levels, and other health metrics. For instance, AI-driven wearable devices have been employed to monitor diabetic patients, assisting in calorie tracking and insulin management with minimal human intervention (Kumar et al., 2022). Such innovations empower patients to take a proactive role in their care while reducing the burden on healthcare providers. AI-powered chatbots and virtual assistants extend remote monitoring capabilities by providing personalized guidance and support. These tools interact with patients to assess symptoms, provide health advice, and even flag potential complications. For example, cognitive agents designed for mental health monitoring engage users through tailored conversations, reducing barriers to care and enhancing accessibility (Cheng & Jiang, 2020). By enabling continuous interaction, these AI systems bridge the gap between patients and providers, ensuring timely interventions when needed.

In chronic disease management, remote monitoring systems supported by AI enhance patient outcomes by facilitating early detection of complications. Predictive analytics tools integrated into monitoring platforms can identify warning signs of deteriorating health, prompting timely medical attention. For instance, remote monitoring solutions for cardiovascular patients use AI to analyze heart rate and blood pressure trends, alerting providers to potential risks before they escalate (Chattu, 2021; Thakur et al., 2024). These capabilities exemplify how AI supports preventive care and reduces hospital admissions. The integration of remote monitoring into healthcare workflows also improves operational efficiency. By reducing the need for frequent in-person visits, AI-enabled systems save time for both patients and providers. This is particularly valuable in rural or resource-limited settings where access to healthcare facilities may be challenging. Remote monitoring tools ensure continuity of care while minimizing logistical constraints and enhancing healthcare equity and efficiency (Cheng & Jiang, 2020; Kumar et al., 2022). AI-driven remote monitoring also plays a vital role in emergency response and public health management. For example, chatbots and monitoring systems have been used to support populations during crises, such as natural disasters or pandemics, by providing real-time updates and health assessments.

Challenges and Limitations

Integrating AI into health care is linked to challenges and limitations that must be navigated to unlock its full potential. These obstacles, ranging from data-related issues to ethical and operational complexities, reflect the need for a comprehensive approach to ensure effective and equitable AI deployment. A fundamental challenge lies in the quality and availability of healthcare data. AI systems rely on large data sets for training, yet inconsistencies, missing values, and a lack of standardization plague healthcare data sets. These issues necessitate extensive preprocessing, including techniques like data imputation and normalization, to ensure model reliability (Gollapalli et al., 2024). Moreover, the scarcity of diverse and representative data sets limits the generalizability of AI systems, raising concerns about their effectiveness in varied populations (Roppelt et al., 2023). Scalability and integration also present significant barriers. AI models often struggle to transition from controlled development environments to real-world applications due to differences in infrastructure and workflows. Many healthcare systems, particularly those in resource-constrained settings, face challenges adapting outdated IT systems to accommodate advanced AI tools (Fontes et al., 2022; Martins et al., 2020). These scalability constraints hinder the widespread adoption of AI, even in areas where it could have a substantial impact. The "black box" nature of many AI systems creates additional challenges in interpretability and trust. Complex algorithms often lack transparency, making it difficult for physicians to understand how decisions are reached. This opacity can undermine confidence in AI tools and limit their use in clinical settings. For example, cognitive agents developed for diagnostic support faced resistance due to their lack of explainability, highlighting the importance of developing AI frameworks that provide clear and interpretable insights (Reis et al., 2020).

Generalizability remains a persistent limitation, with AI models often performing inconsistently across different demographic groups or healthcare settings. For instance, systems trained on specific populations may struggle to deliver accurate results in diverse environments, emphasizing the need for data sets that capture a broad range of patient characteristics (Roppelt et al., 2023). Addressing this limitation is critical for ensuring that AI technologies are equitable and effective for all patients. In parallel, ethical and regulatory challenges demand urgent attention. The lack of universally accepted regulatory frameworks for AI implementation creates a fragmented landscape, leading to standard variability across regions and healthcare institutions. Establishing robust policies ensures AI systems align with ethical principles, clinical guidelines, and legal requirements (Misra et al., 2023).

Ethical and regulatory challenges further complicate the deployment of AI in health care. The absence of clear guidelines on AI accountability creates uncertainty, deterring adoption and raising questions about liability in cases of error or harm. Ethical concerns, such as algorithmic bias and the misuse of sensitive patient data, add another layer of complexity. For instance, the European Union's proposed "*AI Act*" highlights the necessity of developing risk-based approaches to ensure high-risk AI applications in health care, such as chatbots used in mental health care, are subject to strict compliance checks to provide accurate, culturally sensitive advice and avoid harm to vulnerable populations, thereby fostering trust and safety in their usage (Basharat & Shahid, 2024).

Financial and resource constraints also pose significant barriers to adopting AI technologies. The costs associated with acquiring, maintaining, and updating AI systems, coupled with the need for specialized training, often exceed the budgets of many healthcare institutions (Apell & Eriksson, 2023). These financial limitations restrict the scaling of AI innovations, particularly in low-resource settings. Finally, resistance to change among healthcare stakeholders remains a notable challenge. Clinicians may hesitate to adopt AI tools due to concerns about reliability, usability, and the potential to undermine human judgment (Dai & Singh, 2020; Reis et al., 2020).

Conclusions

This study addresses a critical gap in the literature by shedding light on how artificial intelligence can enhance clinical and governance decisions in health care. While prior research has primarily emphasized the technical and operational aspects of AI (Meyer et al., 2024; Secinaro et al., 2021; Yin et al., 2021), insufficient attention has been given to its potential to support governance decisions, such as resource allocation, quality and safety standards, risk management, and stakeholder engagement. This study contributes to a more nuanced understanding of AI's role in shaping effective and equitable healthcare systems by bridging this gap. The study aimed to examine AI's impact on healthcare professionals' clinical decisions and supporting governance decisions for managers within healthcare organizations. This approach aimed to synthesize existing knowledge and provide actionable insights into how AI can empower governance to address healthcare's evolving challenges. The methodology followed the guidelines of PRISMA, ensuring a rigorous and transparent review process. A total of 53 peer-reviewed articles were identified, screened, and analyzed, offering a comprehensive view of AI's applications in governance and decision-making within health care. The results reveal that AI holds significant promise in revolutionizing governance by enabling dynamic resource allocation, enhancing quality and safety standards, improving risk management strategies, and facilitating stakeholder engagement. AI-driven tools can optimize decision-making by providing real-time insights, predictive capabilities, and evidence-based frameworks that address the complexity of modern healthcare. However, data quality, algorithmic bias, scalability, and ethical concerns persist, requiring targeted strategies to overcome these barriers.

Theoretical Contributions

From a theoretical point of view, this study contributes to the discourse on artificial intelligence in health care by offering an integrated framework that connects governance, practical application, and associated challenges. It deepens our understanding of how governance decisions interact with technological innovation. It creates a theoretical foundation that bridges the gap between AI's transformative potential and its responsible implementation within healthcare systems. A key theoretical insight is the framing of governance as a multidimensional construct encompassing resource allocation, quality and safety standards, ethical oversight, and stakeholder engagement. These dimensions ensure that AI systems meet operational or clinical objectives and align with governance decisions. This perspective enhances existing theories by illustrating how the identified governance domains can guide AI's ethical and equitable deployment in health care. The study also highlights the need for AI adoption by emphasizing the need to incorporate diverse perspectives from clinicians, technologists, policymakers, and patients. This inclusivity highlights the socio-technical dynamics that shape AI implementation, providing a robust lens for examining the interplay between technology, human actors, and organizational processes. Doing so lays a foundation for future research to explore these interconnected dimensions.

Practical Implications

The study provides actionable insights for policymakers, healthcare providers, and technology developers, emphasizing a collaborative approach to AI adoption in health care. For Policymakers, the findings stress the need for robust governance frameworks that balance innovation with ethical oversight. Clear and adaptable regulations addressing accountability, fairness, data security, and algorithmic transparency are essential to foster patient trust and safety. Policies must also anticipate evolving risks, such as data misuse and algorithmic opacity, to create a stable foundation for AI integration. For Healthcare Providers, the study underscores AI's potential to enhance operational efficiency and patient outcomes, from diagnostic tools that alleviate clinician workload to predictive analytics optimizing resource use. To realize these benefits, investments in infrastructure and human capital are critical. Training healthcare professionals to effectively use AI tools can bridge the gap between innovation and application, reducing resistance and fostering acceptance. For Technology Developers, the study highlights the importance of designing scalable and interpretable AI systems. Addressing the "black box" nature of algorithms by prioritizing explainability ensures broader accessibility and reliability. Collaboration with healthcare IT departments can also mitigate infrastructure challenges, enabling seamless integration of AI technologies. Stakeholder engagement emerges as a unifying practical imperative. Actively involving clinicians, patients, and key stakeholders in AI system design and deployment ensures alignment with real-world needs. For example, incorporating patient feedback can enhance the usability and acceptance of AI tools, particularly in underserved communities. Similarly, engaging clinicians during implementation can address concerns about professional autonomy and foster trust.

References

Agarwal, R., Dugas, M., & Gao, G. (2024). Augmenting physicians with artificial intelligence to transform healthcare: Challenges and opportunities. *Journal of Economics & Management Strategy, 33*(2), 360–374. https://doi.org/10.1111/jems.12555

Akter, S., Hossain, M. A., Sajib, S., Sultana, S., Rahman, M., Vrontis, D., & McCarthy, G. (2023). A framework for AI-powered service innovation capability: Review and agenda for future research. *Technovation, 125*, 102768. https://doi.org/10.1016/j.technovation.2023.102768

Alnasser, A. H., Hassanain, M. A., Alnasser, M. A., & Alnasser, A. H. (2024). Critical factors challenging the integration of AI technologies in healthcare workplaces: A stakeholder assessment. *Journal of Health Organization and Management*. https://doi.org/10.1108/JHOM-04-2024-0135

Alnsour, Y., Johnson, M., Albizri, A., & Harfouche, A. H. (2023). Predicting patient length of stay using artificial intelligence to assist healthcare professionals in resource planning and scheduling decisions. *Journal of Global Information Management (JGIM), 31*(1), 1–14. https://doi.org/10.4018/JGIM.323059

Apell, P., & Eriksson, H. (2023). Artificial intelligence (AI) healthcare technology innovations: The current state and challenges from a life science industry perspective. *Technology Analysis & Strategic Management, 35*(2), 179–193. https://doi.org/10.1080/09537325.2021.1971188

Basharat, I., & Shahid, S. (2024). AI-enabled chatbots healthcare systems: An ethical perspective on trust and reliability. *Journal of Health Organization and Management*. Ahead-of-print. https://doi.org/10.1108/JHOM-10-2023-0302

Basile, L. J., Carbonara, N., Panniello, U., & Pellegrino, R. (2024a). How can technological resources improve the quality of healthcare service? The enabling role of big data analytics capabilities. *IEEE Transactions on Engineering Management, 71*, 5771–5781. https://doi.org/10.1109/TEM.2024.3366313

Basile, L. J., Carbonara, N., Panniello, U., & Pellegrino, R. (2024b). The role of big data analytics in improving the quality of healthcare services in the Italian context: The mediating role of risk management. *Technovation, 133*, 103010. https://doi.org/10.1016/j.technovation.2024.103010

Basile, L. J., Carbonara, N., Pellegrino, R., & Panniello, U. (2023). Business intelligence in the healthcare industry: The utilization of a data-driven approach to support clinical decision making. *Technovation, 120*, 102482. https://doi.org/10.1016/j.technovation.2022.102482

Buaka, E. S. D., & Moid, M. Z. I. (2024). AI and medical imaging technology: Evolution, impacts, and economic insights. *The Journal of Technology Transfer.* https://doi.org/10.1007/s10961-024-10100-x

Çetin, E. (2024). Public perceptions and acceptance of artificial intelligence humanoid bots/robots: Evidence from Turkey. *Technological Forecasting and Social Change, 208*. Scopus. https://doi.org/10.1016/j.techfore.2024.123678

Chatterjee, S., Chaudhuri, R., Gupta, S., Sivarajah, U., & Bag, S. (2023). Assessing the impact of big data analytics on decision-making processes, forecasting, and performance of a firm. *Technological Forecasting and Social Change, 196*. Scopus. https://doi.org/10.1016/j.techfore.2023.122824

Chattu, V. K. (2021). A review of artificial intelligence, big data, and blockchain technology applications in medicine and global health. *Big Data and Cognitive Computing, 5*(3), 41. https://doi.org/10.3390/bdcc5030041

Cheng, Y., & Jiang, H. (2020). AI-Powered mental health chatbots: Examining users' motivations, active communicative action and engagement after mass-shooting disasters. *Journal of Contingencies and Crisis Management, 28*(3), 339–354. https://doi.org/10.1111/1468-5973.12319

Dai, T., & Singh, S. (2020). Conspicuous by its absence: Diagnostic expert testing under uncertainty. *Marketing Science, 39*(3), 540–563. https://doi.org/10.1287/mksc.2019.1201

Dal Mas, F., Massaro, M., Rippa, P., & Secundo, G. (2023). The challenges of digital transformation in healthcare: An interdisciplinary literature review, framework, and future research agenda. *Technovation, 123*, 102716. https://doi.org/10.1016/j.technovation.2023.102716

de Carvalho, L. S. F., Gioppato, S., Fernandez, M. D., Trindade, B. C., Silva, J. C. Q. E., Miranda, R. G. S., de Souza, J. R. M., Nadruz, W., Avila, S. E. F., & Sposito, A. C. (2020). Machine learning improves the identification of individuals with higher morbidity and avoidable health costs after acute coronary syndromes. *Value in Health, 23*(12), 1570–1579. https://doi.org/10.1016/j.jval.2020.08.2091

Dicuonzo, G., Donofrio, F., Fusco, A., & Shini, M. (2023). Healthcare system: Moving forward with artificial intelligence. *Technovation, 120.* https://doi.org/10.1016/j.technovation.2022.102510

Fontes, C., Hohma, E., Corrigan, C. C., & Lütge, C. (2022). AI-powered public surveillance systems: Why we (might) need them and how we want them. *Technology in Society, 71*, 102137. https://doi.org/10.1016/j.techsoc.2022.102137

Galetsi, P., Katsaliaki, K., & Kumar, S. (2023). Exploring benefits and ethical challenges in the rise of mHealth (mobile healthcare) technology for the common good: An analysis of mobile applications for health specialists. *Technovation, 121*, 102598. https://doi.org/10.1016/j.technovation.2022.102598

Ghouri, A. M., Khan, H. R., Mani, V., ul Haq, M. A., & de Sousa Jabbour, A. B. L. (2023). An Artificial-Intelligence-Based omnichannel blood supply chain: A pathway for sustainable development. *Journal of Business Research, 164*, 113980. https://doi.org/10.1016/j.jbusres.2023.113980

Gollapalli, M., Rahman, A., Kudos, S. A., Foula, M. S., Alkhalifa, A. M., Albisher, H. M., Al-Hariri, M. T., & Mohammad, N. (2024). Appendicitis diagnosis: Ensemble machine learning and explainable artificial intelligence-based comprehensive approach. *Big Data and Cognitive Computing, 8*(9), 108. https://doi.org/10.3390/bdcc8090108

Gupta, A. K., & Srivastava, M. K. (2024). Framework for AI adoption in health care sector: Integrated DELPHI, ISM-MICMAC Approach. *IEEE Transactions on Engineering Management.* https://doi.org/10.1109/TEM.2024.3386580

Kumar, K., Gudivada, V. K., Thimmaiah, B. C., Bonthu, K., & Thakur, R. (2022). A role of artificial intelligence in healthcare data for diabetic people affected by COVID-19. *International Journal of Operations Research and Information Systems (IJORIS), 13*(2), 1–13. https://doi.org/10.4018/IJORIS.306196

Lam, H. Y., Ho, G. T. S., Mo, D. Y., & Tang, V. (2021). Enhancing data-driven elderly appointment services in domestic care communities under COVID-19. *Industrial Management and Data Systems*. Scopus. https://doi.org/10.1108/IMDS-07-2020-0392

Liu, X., He, X., Wang, M., & Shen, H. (2022). What influences patients' continuance intention to use AI-powered service robots at hospitals? The role of individual characteristics. *Technology in Society, 70*, 101996. https://doi.org/10.1016/j.techsoc.2022.101996

Liu, Y., Zhang, J., & Chan, F. T. (2024). AI-enhanced robust method for integrated healthcare resource pre-positioning and patient scheduling. *International Journal of Production Research, 63*(2), 729–757. https://doi.org/10.1080/00207543.2024.2309312

Mahdi, S. S., Battineni, G., Khawaja, M., Allana, R., Siddiqui, M. K., & Agha, D. (2023). How does artificial intelligence impact digital healthcare initiatives? A review of AI applications in dental healthcare. *International Journal of Information Management Data Insights, 3*(1), 100144. https://doi.org/10.1016/j.jjimei.2022.100144

Martins, S. M., Ferreira, F. A., Ferreira, J. J., & Marques, C. S. (2020). An artificial-intelligence-based method for assessing service quality: Insights from the prosthodontics sector. *Journal of Service Management, 31*(2), 291–312. https://doi.org/10.1108/JOSM-03-2019-0084

Marzi, G., Balzano, M., Caputo, A., & Pellegrini, M. M. (2024). Guidelines for bibliometric-systematic literature reviews: 10 steps to combine analysis, synthesis and theory development. *International Journal of Management Reviews*. https://doi.org/10.1111/ijmr.12381

Mauro, M., Noto, G., Prenestini, A., & Sarto, F. (2024). Digital transformation in healthcare: Assessing the role of digital technologies for managerial support processes. *Technological Forecasting and Social Change, 209*, 123781. https://doi.org/10.1016/j.techfore.2024.123781

Meyer, L. M., Stead, S., Salge, T. O., & Antons, D. (2024). Artificial intelligence in acute care: A systematic review, conceptual synthesis, and research agenda. *Technological Forecasting and Social Change, 206*. Scopus. https://doi.org/10.1016/j.techfore.2024.123568

Mikalef, P., van de Wetering, R., & Krogstie, J. (2021). Building dynamic capabilities by leveraging big data analytics: The role of organizational inertia. *Information & Management, 58*(6), 103412. https://doi.org/10.1016/j.im.2020.103412

Misra, S. K., Sharma, S. K., Gupta, S., & Das, S. (2023). A framework to overcome challenges to the adoption of artificial intelligence in Indian Government Organizations. *Technological Forecasting and Social Change, 194*, 122721. https://doi.org/10.1016/j.techfore.2023.122721

Moher, D., Liberati, A., Tetzlaff, J., & Altman, D. G. (2009). Preferred reporting items for systematic reviews and meta-analyses: The PRISMA statement. *Journal of Clinical Epidemiology, 62*(10), 1006–1012. https://doi.org/10.1016/j.jclinepi.2009.06.005

Musleh, D., Alkhwaja, A., Alkhwaja, I., Alghamdi, M., Abahussain, H., Albugami, M., Alfawaz, F., El-Ashker, S., & Al-Hariri, M. (2024). Machine learning approaches for predicting risk of cardiometabolic disease among university students. *Big Data and Cognitive Computing, 8*(3), 31. https://doi.org/10.3390/bdcc8030031

Nasir, S., Khan, R. A., & Bai, S. (2024). Ethical framework for harnessing the power of AI in healthcare and beyond. *IEEE Access, 12*, 31014–31035. https://doi.org/10.1109/ACCESS.2024.3369912

O'Connor, S., Gasteiger, N., Stanmore, E., Wong, D. C., & Lee, J. J. (2022). Artificial intelligence for falls management in older adult care: A scoping review of nurses' role. *Journal of Nursing Management, 30*(8), 3787–3801. https://doi.org/10.1111/jonm.13853

Qin, H., Zhu, Y., Jiang, Y., Luo, S., & Huang, C. (2024). Examining the impact of personalization and carefulness in AI-generated health advice: Trust, adoption, and insights in online healthcare consultations experiments. *Technology in Society, 79*, 102726. https://doi.org/10.1016/j.techsoc.2024.102726

Reis, L., Maier, C., Mattke, J., Creutzenberg, M., & Weitzel, T. (2020). Addressing user resistance would have prevented a healthcare AI project failure. *MIS Quarterly Executive, 19*(4), 279–236. https://doi.org/10.17705/2msqe.00038

Roppelt, J. S., Kanbach, D. K., & Kraus, S. (2023). Artificial intelligence in healthcare institutions: A systematic literature review on influencing factors. *Technology in Society*. https://doi.org/10.1016/j.techsoc.2023.102443

Saraswat, D., Bhattacharya, P., Verma, A., Prasad, V. K., Tanwar, S., Sharma, G., Bokoro, P. N., & Sharma, R. (2022). Explainable AI for healthcare 5.0: Opportunities and challenges. *IEEE Access, 10*, 84486–84517. https://doi.org/10.1109/ACCESS.2022.3197671

Schillaci, C. E., De Cosmo, L. M., Piper, L., Nicotra, M., & Guido, G. (2024). Anthropomorphic chatbots' for future healthcare services: Effects of personality, gender, and roles on source credibility, user satisfaction, and intention to use. *Technological Forecasting and Social Change, 199*, 123025. https://doi.org/10.1016/j.techfore.2023.123025

Secinaro, S., Calandra, D., Secinaro, A., Muthurangu, V., & Biancone, P. (2021). The role of artificial intelligence in healthcare: A structured literature review. *BMC Medical Informatics and Decision Making, 21*(1), 125. https://doi.org/10.1186/s12911-021-01488-9

Singha, S., Arha, H., & Kar, A. K. (2023). Healthcare analytics: A techno-functional perspective. *Technological Forecasting and Social Change, 197*. Scopus. https://doi.org/10.1016/j.techfore.2023.122908

Thakur, K., Sandhu, N. K., Kumar, Y., & Thakkar, H. K. (2024). An automated multi-classification of communicable diseases using ensemble learning for disease surveillance. *International Journal of System Assurance Engineering and Management, 15*, 3737–3756. https://doi.org/10.1007/s13198-024-02373-0

Vishwakarma, L. P., Singh, R. K., Mishra, R., & Kumari, A. (2023). Application of artificial intelligence for resilient and sustainable healthcare system: Systematic literature review and future research directions. *International Journal of Production Research, 63*(2), 822–844. https://doi.org/10.1080/00207543.2023.2188101

World Health Organization. (2021). *Ethics and governance of artificial intelligence for health*. World Health Organization. https://www.who.int/publications/i/item/9789240029200

Yin, J., Ngiam, K. Y., & Teo, H. H. (2021). Role of artificial intelligence applications in real-life clinical practice: Systematic review. *Journal of Medical Internet Research, 23*(4), e25759. https://doi.org/10.2196/25759

Zahlan, A., Ranjan, R. P., & Hayes, D. (2023). Artificial intelligence innovation in healthcare: Literature review, exploratory analysis, and future research. *Technology in Society*. https://doi.org/10.1016/j.techsoc.2023.102321

Exploring Ethical Dimensions of AI in Tourism

Álvaro Hernández-Tamurejo, Alicia Orea-Giner, and Sudhir Rana

Introduction

Tourism has undergone significant transformations in recent years, driven by heightened competition among destinations, an increase in the number of tourism agents, and rapid digitalization (Filipiak et al., 2023). This digital revolution has significantly reshaped business operations, tourist behavior, and service delivery within the industry. The integration of digital tools has streamlined, among others, operations, fostered innovation, and enabled real-time management of tourism services (Kar et al., 2023).

A significant development in this digitalization process is the rise of platforms such as Airbnb, TripAdvisor, and Booking.com. These platforms have allowed access to travel services, empowering consumers with more choices and greater transparency (Pencarelli, 2020). Moreover, they have allowed destinations to better manage visitor flows, enhance visitor experiences, and implement sustainable practices (Rodrigues et al., 2023). The digitalization of tourism has also created a dynamic ecosystem where vast amounts of data are generated, enabling personalized experiences and improving decision-making (Rahmadian et al., 2022). Unlocking the full potential of this data requires advanced analytical tools and robust data processing capabilities (Ranjan & Foropon, 2021).

Within this context, the adoption of Big Data, artificial intelligence (AI), and the Metaverse is becoming increasingly prevalent in the tourism sector. These

Á. Hernández-Tamurejo (✉) · A. Orea-Giner
Rey Juan Carlos University, Madrid, Spain
e-mail: alvaro.hernandez@urjc.es; alicia.orea@urjc.es

S. Rana
Gulf Medical University, Ajman, UAE
e-mail: dr.sudhir@gmu.ac.ae

J. R. Saura (ed.), *Global Perspectives on AI, Ethics, and Business Economics*, Contributions to Management Science,
https://doi.org/10.1007/978-3-031-88781-9_8

technologies, especially AI, are revolutionizing various aspects of the industry, including marketing, customer service, destination management, revenue management, and sustainable development (Kar et al., 2023). AI is being used for all tourism agents for different purposes; however, the increasing use of AI in tourism raises significant ethical concerns that need to be addressed.

However, it is worth noting that the usage of AI raises key issues related to privacy, data security, transparency, and bias (Hu & Min, 2023; Saura, 2024). The collection and use of vast amounts of personal data by AI systems could infringe on individual privacy rights, especially if the data is used in unintended ways (Blauth et al., 2022). Additionally, AI systems trained on biased data may perpetuate existing biases, leading to unfair treatment of certain groups (Ferrer et al., 2021). Also, the lack of transparency complicates understanding how AI decisions are made and whether they are fair (van Nood & Yeomans, 2021). These issues are at the core of ethical discussions, as they challenge fundamental principles such as fairness, accountability, and respect for individual rights, highlighting the need for responsible AI implementation in the tourism sector (Knani et al., 2022). For example, AI-powered recommendation systems could prioritize certain accommodations or destinations based on certain factors, unintentionally disadvantaging businesses owned by minorities or underrepresented groups. This could lead to reduced visibility and fewer opportunities for these organizations to fairly compete. Also, if travel platforms use personal data collected during bookings to create detailed user profiles without explicit consent, potentially leading to unwanted targeted advertising or data being shared with third parties. Additionally, dynamic pricing algorithms could lack transparency, charging higher prices to users based on their search history or device type, creating perceptions of unfair treatment and reducing consumer trust in these recommendation systems. This study, therefore, aims to begin filling this gap by analysing the current state of the art, providing a solid foundation for future research that is necessary to advance the key aspect of the proper implementation of AI in tourism. Considering ethical aspects is necessary to ensure responsible AI practices, align with regulatory requirements, and facilitate consumer trust in AI adoption by tourism agents. A correct identification of the ethical dimensions is needed to address potential risks and to develop frameworks that guide tourism agents in their AI strategies.

This study aims to conduct a bibliometric study around artificial intelligence, ethics, and tourism research. This bibliometric study examines the literature published in the Web of Science Core Collection (WoS) and the Scopus database from 2000 to June 13, 2024. Thus, this study aims to respond to the following Research Questions (RQs)—RQ1: How has the scholarly conversation around artificial intelligence and ethics evolved within the field of tourism? RQ2: How have emerging topics related to artificial intelligence and ethics been developed within tourism research? RQ3: What gaps exist in the current research on artificial intelligence and ethics in tourism, and which emerging topics are gaining traction?

This study provides an introductory section and a literature review, followed by a detailed explanation of the technique used to conduct the bibliometric study. Next, the findings are displayed. The study of publications encompasses an analysis of their historical development, the most often referenced journals, and the subjects of research they focus on. In addition, the region was systematically categorized thematically using co-occurrence analysis (VOSviewer) to discover study themes and their progression. The study plan is developed by identifying key topics, which includes a thorough examination of the outcomes.

Literature Review

Digitalization in Tourism

In recent years, the tourism industry has undergone significant transformation due to the high competition among tourism destinations (Streimikiene et al., 2021), the increasing number of tourism agents participating in the delivery of the service, and recently the rapid pace of digitalization (Filipiak et al., 2023). The digital revolution introduced to the industry has reshaped tourism business operations, tourist behavior on planning and experiences, and how destinations and tourism agents manage the service delivery. Digitalization encompasses a wide of technologies and innovations that in tourism includes online booking systems, mobile applications, digital marketing, or consumer relationship management, which allows a more accessible, personalized (Saura et al., 2024a), and efficient industry and real-time management (Kar et al., 2023; Moreno-Izquierdo et al., 2022). Digitalization in tourism has streamlined operational processes and has brought new opportunities for innovation and growth (Troisi et al., 2023). In terms of distribution, digital platforms have emerged such as Airbnb, TripAdvisor, or Booking.com to democratize society access to travel services and information, empowering consumers with more choices and greater transparency (Pencarelli, 2020). The adoption of digital reservation systems can not only enhance efficiency but also lead to the creation of sustainable knowledge, improve prediction of services and demand, and therefore boost sustainability and circular economy (Saura et al., 2024b). Additionally, digitalization has enabled destinations to better manage visitor flows, enhance visitor experiences, and adopt sustainable tourism practices by monitoring and minimizing environmental impacts (Rodrigues et al., 2023).

However, digitalization in tourism creates a dynamic digital interaction ecosystem, generating vast amounts of data that empower personalized experiences and enhance decision-making (Rahmadian et al., 2022). This data-rich environment enables businesses to tailor services to individual preferences, improving customer satisfaction and loyalty (Hadjielias et al., 2022). Moreover, the abundance of information allows for more informed, data-driven decisions, optimizing marketing strategies, resource allocation, and operational efficiency (Saura et al., 2023). However, the effective utilization of this data requires robust data processing capabilities and advanced analytical tools to unlock its full potential (Ranjan & Foropon, 2021). In this sense, the adoption of new technologies such as Big Data, artificial intelligence (AI), and the Metaverse is becoming increasingly prevalent. These technologies are revolutionizing various aspects of the tourism sector, from marketing and customer service to destination management and sustainable development. Big Data allows for the analysis of vast amounts of information to predict trends, personalize services, and optimize operations, providing deep insights into traveler behavior, preferences, and trends (Ardito et al., 2019). AI has gained significant attention for its potential to enhance decision-making, automate routine tasks, and create more personalized and engaging experiences for tourists (Giuggioli & Pellegrini, 2022). The emergence of the Metaverse, a virtual reality space where users can interact with digital environments and each other, presents new opportunities for immersive and innovative tourism experiences (Talwar et al., 2023).

AI Applications in Tourism

The latest research trend related to tourism and new technologies goes for the applications and usage of AI by the industry. AI applications in the tourism sector are diverse and can be observed across different agents, including travel agencies, hotels, airlines, and destination managers (Li et al., 2021). For example, AI-powered chatbots and virtual assistants are being used to provide 24/7 customer support, answer inquiries, and assist with bookings (Zhu et al., 2023). In hotels, AI-driven systems are enhancing guest experiences through personalized recommendations, smart room controls, or predictive maintenance (Rawat et al., 2024). Airlines are leveraging AI for optimizing flight schedules, pricing, and customer service. Destination management organizations use AI to analyze visitor data, forecast demand, and manage resources more effectively (Ivanov & Webster, 2019; Zhu et al., 2023). Besides, given the nature of this industry, AI is also being implemented for revenue management through pricing to optimize revenues for the agents in the value chain (van der Rest et al., 2020). In short, these applications improve businesses operations and efficiency, as well as its value proposal creating more tailored and seamless experiences for tourists, thereby enhancing satisfaction and loyalty (Hadjielias et al., 2022; Tussyadiah, 2020).

Ethical Challenges of AI

However, the usage of AI in tourism raises several concerns, including ethical challenges that need to be addressed related to how the information is managed and used by agents (Grundner & Neuhofer, 2021). General discussion includes issues related to privacy, data security, transparency, or bias (Hu & Min, 2023). For example, the collection, analysis, and usage of vast amounts of personal data by AI systems may infringe on individuals 'privacy rights if it's used in ways that were not initially intended' (Blauth et al., 2022). Moreover, AI systems can perpetuate existing biases if they are trained on biased data, leading to unfair treatment of certain groups of people (Ferrer et al., 2021). The usage of AI in the decision-making can result on a lack of accountability (Novelli et al., 2023). The lack of transparency, often referred to "black box" issues (von Eschenbach, 2021), may make difficult to understand how decisions are made and if there are fair enough for consumers (van Nood & Yeomans, 2021).

To be more precise, ethics, in this context, refers to the principles and standards that guide the development, deployment, and use of AI technologies to ensure that they are aligned with societal values and do not cause harm (Gabriel, 2020). The ethical dimensions of AI encompass a wide range of considerations. According to Morley et al. (2020), explicability should be considered, since AI systems have to be transparent. For example, a hotel booking platform using AI to recommend accommodations must clearly explain why specific options are prioritized, helping users to understand the reasoning behind the suggestions. Another relevant aspect refers to fairness since removing bias from a model is necessary to ensure that an AI model treats everybody fairly (Prem, 2023). Fairness can involve ensuring that AI-driven algorithms do not disadvantage small or minority-owned businesses by systematically prioritizing larger, better-known chains. However, fairness has many interpretations making the definition of mathematical functions fairness hard to conceptualize (Lee et al., 2021). Privacy is another relevant element that refers to data security and personal information management given the confidential information that is shared with AI models (Chen et al., 2024); this is applicable to both final consumers and providers upon the need of feeding AI models with specific information about the business. Actually, users are becoming increasingly aware of privacy and security issues on platforms that require information sharing (Jain et al., 2021). Besides, accountability has been identified as another element of ethics to be considered for AI implementations. According to Shin et al. (2022), the concept of accountability is the measure aimed at holding the providers of automated decision systems responsible for the results generated by their programmed decision-making. Accountability might involve a travel agency being held responsible if an AI-powered itinerary planning tool fails to consider accessibility needs, causing inconvenience to travelers with disabilities. Human rights are also recognized by other authors as key principles in policy guidelines for AI development, and it relates to the balance of ethical implications of autonomy and privacy (Vesnic-Alujevic et al., 2020).

As AI technologies become more relevant in the tourism sector (Jabeen et al., 2022), it is key to examine these ethical issues and develop guidelines and frameworks that can help mitigate potential risks and ensure that AI is used responsibly and ethically (Eitel-Porter, 2021). Ensuring that AI systems are designed and implemented in an ethical manner is crucial for maintaining consumer trust, protecting individuals' rights, and fostering sustainable development in any industry (Stahl, 2022). In terms of the tourist sector, these ethical principles are applicable but specific considerations to tourism sector are scarce. According to Knani et al. (2022), it is needed to "define ethical privacy standards and boundaries related to AI ecosystems; examine tourists' perceptions of (and trust toward) the use of their personal information; and develop an ethical framework and guidelines (good practices) for ethical data management in tourism and hospitality companies." Recent research is emerging to explore ethics in hospitality and tourism sector on the AI application focusing on compliance with data ethics and data governance (Yallop et al., 2023).

Methodology

WoS and Scopus are recognized for their extensive coverage of scholarly journals. These databases are the primary sources of publication metadata and bibliometric indicators used universally for evaluating research output and impact (Pranckute, 2021). Both databases provide stable and highly correlated bibliometric indicators, such as the number of papers and citations received by countries. This stability is key for reliable bibliometric analysis and research evaluations (Archambault et al., 2009). Considering the previous facts, the documents used to conduct this analysis were retrieved from the Web of Science and Scopus between 2000 and June 2024.

The Scopus search was focused on this search stream: (TITLE-ABS-KEY ("artificial intelligence" OR "AI") AND TITLE-ABS-KEY ("tourism" OR "hospitality" OR "Hotel" OR "destination" OR "Tourist" OR "trip" OR "travel") AND TITLE-ABS-KEY ("ethic")). The WoS search was focused on this search stream: ((TS=("artificial intelligence" OR "AI")) AND TS=("tourism" OR "hospitality" OR "hotel" OR "destination" OR "tourist" OR "trip" OR "travel")) AND TS=(ethic). All the searches were done considering the title, abstract, and keywords.

The PRISMA model was employed to screen and select relevant literature on the ethical considerations of AI in tourism and hospitality, ensuring that comprehensive coverage and a rigorous exclusion process are adhered to for quality assurance in synthesizing the final review. In total, 102 documents were found, including 36 from WoS and 66 from Scopus. The authors double-checked the results to validate the link to the research topic. The duplicated documents were eliminated ($n = 13$) as well as the articles not related to the field analyzed ($n = 5$). After this process, we considered a total sample of 89 documents. Figure 1 summarizes this process.

Bibliometric Analysis Methods

The applied bibliometric analysis approach integrates the examination of historical progression, frequently referred journals, research subjects, and co-occurrence networks. Previous research on tourism studies was focused on implementing these bibliometric analysis methods (Knani et al., 2022; Shin & Kang, 2023).

By using co-occurrence analysis as a methodology, this chapter conducts a bibliometric study to outline the theme contours of the scientific literature within a specific subject. Co-occurrence networks reveal the temporal evolution of research disciplines and highlight the emergence of research fronts and intellectual bases (Sedighi, 2016). By focusing on manuscripts with the highest frequency of keyword

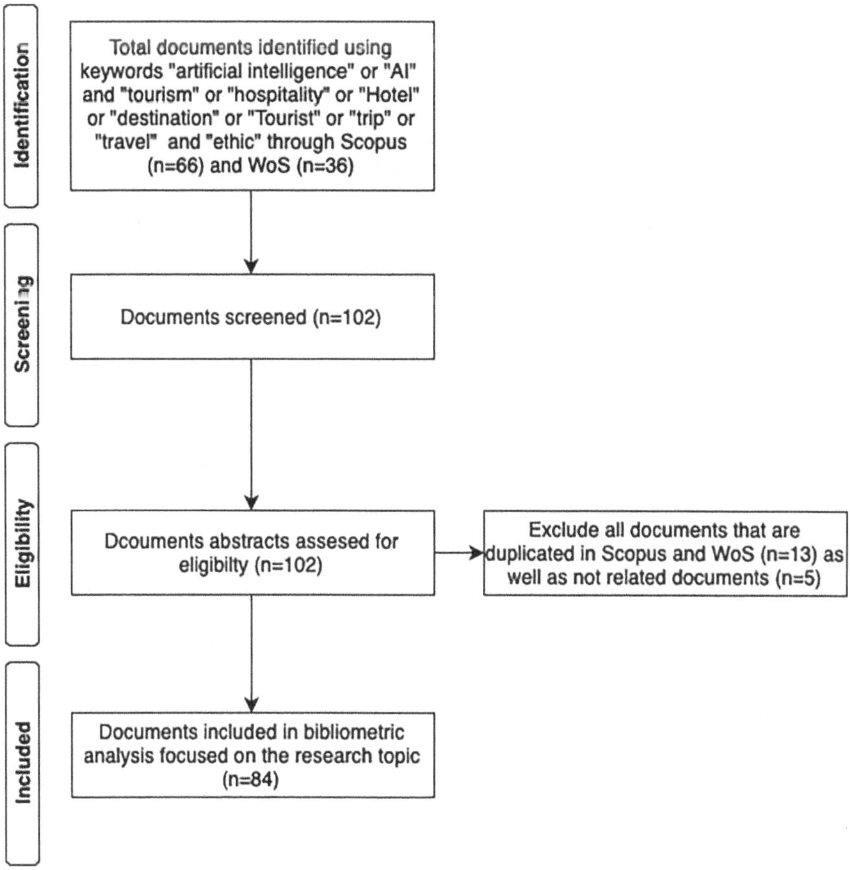

Fig. 1 PRISMA flow chart. *Source*: Own elaboration

co-occurrences, this approach may use these correlations to map the domain's conceptual structure and track its thematic progression. This approach is valuable for tracking how research topics develop and interconnect over time (Liu & Mei, 2016).

In addition, the analysis of publications is conducted using the overlay mapping approach, which enables the visualization of the chronological development and thematic changes within a certain study field. This approach successfully displays the ever-changing character of study disciplines and unveils how specific subjects become more prominent over time (McAllister et al., 2022).

To conduct the co-occurrence and overlay mapping analysis, VOSviewer was utilized for its ability to map thematic networks and visualize keyword relationships over time (Stopar and Bartol, 2019). VOSviewer offers superior capabilities for creating intuitive visualizations and managing large data sets, making it particularly suited for this study compared to other softwares such as Gephi or CiteSpace. The analysis involved harmonizing terms using a thesaurus to ensure consistency across keywords. Variations such as "AI ethics" and "artificial intelligence ethics" were standardized, while non-specific terms like "review" and "study" were excluded to maintain focus. While WoS and Scopus provide extensive coverage, their focus on peer-reviewed journals may exclude relevant gray literature or studies published in non-indexed sources. Additionally, the choice of search terms, although broad, may have unintentionally excluded documents addressing related concepts using alternative terminology.

Results

Descriptive Analysis

This section presents a detailed descriptive analysis of publication records from 2000 to 2024, regarding various aspects of research activity within the analyzed field. The data includes the annual number of published articles, the geographical distribution of research contributions, and the categorization of reference types. The primary objective is to identify trends in research output, highlight key contributing countries, and understand the types of sources cited.

Figure 2 shows a clear trend in the number of articles published per year from 2000 to 2024. Initially, the publication frequency is low, with sporadic articles appearing in 2000, 2003, 2008, 2011, and 2015. However, starting from 2017, there is a noticeable increase in the number of articles published. The significant increase in research publications observed post-2017 may be linked to the growing influence

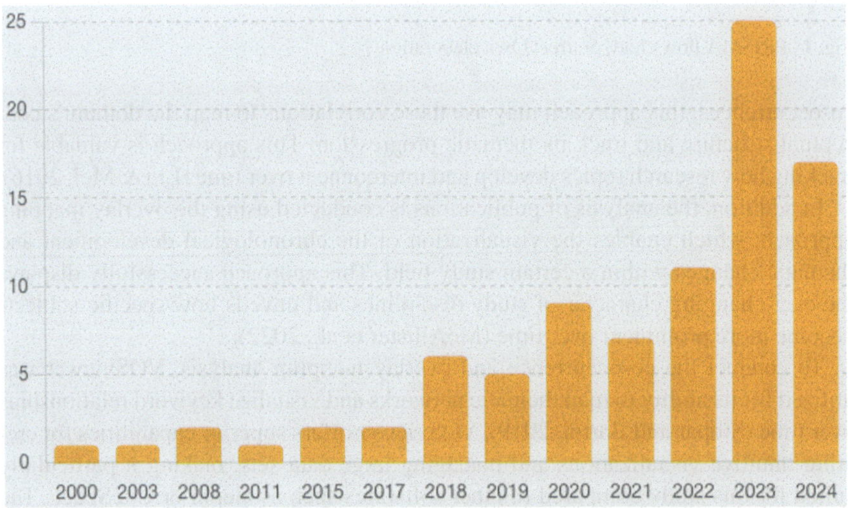

Fig. 2 Number of articles published per year (2000–2024). *Source*: Own elaboration

of AI technologies in tourism research and heightened global discourse on ethical and sustainability issues. For instance, 2020–2021 saw a surge in AI-related publications during the COVID-19 pandemic, as scholars explored digital tools to address challenges in tourism management (Gretzel et al., 2020). This upward trend continues, peaking in 2020 and 2021, and then significantly spiking from 2022 onward. The most substantial growth is observed in 2023 and 2024, indicating a dramatic rise in research output during these years. The spike in 2023–2024 corresponds with advancements in AI ethics and the implementation of policy frameworks like the European Union's AI Act (2023), emphasizing responsible technological applications in tourism. This overall trend suggests a significant increase in research activity, possibly driven by heightened academic interest, more funding opportunities, or expanding research fields. Given the sharp rise in 2023 and 2024, it is likely that this trend may continue in the future, reflecting a dynamic and growing field of study.

The geographical distribution of research, as illustrated in Fig. 3, reveals significant contributions from a variety of countries. Australia and Canada lead with the highest number of publications, each contributing over 13 articles. France and China also show strong contributions, each with around 12 articles. The United States, Spain, and Italy follow, each contributing between nine and ten articles. The UK, Germany, and India also feature in the distribution, though with relatively fewer publications, each contributing between seven and eight articles.

Australia and Canada's prominence in the data set reflects robust academic infrastructures, significant research funding (e.g., Australia Research Council, SSHRC in Canada), and their established focus on tourism as a critical economic sector. Besides, countries like France and China benefit from government-driven investments in tourism research and their global positioning as major tourist destinations.

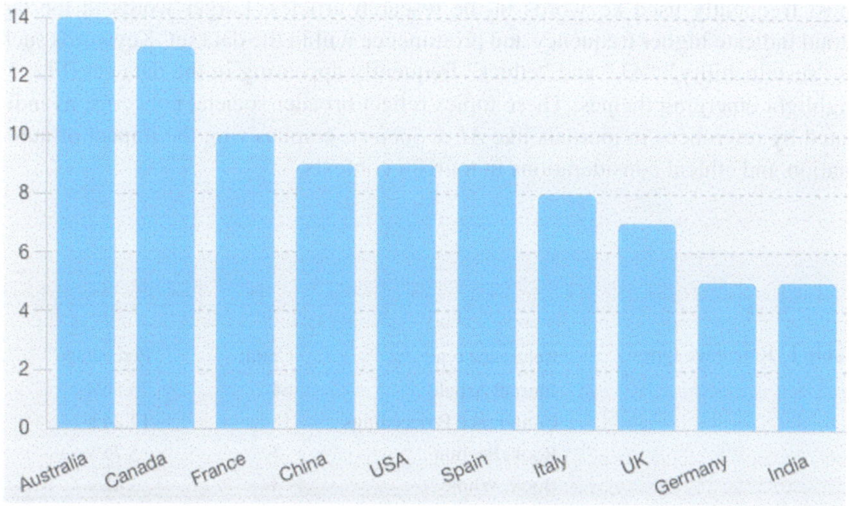

Fig. 3 Distribution of research. *Source*: Own elaboration

Their economic reliance on tourism and strong publication ecosystems, including leading universities in hospitality and tourism.

Considering the previous results as well as the dominance of contributions from high-income regions, it is possible to highlight disparities in how ethical and practical AI applications are addressed globally. For instance, countries leading in AI ethics research (e.g., USA, Australia) may set standards that fail to consider resource constraints and cultural contexts in low- and middle-income countries, limiting the global applicability of findings. This raises critical questions about the cultural relevance of AI ethics, necessitating region-specific research and collaboration between the Global North and South.

Table 1 categorizes the references into four types: journal articles, conference proceedings, book sections, and whole books. The data reveals a clear predominance of journal articles, with a total count of 64, indicating that the bulk of the referenced works are scholarly articles published in academic journals. This suggests a strong focus on peer-reviewed, research-intensive outputs. Conference proceedings, which total 15, represent a significant portion but are considerably less frequent than journal articles. This highlights the role of conferences as important venues for disseminating research, though not as central as journal publications in this context. Book sections, numbering 5, and whole books, with 3 entries, are the least common reference types. This could suggest that while books and book chapters are valuable, they are not the primary source of references in this data set.

Table 2 reveals a diverse range of journals, indicating a multidisciplinary appeal. Most of the journals fall under the research area of Business, Management, and Accounting, specifically within the sub-research area of Tourism, Leisure, and Hospitality Management. This concentration suggests that the tourism sector is a significant focus of scholarly interest within this field.

Figure 4 represents a keyword tag cloud, providing a visual representation of the most frequently used keywords in the research articles. Larger words in the tag cloud indicate higher frequency and prominence within the data set. Keywords such as "sustainability," "AI," and "ethics" frequently appearing in the data set (Fig. 4) highlight emerging themes. These topics reflect broader societal concerns, as indicated by references in journals like *AI & Society*, emphasizing the impact of automation and ethical considerations in tourism contexts.

Table 1 Reference types

Reference type	Count	Percentage
Journal Article	64	73.56%
Conference Proceedings	15	17.24%
Book, Section	5	5.75%
Book, Whole	3	3.45%

Source: Own elaboration

Table 2 Most frequent journals and research areas

Journal	Research area	Sub-research area	Count
Tourism Review	Business, Management, and Accounting	Tourism, Leisure, and Hospitality Management	4
Tourism Geographies	Business, Management, and Accounting	Tourism, Leisure, and Hospitality Management	4
Annals of Tourism Research	Business, Management, and Accounting	Tourism, Leisure, and Hospitality Management	3
AI and Society	Computer Science	Artificial Intelligence Human–Computer Interaction	3
International Journal of Contemporary Hospitality Management	Business, Management, and Accounting	Tourism, Leisure, and Hospitality Management	2

Source: Own elaboration

Fig. 4 Tag cloud. *Source*: Own elaboration

Bibliometric Analysis: Co-occurrence Network and Overlay Mapping

The bibliometric analysis depends on the use of a co-occurrence network and an overlay mapping. The VOSviewer software employs these methodologies to perform a thematic analysis. A co-word analysis is performed to determine the prominent areas of research at the intersection of artificial intelligence and ethics within the tourist business. The VOSviewer software determined the intensity of connections among the terms, resulting in the formation of clusters. The total link strength is a metric utilized to quantify the intensity of the connections between the keywords.

Co-occurrence Network

The analysis yielded five groups of terms, each denoted by a distinct color (refer to Fig. 5). The blue cluster is focused on "ethical and decision-making frameworks in artificial intelligence," exploring how ethical guidelines can influence the development and implementation of AI, particularly in the tourism sector. The green cluster, titled "future directions in conversational ai and computer science," delves into advancements in AI technologies that enhance interactions between tourists and service providers. In the yellow cluster, the theme is "technological advancements in hospitality and web 3.0," which investigates how blockchain, IOT, and other emerging technologies are transforming hospitality services. The red cluster, named "human-centered sustainability in technology and tourism," examines sustainable practices in tourism that utilize technology to benefit local communities and preserve cultural heritage. Finally, the purple cluster addresses "privacy and social media dynamics in tourism technologies," focusing on the challenges of balancing user engagement through social media with privacy concerns in the digital age.

The blue and purple clusters focus heavily on ethics, privacy, and decision-making frameworks. These topics are closely linked, suggesting a strong focus on how AI should operate within predefined ethical boundaries, particularly in sensitive applications such as in tourism, where personal data and human interaction are involved. Consumer decisions in situations with uncertain benefits are influenced by views of ethics (Mkono & Hughes, 2024). However, while there is a robust emphasis on privacy protection and ethical AI, gaps remain in addressing real-world implementation challenges, such as the regulation and enforcement of ethical AI in

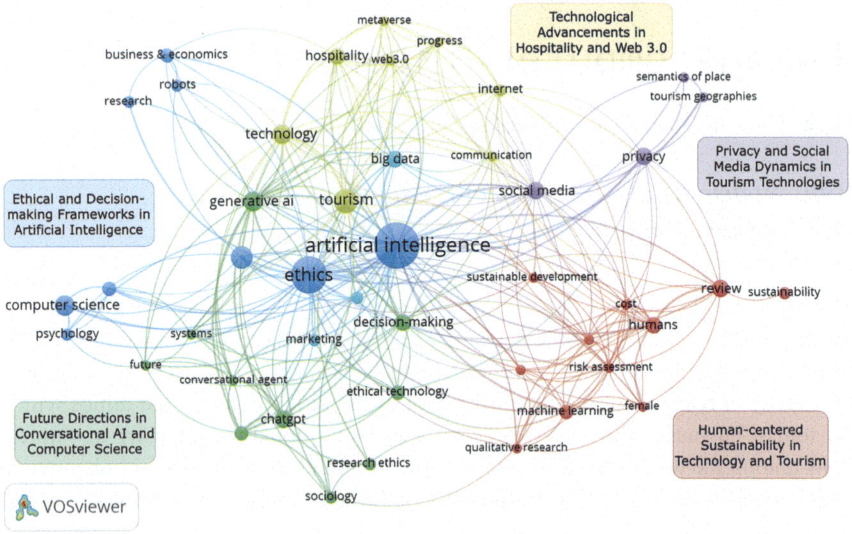

Fig. 5 Co-occurrence network. *Source*: Own elaboration using VOSviewer

developing countries, as well as disparities in global privacy laws. This suggests that more research is needed to bridge theory and practice, particularly in areas like algorithmic transparency and data consent mechanisms. Ethical challenges in AI for tourism primarily revolve around data privacy, user consent, and transparency in how AI algorithms make decisions affecting tourists' choices and experiences (Milwood et al., 2023). These technologies must be utilized ethically, privacy-centrically, and socially responsibly to shape a future that is both technologically sophisticated and ethical (Chon & Hao, 2024).

The green cluster connects conversational AI with computer science, highlighting on-going developments in AI technologies that aim to enhance how humans interact with machines, particularly in service-oriented industries like tourism. Inversini (2024) states that to develop a research agenda with a horizon of 2050, identified research is centered on examining the ideas of digital technology control, participation, education, and ethics. According to Inversini (2024), social science researchers in the field of travel can only fulfill the "high-tech for high-touch" promise—that is, promoting an encounter between humans that is both enhanced and compromised by digital technology—by adopting a human-centered digital transformation viewpoint. Research should explore the dual-use nature of conversational AI, ensuring ethical guidelines are implemented to prevent data misuse while leveraging its benefits for personalized and human-centered experiences. AI tools like ChatGPT are likely to be in the green cluster. Researchers interested in the potential for ChatGPT to generate quantitative data sets for the purpose of engaging in unethical data fabrication can find this technology under scrutiny (Sop & Kurçer, 2024). Within the framework of tourism research, Sop and Kurçer (2024) examine the wider ramifications of utilizing AI to alter or generate data, which could impact the integrity of personal data.

The yellow cluster's emphasis on Web 3.0 and blockchain demonstrates significant technological advancements. Some suppliers of hospitality IT are already developing solutions that incorporate decision-making AI agents, being led to automated room assignments and the dissemination of customer preference data across various channels (Morosan & Dursun-Cengizci, 2024). However, the results show a neglection of broader ethical implications such as data decentralization risks and inclusivity for marginalized communities. Research should explore whether the integration of technologies like IoT and blockchain inadvertently promotes inequality or neglects local cultural and economic contexts.

The red cluster connects sustainability and humans, being focused on applying technology to enhance sustainable practices in tourism, ensuring that technology adoption benefits local communities and preserves the environment. The relationship between digitalization and sustainability has been extensively debated in academic literature, with papers advocating for further research (Bulchand-Gidumal et al., 2023). As the industry consolidates and systems become more interconnected, comprehending the factors that drive the adoption of technological agencies in one sector can assist other sectors in developing goods that utilize customers' AI systems (Morosan & Dursun-Cengizci, 2024). This can be achieved through initiatives such as encouraging the use of local amenities, employing local staff, and promoting sustainable transport options, which align with the broader goals of environmental consciousness and corporate responsibility outlined by Menegaki and Agiomirgianakis (2019). This red cluster emphasizes the combination of technology with sustainable tourism practices, with the capacity to tackle social equity by fostering local resources and employment opportunities. However, it is still ambiguous how emerging AI technologies, particularly those in the green and yellow clusters, correspond with or contest the sustainability objectives delineated throughout.

The purple cluster is concentrated on privacy, social media, and tourism. This cluster explores the tensions between leveraging social media for business purposes in tourism and protecting individual privacy. Privacy concerns in the purple cluster are particularly relevant to the green cluster's focus on conversational AI, as these tools increasingly rely on personal data. About privacy in tourism services such as hotels, Liu et al. (2024) emphasize the importance of privacy problems, particularly in relation to AI concierges' capacity to acquire and analyze extensive personal data. This raises ethical questions regarding the appropriate handling and potential abuse of such data. When developing AI-driven tourist applications, it is important to prioritize ethical considerations, such as safeguarding privacy and fostering diversity (Milwood et al., 2023).

Overlay Mapping

The overlay mapping (Fig. 6) provided using VOSviewer offers a visual analysis of the key research themes within the domain of artificial intelligence as it intersects with technology and tourism through the time. This mapping is instrumental in revealing the core areas of focus and their evolution over time, which is reflected through the color gradient from 2019 to 2024. The colors of the nodes and links shift from blue to green over time, from 2019 to 2024, indicating the progression and evolving focus of research. Blue indicates earlier research, while green signifies more recent studies. This gradient could illustrate the shifting focus or emerging trends over these years.

This map places "artificial intelligence" in the middle and shows its impact on several fields. Though ubiquitous and linked to several clusters, its widespread use may indicate AI over-generalization. Further studies may benefit from a clearer definition of AI's roles in travel and technology. Inter-cluster linkages demonstrate a multidisciplinary approach, but link strength and density vary. This visualization should spark discussions about strengthening these ties or finding new connections between seemingly unrelated sectors, like conversational AI and environmental policies.

While ethics in artificial intelligence are commendable in some areas, a more complex study on how tourism's legal and cultural systems modify these ethical rules is needed. The Web 3.0 and hospitality cluster highlights technological advances but may overlook socioeconomic barriers to technology adoption in developing travel markets.

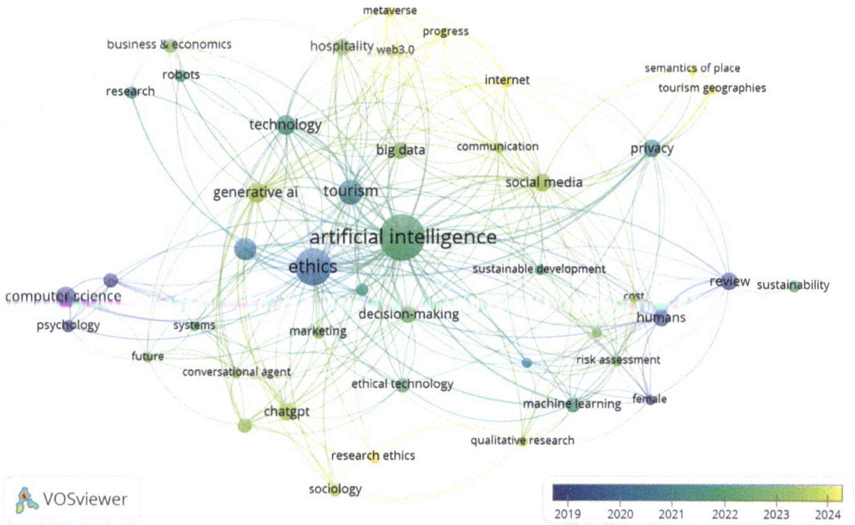

Fig. 6 Overlay mapping. *Source*: Own elaboration using VOSviewer

Future studies should focus on sustainability and human-centric designs, but they should also assess whether they produce theoretical or pragmatic, scalable solutions. Also important is the social media dynamics and privacy cluster. More critical study of privacy management in practical applications and technology-related hazards is needed.

Discussion and Research Agenda

This research has allowed us to understand the most relevant aspects of ethics in the use of AI within the tourism sector, as reflected in the existing literature. Our bibliometric analysis reveals that while there is a notable intersection between ethics, AI, and tourism, specific studies focusing on ethics in AI within this sector remain limited. Although the convergence of these themes is significant, it is not yet predominant in the body of research. The increasing number of publications suggests a growing interest among researchers in exploring this topic. However, there remains a noticeable gap in the literature concerning specific studies on the intersection of ethics, AI, and tourism. This gap highlights the need for more targeted research to better understand and address the ethical challenges unique to this sector.

According to Milwood et al. (2023), the primary ethical challenges in AI for tourism revolve around data privacy, user consent, and transparency in how AI algorithms make decisions that affect tourists' choices and experiences. Privacy dilemmas have emerged in cases where traveler data collected by AI-powered platforms was repurposed for targeted advertising without user consent, raising questions about trust and accountability. In contrast, successful examples of sustainable AI include destination management systems that use AI to monitor tourist flows, reducing environmental impact while enhancing visitor experiences. Our bibliometric analysis confirms that these elements have been identified as central concerns in literature. Furthermore, fairness is increasingly recognized as an affecting aspect, with studies emphasizing the need to eliminate bias from AI models to ensure equitable treatment for all users, as highlighted by Prem (2023).

Furthermore, privacy emerged as a critical component in understanding the ethics of AI in tourism. Blauth et al. (2022) point out potential privacy issues related to the collection, analysis, and use of personal data. Our analysis supports this, identifying privacy concerns as a significant topic within the "blue cluster" of our bibliometric data. In addition to data privacy, the management of social media in the tourism sector has been highlighted as another dimension where ethical considerations are paramount. According to Milwood et al. (2023), when developing AI-driven tourist applications, it is important to prioritize ethical considerations, such as safeguarding privacy and promoting diversity.

On the other hand, the field of computer science is also exploring ethics from a technological perspective, particularly concerning conversational AI. Ethics is being increasingly incorporated into discussions about the management of these technologies. For instance, Sop and Kurçer (2024) discuss the ethical implications of using AI tools like ChatGPT to generate quantitative data sets, particularly concerning the potential for unethical data fabrication and the integrity of personal data.

Ethics is also being integrated into the implementation of AI technology aimed at improving efficiency and customer experiences. However, our analysis indicates that ethical considerations in this area are often included only vaguely, as reflected in the "yellow cluster." Another significant finding from our bibliometric analysis is the growing focus on sustainability and human capital, which are emerging as important dimensions that could be integrated into ethical considerations. According to Bulchand-Gidumal et al. (2023), the digitalization and sustainability debate covers various areas, and our results suggest that the implementation of AI in tourism must also adopt sustainable practices to ensure that technology benefits local communities and preserves the environment. This underscores the ethical imperative of incorporating sustainability into technology implementation to guarantee that all stakeholders' interests are considered.

Finally, Morosan and Dursun-Cengizci (2024) highlight that understanding the factors driving the adoption of technology in one sector can inform the development of AI systems in other sectors, further emphasizing the interconnectedness of ethical considerations across different domains of AI application. Table 3 offers a detailed overview of identified research gaps and proposes potential directions for future research based on the bibliometric analysis conducted.

Table 3 Research gaps and future research lines

Cluster	Topic	Research gaps	Future research lines
Blue. Ethical and decision-making frameworks in artificial intelligence	Ethical and decision-making frameworks in artificial intelligence	There is a gap in empirical research assessing the impacts of AI applications on ethical issues within tourism. This includes understanding how AI affects employment, local cultures, and tourist experiences from an ethical standpoint	Future studies should develop and test frameworks that evaluate AI's impact on job displacement, cultural integrity, and equitable tourist experiences, focusing on creating ethical AI guidelines specific to tourism
Green. Future directions in conversational AI and computer science	Future directions in conversational AI and computer science	Transparency of AI algorithms used in tourism. Understanding and disclosing how decisions are made by AI systems is crucial for ethical considerations and trust-building among users	Research should aim to create transparent AI models where the decision-making processes are visible and understandable to users, with methods for users to influence these processes in tourism contexts
Yellow. Technological advancements in hospitality and web 3.0	Technological advancements in hospitality and web 3.0	There is a gap in the ability of AI-based systems to authentically replicate human emotional response	Research should focus on enhancing AI's emotional intelligence, possibly through neuro-linguistic programming and emotional data training to better replicate human emotional responses in service interactions
Red. Human-centered sustainability in technology and tourism	Human-centered sustainability in technology and tourism	The hotel sector requires extensive studies that integrate numerous sustainability practices and their implications in order to implement sustainable technologies effectively	Future research should investigate multi-dimensional sustainability frameworks that include economic, environmental, and social aspects, assessing their practical application in the hotel industry for technology integration
Purple. Privacy and social media dynamics in tourism technologies	Privacy and social media dynamics in tourism technologies	Data privacy and security issues related to AI in tourism	Studies should investigate the specific privacy concerns of tourists using AI-driven platforms, exploring mechanisms for data protection and trust-building, particularly in social media contexts within tourism

Source: Own elaboration

Conclusions

This bibliometric analysis provides valuable insights into the current state of research on the ethical implications of artificial intelligence (AI) in the tourism sector. The findings reveal that, although there is a growing interest in this topic, specific research focusing on the intersection of ethics, AI, and tourism remains limited. Key ethical challenges, such as data privacy, user consent, transparency, and fairness, stand out as critical concerns for the responsible application of AI in tourism.

The findings offer valuable insights for policymakers and tourism practitioners. Integrating ethical principles into AI development requires clear guidelines, such as prioritizing transparency in algorithmic decision-making and ensuring accountability in data management. Industry partnerships, involving academic researchers, technology developers, and tourism professionals, could bring collaboration to advance ethical AI research and application. Implementing these frameworks is not without challenges. Practical obstacles include the financial costs of ethical AI development, the complexity of navigating regulatory requirements across different regions, and resistance to organizational change within the tourism sector. Addressing these barriers will require strategic planning and capacity building among private and public stakeholders of the industry from a multidisciplinary approach. Furthermore, this study allows relevant contributions by identifying underexplored thematic clusters, such as the intersection of AI ethics and sustainable tourism practices, and by proposing interdisciplinary approaches that combine ethical theory, technological innovation, and practical applications. These contributions lay a foundation for future research aimed at bridging the gap between technological advancements and ethical imperatives in tourism.

The study acknowledges some limitations inherent to the bibliometric approach. The reliance on WoS and Scopus databases may introduce biases by excluding gray literature, non-indexed sources, or publications in languages other than English, potentially overlooking diverse perspectives. These constraints highlight the need for complementary methodologies in future research. Future research should seek to bridge these gaps by conducting in-depth, interdisciplinary investigations into specific ethical challenges, employing both qualitative and quantitative methods. The development of comprehensive, context-specific frameworks will be pivotal to guide the ethical design, implementation, and evaluation of AI technologies in tourism. These frameworks should incorporate principles of fairness, transparency, and inclusivity, ensuring that AI meets technical and operational standards and aligns with the diverse needs and values of all stakeholders, thereby maximizing its social and economic benefits linked to the tourism industry.

References

Archambault, I., Janosz, M., Morizot, J., & Pagani, L. (2009). Adolescent behavioral, affective, and cognitive engagement in school: Relationship to dropout. *Journal of School Health, 79*(9), 408–415. https://doi.org/10.1111/j.1746-1561.2009.00428.x

Ardito, L., Cerchione, R., Del Vecchio, P., & Raguseo, E. (2019). Big data in smart tourism: challenges, issues and opportunities. *Current Issues in Tourism, 22*(15), 1805–1809. https://doi.org/10.1080/13683500.2019.1612860

Blauth, T. F., Gstrein, O. J., & Zwitter, A. (2022). Artificial intelligence crime: An overview of malicious use and abuse of AI. *IEEE Access, 10*, 77110–77122. https://doi.org/10.1109/ACCESS.2022.3191790

Bulchand-Gidumal, J., Secin, E. W., O'Connor, P., & Buhalis, D. (2023). Artificial intelligence's impact on hospitality and tourism marketing: exploring key themes and addressing challenges. *Current Issues in Tourism*. https://doi.org/10.1080/13683500.2023.2229480

Chen, C., Li, Y., Wu, Z., Mai, C., Liu, Y., Hu, Y., Kang, J., & Zheng, Z. (2024). Privacy computing meets metaverse: Necessity, taxonomy and challenges. *Ad Hoc Networks, 158*, 103457. https://doi.org/10.1016/j.adhoc.2024.103457

Chon, K. K. S., & Hao, F. (2024). Technological evolution in tourism: a Horizon 2050 perspective. *Tourism Review*. https://doi.org/10.1108/TR-10-2023-0753

Eitel-Porter, R. (2021). Beyond the promise: implementing ethical AI. *AI and Ethics, 1*(1), 73–80. https://doi.org/10.1007/s43681-020-00011-6

European Union. (2023). *Artificial Intelligence Act*. Official Journal of the European Union. Retrieved from https://eur-lex.europa.eu

Ferrer, X., Van Nuenen, T., Such, J. M., Coté, M., & Criado, N. (2021). Bias and discrimination in AI: a cross-disciplinary perspective. *IEEE Technology and Society Magazine, 40*(2), 72–80. https://doi.org/10.1109/MTS.2021.3056293

Filipiak, B. Z., Dylewski, M., & Kalinowski, M. (2023). Economic development trends in the EU tourism industry. Towards the digitalization process and sustainability. *Quality & Quantity, 57*(Suppl 3), 321–346. https://doi.org/10.1007/s11135-020-01056-9

Gabriel, I. (2020). Artificial intelligence, values, and alignment. *Minds and Machines, 30*(3), 411–437. https://doi.org/10.1007/s11023-020-09539-2

Giuggioli, G., & Pellegrini, M. M. (2022). Artificial intelligence as an enabler for entrepreneurs: a systematic literature review and an agenda for future research. *International Journal of Entrepreneurial Behavior & Research, 29*(4), 816–837. https://doi.org/10.1108/IJEBR-05-2021-0426

Gretzel, U., Fuchs, M., Baggio, R., Hoepken, W., Law, R., Neidhardt, J., et al. (2020). e-Tourism beyond COVID-19: A call for transformative research. *Information Technology & Tourism, 22*, 187–203. https://doi.org/10.1007/s40558-020-00181-3

Grundner, L., & Neuhofer, B. (2021). The bright and dark sides of artificial intelligence: A futures perspective on tourist destination experiences. *Journal of Destination Marketing & Management, 19*, 100511. https://doi.org/10.1016/j.jdmm.2020.100511

Hadjielias, E., Christofi, M., Christou, P., & Drotarova, M. H. (2022). Digitalization, agility, and customer value in tourism. *Technological Forecasting and Social Change, 175*, 121334. https://doi.org/10.1016/j.techfore.2021.121334

Hu, Y., & Min, H. K. (2023). The dark side of artificial intelligence in service: The "watching-eye" effect and privacy concerns. *International Journal of Hospitality Management, 110*, 103437. https://doi.org/10.1016/j.ijhm.2023.103437

Inversini, A. (2024). Human centered digital transformation in travel: a horizon 2050 paper. *Tourism Review*. https://doi.org/10.1108/TR-12-2023-0886

Ivanov, S., & Webster, C. (Eds.). (2019). *Robots, artificial intelligence, and service automation in travel, tourism and hospitality*. Emerald. https://doi.org/10.1108/978-1-78756-687-320191014

Jabeen, F., Al Zaidi, S., & Al Dhaheri, M. H. (2022). Automation and artificial intelligence in hospitality and tourism. *Tourism Review, 77*(4), 1043–1061. https://doi.org/10.1108/TR-09-2019-0360

Jain, A. K., Sahoo, S. R., & Kaubiyal, J. (2021). Online social networks security and privacy: comprehensive review and analysis. *Complex & Intelligent Systems, 7*(5), 2157–2177. https://doi.org/10.1007/s40747-021-00409-7

Kar, A. K., Choudhary, S. K., & Ilavarasan, P. V. (2023). How can we improve tourism service experiences: insights from multi-stakeholders' interaction. *Decision, 50*(1), 73–89. https://doi.org/10.1007/s40622-023-00338-z

Knani, M., Echchakoui, S., & Ladhari, R. (2022). Artificial intelligence in tourism and hospitality: Bibliometric analysis and research agenda. *International Journal of Hospitality Management, 107*, 103317. https://doi.org/10.1016/j.ijhm.2022.103317

Lee, M. S. A., Floridi, L., & Singh, J. (2021). Formalising trade-offs beyond algorithmic fairness: lessons from ethical philosophy and welfare economics. *AI and Ethics, 1*(4), 529–544. https://doi.org/10.1007/s43681-021-00067-y

Li, M., Yin, D., Qiu, H., & Bai, B. (2021). A systematic review of AI technology-based service encounters: Implications for hospitality and tourism operations. *International Journal of Hospitality Management, 95*, 102930. https://doi.org/10.1016/j.ijhm.2021.102930

Liu, L., & Mei, S. (2016). Visualizing the GVC research: A co-occurrence network based bibliometric analysis. *Scientometrics, 109*, 953–977. https://doi.org/10.1007/s11192-016-2100-5

Liu, S. Q., Vakeel, K. A., Smith, N. A., Alavipour, R. S., Wei, C., & Wirtz, J. (2024). AI concierge in the customer journey: what is it and how can it add value to the customer? *Journal of Service Management, 35*(6), 136–158. https://doi.org/10.1108/JOSM-12-2023-0523

McAllister, J. T., Lennertz, L., & Atencio Mojica, Z. (2022). Mapping a discipline: A guide to using VOSviewer for bibliometric and visual analysis. *Science & Technology Libraries, 41*(3), 319–348. https://doi.org/10.1080/0194262X.2021.1991547

Menegaki, A. N., & Agiomirgianakis, G. M. (2019). Sustainable technologies in tourist accommodation: A qualitative review. *Progress in Industrial Ecology, 13*(4), 373–400. https://doi.org/10.1504/PIE.2019.102858

Milwood, P. A., Hartman-Caverly, S., & Roehl, W. S. (2023). A scoping study of ethics in artificial intelligence research in tourism and hospitality. In *ENTER22 e-tourism conference* (pp. 243–254). Springer. https://doi.org/10.1007/978-3-031-25752-0_26

Mkono, M., & Hughes, K. (2024). A state-of-the-art-review of animals in tourism: key debates and future directions. *Tourism Geographies*. https://doi.org/10.1080/14616688.2024.2342462

Moreno-Izquierdo, L., Ramón-Rodríguez, A. B., & Más-Ferrando, A. (2022). Digitalization and the transformation of tourism economics. In Z. Xiang, M. Fuchs, U. Gretzel, & W. Höpken (Eds.), *Handbook of e-tourism* (pp. 1–19). Springer. https://doi.org/10.1007/978-3-030-05324-6_139-1

Morley, J., Floridi, L., Kinsey, L., & Elhalal, A. (2020). From what to how: an initial review of publicly available AI ethics tools, methods and research to translate principles into practices. *Science and Engineering Ethics, 26*(4), 2141–2168. https://doi.org/10.1007/s11948-019-00165-5

Morosan, C., & Dursun-Cengizci, A. (2024). Letting AI make decisions for me: an empirical examination of hotel guests' acceptance of technology agency. *International Journal of Contemporary Hospitality Management, 36*(3), 946–974. https://doi.org/10.1108/IJCHM-08-2022-1041

Novelli, C., Taddeo, M., & Floridi, L. (2023). Accountability in artificial intelligence: what it is and how it works. *AI & Society*, 1–12. https://doi.org/10.1007/s00146-023-01635-y

Pencarelli, T. (2020). The digital revolution in the travel and tourism industry. *Information Technology & Tourism, 22*(3), 455–476. https://doi.org/10.1007/s40558-019-00160-3

Pranckute, R. (2021). Web of Science (WoS) and Scopus: The titans of bibliographic information in today's academic world. *Publications, 9*(1), 12. https://doi.org/10.3390/publications9010012

Prem, E. (2023). From ethical AI frameworks to tools: a review of approaches. *AI and Ethics, 3*(3), 699–716. https://doi.org/10.1007/s43681-023-00258-9

Rahmadian, E., Feitosa, D., & Zwitter, A. (2022). A systematic literature review on the use of big data for sustainable tourism. *Current Issues in Tourism, 25*(11), 1711–1730. https://doi.org/10.1080/13683500.2021.1974358

Ranjan, J., & Foropon, C. (2021). Big data analytics in building the competitive intelligence of organizations. *International Journal of Information Management, 56*, 102231. https://doi.org/10.1016/j.ijinfomgt.2020.102231

Rawat, A., Kukreti, R., Dimari, A., & Dani, R. (2024, May). Artificial intelligence in HMI system. In *2024 4th international conference on advance computing and innovative technologies in engineering (ICACITE)* (pp. 1362–1367). IEEE. https://doi.org/10.1109/ICACITE60783.2024.10617209

Rodrigues, V., Eusébio, C., & Breda, Z. (2023). Enhancing sustainable development through tourism digitalisation: a systematic literature review. *Information Technology & Tourism, 25*(1), 13–45. https://doi.org/10.1007/s40558-022-00241-w

Saura, J. R. (2024). Algorithms in digital marketing: Does smart personalization promote a privacy paradox? *FIIB Business Review, 13*(5), 499–502. https://doi.org/10.1177/231971452412768

Saura, J. R., Palacios-Marqués, D., & Ribeiro-Soriano, D. (2023). Digital marketing in SMEs via data-driven strategies: Reviewing the current state of research. *Journal of Small Business Management, 61*(3), 1278–1313. https://doi.org/10.1080/00472778.2021.1955127

Saura, J. R., Ribeiro-Soriano, D., & Palacios-Marqués, D. (2024a). Adopting digital reservation systems to enable circular economy in entrepreneurship. *Management Decision, 62*(8), 2388–2408. https://doi.org/10.1108/MD-02-2022-0190

Saura, J. R., Škare, V., & Dosen, D. O. (2024b). Is AI-based digital marketing ethical? Assessing a new data privacy paradox. *Journal of Innovation & Knowledge, 9*(4), 100597. https://doi.org/10.1016/j.jik.2024.100597

Sedighi, M. (2016). Application of word co-occurrence analysis method in mapping of the scientific fields (case study: the field of Informetrics). *Library Review, 65*(1/2), 52–64. https://doi.org/10.1108/LR-07-2015-0075

Shin, D., Rasul, A., & Fotiadis, A. (2022). Why am I seeing this? Deconstructing algorithm literacy through the lens of users. *Internet Research, 32*(4), 1214–1234. https://doi.org/10.1108/INTR-02-2021-0087

Shin, H., & Kang, J. (2023). Bridging the gap of bibliometric analysis: The evolution, current state, and future directions of tourism research using ChatGPT. *Journal of Hospitality and Tourism Management, 57*, 40–47. https://doi.org/10.1016/j.jhtm.2023.09.001

Sop, S. A., & Kurçer, D. (2024). What if ChatGPT generates quantitative research data? A case study in tourism. *Journal of Hospitality and Tourism Technology, 15*(2), 329–343. https://doi.org/10.1108/JHTT-08-2023-0237

Stahl. (2022). ESG report 2022. https://esg2022.stahl.com/esg-report-2022/start.html

Stopar, K., & Bartol, T. (2019). Digital competences, computer skills and information literacy in secondary education: Mapping and visualization of trends and concepts. *Scientometrics, 118*(2), 479–498. https://doi.org/10.1007/s11192-018-2990-5

Streimikiene, D., Svagzdiene, B., Jasinskas, E., & Simanavicius, A. (2021). Sustainable tourism development and competitiveness: The systematic literature review. *Sustainable Development, 29*(1), 259–271. https://doi.org/10.1002/sd.2133

Talwar, S., Kaur, P., Nunkoo, R., & Dhir, A. (2023). Digitalization and sustainability: virtual reality tourism in a post pandemic world. *Journal of Sustainable Tourism, 31*(11), 2564–2591. https://doi.org/10.1080/09669582.2022.2029870

Troisi, O., Visvizi, A., & Grimaldi, M. (2023). Digitalizing business models in hospitality ecosystems: toward data-driven innovation. *European Journal of Innovation Management, 26*(7), 242–277. https://doi.org/10.1108/EJIM-09-2022-0540

Tussyadiah, I. (2020). Una revisión de la investigación sobre automatización en el turismo: lanzamiento de la colección curada de Annals of Tourism Research sobre inteligencia artificial y robótica en el turismo. *Annals of Tourism Research, 81*, 102883. https://doi.org/10.1016/j.annals.2020.102883

van der Rest, J. P., Wang, L., & Miao, L. (2020). Ethical concerns and legal challenges in revenue and pricing management. *Journal of Revenue and Pricing Management, 19*, 83–84. https://doi.org/10.1057/s41272-020-00239-1

van Nood, R., & Yeomans, C. (2021). Fairness as equal concession: critical remarks on fair AI. *Science and Engineering Ethics, 27*(6), 73. https://doi.org/10.1007/s11948-021-00348-z

Vesnic-Alujevic, L., Nascimento, S., & Polvora, A. (2020). Societal and ethical impacts of artificial intelligence: Critical notes on European policy frameworks. *Telecommunications Policy, 44*(6), 101961. https://doi.org/10.1016/j.telpol.2020.101961

Von Eschenbach, W. J. (2021). Transparency and the black box problem: Why we do not trust AI. *Philosophy & Technology, 34*(4), 1607–1622. https://doi.org/10.1007/s13347-021-00477-0

Yallop, A. C., Gică, O. A., Moisescu, O. I., Coroş, M. M., & Séraphin, H. (2023). The digital traveller: implications for data ethics and data governance in tourism and hospitality. *Journal of Consumer Marketing, 40*(2), 155–170. https://doi.org/10.1108/JCM-12-2020-4278

Zhu, Y., Zhang, R., Zou, Y., & Jin, D. (2023). Investigating customers' responses to artificial intelligence chatbots in online travel agencies: The moderating role of product familiarity. *Journal of Hospitality and Tourism Technology, 14*(2), 208–224. https://doi.org/10.1108/JHTT-02-2022-0041

Artificial Intelligence in Social Media Marketing

Oleksii Lyulyov, Tetyana Pimonenko, and Aleksy Kwilinski

Introduction

With more than 5.1 billion active users on social media platforms worldwide (approximately 60% of the total global population), these channels have become critical sources of data on consumer behavior, preferences, and real-time engagement (DataReportal, 2024). This vast data environment has driven a marketing paradigm shift toward data-centric decision-making, where marketers leverage these insights to develop targeted strategies. As this shift takes hold, global investment in AI solutions has surged, reaching $184 billion in 2024—a significant increase of nearly $50 billion compared with that in 2023 (Statista, 2024). A substantial portion of this investment has been allocated to social media analytics and automation tools (Chaffey, 2022). Gentsch (2018) reported that companies adopting AI-driven marketing solutions experienced up to a 20% increase in consumer engagement and over a 30% increase in conversion rates. The importance of AI in marketing is further emphasized by a survey by Statista (2022), which revealed that 76% of marketers consider AI a vital component of their strategy. This widespread adoption highlights its role in maintaining a competitive edge within the digital landscape.

O. Lyulyov · T. Pimonenko (✉)
WSB University, Dabrowa Gornicza, Poland

Sumy State University, Sumy, Ukraine
e-mail: alex_lyulev@econ.sumdu.edu.ua; tetyana_pimonenko@econ.sumdu.edu.ua

A. Kwilinski
WSB University, Dabrowa Gornicza, Poland

Sumy State University, Sumy, Ukraine

The London Academy of Science and Business, London, UK
e-mail: a.kwilinski@biem.sumdu.edu.ua

J. R. Saura (ed.), *Global Perspectives on AI, Ethics, and Business Economics*, Contributions to Management Science,
https://doi.org/10.1007/978-3-031-88781-9_9

McKinsey's Global AI Survey (2021) corroborates these findings, revealing that companies employing advanced AI-driven personalization strategies reported 10–15% greater revenue growth than their peers did. Bilan (2024) further supported this by noting that 61% of high-performing marketers utilize predictive analytics and AI to anticipate customer needs and tailor interactions, leading to stronger customer loyalty and retention.

Machine learning algorithms have also enhanced the capabilities of social media monitoring, achieving up to 90% precision in sentiment analysis and allowing marketers to identify shifts in consumer sentiment with remarkable accuracy (Forrester, 2022). These advancements enable real-time campaign adjustments, optimizing marketing strategies for maximum impact and responsiveness. Moreover, the integration of AI into social media platforms has refined influencer marketing strategies. A report from Influencer Marketing Hub (2022) revealed that brands that use AI to identify and collaborate with suitable influencers experienced an average 25% increase in return on investment (ROI), illustrating the technology's effectiveness in enhancing audience targeting and engagement. The ongoing evolution of AI technologies underscores their deepening influence on digital marketing (Elsayed Fayed, 2021). These tools not only inform strategy but also increase the customer journey at every stage, offering more sophisticated and effective means of connecting with global audiences. As AI capabilities continue to advance, their role in social media marketing will only grow, transforming how marketers engage with and respond to consumer behaviors and preferences.

This chapter has the following structure: literature review—analysis of the theoretical background on AI in SMM; materials and methods—outlining the data, instruments, and methods of bibliometric analysis; results—exploration of the dynamics of paper publications, the prolific authors and investigations, and the core scientific patterns in the investigations on AI and SMM; discussions—comparison analysis of the obtained results with the previous investigations; conclusions—summarizing core results, limitations, and directions for future investigations.

Literature Review

Research shows that AI optimizes various aspects of social media marketing through ML, NLP, and data analytics, enabling marketers to better understand and predict user behavior (Kaplan & Haenlein, 2019; Hammou et al., 2020; Titko et al., 2023). Advanced AI platforms employ NLP to customize messages, captions, and visual content, allowing brands to scale personalized campaigns and respond to changes in engagement and sentiment (Sadiq et al. 2020; Nyenno et al., 2023; Saura et al., 2024). ML models have become central to AI applications in social media marketing, enabling the analysis of demographic and behavioral data to inform adaptive and personalized strategies (Davenport et al., 2020). These tools surpass traditional demographic-based segmentation by focusing on behaviors, interests, and real-time interactions, which support increased engagement and conversion rates (Bucklin &

Sismeiro, 2009). Predictive analytics further enhance these capabilities by providing insights into optimal engagement times and probable purchasing decisions (Rygielski et al., 2002).

Digital tools, which employ NLP, generate content that resonates with audience segments and enhances engagement across diverse social channels (Trofymenko et al., 2023; Senyah, 2023; Jurafsky & Martin, 2024). In addition, the literature highlights AI's contribution to automating workflows, reducing errors, and scaling operations by handling tasks traditionally performed by human agents (Nesterenko & Olefirenko, 2023). This automation extends to content creation, audience segmentation, and customer support. AI-driven chatbots efficiently manage large volumes of routine inquiries with precision and escalate complex inquiries to human agents as needed, thereby increasing user satisfaction and optimizing resource allocation (Huang & Rust, 2021). Additionally, AI's ability to continuously analyze user-generated content, such as comments and posts, enables sentiment analysis, allowing brands to monitor and adjust their messages in response to real-time user feedback (Sterne, 2017; Lukowicz & Strzelecki, 2020). Research has highlighted the real-time adaptability of AI, with AI-driven systems adjusting ad spending, tailoring content, and refining personalization strategies on the basis of changes in user engagement. Reinforcement learning techniques, as noted by Davenport et al. (2020), allow AI models to continuously learn and improve, increasing the relevance and effectiveness of marketing efforts (Russell & Norvig, 2016). The continuous optimization enabled by AI aligns marketing strategies with dynamic user behavior, positioning brands to engage users in more precise and timely ways (Kaplan & Haenlein, 2019). As AI technologies continue to evolve, their increasing sophistication means that they are capable of not only performing repetitive tasks but also adapting to complex data patterns and facilitating deeper, ongoing interactions with users. Such interactions enhance customer satisfaction and engagement, but they also pose ethical challenges, including potential algorithmic biases and risks to user privacy, highlighting the importance of responsible AI practices in marketing (Gentsch, 2018; Chaffey, 2022; Owusu et al., 2023).

Materials and Methods

Previous studies (Al-Ghamdi, 2021; Andrews et al., 2023; Gera & Kumar, 2023; Veckalne et al., 2023; Bartoloni & Ancillai, 2024; Veckalne et al., 2023) have analyzed the theoretical landscape of AI and SMM via bibliometric analysis. This method is used to quantitatively assess the academic literature on a particular topic by examining the patterns, trends, and structures within published works. It involves the statistical analysis of publications, citations, and other bibliographic data to measure the impact of research articles, authors, journals, and institutions. This method allows the identification of influential papers, prolific authors, collaborations, and emerging trends in a field of study. Bibliometric analysis includes techniques such as citation analysis, co-citation analysis, co-authorship networks, and

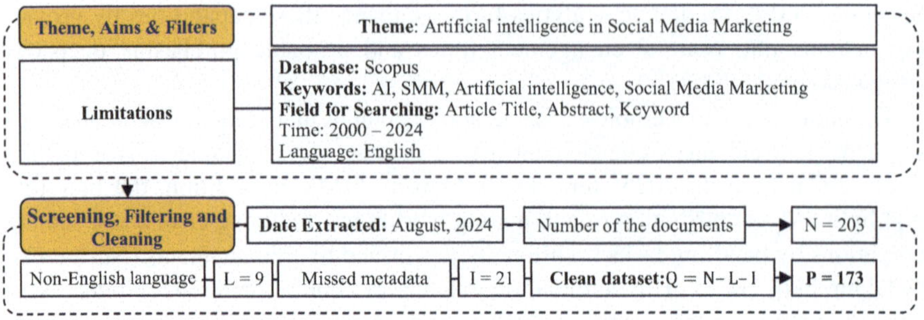

Fig. 1 Framework of the bibliometric analysis of the theoretical background of AI and SMM. *Source*: Developed by the authors

keyword analysis to visualize and map the intellectual structure and evolution of a research area. By providing insights into the volume, growth, and influence of research outputs, bibliometric analysis serves as a valuable tool for understanding the development and impact of knowledge within an academic discipline.

In accordance with the PRISMA guidelines, the following stages were followed (Fig. 1):

1. Data collection. This initial stage involves gathering relevant articles from the Scopus database via specific keywords such as "AI," "Artificial Intelligence," "Social Media Marketing," and "SMM." Boolean operators (AND, OR) are applied to refine the search, ensuring a comprehensive set of records.
2. Screening and filtering. After the initial set of publications is collected, the data undergo a screening process to remove duplicates, irrelevant records, and documents that do not meet language or thematic requirements (e.g., non-English publications or articles outside the focus of AI in social media marketing).
3. Data cleaning: This stage addresses any missing metadata or inconsistencies in the data set, resulting in a clean, standardized data set for analysis.
4. Analysis and visualization. The final, cleaned data set is analyzed via bibliometric methods, including citation analysis, co-citation analysis, and keyword analysis, to identify trends, influential authors, and emerging topics. Visualizations such as co-authorship networks or topic overlays are generated to map the intellectual structure and evolution of the research area.

Results

Dynamics of Paper Publications on AI and SMM

The results of the analysis of the publication trend over time for research on AI and SMM from 2000 to 2024 allow us to explore the three core timeframes:

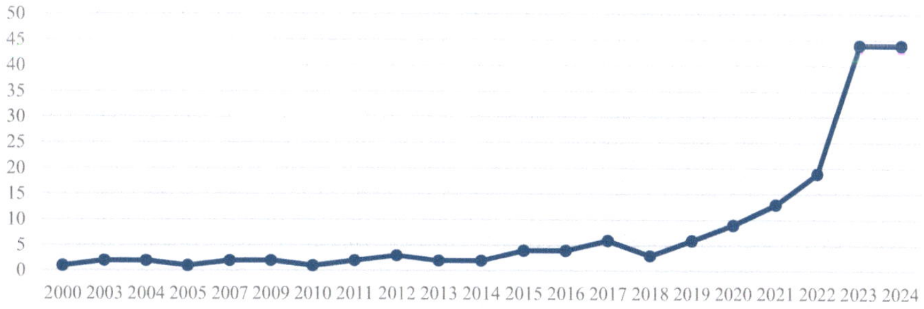

Fig. 2 Publication dynamics of AI and SMM. *Source*: Developed by the authors

1. Steady low growth (2000–2017): From 2000 to 2017, the number of publications on AI and SMM remained relatively low, fluctuating slightly but never exceeding approximately five publications per year. This period likely reflects the early stages of research in this combined field or a lack of integration between AI and SMM topics at that time.
2. Gradual increase (2018–2020): Starting in 2018, there was a gradual rise in publications, indicating a growing interest in the application of AI within social media marketing. This uptick could be due to advancements in AI technologies and their increasing relevance for digital marketing.
3. Rapid growth (2021–2024): A significant spike in publications is observed from 2021 onward, reaching nearly 45 publications by 2023 and 2024. This sharp increase suggests that AI in social media marketing has become a highly relevant research area, likely driven by the expansion of AI applications in consumer engagement, data analytics, and digital marketing strategies. The accelerated growth during these years may also reflect broader trends in AI adoption across industries and the role of social media in digital economies.

Figure 2 reveals that research on AI and SMM has experienced explosive growth in recent years, highlighting the increasing importance and application of AI in social media marketing. This trend likely corresponds with technological advancements, increased data availability, and a demand for more sophisticated marketing strategies.

The Prolific Authors and Investigations of AI and SMM

Table 1 lists the leading scientists contributing to the fields of artificial intelligence (AI) and social media marketing (SMM), ranking them by their publications in this specific area, total document count, and h-index. Cambria E. leads with six AI and SMM publications, a total of 480 documents, and a remarkable h-index of 95, indicating high impact and citation across his research. Hussain A. follows closely with

Table 1 Top 10 prolific authors on AI and SMM

Authors	Affiliation, Country	Published documents		h-index
		on AI and SMM	Total	
Cambria E.	Nanyang Technological University, Singapore City, Singapore	6	480	95
Hussain A.	Edinburgh Napier University, Edinburgh, United Kingdom	3	620	64
Capatina A.	Universitatea Dunarea de Jos din Galati, Galati	2	60	12
Chen H.H.	Taipei Medical University Hospital, Taipei, Taiwan	2	92	21
Chen T.H.		2	111	26
Chen T.W.	Wei Gong Memorial Hospital, Miao-li, Taiwan	2	118	25
Chen Y.T.	Taipei Medical University Hospital, Taipei, Taiwan	2	5	5
Feigh K.M.	Georgia Institute of Technology, Atlanta, United States	2	150	17
Havasi C.	Massachusetts Institute of Technology, United States	2	47	18
Jacobson J.	Ted Rogers School of Management, Toronto, Canada	2	38	15

Source: Developed by the authors via Scopus

three AI and SMM documents, 620 total publications, and an h-index of 64, suggesting an extensive influence in AI that extends beyond SMM.

The other scientists on the list each have two publications focused on AI and SMM. Capatina A. has a total of 60 publications and an h-index of 12, reflecting a moderate level of research activity. Chen H.H., Chen T.H., and Chen T.W. presented h-indices between 21 and 26, with broader contributions ranging from 92 to 118 total documents, demonstrating established influence in their areas. Chen Y.T. has published five total documents with an h-index of five, suggesting that they are either newer to research or have had more limited reach. Feigh K.M. contributed a substantial number of 150 documents, achieving an h-index of 17. Moreover, Havasi C. and Jacobson J. have moderate h-indices of 18 and 15, indicating focused yet impactful contributions. Cambria E. and Hussain A. stand out for their extensive contributions and high academic influence in AI and SMM, whereas the other scientists showcase varied levels of specialization and reach across related research domains.

Table 2 presents the top 10 most-cited papers by scientists in AI and social media marketing (SMM), showcasing their influence on citation counts, publication venues, and journal quality.

The leading paper by Dwivedi et al. (2021), with an impressive 925 citations, was published in the *International Journal of Information Management*, a top-tier Q1 journal, highlighting its major impact on both the AI and SMM fields. Poria et al. (2014) and Poria et al. (2015), with 217 and 113 citations, respectively. These studies have advanced concept-level sentiment analysis and sentiment data

Table 2 Top 10 most-cited papers on AI and SMM

Papers	Citations	Journal	
		Title	Quartile SJR
Dwivedi et al. (2021)	925	*International Journal of Information Management*	Q1
Ye et al. (2019)	279	*Smart Structures and Systems*	Q2
Poria et al. (2014)	217	*Knowledge-Based Systems*	Q1
Cambria et al. (2012b)	197	*Proceedings of the 25th International Florida Artificial Intelligence Research Society Conference, FLAIRS-25*	–
Cambria et al. (2012a)	129	*Multimedia Tools and Applications*	Q1
Luo et al. (2015)	104	*32nd International Conference on Machine Learning, ICML 2015*	–
Poria et al. (2015)	113	*IEEE Computational Intelligence Magazine*	Q1
Sands et al. (2022)	93	*Business Horizons*	Q1
Capatina et al. (2020)	88	*Technological Forecasting and Social Change*	Q1
Vincent et al. (2010)	85	*IEEE Transactions on Medical Imaging*	Q1

Source: Developed by the authors via Scopus

flow—essential areas for understanding consumer sentiment in SMM. Cambria et al. (2012a), with 129 citations, underscore the role of affective computing in SMM. A central contribution is the development of Sentic Computing and SenticNet, which employ natural language processing (NLP), affective computing, and semantic analysis to capture deeper, concept-based insights into human emotions, opinions, and sentiments. Cambria et al. (2012a) introduced Sentic computing as a novel AI approach that leverages cognitive and affective data to analyze and respond to consumer sentiment on social media, helping marketers gauge customer opinions, uncover brand perceptions, and create targeted campaigns. Extending this approach, Cambria et al. (2012b) present SenticNet 2, a semantic and affective resource that enables AI models to recognize nuanced sentiments by mapping words to emotional meanings, enhancing the real-time detection of consumer mood and sentiment trends. Cambria and Melfi (2015) advanced this work by developing a method for identifying outliers in sentiment data, thus improving sentiment analysis accuracy by filtering noise and focusing on the most meaningful consumer expressions.

Scientists such as Capatina et al. (2020), Sands et al. (2022), and Vincent et al. (2010) have shown the interdisciplinary reach of AI for SMM, with applications spanning technology, forecasting, and business. Ye et al. (2019), with 279 citations, indicate substantial influence even from a lower-ranked journal.

Poria et al. (2015) propose dynamic linguistic patterns to assess sentiment data flow, aiding marketers in tracking sentiment shifts over time—an essential tool for time-sensitive SMM campaigns. In another study, Poria et al. (2014) introduce dependency-based sentiment patterns, which map the relationships between words for improved context understanding in sentiment analysis, offering SMM practitioners' insights into brand-specific themes. Qazi et al. (2014) demonstrate how

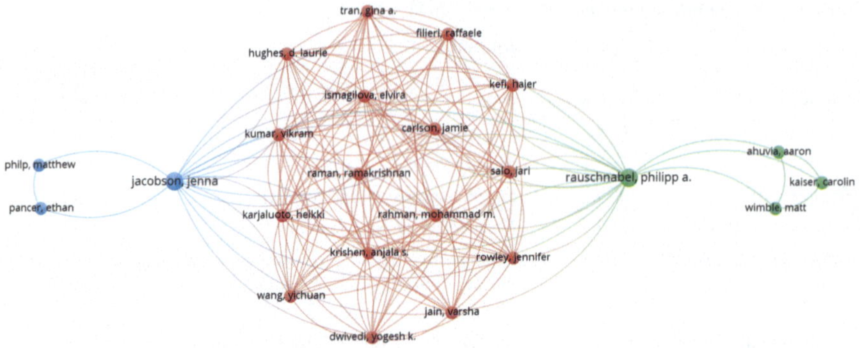

Fig. 3 Collaboration patterns among researchers in the analysis of AI and SMM. *Source*: Developed by the authors

sentiment analysis can enhance business intelligence by analyzing consumer reviews to generate actionable insights, providing guidance for SMM strategies that address consumer preferences and optimize product positioning. The results highlight that scientists leading AI and SMM research are published primarily in high-quality Q1 journals, with additional contributions from influential conference papers. The interdisciplinary nature of these studies reflects the broad academic interest in applying AI to social media marketing.

The co-authorship network visualization highlights the collaboration patterns among researchers in a specific field related to AI and SMM (Fig. 3). The nodes represent individual researchers, and the edges (connecting lines) indicate co-authorship relationships. The color coding of the nodes suggests distinct clusters or groups of researchers who frequently collaborate within their groups but less so with researchers from other clusters.

The results allow the identification of three main clusters: blue cluster centers around Jenna Jacobson with connections to Matthew Philp and Ethan Pancak; red cluster—the largest and most densely connected, revolving around multiple authors with strong interconnected relationships. Notable names here include Jamie Carlson, Heikki Karjaluoto, and Mohammad M. Rahman, among others. This dense network indicates a group with a high level of collaboration within itself; the green cluster is centered on Philip A. Rausehnabel, who collaborates closely with Aaron Ahuvia, Carolin Kaiser, and Matt Wimble. This is another smaller cluster with fewer connections to the larger red network.

The red cluster has the most interconnections, suggesting a strong collaborative network among these researchers, potentially focused on similar research themes or projects. The blue and green clusters have fewer interconnections within their groups and limited links to the central red cluster. There are limited cross-cluster connections, indicating that while some researchers may be aware of each other's work, collaboration tends to remain within the identified clusters. The centrality of researchers such as Jenna Jacobson and Philipp A. Rauschnabel in their respective clusters suggests that they are influential within their groups but have less collaborative overlap with the red cluster.

The Core Scientific Patterns in Investigations of AI and SMM

The network of research topics highlights the connections among key terms and fields relevant to AI and its applications in marketing and human behavior analysis (Fig. 4). The different colors denote thematic clusters: green for marketing and consumer-focused economics, blue for machine learning and analytical methods, and red for human-centered applications and healthcare economics.

The connections among these clusters show how AI serves as a bridge, linking different areas of economic research. For example, AI connects social media marketing and digital marketing, on the one hand, with human- and computer-assisted diagnosis, on the other hand, highlighting its versatility and interdisciplinary relevance in both market- and human-centered economic studies.

AI is the central and largest node, symbolizing its foundational role in modern economic research, particularly in the analysis of market behavior, consumer trends, and decision-making processes. Around AI, the clusters Marketing, Social Media Marketing, Machine Learning, and Human Interaction are located close to each other, which reflects the broad applicability of AI in economic studies, from market predictions to consumer insights.

To the left of AI, there is a dense cluster encompassing marketing, social media marketing, and digital marketing. This group is linked to terms such as influencer marketing, mobile marketing, consumer behavior, and advertising, all of which are highly relevant to economists studying digital economies and market dynamics.

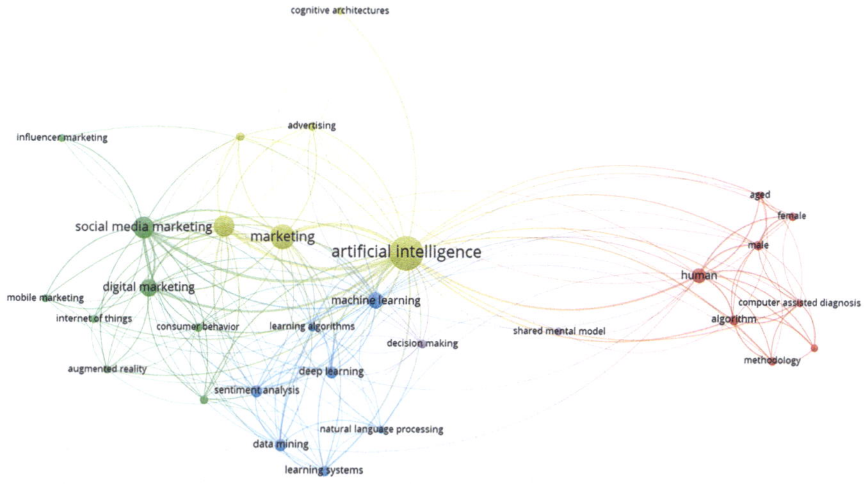

Fig. 4 Research patterns in the analysis of AI and SMM. *Source*: Developed by the authors

These connections illustrate how AI is utilized to understand consumer behavior patterns, predict demand, and develop targeted marketing strategies.

Terms such as sentiment analysis, data mining, and the Internet of Things suggest the integration of AI with big data analytics in marketing, enabling economic researchers to analyze consumer sentiment and collect data from connected devices for more informed economic modeling and forecasting.

Below AI, the cluster of terms related to machine learning, deep learning, learning systems, and natural language processing reflect the technical methodologies that economists employ to analyze large data sets, detect trends, and create predictive models. These AI techniques are essential for modern economic analysis, particularly in understanding market trends, consumer segmentation, and economic decision-making processes. Links to decision-making and learning algorithms emphasize the role of AI in assisting economists with economic forecasting and scenario planning.

On the right side, the human cluster, which connects to terms such as male, female, aged, and computer-assisted diagnosis, represents areas where AI intersects with studies on human demographics and healthcare economics. Economists in this domain may use AI to understand the economic impacts of demographic shifts, healthcare advancements, and human-centered technology applications. The presence of terms such as shared mental models and methodology suggests an interdisciplinary approach that combines AI with economic theories on human behavior and social factors, which is relevant for areas such as labor economics and public health economics.

The color gradient in the overlay visualization (Fig. 5), ranging from blue (indicating older topics) to yellow (representing more recent topics), reveals temporal trends and emerging interests in AI and related fields.

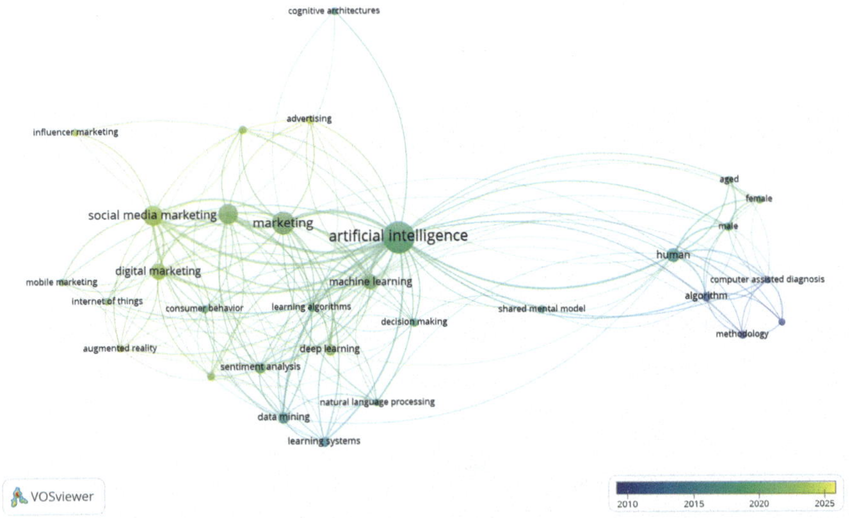

Fig. 5 Overlay visualization of research patterns in the analysis of AI and SMM. Source: Developed by the authors

Older topics (before 2010), shaded in blue, include Humans, Computer-assisted Diagnosis, and Algorithms, indicating early applications focused on health care and human-centered AI. In contrast (after 2024), recent topics shown in yellow, such as Social Media Marketing, Influencer Marketing, Advertising, and Augmented Reality, highlight a shift toward consumer engagement and digital marketing. This progression reflects AI's evolving role, moving from foundational applications to more recent interest in analyzing and influencing consumer behavior in digital spaces.

This chapter reaffirms that the application of AI in social media marketing (SMM) is not merely an enhancement of current methodologies but also a pivotal evolution that reshapes the strategic landscape of digital marketing. The bibliometric analysis on the field's progression from 2000 to 2024 highlights three distinct growth phases. Initially, the early 2000s reflected sporadic interest, with fewer than five publications annually. However, after 2021, the field experienced exponential growth, driven by the increasing sophistication of AI algorithms, the availability of big data, and a shift toward real-time, data-driven marketing solutions.

Discussion

The analysis of publication trends in AI and SMM from 2000 to 2024 highlights three distinct phases: steady low growth (2000–2017), gradual increase (2018–2020), and rapid growth (2021–2024). Early research in the field was sparse, aligning with studies such as Dwivedi et al. (2021) and Cambria et al. (2012a, 2012b), which observed limited integration of AI in marketing during its infancy, primarily focusing on foundational frameworks such as Sentic computing for sentiment analysis. The gradual rise in publications after 2018 reflects advancements in AI technologies, such as natural language processing (NLP) and machine learning, which became more accessible and applicable in marketing, as emphasized by Poria et al. (2014) and Ye et al. (2019). The exponential growth after 2021, reaching nearly 45 publications annually by 2024, indicating the increasing importance of AI-driven analytics for consumer engagement, predictive modeling, and real-time marketing.

The dominance of influential researchers such as Cambria E., Hussain A., and Poria S. underscores the foundational role of their contributions in advancing the field. Sentic computing and dynamic linguistic models for sentiment analysis, as introduced in Cambria et al. (2012b) and Poria et al. (2015), have provided essential tools for understanding consumer sentiment and optimizing SMM strategies. Additionally, studies such as Luo et al. (2015) and Vincent et al. (2010) have highlighted the interdisciplinary applications of AI, bridging marketing, healthcare, and computational intelligence. The thematic clusters identified in the research, which focused on marketing, human behavior, and AI techniques, highlight the interdisciplinary nature of the field. These clusters align with findings by Qazi et al. (2014), who emphasized the need for sentiment analysis to enhance business intelligence, and Capatina et al. (2020), who explored AI's role in forecasting and technological applications. Emerging topics, such as influencer marketing, augmented reality, and advertising, as highlighted in recent studies such as Sands et al. (2022) and Vincent et al. (2010), point to the evolving applications of AI in digital marketing. The overlay visualization further supports these findings, with recent trends showing a shift from foundational AI applications, such as health care and algorithm development, to more consumer-focused tools for digital economies, as reported by Rauschnabel (2023).

The co-authorship networks reveal localized collaboration within key clusters, echoing patterns identified by Qazi et al. (2014) and extended by Rauschnabel (2023), but they show limited cross-disciplinary connections. This suggests opportunities for broader collaboration to bridge isolated research efforts and integrate diverse AI methodologies into SMM. The predominance of high-impact papers in Q1 journals, including works by Dwivedi et al. (2021), Cambria et al. (2012b), and Sands et al. (2022), underscores the academic maturity and significance of the field.

Conclusions

In recent years, the integration of AI into SMM has emerged as a transformative research area, addressing the challenges of optimizing consumer engagement, sentiment analysis, and predictive marketing strategies within a rapidly evolving digital economy. This issue resides at the intersection of technological advancement and marketing innovation, where a comprehensive understanding of AI's application to SMM is vital for driving both theoretical advancements and practical solutions. Through a bibliometric analysis of research spanning from 2000 to 2024, this study identified three distinct phases in the field's evolution: steady low growth (2000–2017), a gradual increase (2018–2020), and a rapid expansion (2021–2024). This progression reflects the growing sophistication of AI technologies and their expanding relevance in digital marketing. By examining influential studies, thematic clusters, and collaboration networks, the analysis underscores a shift from foundational AI applications to advanced, consumer-focused tools that leverage real-time data for hyperpersonalized marketing strategies. Contributions such as sentiment computing and concept-level sentiment analysis exemplify the interdisciplinary and practical impact of AI on SMM, facilitating more nuanced and dynamic consumer engagement. Despite these advancements, the field faces significant challenges, including ethical concerns related to algorithmic biases, data privacy, and the transparency of AI-driven systems. These issues underscore the need for interdisciplinary research that integrates ethical frameworks, legal standards, and consumer rights to ensure responsible AI usage in marketing. Dwivedi et al. (2021) and Gentsch (2018) emphasize the importance of developing frameworks that uphold transparency, fairness, and accountability; mitigate biases; and maintain consumer trust in AI-driven campaigns.

Future research should address these limitations by exploring mechanisms to reduce biases in AI algorithms and developing data governance models that align with global privacy standards. Investigations into ethical AI frameworks can provide actionable insights to bridge the gap between technological advancements and consumer trust.

Emerging trends point toward the integration of AI with immersive technologies, such as augmented reality and virtual influencers, which are reshaping consumer–brand interactions. As highlighted in the overlay visualization of research clusters from 2000 to 2024, the field has transitioned from early focus areas such as algorithm development and healthcare applications to newer interests in influencer marketing and AR-enhanced experiences. These trends suggest an expanding role for AI in crafting highly interactive and engaging marketing strategies. For example, AR-driven marketing, combined with real-time AI analytics, could create fully immersive shopping experiences tailored to individual consumer preferences.

Future research directions include exploring the synergy between AI and immersive technologies, focusing on the consumer psychological impact and return on investment for brands. Moreover, investigating the potential of generative AI, such as ChatGPT and other language models, for automating and enhancing real-time consumer interactions can add to the practical applications of AI in SMM. Expanding research into AI's role in enhancing ethical marketing practices, such as green marketing and sustainability-focused branding, would also align with growing consumer preferences for socially responsible companies.

While advancements in AI and SMM have redefined marketing strategies through predictive analytics, continuous learning, and sentiment analysis, addressing ethical challenges and broadening the application scope with technologies such as AR and generative AI represent essential future directions. These efforts ensure that AI continues to enhance marketing while maintaining transparency, consumer trust, and ethical alignment.

References

Al-Ghamdi, L. M. (2021). Towards adopting AI techniques for monitoring social media activities. *Sustainable Engineering and Innovation, 3*(1), 15–22.

Andrews, R. W., Lilly, J. M., Srivastava, D., & Feigh, K. M. (2023). The role of shared mental models in human-AI teams: a theoretical review. *Theoretical Issues in Ergonomics Science, 24*(2), 129–175.

Bartoloni, S., & Ancillai, C. (2024). Twenty years of social media marketing: A systematic review, integrative framework, and future research agenda. *International Journal of Management Reviews, 26*(3), 435–457.

Bilan, M. (2024). Artificial intelligence statistics: Essential insights for business success. *Master of Code Global*. https://masterofcode.com/blog/ai-statistics

Bucklin, R. E., & Sismeiro, C. (2009). Click here for internet insight: Advances in clickstream data analysis in marketing. *Journal of Interactive Marketing, 23*(1), 35–48.

Cambria, E., Grassi, M., Hussain, A., & Havasi, C. (2012a). Sentic computing for social media marketing. *Multimedia Tools and Applications, 59*(2), 557–577. https://doi.org/10.1007/s11042-011-0815-0

Cambria, E., Havasi, C., & Hussain, A. (2012b). SenticNet 2: A semantic and affective resource for opinion mining and sentiment analysis. In *Proceedings of the 25th International Florida Artificial Intelligence Research Society Conference, FLAIRS-25* (pp. 202–207).
Cambria, E., & Melfi, G. (2015). Semantic outlier detection for affective common-sense reasoning and concept-level sentiment analysis. In *Proceedings of the 28th International Florida Artificial Intelligence Research Society Conference, FLAIRS 2015* (pp. 276–281).
Capatina, A., Kachour, M., Lichy, J., Micu, A., Micu, A.-E., & Codignola, F. (2020). Matching the future capabilities of an artificial intelligence-based software for social media marketing with potential users' expectations. *Technological Forecasting and Social Change, 151*. https://doi.org/10.1016/j.techfore.2019.119794
Chaffey, D. (2022). *Digital marketing: Strategy, implementation and practice* (8th ed.). Pearson Education.
DataReportal. (2024). Global social media statistics. *DataReportal*. https://datareportal.com/social-media-users
Davenport, T. H., Guha, A., Grewal, D., & Bressgott, T. (2020). How artificial intelligence will change the future of marketing. *Journal of the Academy of Marketing Science, 48*, 24–42.
Dwivedi, Y. K., Ismagilova, E., Hughes, D. L., Carlson, J., Filieri, R., Jacobson, J., Jain, V., Karjaluoto, H., Kefi, H., Krishen, A. S., Tran, G. A., & Wang, Y. (2021). Setting the future of digital and social media marketing research: Perspectives and research propositions. *International Journal of Information Management, 59*. https://doi.org/10.1016/j.ijinfomgt.2020.102168
Elsayed Fayed, A. (2021). Artificial intelligence for marketing plan: The case for E-marketing companies. *Marketing and Management of Innovations, 1*, 81–95. https://doi.org/10.21272/mmi.2021.1-07
Forrester. (2022). The Forrester Wave™: AI-Based Text Analytics Platforms, Q2 2020
Gentsch, P. (2018). *AI in marketing, sales and service: How marketers without a data science degree can use AI, Big Data and Bots*. Springer.
Gera, R., & Kumar, A. (2023). Artificial intelligence in consumer behaviour: A systematic literature review of empirical research papers published in marketing journals (2000-2021). *Academy of Marketing Studies Journal, 27*(S1).
Hammou, I., Aboudou, S., & Makloul, Y. (2020). Social media and intangible cultural heritage for digital marketing communication: Case of Marrakech crafts. *Marketing and Management of Innovations, 1*, 121–127. https://doi.org/10.21272/mmi.2020.1-09
Huang, M. H., & Rust, R. T. (2021). Engaged to a robot? The role of AI in service. *Journal of Service Research, 24*(1), 30–41.
Influencer Marketing Hub. (2022). The state of AI in influencer marketing: A comprehensive benchmark report.
Jurafsky, D., & Martin, J. H. (2024). *Speech and language processing: An introduction to natural language processing, computational linguistics, and speech recognition* (3rd ed.). Retrieved from https://web.stanford.edu/~jurafsky/slp3/
Kaplan, A., & Haenlein, M. (2019). Siri, Siri, in my hand: Who's the fairest in the land? On the interpretations, illustrations, and implications of artificial intelligence. *Business Horizons, 62*(1), 15–25.
Lukowicz, K., & Strzelecki, A. (2020). User statisfaction on social media profile of E-sports organization. *Marketing and Management of Innovations, 4*, 61–75. https://doi.org/10.21272/mmi.2020.4-05
Luo, L., Xie, Y., Zhang, Z., & Li, W.-J. (2015). Support matrix machines. In *32nd International Conference on Machine Learning, ICML 2015* (Vol. 2, pp. 938–947).
McKinsey & Company. (2021). *The State of AI in 2021*. McKinsey Global Institute. Retrieved from https://www.mckinsey.com
Nesterenko, V., & Olefirenko, O. (2023). The impact of AI development on the development of marketing communications. *Marketing and Management of Innovations, 1*, 169–181. https://doi.org/10.21272/mmi.2023.1-15

Nyenno, I., Truba, V., & Tokarchuk, L. (2023). Managerial future of the artificial intelligence. *Virtual Economics, 6*(2), 72–88. https://doi.org/10.34021/ve.2023.06.02(5)

Owusu, E., Arthur, J. L., & Amofah, K. (2023). Cross-cultural communication strategies in the digital era: A bibliometric analysis. *Virtual Economics, 6*(2), 55–71. https://doi.org/10.34021/ve.2023.06.02(4)

Poria, S., Cambria, E., Gelbukh, A., Bisio, F., & Hussain, A. (2015). Sentiment data flow analysis by means of dynamic linguistic patterns. *IEEE Computational Intelligence Magazine, 10*(4), 26–36. https://doi.org/10.1109/MCI.2015.2471215

Poria, S., Cambria, E., Winterstein, G., & Huang, G.-B. (2014). Sentic patterns: Dependency-based rules for concept-level sentiment analysis. *Knowledge-Based Systems, 69*(1), 45–63. https://doi.org/10.1016/j.knosys.2014.05.005

Qazi, A., Raj, R. G., Tahir, M., Cambria, E., & Syed, K. B. S. (2014). Enhancing business intelligence by means of suggestive reviews. *Scientific World Journal, 2014*. https://doi.org/10.1155/2014/879323

Rauschnabel, P. A. (2023). Boosting brands with augmented reality: Why and when it works. *NIM Marketing Intelligence Review*, 15(2), 24–29.

Russell, S. J., & Norvig, P. (2016). *Artificial intelligence: A modern approach*. Pearson.

Rygielski, C., Wang, J.-C., & Yen, D. C. (2002). Data mining techniques for customer relationship management. *Technology in Society, 24*(4), 483–502.

Sadiq, W., Abdullah, I., Aslam, K., & Zulfiqar, S. (2020). Engagement marketing: The innovative perspective to enhance the viewer's loyalty in social media and blogging E-Commerce websites. *Marketing and Management of Innovations, 1*, 149–166. https://doi.org/10.21272/mmi.2020.1-12

Sands, S., Ferraro, C., Demsar, V., & Chandler, G. (2022). False idols: Unpacking the opportunities and challenges of falsity in the context of virtual influencers. *Business Horizons, 65*(6), 777–788. https://doi.org/10.1016/j.bushor.2022.08.002

Saura, J. R., Škare, V., & Dosen, D. O. (2024). Is AI-based digital marketing ethical? Assessing a new data privacy paradox. *Journal of Innovation & Knowledge, 9*(4), 100597. https://doi.org/10.1016/j.jik.2024.100597

Senyah, M. M. (2023). Digitalization, gender, and career intentions: Knowledge mapping. *Virtual Economics, 6*(3), 38–55. https://doi.org/10.34021/ve.2023.06.03(3)

Statista. (2022). *AI usage in marketing survey*. Retrieved from https://www.statista.com

Statista. (2024). Artificial intelligence (AI) market size worldwide from 2020 to 2030. *Statista*. https://www.statista.com/forecasts/1474143/global-ai-market-size

Sterne, J. (2017). *Artificial intelligence for marketing: practical applications*. John Wiley & Sons.

Titko, J., Steinbergs, K., Achieng, M., & Uzule, K. (2023). Artificial intelligence for education and research: Pilot study on perception of academic staff. *Virtual Economics, 6*(3), 7–19. https://doi.org/10.34021/ve.2023.06.03(1)

Trofymenko, M., Bulatova, O., Trofymenko, A., & Vyshniakov, O. (2023). Digital development and technological innovations: Inequality and asymmetry. *Marketing and Management of Innovations, 14*(3), 215–229. https://doi.org/10.21272/mmi.2023.3-19

Veckalne, R., Kapustins, M., & Tambovceva, T. (2023). Smart cities, green diets: How the Lucy Veg App supports Valencia's Vegan Community and contributes to SDGs. *Virtual Economics, 6*(2), 7–22. https://doi.org/10.34021/ve.2023.06.02(1)

Vincent, T., Risser, L., & Ciuciu, P. (2010). Spatially adaptive mixture modelling for analysis of fMRI time series. *IEEE Transactions on Medical Imaging, 29*(4), 1059–1074. https://doi.org/10.1109/TMI.2010.2042064

Ye, X. W., Jin, T., & Yun, C. B. (2019). A review on deep learning-based structural health monitoring of civil infrastructures. *Smart Structures and Systems, 24*(5), 567–585. https://doi.org/10.12989/sss.2019.24.5.567

Mapping Brain Science Research and Its Influence on Public Governance: Increasing the Effectiveness of Public Policies Through Behavioural Change

Sonia Cea Quintana

Introduction

Recent advances in genetic, genomic, and behavioural approaches have revolutionized modern neuroscience, providing a viable avenue for multidimensional studies of the brain (Baratta et al., 2022). The increased use of technology in recent decades has led to the rapid development of neuroscience (Tymoczko, 2012; Mehonic & Kenyon, 2022). This science is dedicated to the study of the nervous system and how its different elements interact, giving rise to the biological basis of cognition and behaviour (Manes, 2023). In recent decades, technological developments have made it possible to observe brain function in healthy individuals, monitor brain function, document neural pathways, and even track the activity of specific neurons (Tymoczko, 2012). These advances have made neuroscience a frame of reference through which all sorts of social and political phenomena are rearticulated (Farrugia & Fraser, 2017). For example, in 1988, the US Congress decided that the decade of the 1990s should be considered the decade of the brain (Jones & Mendell, 1999). Thus, in everyday life, ideas about the brain, neurochemistry, and the biological basis of life are increasingly becoming prominent cultic phenomena (Vrecko, 2010). For all these reasons, our societies are experiencing the emergence of a brain culture (Taylor, 2011; Thornton, 2011). This phenomenon is defined as the way in which brain knowledge, images, and representations shape our identities and create new ways of understanding and exercising governance (Pykett, 2016).

In this context, it is worth highlighting the notion of behavioural governance, which is emerging to indicate the development of policies guided by a better understanding of the thinking and decision-making processes of citizens

S. C. Quintana (✉)
Rey Juan Carlos University, Madrid, Spain
e-mail: s.cea@alumnos.urjc.es

J. R. Saura (ed.), *Global Perspectives on AI, Ethics, and Business Economics*, Contributions to Management Science,
https://doi.org/10.1007/978-3-031-88781-9_10

(Dąbrosz-Drewnowska, 2021). In order to gain this knowledge, public policymakers make use of sciences such as cognitive neuroscience, which is dedicated to the study of the genetic/neuronal mechanisms underlying cognitive functions (Lavazza & De Caro, 2009). Amongst its applications, neuropolitics (Somit & Peterson, 2012) refers to the application of genetic and neuroscientific techniques and findings to the study of behaviour and decision-making with relevance to the theory and analysis of political science.

In the face of this paradigm, policies explicitly aimed at changing people's behaviour and reformulating the relationship between the state and citizens are becoming increasingly common (Pykett, 2016). In line with these applications, the notion of "soft paternalism" or "libertarian paternalism" (Thaler & Sunstein, 2003; Thaler & Sunstein, 2008) is emerging, focusing on the development of new "soft policies" to govern through behavioural change (Pykett, 2011). In this context, the United Kingdom has been recognized as a social laboratory for innovations in public policy and practice that draw on behavioural science and neuroscience for their rationale (Pykett, 2011). Internationally, the government's 2013 "BRAIN" project, which aims to establishing the 2010s as the new decade of the brain, is also noteworthy. As well as the "Human Brain" (2013–2016) project funded by the European Commission with similar objectives, amongst which the study of behaviour has been highlighted (Pykett, 2016).

For all these reasons, brain research is currently being presented as a fundamental research area, not only for individual and collective health but also for understanding how societies behave. In this context, neuroscience, and brain scanning, in particular, has begun to transform the world around us, including our institutions, governmental practices, social attitudes, and notions of self (Pykett, 2016).

However, authors such as Pykett (2011) warn against the plethora of unsupported claims about the study of the human brain and its possible relationship with political and social behaviour. Similarly, authors such as Rose (2013) stress the dangers of reducing human beings to "simple puppets" in the hands of their brains (Klein, 2009). Meanwhile authors such as Lavazza and De Caro (2009) warn that the exclusive use of neuroscientific data to interpret the individual can lead to harmful consequences when applied to the design of public policies.

Focusing on our object of study, the expectations regarding the impact of the results are overwhelming, even in fields traditionally sheltered from neurobiological explanations, such as political theory (Meloni, 2011). For all these reasons, authors such as Edelman (2006) argue that a conceptual and methodological reflection on how to work at this stage, when neuroscience and political theory can influence decision-making in public governance, is indispensable. In the same vein, Holmes and Panagopoulos (2013) point out that neuroscience has made significant contributions to political science, but discuss its practical application to relevant issues. Similarly, Seymour and Vlaev (2012) argue that there is little evidence of the use of neuroscience in current politics.

Therefore, with the purpose of contributing knowledge to the use of neuroscience in politics and filling the gap in the literature regarding the study of its use in political action, this study aims to identify which advances contributed by cognitive neuroscience are being taken into account in public administration and governance decisions.

Three research questions (RQs) are therefore proposed to address the research objective: RQ1: What are the main contributions and findings of neuroscience research in the study of citizen behaviour? RQ2: How do these contributions influence the creation of new forms of governance and the design of new public policies? and RQ3: In which areas of governance are the main developments taking place? RQ4: What future research directions are suggested by current findings in the neuroscience of citizen behaviour and their implications for governance and policymaking?

There are scientific contributions (Villarejo & Camacho, 2009; Pykett, 2016) that focus on investigating the relationship between neuroscience and politics and theorizing about its possible application. Despite this, the authors have not found any studies that provider an updated state of the art that would allow analysing its practical application in different fields. Therefore, the originality of this study lies in its ability to link neuroscience findings to different areas of government policy. It gives examples of its use and warns of both its potential and its drawbacks. It also identifies new social problems where its implementation could be successful.

Therefore, based on the above objectives, the research objectives of this study are as follows:

- To generate knowledge about neuroscience applied to the study of citizen behaviour.
- To provide evidence of links between neuroscience and the implementation of public policy.
- To explore new ways to identify future challenges where the use of neuroscience will help to improve the effectiveness of public policy.

To achieve the objectives presented, we adopt an approach known as bibliometric analysis (Linnenluecke et al., 2020 cited by Lafont et al., 2023). The bibliometric analysis is developed using VOS Viewer on a data set composed of scientific contributions (N = 212 studies) published between 01-01-1995 and 31-12-2022 in Web of Sciences (WoS) using the Boolean operators "AND" and "OR". The query in the WoS database is as follows: "TS = (Neurosciences) AND TI = (Politics)" In this way, three analyses are carried out in order to understand the most relevant contributions made so far in the literature and to answer the research questions and objectives: (i) co-citation of authors, (ii) bibliographic coupling, and (iii) co-occurrence of keywords (Ding & Yang, 2020; Oyewola & Dada, 2022; McAllister et al., 2022 cited by Lafont et al., 2023). This approach focuses on understanding the most relevant authors who have published contributions related to neuroscience applied to policy to date. In addition, we also seek to understand the main sources that publish information related to neuroscience applied to policy, as well as the main keywords and areas of development.

This introduction is followed by a presentation of the theoretical framework and an explanation of the key concepts that have been influential in the application of neuroscientific findings to policy. The methodology is then presented. Next, the main findings are reported in order to move on to their analysis. The article concludes with a discussion section, in which both the limitations of this study and a number of areas with practical examples are offered. A synthetic research agenda is also developed. Finally, we outline the conclusions of the work.

Theoretical Framework

In order to understand the theoretical framework that encompasses the development of policies based on knowledge of citizens' behaviour, this section reviews biopolitics and biopower (Foucault, 2008; Rose, 2009; Rose & Abi-Rached, 2013), the plasticity of the brain and its capacity for optimization (Malabou, 2008; Papadopoulos, 2011), the end of the Cartesian paradigm that points to the influence of emotions in citizens' decisions (Damasio, 1994; Ledoux, 1998; Westen, 2008; Somit & Peterson, 2005; Papadopoulos, 2011) and the birth of behavioural governance and libertarian paternalism as new forms of governance in the search for the optimization of the citizen and the victory over the unthinking self (Dąbrosz-Drewnowska, 2021; Thaler & Sunstein, 2008; Pykett, 2011, 2016).

To provide a better understanding of how these findings are influencing the design of new policies, Table 1 summarizes the areas in which they have been applied, their objectives, and examples of their use.

Biopolitics, Neuroscience, and Optimization

Biopolitics is a way of governing the life of bodies and populations (Foucault, 2008). In turn, it requires a new kind of political knowledge, in which modern sciences inform policy and define political goals (Millei & Joronen, 2016). Currently, the knowledge produced by the neurosciences and biosciences has enabled these tactics of biopolitics to become policy in new fields (Rose & Abi-Rached, 2013). In this way, the new brain and behavioural sciences are setting up new ways of understanding ourselves, while at the same time being linked to techniques that help us to correct or improve the kind of people we want to be (Rose, 2009).

Plasticity as Practice and as Political Promise: Neuro-citizenship and Embodied Control

Brain plasticity or neuroplasticity refers to the ability of the brain to change in response to changes in its functioning or environment (Pitts-Taylor, 2010). In this way, plasticity contradicts rigidity and leads us to think of our brains as simultaneously modifiable, malleable, and formative (Malabou, 2008). This plasticity establishes a potential interface of relationship and modification between the brain and

Table 1 Actual government actions and policies based on behaviour change

Area	Target	Development
Welfare construction policies.	• The use of happiness and positive psychology as a cause for government policies, that aim to improve the well-being of citizens (Seligman, 2019) Happiness: – Improves immune system function (Diener & Chan, 2011; Pressman & Cohen, 2005) – Associated with fewer sick days (Lyubomirsky et al., 2005) – Improved health behaviours (Diener et al., 2017; Lyubomirsky et al., 2005) – It predicts income gains (De Neve et al., 2013)	• France: Commission to recommend national success measures (see Seligman, 2019) • England: measuring citizens' well-being every three months to gauge the success of government policies (see Seligman, 2019) • USA: resilience training for soldiers. Those who received it were significantly less likely to be diagnosed with post-traumatic stress disorders, anxiety or depression (see Harms et al., 2013)
Urban policies: redesigning cities	• Building "living places" to ensure the creation of quality of life through "cleaner, safer, and greener" public spaces (Kraftl, 2014) • Creating public spaces that stimulate public participation and a sense of belonging to the urban environment (Adli & Schöndorf, 2020) • Promoting accessibility to green spaces, which have a positive impact on all-cause and cardiovascular mortality (Gascon et al., 2016), contribute to the reduction of obesity (Lachowycz & Jones, 2011), reduce the release of stress hormones (Hunter et al., 2019), generate a lower risk of mental illness in adulthood (Engemann et al., 2019) and have a protective effect on the risk of depression (Cohen-Cline et al., 2015)	• UK: Transformative projects of urban habitats, to address local, economic, social, political and environmental issues simultaneously (see Raco, 2005) Example of "Sustainable Communities" plan (see Kraftl, 2014; ODPM, 2003) • Germany: Creation of the "Interdisciplinary Forum on Neurourbanism". Creation of working groups consisting of university professors, scientists and professionals from the fields of psychiatry, urban planning, psychology, neuroscience, architecture, sociology, philosophy and ethnography, to design cities that are beneficial to people's mental health and produce policy advice (see Interdisciplinary Forum Neurourbanism, n.d.)

(continued)

Table 1 (continued)

Area	Target	Development
Defense policies:	• Human performance enhancement and degradation (Howell, 2016)	• USA: Funding of neuroscience projects by the Defense Advanced Research Projects Agency (DRAPA) to prevent the effects of sleep deprivation, enable resilience to stress, or improve recruit selection by prioritizing those with better brain capacities to learn fast or take risks (see Howell, 2016) • Russia: Use of neuropharmaceuticals against enemy forces (opioids in response to Moscow been threatened with bombing by Chechen terrorists) • Application of oxytocin to interrogates in order to produce feelings of trust that induce confession (see Howell, 2016)
Crime management policies	• Increasing the security of its population (Pieri & Levitt, 2008) • Using advances in neuroscience and the application of new imaging techniques together with DNA analysis to identify behavioural biomarkers (Pieri & Levitt, 2008) • Determine relevant risk factors and develop effective crime prevention and intervention strategies (Dressing et al., 2008) Search for the “candidate gene” (Eastman & Campbell, 2006)	• USA: Courts reluctant to consider neuroimaging sufficient to prove insanity or incompetence, but relatively lenient in death penalty hearings. No allowance for magnetic resonance image (MRI) to prove deception or truthfulness, but to identify physiological structures, trauma and certain diseases. New neuroimaging: Doubt about the evidential reliability of PET and SPECT scans and P300 wave until some degree of certainty is achieved (see Moriarty, 2008) • Current trend in the courts: Distinction between brain, mind and personality, assuming that people are free and therefore responsible for their actions (Pieri & Levitt, 2008)

Educational policies	• Neuroplasticity: children's brains can change and improve in response to certain classroom activities • Parenting as a planning project to anticipate and manage risks (Beck-Gernsheim, 2002) Young children's brains as the building of a "hopeful ethos" for society (Rose & Abi-Rached, 2013) • Producing an enterprising and healthy future workforce, fostering neurological developments that stimulate synaptic growth and lead to optimal brain architecture in children (Shonkoff & Phillips, 2000) • Neuroparenting: government-sponsored early intervention practices with a particular focus on the preschool child, so that parents can optimize their own children's development (Rawdin, 2019) • Strategies based on the use of artificial intelligence in the classroom to enhance knowledge and improve learning capacity (see Ali et al., 2024)	• Australia: Identification of early childhood as a priority area to maintain international competitiveness. Calculation of the return on investment devoted to these policies in terms of savings in social expenditure such as crime, employment, social services and health (see Millei & Joronen, 2016). State of Ontario, launch of Healthy Baby/Healthy Brain, a parent-oriented campaign focused on children's emotional brain development and self-regulation through attachment techniques (Wall, 2017) • UK: Policy initiatives and legislation. Sure start: aims to implement a series of combined policy to give children the best start. Every Child Matters: comprehensive development for children up to the age of 18 in all its formative and health aspects. (Rawdin, 2019) • Currently, human capital theory (HCT) and neuroscientific reasoning are the dominant frameworks in education policymaking and early childhood care around the world (Millei & Joronen, 2016)
Health policies (Policies against addictions and generation of healthy lifestyles)	• Change of focus: – Failure of policies based on an individual focus, leaving aside interest in understanding how neighbourhood, family or poverty or experiences of discrimination and violence affect addiction (Metzl & Hansen, 2014) – Development of policies from a transdisciplinary perspective. Creation of relational policies that influence the importance of the individual's relationship with his or her environment when making a decision (Farrugia & Fraser, 2017)	• USA: Policies developed to treat gambling addiction from a neurological point of view. The National Centre for Responsible Gambling is set up to fund scientific research on peers, with the gambling industry itself as its main benefactor. It helped to recognize the ineffectiveness of policies based on its neuroreductionist vision (see Vrecko, 2008) • Tobacco consumption control: a set of interventions in the systems involved, such as industry, markets, advertising, human preferences, group behaviour and individual actors (Farrugia & Fraser, 2017) • Obesity: Creation of "Childhood obesity: a plan for action", which addresses the issue of childhood obesity through a range of actions focusing on children's environment and their development (see Her Majesty's Government, 2016). The National Institute for Health and Care Excellence has produced a guide to tackling obesity by working with local communities, businesses, authorities and community leaders (see NICE, 2012)

Source: The authors adapted from Pykett (2011, 2016) areas

the social world (Youdell et al., 2017). Similarly, it opens up a space in which we can be self-managing, self-optimizing, and self-governed by our brains (Isin, 2004).

This understanding of plasticity as self-optimization is introduced into the cultural imaginary of the global North as a promise, practice, and as a condition of the liberal individualism embodied in our societies (Papadopoulos, 2011). Thus, for various authors in these Western societies, control is embodied and exercised by being placed in a constant process of modification of our own material existences (Pitts-Taylor, 2010; Cromby et al., 2011). With regard to the citizen himself and his relationship with power, Vidal coins the term "brainhood" to refer to the anthropological figure of a new modernity that places the highest value on the individual as an autonomous agent of choice and initiative (2009).

As a result, of applying all these concepts, the "neurocitizen" emerges as a subject of the brain world and an object of neurologically informed governance in specific spheres of policy and practice (Pykett, 2016).

Emotion and Politics: The Unthinking Citizen

Contemporary advances in the field of neuroscience provide us with a deeper understanding of the relationships between the external environment, human emotion, and brain function, which are of great political importance (Somit & Peterson, 2012).

In 1994, the neuroscientist Antonio Damasio put an end to the Cartesian paradigm according to which the mind is separate from the body and emotions (Damasio, 1994). In line with this assertion, Ledoux (1998) argues that the brain is a whole and that emotions are not only necessary, but can often take over the rational part. More recent studies confirm the dominant role of emotion in decision-making (Somit & Peterson, 2012). Drew Westen (2008) demystifies the idea of the political brain as a dispassionate calculating machine that objectively analyses facts, figures, and policies to make a reasoned decision, describing it as an eminently emotional brain. Therefore, the assumption that the brain makes political decisions after a rational evaluation process is not related to the way it actually works, as emotions play a central role in how citizens perceive politics (Maneiro, 2017).

For all these reasons, rational economic man has been replaced by a universal irrational subject, but the ideal subject of the new embodied governments is still the one who can control his own temptations through a reflexive victory over his limbic system (Pykett, 2011).

Behavioural Governance: Addressing the Irrational Brain, Behavioural Change

As mentioned, above, the term behavioural governance to denote the development of policies guided by a better understanding of citizens' thinking and decision-making processes (Dąbrosz-Drewnowska, 2021). To deepen the knowledge of this behaviour, governors use the insights offered by neuroscience, psychology, and behavioural economics (Pykett, 2011). In this way, managers, aware of the limited rationality of citizens, use these inputs to encourage the desired behaviour (Dąbrosz-Drewnowska, 2021). Thus, the employment of these policies aims to control the irrational brain through affective interventions and to cultivate the rational and reflective aspects of the mind (Pykett, 2011). The most common tool for changing behaviour is the so-called nudge theory (Sunstein & Thaler, 2008). This theory encompasses a set of actions designed to make citizens behave and choose in the desired way, leaving them free to choose (Haber & Olejniczak, 2014; Saura, 2024).

In line with this theory, the notion of "soft paternalism" or "libertarian paternalism" (Thaler & Sunstein, 2003; Thaler & Sunstein, 2008) emerges as a distinctive arrangement between the state and the citizen, focusing on new cultural practices of governance through behavioural change (Pykett, 2011). This form of governance has achieved some notoriety in the UK since 2004, under both Labour and Conservative governments, as well as in the Obama administration (Pykett, 2011). Its development on both sides of the political spectrum has led to this libertarian paternalism be seen as a "third way" (Thaler & Sunstein, 2008, p. 252).

The global financial crisis of 2008 vindicated the need for new regulatory and governance tools, thus launching the behavioural revolution in public policy (Dąbrosz-Drewnowska, 2021). Employment, health, crime, and education have been identified as policy areas where the behavioural change approach would be particularly appropriate (Pykett, 2011; González-Padilla et al., 2024), as well as welfare, education, public health, military training, law and more recently, architecture as areas where this brain culture has already taken hold (Pykett, 2011, 2016). Similarly, these emerging methodologies exist within a political milieu wherein the improvement of decision-making through artificial intelligence (Valle-Cruz et al., 2020; Saura et al., 2024), the use of open data (Corrales-Garay et al., 2019), and the implementation of chatbots to engage with citizens under conditions of trust are being evaluated and strategically planned (Aoki, 2020). Finally, the recent COVID-19 crisis and its impact have given rise new ways of organizing information, leading to significant changes in all societal domains that need to be taken into account (Dwivedi et al., 2020).

Actual Government Actions and Policies Based on Behaviour Change

In the following, we will use the areas previously identified by Pykett (2011, 2016) to provide a number of practical examples of these policies that we have encountered in conducting our SLR.

Methodology

Bibliometric Analysis

Sampling and Data Description

As mentioned above, this study uses the Web of Science (WoS) academic database. As pointed out by authors such as Yuan and Sun (2020), this database is one of the most widely used to obtaining and developing bibliometric sources and studies, due to its international prestige in science. The prestigious JCR ranking, which indexes the best and most prestigious academic journals, can also be found in this database. In terms of data collection, the final queries were carried out on 30 January 2023. During this session, data is extracted and downloaded from the database, using a time horizon for the query in which Boolean operators are used. In this way, the set of academic contributions made to date on neuroscience, policy, and its relationship with public governance was compiled.

Therefore, the following search is performed using the Boolean operator "AND". The query performed in the WoS database is as follows: "TS = (Neuroscience*) AND TI = (Politics)". This search in the WoS Core Collection returned 212 results. Considering the subject of study as an emerging topic, it was decided to perform a broad search in terms of the types of documents registered, analysing articles, proceedings, book chapters, editorial material, book reviews, review articles, books, early access, as well as the meeting abstracts found. A time limit was set to study the publications between 01-01-1995 and 31-12-2022, because the first valid publication for our object of study, entitled "From inclusive fitness to neuroscience: proximate mechanisms, feminism and the politics of gender", was found in 1995 (Masters, 1995).

According to Gorraiz and Schloegl (2008), in bibliometric analyses, the sample is determined according to the number of valid contributions and identified in the databases used, with a value of 175 valid studies, from studies such as Shi et al. (2019) and Kraus et al. (2020). In addition, Fig. 1 can be used to identify the main

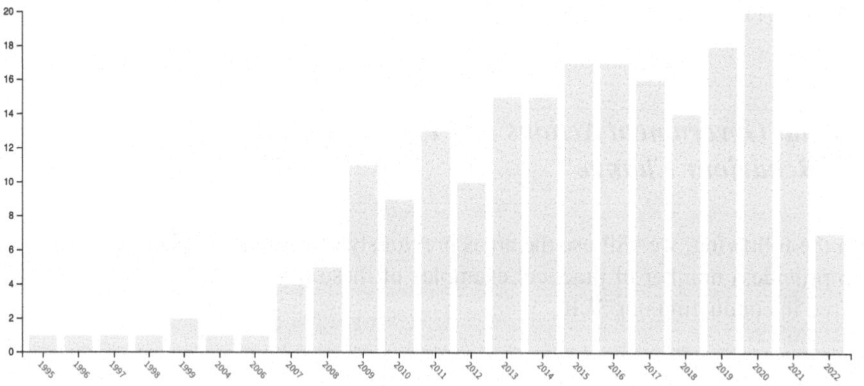

Fig. 1 Number of articles published by year from January 1995 to December 2022. *Source*: WoS, accessed 17 January 2023

contributions in the scientific literature in the selected years. It should be noted that the year with the most publications is 2020, with 8.68%, corresponding to 27 research papers, followed by 2013 with 26 identified scientific contributions and corresponding to 8.36%. In third place would be 2019 with 23 references (7.39%), in fourth place, 2018: 23 references (7.39%), in fifth place, 2017: 23 references (7.39%); sixth place, 2016: 21 references (6.75%); seventh place, 2015: 20 references (6.43%); eighth place, 2014: 19 references (6.1%); ninth place, 2022: 18 references (5.78%); and finally, in tenth place, 2007: 18 references (5.78%).

Figure 1 shows that 2020 (9.4%) and 2019 (8.4%) are the years that contribute most to the study of neuroscience applied to politics. As we have commented, the measurement starts with 1995 as the first year of study, because the first relevant article was registered on that date. Recall that on 25 February 1989, the US Congress agreed to call the 1990s "the decade of the brain", which led to an increase in funding and studies related to the creation of knowledge about neuroscience and its derived applications (Jones & Mendell, 1999). Subsequently, in April 2013, President Obama pledged an initial investment of $100 million to establish the 2010s, while in the same year, the EU BRAIN initiative emerged with similar objectives (Pykett, 2016). Both facts, as shown, seem to have encouraged the creation of scientific knowledge in our field of study, causing them to gradually increase the number of records, in an upward trend that charges its highest record in 2020, with a total of 20 published articles and 416 citations.

Thus, as can be seen in Fig. 2, the great results obtained in 2020 manage to maintain the upward trend in 2021, despite the low number of publications recorded that year (13 publications), but also in that year, the highest number of citations obtained during the entire progress under study (482). In 2022, the desire to publish continues to decline, with the lowest number of publications since 2008 (7), but a high records in the number of citations (442). These data show a slight decline in interest in this field.

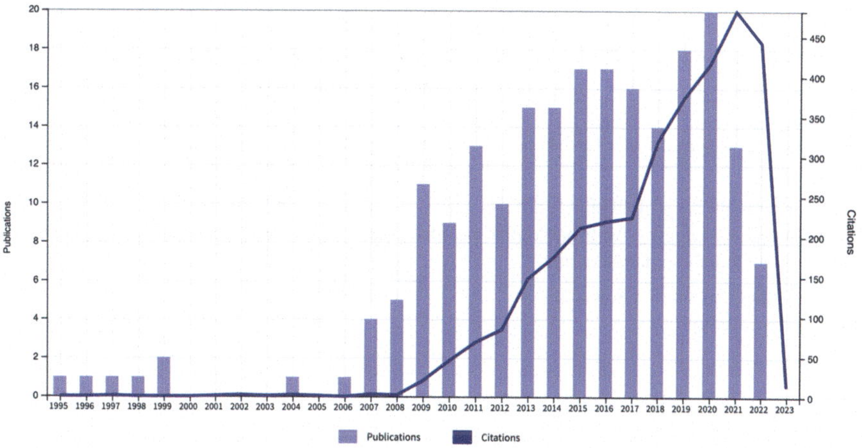

Fig. 2 Number of citations and publications over time from January 1995 to December 2022. *Source*: WoS, accessed 17 January 2023

In terms of the number of categories in which scientific contributions related to neuroscience and its relationship with politics are published, the research categories related are the following. In first place is Political Science, with 28 entries (13.20% of the total). The second category is History Philosophy of Science with 18 entries (8.4%). Next is Social Science Biomedical with 15 entries (7.07%). This is followed by Education Educational Research, with 14 entries (6.60%). In fifth place, International Relations with 14 contributions (6.60%). Sixth place would go to Social Issues with 14 entries (6.60%). Seventh place would go to Social Sciences Interdisciplinary with 12 entries (5.60%), followed by Sociology with 11 results (5.2%), Humanities Multidisciplinary with 10 entries (4.72%). Ninth place would go to Humanities Multidisciplinary with 10 entries (4.72%) and the list of the top 10 categorical places would be completed by Psychology Multidisciplinary with 10 entries (4.72%) (Table 2).

Table 2 WoS categories, percentage of records, and most cited articles

WoS categories	Number of records	of total
Political Science	28	13,21
History Philosophy of Science	18	8,49
Social Sciences Biomedical	15	7,07
Education Educational Research	14	6,60
International Relations	14	6,60
Article	**Author**	**Quotations**
The Perils of Ignoring History: Big Tobacco Played Dirty and Millions Died. How Similar Is Big Food?	Brownell and Warner (2009)	438
The Future of Sex and by Psychology Gender in Psychology: five Challenges to the Gender Binary	Hyde et al. (2019)	275
The logic of habit in International Relations	Hopf (2010)	253
The Human Sciences in a Biological Age	Rose (2013)	190
The plastic brain: Neoliberalism and the neuronal self	Pitts-Taylor (2010)	126
Rethinking Interdisciplinarity across the Social Sciences and Neurosciences	Callard and Fitzgerald (2015)	111
Critical medical humanities: embracing entanglement, taking risks	Viney et al. (2015)	89
Mapping the new molecular landscape: social dimensions of epigenetics	Pickersgill et al. (2013)	66
Positive Psychology: A personal history	Seligman (2019)	65
Situating local biologies: Anthropological perspectives on environment/human entanglements	Niewöhner and Lock (2018)	54

Source: data from Web of Sciences
Elaboration: the authors

Analysis of Results

Analysis of Joint Appointments

Following the study of Hou et al. (2018), we identify the most cited references amongst the studies that make up the database. Table 3 therefore presents the ten most relevant articles, as identified by their frequency of co-citation amongst their

Table 3 Results of reference matching and author matching

Reference co-citations				Author's co-citations		
Title	Author(s)	Quotations	Link strength	Author(s)	Quotations	Link strength
1. 1. Critical neuroscience: A Handbook of the Social and Cultural Context of Neuroscience	Choudhury and Slaby (2016)	10	43	Rose, N	47	427.00
2. Picturing personhood: brain scans and biomedical identity	Dumit (2004)	11	38	Choudhury, S	30	404.00
3. Critical neuroscience: Linking Neuroscience and Society through critical practice	Choudhury et al. (2009)	10	37	Callard, F	19	317.00
4. Social Science and Neuroscience beyond interdisciplinary: experimental entanglements	Fitzgerald and Callard (2015)	11	37	Cacciopo, JT	29	306.00
5. What should we do with our brains?	Malabou (2008)	9	33	Fitzgerald, D	20	280.00
6. Brainhood, anthropological figure of modernity	Vidal (2009)	11	32	Foucault, M	35	251.00
7. The new brain and the management of the mind	Rose and Abi-Rached (2013)	14	32	Ortega, F	18	246.00
8. The plastic brain: Neuroliberalism and the neuronal self	Pitts-Taylor (2010)	9	23	Dumit, J	20	242.00
9. The politics of life itself	Rose (2007)	12	22	Cromby, J	14	238.00
10. Descartes' error	Damasio (1994)	11	16	Haidt, J	20	228.00

Source: Authors

authors. These studies are significant not because of their direct relevance to the research questions posed in this study, but because of their connection to the general theme of this research, which other authors frequently utilize in their scientific contributions to establish and develop their theoretical frameworks related to the general theme of this study. These ten exemplary contributions are specifically related to neuroscience as it applies to policy.

The most cited contribution is that of Choudhury and Slaby (2016) with 10 citations and a link strength of 43.00. This book provides a frame of reference for the importance and development of neuroscience in the social and cultural context of our time. It also draws attention to the phenomenon of "neuromania", which, according to the author, characterizes our popular culture.

The next source is Dumit (2004), which has been cited 11 times and has a link strength of 38.00. The study in question analyses focuses images obtained through brain scanning techniques (PET) and their impact on our conceptualization of the mind. He subsequently examines how these assumptions are transported beyond the laboratory and exert influence on social debates, thereby contributing to a societal dependence on scientific authority.

The third-most frequently cited paper is that of Choudhury et al. (2009), which has been referenced 10 times and a link strength of 37.00. This study presents the formulation of a conceptual framework for critical neuroscience research, addressing the social, cultural, and political challenges posed by advancements in behavioural and brain sciences. In fourth place is the study by Fitzgerald and Callard (2015) which has been cited 11 times and a link strength of 37.00. This research advocates for collaborative efforts between neuroscience and the social sciences.

Vidal (2009) is in fifth place with nine citations and a link strength of 33.00. The article explores the novel subjectivities that have emerged in the present century in the wake of the growing relevance of neuroscience. Consequently, it delves into the concept of the "cerebral self" as the location of the "modern self", an anthropological construct intrinsic to the new modernity.

In sixth place are the studies of Malabou (2008), which have been cited 11 times and have a linking strength of 32.00. This quality is of vital importance for the development and learning of the human brain throughout the lifespan. Likewise, it stablishes a direct interconnection between the nervous system and the political and social organization that shape and are shaped by human experience. As a result of this relationship, the book outlines the concept of human brain as "historical product".

In seventh place, we find Rose and Abi-Rached (2013) with 14 citations and a link strength of 32.00. The book presents an extensive analysis of the evolution of neurosciences and their implications for the comprehension of human behaviour. It explores how this influence defines new policies and new forms of social interaction. It cites as examples the influence on the penal system and the creation of new models of education and parenthood.

In eighth place, with nine citations and a linking strength of 23.00, is Pitts-Taylor (2010), whose work focuses on the popular discourse surrounding brain plasticity and its reflection on neoliberalism practices. In ninth place is Rose (2009) and his

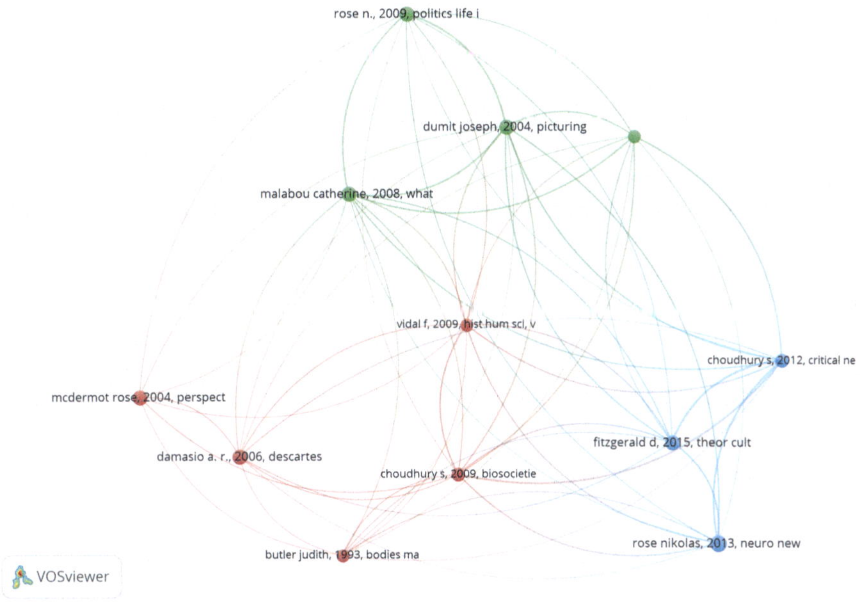

Fig. 3 Co-citation analysis of references. *Source*: Authors based on VOS Viewer results

"politics of life itself", with 12 citations and a strength of 22.00. The book develops Foucault's concept of biopolitics and highlights how the latest findings in neuroscience define a new subjectivity "the neural self", while marking a new mode of governance in neoliberal societies.

Finally, in tenth place, with 11 citations and a link strength of 16.00, we find Damasio (2005). The research developed in this book suggests putting an end to the "Cartesian error". The author demonstrates the indissoluble relationship between reason and emotion in the brain in decision-making.

Therefore, in Table 3, the inclusion criterion for the co-citation analysis reference is a minimum of 9 co-citation references, with a total of 12 papers meeting the threshold. The number of co-citations and the total strength of the link are highlighted in Table 3. For the author co-citation in Table 3, a minimum of 13 citations is set for each author, out of a total of 9382 authors in the database, 44 meeting the threshold.

In this sense, to continue with the co-citation analysis, Fig. 3 shows a visual and graphical map that identifies clusters related to the co-citation of references in the analysed database. In this way, it is possible to understand different links between the variables that make up the clusters. Figure 2 shows a total of 12 references included in the neural network. Different filters and criteria were used to include them in the neural network in order to optimize the results. The minimum number of citations obtained for each reference included in Fig. 2 was 9. Based on this criterion, a total of 12,835 cited references are obtained. After this filtering, 36 optimal references were included in the neural network. Of these, 12 references were included because they were considered relevant and form clusters amongst themselves. Based on the results, a total of 60 links were obtained, representing 100% of the connections between the 12 identified inputs. Similarly, the total strength of the links taken into account is 168 points, and the degree of representation is 100.

As posited by Gorraiz and Schloegl (2008), the visual representation of databases in bibliometric analysis is crucial to elucidating the interconnections between the contents published in each selected paper. Thus, Fig. 3 identifies a total of three clusters. The first, in terms of weight, is shown in red, in the middle and left side of the figure. This cluster is formed by Vidal, F., Damasio, A., Choudhury, S., Butler, J., Mcdermot, R., it is focused on the development of neuroscience, is characterized by the study of emotions in decision-making. Next, we find the green cluster (top of the figure) composed by Rose, N., Dumit, J., Malabou, C., and Pitts-Taylor, V., this cluster is characterized by an emphasis on the study of brain plasticity and its potential role in optimizing the individual. This characteristic will influence both the formation of new identities and the way of being governed. The final cluster, in blue (bottom right), is led by Choudhury, S., Fitzgerald, D., and Rose, N, focused on the critical study of the application of these phenomena and the commitment to transdisciplinarity.

Furthermore, in order to complete the reference co-citation analysis, the most relevant authors in terms of citations and link strength have also been identified. The link strength in the variable determines the importance of the connections between these authors and other published research in this field. Consequently, these authors can be considered the most representative of this field in the literature identified.

Please refer to Table 3, fourth column, for a list of the authors. First, we find Rose, N., who has been cited 47 times and has link strength of 427.00. Second, Choudhury, S., with 33 citations and a total link strength of 404.00. Subsequently, Callard, F. is listed with 19 citations and a binding strength of 317.00. The fourth ranked author is Cacciopo, JT., with 29 citations and a link strength of 306.00. In fifth place is Fitzgerald, D., with 20 citations and a link strength of 280.00. In sixth place, Foucault, M., with 35 citations and 251.00 link strength. Ortega, F., is in seventh place with 18 citations and a link strength of 246.00. In eighth place is Dumit, J., with 20 citations and 242.00 link strength. In ninth place, Cromby, J., with 14 citations and a link strength of 238.00. In the final position Haidt, J., with 20 citations and 228.00 linking strength.

Furthermore, the neural map of author citation density is also calculated. In order to achieve this, parameters are established to ensure the correct computation of the study, whereby references that have received at least 16 citations are identified as a variable. In accordance with the aforementioned selection criteria, 29 authors out of a total of 9382 were identified as meeting the specified criterion from the database utilized. Consequently, a total of 254 links were identified, representing 90% of the density observed in the map.

The total link strength of the connections represented in Fig. 4 is 1957. In accordance with the findings yielded by the aforementioned criteria, a total of three clusters have been identified in relation to the author density neural map. The centres of the clusters identified in Fig. 4 are composed of connections between authors and

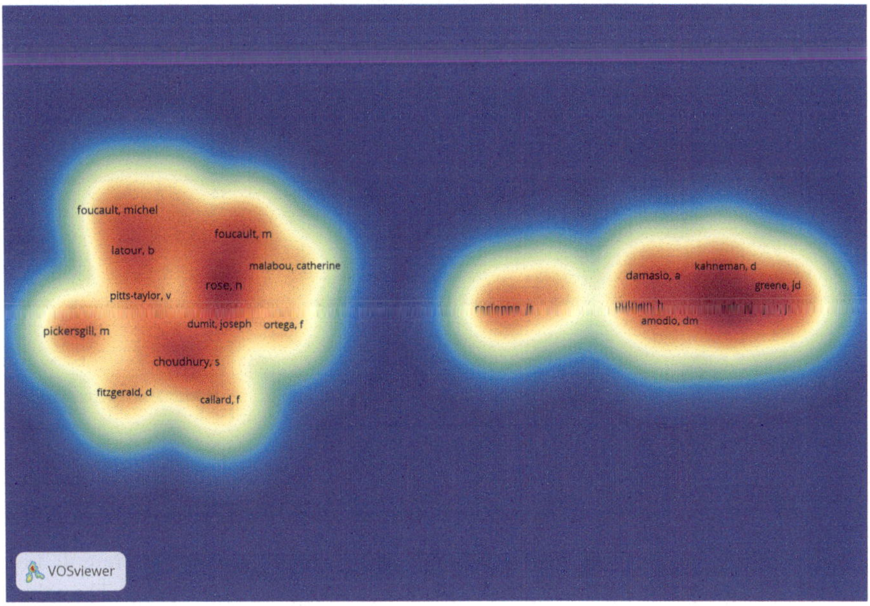

Fig. 4 Density map of the authors' co-citation analysis. *Source*: Authors based on VOS Viewer results

groups of authors who cite each other. The colour of the density indicates the relevance and the number of citations obtained. Consequently, the most frequently cited authors are indicated in red within the clusters, whereas those authors who appear in orange, yellow, or who are not directly linked to a cluster with a high density of authors are cited to a lesser extent.

Two clusters converge in the left zone, marked by the influence of Rose, and Foucault, as well as Choudhury. This evidences the importance of biopolitics and theories of the politics of life itself, for the creation of the concept, as well as its development within the more critical version. The third cluster, located on the right side of the image, is marked by the importance of Damasio, Cacioppo, and Amodio. This cluster focuses more on the study of emotions and their influence on the decisions of citizens and their behaviour, while generating new ways of doing and understanding politics. Therefore, this cluster, represents the most practical application.

Bibliographic Coupling

In order to understand the main journals that have published the most relevant papers related to neuroscience and policy, the present bibliometric analysis develops and calculates the so-called bibliographic source linkage. This type of analysis

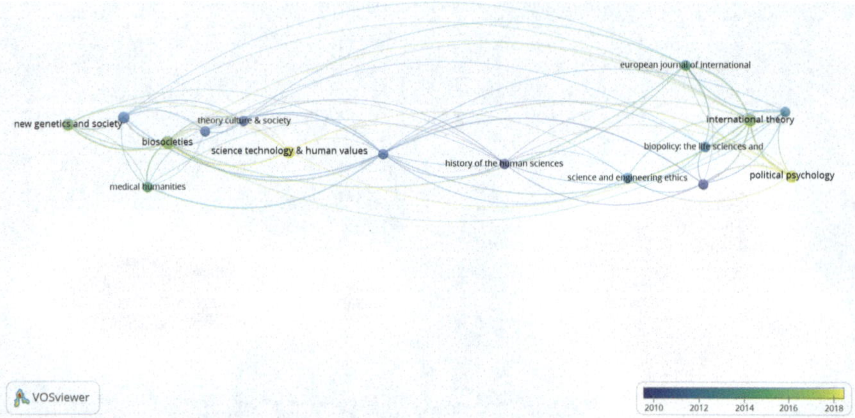

Fig. 5 Bibliographic matching of sources by average year of publication. *Source*: Authors based on VOS Viewer results

aims to identify the most relevant papers in terms of citations and link strength. For the correct calculation of this analysis, the following filters are applied. The minimum number of documents per journal is set at a minimum of 2 points, and the minimum number of citations per source is set at 3. Out of a total of 251 journals in the database, 25 meet this criterion. From the total of 26 journals appearing in the database, 16 journals were selected for visual representation in Fig. 5.

All the journals have links with each other, so Fig. 5 shows a total of 16 journals directly related to the objectives of the study. In addition, the results identified two clusters with a total of 73 links between them, with a total link strength of 291 points. Table 4 presents the journals with the metrics and indicators obtained for each of them.

Amongst the results obtained; the following stand out. In terms of link strength, three journals stand out: Biosocieties (link strength of 89.00), Subjectivity (link strength of 88.00), and International Theory (link strength of 52.00). These three journals are the top three in terms of relevance to neuroscience in its political application. Of the remaining results, Political Psychology, with 18 citations but a linking strength of 49.00 and Political Research Quarterly, with a total of 38 citations and a link strength of 46.00, also stand out. The remaining journals identified and presented in Table 4 show more moderate results in terms of impact compared to the other cited results.

In order to understand the scientific production in this field of research in recent years, an analysis of the bibliographic links between sources by average year of publication is also presented. As can be seen in Fig. 5; two clusters are identified in which the positions of the journals and the links between them can be seen. In relation to the time horizon analysed, blue represents the year 2010 as the first year represented as relevant in the neuron map. Then, the colour palette changes successively until it reaches yellow, and in this projection, dark blue represents 2012, light blue 2014, green 2016, light green 2018, and yellow represents 2020.

Table 4 Bibliographic coupling of sources

Source	Documents	Quotations	Link strength
Biosocieties	4	69	89.00
Subjectivity	2	41	88.00
International Theory	4	76	79.00
Political Psychology	3	18	49.00
Political Research Quarterly	2	38	46.00
International Studies Perspectives	2	19	42.00
Theory Culture Society	2	205	39.00
Social studies of science	3	92	36.00
Biopolicy: the life science and public policy	2	5	35.00
European Journal of International Relations	2	257	35.00
New genetics and society	3	73	35.00
Medical humanities	2	93	33.00
Science and engineering ethics	2	15	18.00
Science technology and human values	3	19	18.00

Source: Authors based on VOS Viewer results

It can therefore be concluded that the years 2010 to 2020 are the most relevant, scientifically speaking, for neuroscience and how it relates to politics. In this sense, it is interesting to note how, in the years of greatest scientific production, the subject evolved from a biological perspective towards an interest in its relationship with international relations and political psychology (see Fig. 5).

Co-occurrence of Author Keywords

Continuing with the development of the bibliometric analysis, the results related to the calculation and development of the co-occurrence analysis of authors' keywords are presented below. In this way, all the keywords used by the authors in their academic contributions appearing in the database are taken into account with regard to the searches carried out in the Neuroscience related to Politics database.

The author keyword co-occurrence analysis is developed to identify key concepts, types of use/areas of policy development, and the interdisciplinary relationship of related sciences in their development. We therefore link these representations to the objectives and research questions proposed in this study. Table 5 shows the keywords selected as the most relevant in terms of their linkage to the objectives of this research. Regarding the requirements for the publications to be included in this analysis, a minimum number of occurrences of these keywords of 6 is proposed. From the total of 1177 keywords found, 38 were obtained that met these requirements, which were considered valid in this study. These were studied and linked to the research objectives and finally 20 keywords were selected to represent the research objectives (see Table 5).

Table 5 Co-occurrence of author keywords

Key words	Occurrences	Total bond strength
Neuroscience	92	151.00
Politics	58	119.00
Science	33	76.00
Brain	28	61.00
Biology	9	31.00
Psychology	13	30.00
Education	12	29.00
Culture	10	26.00
Policy	9	25.00
Biopolitics	11	22.00
Self	7	22.00
Life	7	21.00
Power	6	20.00
Stress	8	20.00
Emotions	10	19.00
Neurobiology	11	18.00
Sociology	6	18.00
Empathy	6	15.00
Neuropolitics	6	13.00
Decision-making	7	13.00

Source: Authors based on VOS Viewer results

Presentation from the data obtained in Table 5 provides important information on the transdisciplinarity in applying neuroscience to politics. We can see how biology, biopolitics, psychology, neurobiology, and sociology are involved in its development. In addition, and as we will detail in Fig. 7, it is also relevant to see what terms are related to the analysis of citizen decision-making and reinterpret the new politics. Finally, Fig. 8, illustrates the area in which there is currently a greater number of policies being developed under this consideration.

Based on these observations and in order to correctly visualize the relationships between the keywords that will allow us to identify the detailed concepts, we will now present a neural network with the main connections between the keywords identified as most relevant. The number of links identified was 157 with a total link strength of 432 points. On average, 4 clusters are presented, consisting of 26 variables in the form of keywords.

In addition, to link the research findings to the identification of key concepts to investigate citizens' decision-making, we present the following figure. We can see that neurobiology, cognitive neuroscience, neuropolitics, and psychology are key to the creation of knowledge. We also highlight the predominance of fMRI as the most preferred technique for measuring brain activity. On the other hand, we show the importance of the study of emotions in decision-making, to understand both the behaviour of citizens and for improving the effectiveness of public policies.

In terms of policymaking, note how "education" has emerged as the most relevant concept, especially in recent years.

Discussion and Agenda for Future Research

To the best of our knowledge, this study represents a comprehensive and systematic literature review of the application of neuroscience in governmental policies, the first of its kind. The completion of this systematic literature review (SLR) was crucial for a number of reasons. First, as highlighted in the introduction, authors such as Edelman (2006) have called for conceptual and methodological reflection on working in this new stage, while others such as Seymour and Vlaev (2012) have argued that there is a paucity of evidence to suggest that neuroscience is being utilized in contemporary politics. This SLR, has allowed us to address this issue in a comprehensive manner. In the analyses presented, we offer a compilation of different thematic areas in which specific behaviour-based policies have been implemented (Table 1). Moreover, we present another table that displays potential areas for successful policy implementation (see Table 6) and propose new avenues for research to promote their development (see Table 7). In this way, the present study offers a comprehensive view of the subject area, providing researchers and professionals dedicated to the topic with a more organized understanding of concepts, application pathways, opportunities, and new challenges.

Second, by demonstrating the substantial growth that this field has experienced over the past decade (see Fig. 1), this SLR has facilitated an understanding of the evolution of research streams, which have been shaped by the contributions of its authors (see Table 3 and Fig. 2). One set of the studies adopts a critical stance (Choudhury & Slaby, 2016; Rose, 2009; Rose & Abi-Rached, 2013), whereas another emphasizes practical applications, with a focus on brain studies and the role of emotion in decision-making (Damasio, 1994) (see Fig. 4). We believe that our study is beneficial in this regard, as it not only identifies the potential risks associated to these techniques but also offers a broad conceptual framework for understanding and promoting their development, while also taking into account the necessary ethical perspective. In this regard, as various authors have asserted, we believe that the commitment of policy strategists to neuroethics and critical neuroscience is for the utmost importance for this research to be conducted in an ethical manner and with the necessary scientific rigour to continue advancing in the field (Pykett, 2011; Fitzgerald & Callard, 2015).

Third, the results provided in the co-occurrence of keywords also offer intriguing insights for our study (see Table 5). It can be observed that the development of this research field has its origins in various disciplinary areas, including biology, biopolitics, psychology, amongst others (see Fig. 6), furthermore the study of citizen decision-making, which is approached from a diverse array of perspectives, including neurobiology, cognitive science, neuroscience, politics, and neuropolitics (see Fig. 7). This observation is compelling for several reasons. First, this invites a transdisciplinary approach to developing this field of study, converging with the advice provided by Rose (2013). Second, it corroborates the findings of the theoretical framework, which indicated that the most efficacious policies for behavioural change had addressed this from a relational perspective involving various professionals and knowledge domains (Pykett, 2011). Accordingly, in our proposal for

Table 6 Relationship of new areas to generate soft paternalism policies

Area	Problem	Development
Public information communication policies	• Citizens need to be well informed in democratic environments to support their vote, together with the decline in the attention span and retention levels amongst the new generation of digital natives, and the danger of the fake news	• Presentation of political information through the context of humour to improve attention and long-term retention of information (see Young, 2014; Hardy et al., 2014; Kim & Vishak, 2008; Shohamy & Adcock, 2010), increase the likelihood of information sharing amongst peers and improve recall of political information (see Coronel et al., 2021), and increase its reach to a more generalist audience (see Young, 2014) • Generation of trust in information through the use of visual symbols that convey truthfulness (Gaozhao, 2021)
International relations	• Overcoming animosities between regions historically at odds with each other • Acceptance of democratic values in societies inherited from anti-democratic regimes. • Overthrow of authoritarian regimes	• Overcoming fear and established prejudices by fostering the degree of cooperation and empathy between individuals from formerly warring nations (see Crawford, 2009). • Encouraging conscious deliberation to break with the logic of habit (see Wegner & Bargh, 1998). Influencing individuals less rooted in social structures such as children, grandparents and those who have more contacts with other cultures (see Hopf, 2010). • Strategies for overcoming fear and generating resistance networks through hope and humour as cohesive elements of the population (see Helmy & Frerichs, 2013)
Microeconomic policies	• Improve the present and future savings capacity of the population	• Through knowledge of bounded rationality theories and self-control problems (Benartzi & Thaler, 2004) change informed choice by automatic enrolment in pension plans or other policies aimed at encouraging savings (Pykett, 2011). To consider, the personalization-privacy paradox currently facing various microeconomic tools in their interaction with the user (see Alalwan et al., 2023)
Environmental policies	• Need to implement low-emission policies in European cities to apply the new EU regulatory framework	• Generation of relational measures between consumers, industry, companies and institutions to generate a change in the habits of the population (study state policies against obesity highlighted in this article)
Public health promotion and mental health protection policies	• Increase in obesity and sedentary habits in Western societies. Increase in problems related to mental health	• Development of policies to promote physical activity amongst the population through the digitalization of sports facilities. Introduction of gamification in the access applications to these facilities. Positive implications for both public managers and citizens, through increased sporting activity and happiness of the population (see Seligman, 2019)

Source: Authors

Table 7 Research directions and open research questions

Research directions	Research questions
Public information communication policies	• Could political information delivered in the form of humorous content increase the population's knowledge of public affairs? • How does the sustained use of humour in the dissemination of political information impact public perception, civic engagement, and the retention of information over time? • How does fake news affect citizens' feelings of acceptance/rejection of their governments? • Do government fact-checkers increase people's trust in their governments? • Can trust in institutions be enhanced through the use of these verification and transparency techniques?
International relations	• Is it possible to improve the level of empathy between citizens of opposing nations by creating coexistence and cooperation projects? • Through the creation of projects based on conscious deliberation, could we overcome prejudices between members of opposing regions? • Could collaborative projects improve empathy between citizens of opposing nations? • Could initiatives based on conscious deliberation help to overcome prejudices between members of conflicting regions? • Could hope for a common future increase the desire for cooperation between members of opposing regions?
Microeconomic policies	• How do default decisions within financial policies, such as automatic enrolment in pension plans or other savings schemes, affect individuals' saving behaviours? • How do different financial incentives, bonuses, or reward programmes impact individuals' decisions to save? • How does the use of new financial technologies, such as mobile savings apps, automated investment platforms (robo-advisors), cryptocurrencies, or other innovative financial instruments, affect individuals' saving habits and economic decision-making? • How do psychological and social factors, including social norms, emotions, peer influence and risk perception, shape decisions about saving and personal financial management? • Financial education and economic decision-making: What is the impact of financial education programmes on improving individuals' economic and savings decisions?
Environmental policies	• How can the use of specific visual images, graphics, or symbols influence the adoption of sustainable and environmentally friendly behaviours by citizens? • To what extent can gamification strategies applied to environmental programmes encourage citizen participation and promote environmentally beneficial actions? • What types of incentives are most effective in fostering environmentally friendly behaviour? How can these measures be designed to maximize their impact without generating resistance or unintended effects? • How does the design and layout of the physical environment (public spaces, arrangement of recycling bins, accessibility to green transportation) influence individuals' environmental behaviours?

(continued)

Table 7 (continued)

Research directions	Research questions
Policies to promote public health and protect mental health	• Could the digitalization of sports facilities increase the number of people exercising? • How does the digitalization of health-related information and services influence people's behaviour change towards healthier habits? • How could the integration of gamification into health promotion applications and programmes increase user engagement and participation? • What specific relational intervention strategies could promote a positive behaviour change towards physical activity in specific groups, such as youth, older adults, or people with health conditions?

Source: Authors

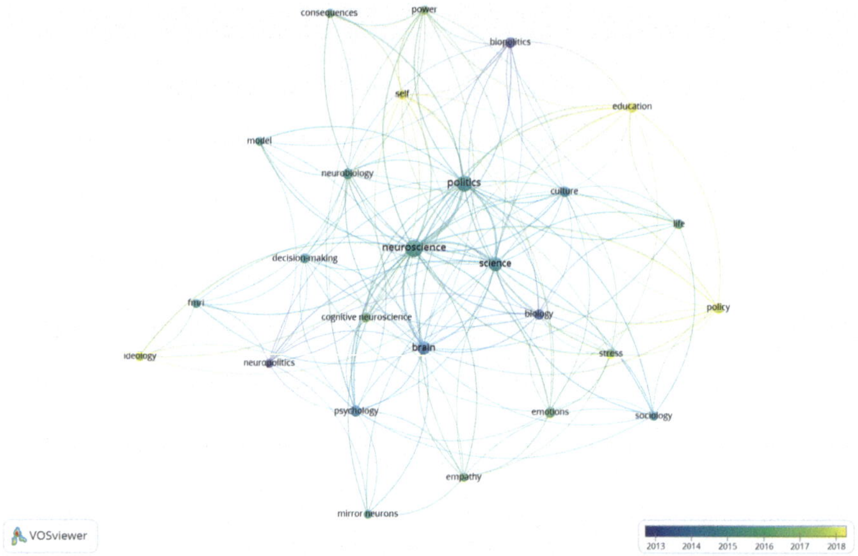

Fig. 6 Co-occurrence of author keywords by average year of publication. *Source*: Authors based on VOS Viewer results

future areas and issues to address with this knowledge (see Tables 6 and 7), we advise that these be approached from a relational dynamic perspective, involving both areas and professionals.

Fourth, it is our contention that this study is relevant in understanding how the latest scientific contributions relate to each other in this field and how they are generating new ways of understanding politics and power. As depicted by the neural network generated by keyword connections (see Fig. 5), the study of emotions and citizens' decision-making processes, in conjunction with analysis by a diverse range of scientists from various disciplines, pave the way for new insights into power relations. Similarly, it can be posited that this interplay influences the formulation of policies and, consequently, the generation of new forms of governance. This result corroborates the findings of prior studies conducted by Damasio (1994) and Ledoux

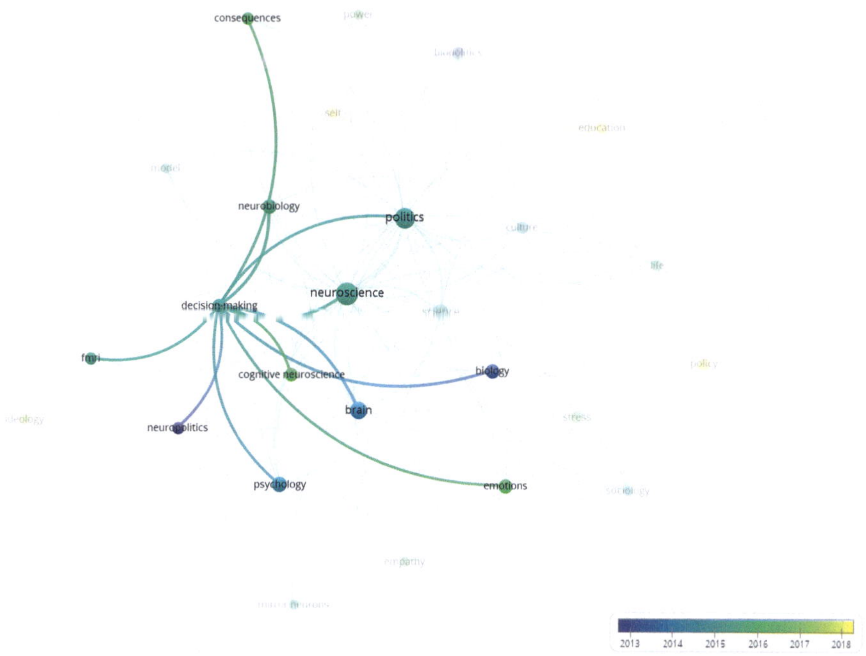

Fig. 7 Decision-making highlighted in author's keyword co-occurrence. *Source*: Authors based on VOS Viewer results

(1998), which underscored the pivotal role of emotions in an individual's decision-making process. When viewed in conjunction with findings in brain plasticity (Malabou, 2008), this suggest that a citizen can make irrational decisions but with behaviour susceptible to change. It is our contention that these relationships provide a foundation for new researchers to comprehend how neuroscience is transforming the manner in which politics are conducted and how it is influencing the relationship with citizens. Finally, before outlining the areas in which these studies could potentially yield optimal results, it is important to highlight possible risks associated with the subject matter.

In our view, under no circumstances should this knowledge lead to a belief in biological determinism, which undermines the notion of individual free will. This is a pivotal element of our democratic systems. The assumption of automaton-like individuals would lead us to a very bleak future (Klein, 2009). Similarly, as demonstrated throughout the study, the belief in biological determinism can have a profoundly adverse impact on the structures of our own penal and educational systems, as well as on the individuals or governments that might cling to it in order to evade their responsibility. Moreover, in order to ascertain the efficacy of these approaches, it is essential to conduct a comprehensive examination of the cognitive biases underlying the acceptance of certain dynamics, this topic was extensively explored by various authors (Oschinsky et al., 2021). Lastly, excessive neuroreductionism, which is not supported by the scientific community, could result in the rejection of further research in this area, leaving the field open to the development of culturally consumable products.

With the aim of compiling knowledge and following the work of Pykett (2011), who highlighted areas where libertarian or soft paternalistic policies could be well developed, this study has provided a set of practical examples organized around those categories (see Table 1). Nevertheless, our research has identified new areas where the application of this knowledge could have positive consequences for the population. Therefore, and with the aim of continuing to promote knowledge generation, we propose a table of new policy areas where we have identified several issues where interdisciplinary working groups, offering relational solutions, could provide very effective support to public policies developers.

Having identified the areas susceptible to introducing these techniques to effect behavioural change amongst citizens, we take as reference the article by Mariani et al. (2023), for the introduction of new lines of research, as set out *in Table 7*. Similarly, building on the opportunities presented by SLR (Paul et al., 2021), we anticipate that in the near future, they may assist researchers in avoiding duplications and delving into the study of diverse areas and the uncertainties they pose.

It is our contention that the development of apps could be an efficacious tool for achieving direct contact with citizens and for promoting the desired behavioural changes. The use of applications has been demonstrated to increase motivation, the desire to set goals, confidence, and control, thereby leading to a perceived change in behaviour (Crookston et al., 2017). Consequently, it would be beneficial to study the characteristics that these governmental apps require in order to achieve acceptance and attain the desired effects.

Theoretical Implications

The objective of this chapter is to elucidate the significant theoretical implications of the growing utilization of neuroscience in public governance. These implications have a profound impact on a multitude of academic disciplines and practical areas (see Table 1). In light of the above, this chapter makes several theoretical contributions.

First, at the forefront of this transformation is the redefinition of citizenship (Rose, 2009; Vidal, 2009; Rose & Abi-Rached, 2013). This perspective posits that citizens are beings whose conduct and decision-making processes are intricately linked with an understanding of their cognitive and affective mechanisms. Such a shift in perspective gives rise to a number of fundamental questions regarding the autonomy and accountability of citizens within a governance system influenced by neuroscience. It also serves to challenge the long-held notions of citizenship and individual autonomy.

Second, the application of neuroscience to governance necessitates a re-evaluation of traditional political and social theories. The infusion of neuroscience introduces novel paradigms of power and control, whereby brain knowledge becomes a pivotal instrument in shaping political landscapes and influencing citizens' behaviours and decisions (Pykett, 2011; Dąbrosz-Drewnowska, 2021). This transition requires a reassessment of decision-making models, as the significant role of emotions and subconscious factors in political choices becomes increasingly evident, challenging the long-standing dominance of rationalist models (Damasio, 1994; LeDoux, 1998; Westen, 2008).

Third, the progression of political and governance methodologies through the lens of neuroscience paves the way for innovative approaches to policy development (Pykett, 2011). This strategy pledges more effective and targeted solutions to a range of social dilemmas, revolutionizing government strategies in areas such as education, public health, and safety (Pykett, 2016). The advent of "soft paternalism" and related methodologies heralds a paradigm shift in governance understanding and practice, endorsing a more interventionist and behaviourally oriented approach within public administration (Thaler & Sunstein, 2003; Thaler & Sunstein, 2008). This evolution represents a significant departure from traditional governance models, with the objective of optimizing citizen behaviour as a means to enhancing individual and collective well-being.

Finally, the integration of neuroscience into policy formulation gives rise to a multitude of intricate ethical considerations. At the core of these concerns lies the delicate balance between guiding citizens towards beneficial decisions and the potential infringement upon individual liberty (Pykett, 2015), as well as the risks posed by neuroreductionism to the formation of our future democracies (Klein, 2007). Consequently, the incorporation of neuroscience into public governance signifies a transformative framework that redefines our comprehension of citizenship, political theories of power and control, and presents novel avenues for the development of innovative policies. However, this integration also gives rise to ethical considerations that cannot be overlooked.

Practical Implications

The practical implications of integrating neuroscience into the development of government policies are multifaceted and far-reaching. This study addresses a series of practical considerations that must be taken into account when applying these policies. It then highlights areas where they may find greater implementation, and finally proposes future tools to promote their development.

First, this study demonstrates the potential of neuroscience, particularly cognitive neuroscience, to inform and guide the creation of policies in governments seeking to promote behavioural change in the population. As evidenced throughout the study, the successful implementation of these policies will depend on the collaboration of experts from a range of disciplines, including biology, sociology, psychology, and political science (see the transdisciplinarity reflected in Table 5, Fig. 6). This approach should aim for a holistic and transdisciplinary understanding of the complexity of the human brain and its capacity to modify and optimize itself in relation to the environment (Malabou, 2008; Papadopoulos, 2011; Youdell et al., 2017). It is therefore imperative that the practical application of these policies should transcend the limitations of neuroreductionist theories and take into account both internal cognitive processes and external factors (such as market dynamics, regulatory frameworks, and environmental characteristics) that guide citizen behaviour in its interaction with the surrounding environment (Pitts-Taylor, 2010).

Second, the study identifies a series of themes where these policies could have the greatest impact due to the benefits they would bring to citizens within our liberal democratic systems, thus providing insight into the most effective areas for development. Consequently, the formulation of policies guided by neuroscience can yield favourable outcomes within the context of public information and communication policies (see Coronel et al., 2021). This approach could assist governments in circumventing the perils of fake news and in fostering more informed citizenry overcoming the consequences of media saturation. By drawing on insights from neuroscience, governments could develop communication strategies that take into account factors such as the public's attention capacity or tools to stimulate their memory (see Young, 2014; Hardy et al., 2014; Kim & Vishak, 2008; Shohamy & Adcock, 2010). Such strategies have the potential to enhance the manner in which information is processed and understood by citizens, thereby improving governmental transparency, citizen participation, and the public's understanding of policies. Similarly, as evidenced by the findings presented in Table 4 and Fig. 5, there is a notable interest in the development of this topic within the field of international relations. In this field, the application of neuroscience can facilitate a deeper understanding of the dynamics between different groups and countries, from the cognitive perspective of the individual. Consequently, neuroscience may assist to overcome deep-rooted mental structures that give rise to fears and prejudices within the population which in turn contribute to the perpetuation of conflicts (see Wegner & Bargh, 1998; Hopf, 2010). Likewise, neuroscience can help in the formulation of action plans aimed at fostering trust and empathy amongst opposed individuals (see Crawford, 2009). This understanding has the potential to inform more effective diplomatic strategies and international cooperation, thereby enhancing conflict resolution capabilities. Other areas where these applications would be successful include microeconomics, where citizens could be guided to make successful decisions in the realm of savings and financial health (see Benartzi & Thaler, 2004; Pykett, 2011); environmental policies, where the application of these transdisciplinary tactics could overcome the solely coercive approach and provoke a true behavioural change in the population (see Farrugia & Fraser, 2017), or health where knowledge of the external factors that mark individual behaviour could improve the success of prevention policies (see Her Majesty's Government, 2016).

Third, we believe that the current development of mobile applications can be a positive tool for governments seeking to bring about behavioural change, as they enable a direct relationship with the citizen. In order to achieve this, it is deemed crucial to identify the factors that need to be taken into account in order to produce a real change in citizen behaviour. In this sense, we encourage the review of various studies to determine how the use of ChatGPT or other artificial intelligence applications improves the quality of apps in other domains within the academic context (Saura & Debasa, 2022; Dwivedi et al., 2023). In the same vein, we encourage the development of these applications in line with new models of technology acceptance that are currently being explored for the advancement of e-government and persuasive technologies (see (Dwivedi et al., 2017; Oyibo & Vassileva, 2020).

Similarly, we urge scholars and policymakers to look at other virtual environments where citizens are already engaged, and where researches are currently underway to understand the basis of their behaviour, including the metaverse and its ability to induce behavioural change in new social interaction experiences outside of the real world (see Dwivedi et al., 2012, 2022; Mishra et al., 2023).

Finally, the application of neuroscience in public governance offers significant opportunities to improve policy effectiveness and address critical societal challenges. However, as we have sought to highlight throughout this study, the importance of considering ethical and social implications in its implementation cannot be overstated.

Conclusions

This study carried out a bibliometric analysis using the VOS Viewer on a data set consisting of published scientific papers indexed in the WoS database. As a result of this approach, three different analyses were carried out: co-citation of authors and references, bibliographic linkage, and co-occurrence of keywords. These have been addressed and investigated according to the questions posed. In relation to the first research question (What are the main contributions and findings of neuroscience research in the study of citizen behaviour?), according to the results obtained from the co-citation of references and authors (Table 3, Fig. 3), the phenomenon of brain plasticity, studies demonstrating the importance of emotions in decision-making, and their development from a relational and transdisciplinary perspective have been key. While the former opens the door to the citizen's capacity for optimization, the latter points to his or her unreflective nature, generating new ways of understanding power and exercising politics.

Regarding the second research question: (How do these findings influence the new shape of public governance?) as shown by the neural network generated by the keyword connections (see Fig. 4), emotions, the study of citizens' decision-making, coupled with the analysis of a wide variety of scholars from different fields, marks new paths in power relations. In the same way, it also influences the realization of their policies and thus the generation of new forms of governance. Returning to the phenomena described in RQ1, they generate new forms of governance by understanding their unreflective nature and the possibility of developing certain policies that can optimize their behaviour.

With regard to the third research question (What are the areas of governance where the main developments are taking place and what practical examples can we cite?), through our literature review, we have identified education as the area where these techniques have attracted the most interest in policymaking, especially in recent years (see Fig. 8). Similarly, it is interesting to note how in the years of higher

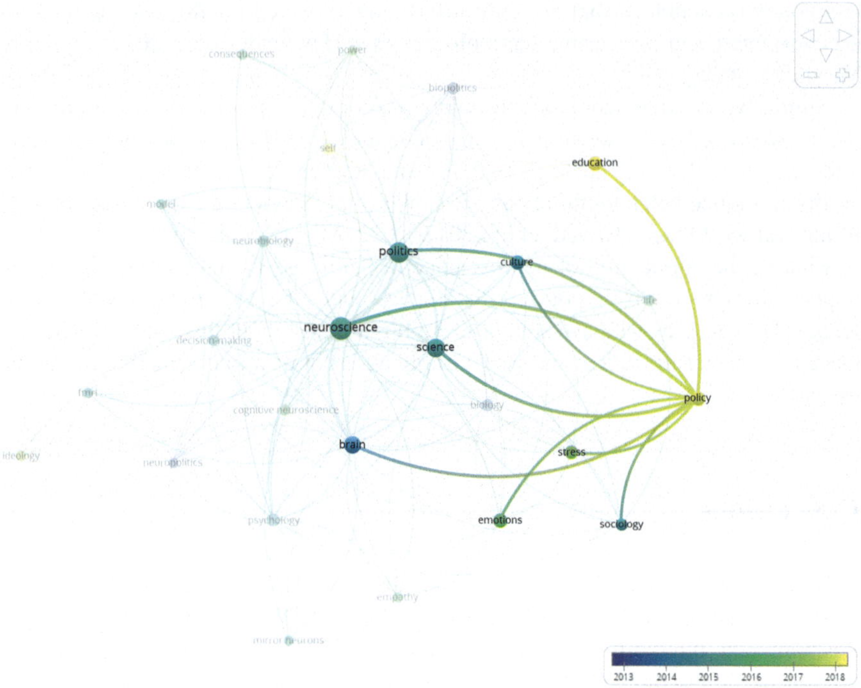

Fig. 8 Policy highlighted in author's keyword co-occurrence. *Source*: Authors based on VOS Viewer results

scientific production (2010–2020), further propelled by state funding (USA, EU), the thematic evolution of the study has shifted from a biological perspective to an interest in the relationship between neuroscience, international relations, and political psychology (see Fig. 5).

Finally, in relation to the fourth research question (What future research directions are suggested by current findings in the neuroscience of citizen behaviour and their implications on governance and policymaking?), the study cites a number of examples of current government actions and policies based on behaviour change (see Table 1), and then identifies a number of new areas in which the generation of soft paternalism policies could be successful, based on the premises for their development (see Table 6). Lastly, it offers a new series of future lines of research (see Table 7) to address social issues such as misinformation, conflict resolution between opposing communities, the improvement of individual economic decisions, or the success of preventive health policies.

Thus, we believe that the creation of successful policies through behavioural knowledge holds great promise for governments honestly committed to improving the welfare of their citizens. It will be the responsibility of a vigilant scientific community to ensure that these are used in a way that respects the rights and freedoms of individuals and of experts committed to generating ethical, interdisciplinary, and practical knowledge to achieve their proper development.

References

Adli, M., & Schöndorf, J. (2020). Macht uns die Stadt krank? Wirkung von Stadtstress auf Emotionen, Verhalten und psychische Gesundheit. *Bundesgesundheitsblatt - Gesundheitsforschung - Gesundheitsschutz, 63*(8), 979–986. https://doi.org/10.1007/s00103-020-03185-w

Alalwan, A. A., Baabdullah, A. M., Al-Debei, M. M., Raman, R., Alhitmi, H. K., Abu-ElSamen, A. A., & Dwivedi, Y. K. (2023). Fintech and contactless payment: Help or hindrance? The role of invasion of privacy and information disclosure. *International Journal of Bank Marketing, 42*(1), 66–93. https://doi.org/10.1108/ijbm-08-2022-0339

Ali, O., Murray, P. A., Momin, M., Dwivedi, Y. K., & Malik, F. T. (2024). The effects of artificial intelligence applications in educational settings: Challenges and strategies. *Technological Forecasting and Social Change, 199*, 123076. https://doi.org/10.1016/j.techfore.2023.123076

Aoki, N. (2020). An experimental study of public trust in AI chatbots in the public sector. *Government Information Quarterly, 37*(4), 101490. https://doi.org/10.1016/j.giq.2020.101490

Baratta, A., Brandner, A., Plasil, S., Rice, R., & Farris, S. (2022). Advancements in genomic and behavioural neuroscience analysis for the study of normal and pathological brain function. *Frontiers in Molecular Neuroscience, 15*. https://doi.org/10.3389/fnmol.2022.905328

Beck-Gernsheim, E. (2002). *Reinventing the family: In search of new lifestyles*. Polity Press.

Benartzi, S., & Thaler, R. (2004). Save more tomorrow: Using behavioural economics to increase employee saving. *Journal of Political Economy, 112*(1), 164–187.

Brownell, K. D., & Warner, K. E. (2009). The perils of ignoring history: big tobacco played dirty and millions died. How similar is big food? *Milbank Quarterly, 87*(1), 259–294. https://doi.org/10.1111/j.1468-0009.2009.00555.x

Callard, F., & Fitzgerald, D. (2015). Rethinking interdisciplinarity across the social sciences and neurosciences. En *Palgrave Macmillan UK eBooks*. https://doi.org/10.1057/9781137407962

Choudhury, S., Nagel, S. K., & Slaby, J. (2009). Critical neuroscience: Linking neuroscience and society through critical practice. *BioSocieties, 4*(1), 61–77. https://doi.org/10.1017/s1745855209006437

Choudhury, S., & Slaby, J. (2016). *Critical neuroscience: A handbook of the social and cultural contexts of neuroscience*. John Wiley & Sons.

Cohen-Cline, H., Turkheimer, E., & Duncan, G. E. (2015). Access to green space, physical activityandmental health: a twin study. *Journal of Epidemiology Community Health, 69*, 523–529.

Coronel, J. C., O'Donnell, M. B., Pandey, P., Delli Carpini, M. X., & Falk, E. B. (2021). Political humor, sharing, and remembering: insights from neuroimaging. *Journal of Communication, 71*(1), 129–161. https://doi.org/10.1093/joc/jqaa041

Corrales-Garay, D., Ortiz-de-Urbina-Criado, M., & Mora-Valentín, E. (2019). Knowledge areas, themes and future research on open data: A co-word analysis. *Government Information Quarterly, 36*(1), 77–87. https://doi.org/10.1016/j.giq.2018.10.008

Crawford, N. C. (2009). Human nature and world politics: Rethinking 'Man'. *International Relations, 23*(2), 271–288. https://doi.org/10.1177/0047117809104639

Cromby, J., Newton, T., & Williams, S. (2011). Special Issue: Subjectivity and neuroscience. *Subjectivity, 4*(3), 215–365.

Crookston, B., West, J., Hall, P., Dahle, K., Heaton, T., Beck, R., & Muralidharan, C. (2017). Mental and emotional self-help technology apps: Cross-sectional study of theory, technology, and mental health behaviors. *JMIR Mental Health, 4*. https://doi.org/10.2196/mental.7262

Dąbrosz-Drewnowska, P. (2021). Behavioural aspects of decision-making and its application in Poland illustrated by the example of the public institutions. *Procedia Computer Science, 192*, 4503–4512. https://doi.org/10.1016/j.procs.2021.09.228

Damasio, A. (1994). *El error de Descartes* (1.a ed.). Ediciones Culturales Paidos S. A. De C. V.

Damasio, A. R. (2005). *Descartes' Error: Emotion, Reason, and the Human Brain*. Penguin.

De Neve, J., Diener, E., Tay, L., & Xuereb, C. (2013). The objective benefits of subjective well-being. *SSRN Electronic Journal*. https://papers.ssrn.com/sol3/Delivery.cfm/SSRN_ID2306651_code944452.pdf?abstractid=2306651

Diener, E., & Chan, M. Y. (2011). Happy people live longer: Subjective well-being contributes to health and longevity. *Applied Psychology: Health and Well-being, 3*(1), 1–43. https://doi.org/10.1111/j.1758-0854.2010.01045.x

Diener, E., Lucas, R. E., & Oishi, S. (2017). Advances and open questions in the science of subjective well-being. *Collabra Psychology, 4*(1). https://doi.org/10.1525/collabra.115

Ding, X., & Yang, Z. (2020). Knowledge mapping of platform research: a visual analysis using VOSviewer and CiteSpace. *Electronic Commerce Research*, 1–23.

Dressing, H., Sartorius, A., & Meyer-Lindenberg, A. (2008). Implications of MRI and genetics for the law and the routine practice of forensic psychiatry. *Neurocase, 14*(1), 7–14. https://doi.org/10.1080/13554790801992800

Dumit, J. (2004). *Picturing Personhood: brain scans and biomedical identity*. https://www.thelancet.com/pdfs/journals/laneur/PIIS1474-4422(04)00828-2.pdf

Dwivedi, Y. K., Hughes, D. L., Coombs, C., Constantiou, I. D., Duan, Y., Edwards, J. S., Gupta, B., Lal, B., Misra, S. K., Prashant, P., Raman, R., Rana, N. P., Sharma, S. K., & Upadhyay, N. (2020). Impact of COVID-19 pandemic on information management research and practice: Transforming education, work and life. *International Journal of Information Management, 55*, 102211. https://doi.org/10.1016/j.ijinfomgt.2020.102211

Dwivedi, Y. K., Hughes, L., Baabdullah, A. M., Ribeiro-Navarrete, S., Giannakis, M., Al-Debei, M. M., Dennehy, D., Metri, B. A., Buhalis, D., Cheung, C. M. K., Conboy, K., Doyle, R., Dubey, R., Dutot, V., Felix, R., Goyal, D., Gustafsson, A., Hinsch, C., Jebabli, I., et al. (2022). Metaverse beyond the hype: Multidisciplinary perspectives on emerging challenges, opportunities, and agenda for research, practice and policy. *International Journal of Information Management, 66*, 102542. https://doi.org/10.1016/j.ijinfomgt.2022.102542

Dwivedi, Y. K., Pandey, N., Currie, W. L., & Micu, A. (2023). Leveraging ChatGPT and other generative artificial intelligence (AI)-based applications in the hospitality and tourism industry: practices, challenges and research agenda. *International Journal of Contemporary Hospitality Management, 36*(1), 1–12. https://doi.org/10.1108/ijchm-05-2023-0686

Dwivedi, Y. K., Rana, N. P., Janssen, M., Lal, B., Williams, M. D., & Clement, M. (2017). An empirical validation of a unified model of electronic government adoption (UMEGA). *Government Information Quarterly, 34*(2), 211–230. https://doi.org/10.1016/j.giq.2017.03.001

Dwivedi, Y. K., Weerakkody, V., & Janssen, M. (2012). Moving towards maturity. *ACM Sigmis Database, 42*(4), 11–22. https://doi.org/10.1145/2096140.2096142

Eastman, N., & Campbell, C. (2006). Neuroscience and legal determination of criminal responsibility. *Nature Reviews Neuroscience, 7*(4), 311–318. https://doi.org/10.1038/nrn1887

Edelman, G. M. (2006). *Second nature: Brain science and human knowledge*. https://ci.nii.ac.jp/ncid/BA83323383

Engemann, K., Pedersen, C. B., Arge, L., Tsirogiannis, C., Mortensen, P. B., & Svenning, J. C. (2019). Residential green space in childhood is associated with lower risk of psychiatric disorders from adolescence into adulthood. *Proceedings of the National Academy of Sciences of the United States of America, 116*, 5188–5193.

Farrugia, A., & Fraser, S. (2017). Young brains at risk: Co-constituting youth and addiction in neuroscience-informed Australian drug education. *BioSocieties, 12*(4), 588–610. https://doi.org/10.1057/s41292-017-0047-2

Fitzgerald, D., & Callard, F. (2015). Social science and neuroscience beyond interdisciplinarity: Experimental entanglements. *Theory, Culture & Society, 32*(1), 3–32. https://doi.org/10.1177/0263276414537319

Foucault, M. (2008). *El nacimiento de la biopolítica*. Palgrave Macmillan.

Gaozhao, D. (2021). Flagging fake news on social media: An experimental study of media consumers' identification of fake news. *Government Information Quarterly, 38*(3), 101591. https://doi.org/10.1016/j.giq.2021.101591

Gascon, M., Triguero-Mas, M., Martínez, D. R., Dadvand, P., Rojas-Rueda, D., Plasència, A., & Nieuwenhuijsen, M. J. (2016). Residential green spaces and mortality: A systematic review. *Environment International, 86*, 60–67. https://doi.org/10.1016/j.envint.2015.10.013

González-Padilla, P., Navalpotro, F. D., & Saura, J. R. (2024). Managing entrepreneurs' behavior personalitics in digital environments: A review. *International Entrepreneurship and Management Journal, 20*, 89–113. https://doi.org/10.1007/s11365-022-00823-4

Gorraiz, J., & Schloegl, C. (2008). A bibliometric analysis of pharmacology and pharmacy journals: Scopus versus Web of Science. *Journal of Information Science, 34*(5), 715–725.

Haber, A., & Olejniczak, K. (2014). (R)ewaluacja 2. Wiedza w działaniu. *Polska Agencja Rozwoju Przedsiębiorczości*, 172.

Hardy, B. W., Gottfried, J. A., Winneg, K. M., & Jamieson, K. H. (2014). Stephen Colbert's civics lesson: How Colbert Super PAC taught viewers about campaign finance. *Mass Communication and Society, 17*(3), 329–353.

Harms, P. D., Herian, M. N., Krasikova, D. V., Vanhove, A. J., & Lester, P. B. (2013). *The Comprehensive Soldier and Family Fitness Evaluation. Report #4: Evaluation of resilience training and mental and behavioural health outcomes*. University of Nebraska- Licoln.

Helmy, M. M., & Frerichs, S. (2013). Stripping the Boss: The powerful role of humor in the Egyptian Revolution 2011. *Integrative Psychological and Behavioural Science, 47*(4), 450–481. https://doi.org/10.1007/s12124-013-9239-x

Her Majesty's Government. (2016). *Childhood obesity: A plan for action*. Retrieved February 20, 2023, from https://www.gov.uk/government/uploads/system/uploads/attachment_data/file/546588/Childhood_obesity_2016__2__acc.pdf

Holmes, M., & Panagopoulos, C. (2013). The social brain paradigm and social norm puzzles. *Journal of Theoretical Politics, 26*(3), 384–404. https://doi.org/10.1177/0951629813502710

Hopf, T. (2010). The logic of habit in International Relations. *European Journal of International Relations, 16*(4), 539–561. https://doi.org/10.1177/1354066110363502

Hou, J., Yang, X., & Chen, C. (2018). Emerging trends and new developments in information science: A document co-citation analysis (2009–2016). *Scientometrics, 115*(2), 869–892.

Howell, A. (2016). Neuroscience and war: Human enhancement, soldier rehabilitation, and the ethical limits of dual-use frameworks. *Millennium: Journal of International Studies, 45*(2), 133–150. https://doi.org/10.1177/0305829816672930

https://www.thersa.org/blog/matthew-taylor/2011/11/the-century-of-the-brain

Hunter, M. R., Gillespie, B. W., & Chen, S. Y. (2019). Urban nature experiences reduce stress in the context of daily life based on salivary biomarkers. *Frontiers in Psychology, 10*. https://doi.org/10.3389/fpsyg.2019.00722

Hyde, J. S., Bigler, R. S., Joel, D., Tate, C. A., & Van Anders, S. M. (2019). The future of sex and gender in psychology: Five challenges to the gender binary. *American Psychologist, 74*(2), 171–193. https://doi.org/10.1037/amp0000307

Isin, E. F. (2004). The neurotic citizen. *Citizenship Studies, 8*(3), 217–235. https://doi.org/10.1080/1362102042000256970

Jones, E. G., & Mendell, L. M. (1999). Assessing the decade of the brain. *Science, 284*(5415), 739. https://doi.org/10.1126/science.284.5415.739

Kim, Y. M., & Vishak, J. (2008). Just laugh! You don't need to remember: The effects of entertainment media on political information acquisition and information processing in political judgment. *Journal of Communication, 58*(2), 338–360.

Klein, N. (2007). *The shock doctrine: The rise of disaster capitalism*. Metropolitan Books.

Klein, O. (2009). From Utopia to Dystopia: Levels of explanation and the politics of social psychology. *Psychologica Belgica, 49*(2–3), 85. https://doi.org/10.5334/pb-49-2-3-85

Kraftl, P. (2014). Liveability and urban architectures: Mol(ecul)ar biopower and the 'becoming lively' of sustainable communities. *Environment and Planning D: Society and Space, 32*(2), 274–292. https://doi.org/10.1068/d21012

Kraus, S., Li, H., Kang, Q., Westhead, P., & Tiberius, V. (2020). The sharing economy: A bibliometric analysis of the state-of-the-art. *International Journal of Entrepreneurial Behavior & Research*.

Lachowycz, K., & Jones, A. M. (2011). Greenspace and obesity: A systematic review of the evidence. *Obesity Reviews, 12*(5), e183–e189. https://doi.org/10.1111/j.1467-789x.2010.00827.x

Lafont, J., Saura, J. R., & Ribeiro-Soriano, D. (2023). The role of cooperatives in sustainable development goals: A discussion about the current resource curse. *Resources Policy, 83*, 103670. https://doi.org/10.1016/j.resourpol.2023.103670

Lavazza, A., & De Caro, M. (2009). Not so fast. On some bold neuroscientific claims concerning human agency. *Neuroethics, 3*(1), 23–41. https://doi.org/10.1007/s12152-009-9053-9

LeDoux, J. (1998). *The emotional brain: The mysterious underpinnings of emotional life*. Simon & Schuster.

Linnenluecke, M. K., Marrone, M., & Singh, A. K. (2020). Conducting systematic literature reviews and bibliometric analyses. *Australian Journal of Management, 45*(2), 175–194.

Lyubomirsky, S., King, L. A., & Diener, E. (2005). The benefits of frequent positive affect: Does happiness lead to success? *Psychological Bulletin, 131*(6), 803–855. https://doi.org/10.1037/0033-2909.131.6.803

Malabou, C. (2008) *What should we do with our brain?* Trans. Rand S. Fordham University Press.

Maneiro, E. (2017). Neuroscience and emotions: New possibilities in the study of political behaviour. *Revista de estudios políticos y sociológicos, 16*(1), 169–188.

Manes, F. F. (2023). *Usar el cerebro: Conocer Nuestra Mente Para Vivir Mejor* (1.ª ed.). Paidós.

Mariani, M. M., Hashemi, N., & Wirtz, J. (2023). Artificial intelligence empowered conversational agents: A systematic literature review and research agenda. *Journal of Business Research, 161*, 113838. https://doi.org/10.1016/j.jbusres.2023.113838

Masters, R. D. (1995). From inclusive fitness to neuroscience: proximate mechanisms, feminism, and the politics of gender. *Politics and the Life Sciences, 14*(2), 180–182. https://doi.org/10.1017/s073093840001902x

McAllister, J. T., Lennertz, L., & Atencio Mojica, Z. (2022). Mapping a discipline: a guide to using VOSviewer for bibliometric and visual analysis. *Science & Technology Libraries, 41*(3), 319–348.

Mehonic, A., & Kenyon, A. J. (2022). Brain-inspired computing needs a master plan. *Nature, 604*(7905), 255–260.

Meloni, M. (2011). Philosophical implications of neuroscience: The space for a critique. *Subjectivity, 4*(3), 298–322. https://doi.org/10.1057/sub.2011.8

Metzl, J. M., & Hansen, H. (2014). Structural competency: Theorizing a New medical engagement with stigma and inequality. *Social Science & Medicine, Structural Stigma and Population Health, 103*(February), 126–133. https://doi.org/10.1016/j.socscimed.2013.06.032

Millei, Z., & Joronen, M. (2016). The (bio)politicization of neuroscience in Australian early years policies: fostering brain-resources as human capital. *Journal of Education Policy, 31*(4), 389–404. https://doi.org/10.1080/02680939.2016.1148780

Mishra, S., Mishra, A., Dubey, A., & Dwivedi, Y. K. (2023). Virtual reality in retailing: a meta-analysis to determine the purchase and non-purchase behavioural intention of consumers. *Industrial Management and Data Systems, 124*(1), 212–252. https://doi.org/10.1108/imds-05-2023-0336

Moriarty, J. C. (2008). Flickering admissibility: neuroimaging evidence in the U.S. courts. *Behavioural Sciences & the Law, 26*(1), 29–49. https://doi.org/10.1002/bsl.795

NICE. (2012). Obesity: Working with local communities. *Public health guideline*. Retrieved February 20, 2023, from https://www.nice.org.uk/guidance/ph42

Niewöhner, J., & Lock, M. (2018). Situating local biologies: Anthropological perspectives on environment/human entanglements. *BioSocieties, 13*(4), 681–697. https://doi.org/10.1057/s41292-017-0089-5

ODPM. (2003). Sustainable communities: Building for the future, Retrieved from: https://www.wellingborough.gov.uk/download/downloads/id/2842/a9_sustainable_communities_plan_-_building_for_the_future_2003.pdf on 3 March 2023

Oschinsky, F. M., Stelter, A., & Niehaves, B. (2021). Cognitive biases in the digital age – How resolving the status quo bias enables public-sector employees to overcome restraint. *Government Information Quarterly, 38*(4), 101611. https://doi.org/10.1016/j.giq.2021.101611

Oyewola, D. O., & Dada, E. G. (2022). Exploring machine learning: a scientometrics approach using bibliometrix and VOSviewer. *SN Applied Sciences, 4*(5), 1–18.

Oyibo, K., & Vassileva, J. (2020). HOMEX: Persuasive technology acceptance model and the moderating effect of culture. *Frontiers in Computer Science, 2*. https://doi.org/10.3389/fcomp.2020.00010

Papadopoulos, D. (2011). The imaginary of plasticity: Neural embodiment, epi genetics and ecomorphs. *The Sociological Review, 59*(3), 432–456. https://doi.org/10.1111/j.1467-954x.2011.02025.x

Paul, S. C., Bartmann, N., & Clark, J. (2021). Customizability in conversational agents and their impact on health engagement. *Human Behaviour and Emerging Technologies, 3*(5), 1141–1152. https://doi.org/10.1002/hbe2.320

Pickersgill, M., Niewöhner, J., Müller, R., Martin, P. J., & Cunningham-Burley, S. (2013). Mapping the new molecular landscape: Social dimensions of epigenetics. *New Genetics and Society, 32*(4), 429–447. https://doi.org/10.1080/14636778.2013.861739

Pieri, E., & Levitt, M. (2008). Risky individuals and the politics of genetic research into aggressiveness and violence. *Bioethics, 22*(9), 509–518. https://doi.org/10.1111/j.1467-8519.2008.00694.x

Pitts-Taylor, V. (2010). The plastic brain: Neoliberalism and the neuronal self. *Health: An Interdisciplinary Journal for the Social Study of Health, Illness and Medicine, 14*(6), 635–652. https://doi.org/10.1177/1363459309360796

Pressman, S. D., & Cohen, S. (2005). Does positive affect influence health? *Psychological Bulletin, 131*(6), 925–971. https://doi.org/10.1037/0033-2909.131.6.925

Pykett, J. (2011). The new maternal state: The gendered politics of governing through behaviour change. *Antipode, 44*(1), 217–238. https://doi.org/10.1111/j.1467-8330.2011.00897.x

Pykett, J. (2015). *Brain culture: Shaping policy through neuroscience*. Policy Press.

Pykett, J. (2016). *Brain culture: Shaping policy through neuroscience (English Edition)* (1.ª ed.). Policy Press.

Raco, M. (2005). Sustainable development, rolled-out neoliberalism and sustainable communities. *Antipode, 37*(2), 324–347. https://doi.org/10.1111/j.0066-4812.2005.00495.x

Rawdin, C. (2019). Towards neuroparenting? An analysis of the discourses underpinning social and emotional learning (SEL) initiatives in English schools. *Educational Review, 73*(3), 279–296. https://doi.org/10.1080/00131911.2018.1557598

Rose, N. (2007). *The politics of life itself: Biomedicine, power, and subjectivity in the twenty-first century*. Princeton University Press.

Rose, N. (2009). *The politics of life itself: biomedicine, power, and subjectivity in the twenty-first century*. Amsterdam University Press.

Rose, N. (2013). The human sciences in a biological age. *Theory, Culture & Society, 30*(1), 3–34. https://doi.org/10.1177/0263276412456569

Rose, N., & Abi-Rached, J. M. (2013). *Neuro. The new brain sciences and the management of the mind*. Princeton University Press.

Saura, J. R. (2024). Algorithms in digital marketing: Does smart personalization promote a privacy paradox? *FIIB Business Review, 13*(5), 499–502. https://doi.org/10.1177/23197145241276898

Saura, J. R., & Debasa, F. (2022). *Handbook of research on artificial intelligence in government practices and processes*. IGI Global. https://doi.org/10.4018/978-1-7998-9609-8

Saura, J. R., Škare, V., & Dosen, D. O. (2024). Is AI-based digital marketing ethical? Assessing a new data privacy paradox. *Journal of Innovation & Knowledge, 9*(4), 100597. https://doi.org/10.1016/j.jik.2024.100597

Seligman, M. E. (2019). Positive psychology: A personal history. *Annual Review of Clinical Psychology, 15*(1), 1–23. https://doi.org/10.1146/annurev-clinpsy-050718-095653
Seymour, B., & Vlaev, I. (2012). Can, and should, behavioural neuroscience influences public policy? *Trends in Cognitive Sciences, 16*(9), 449–451.
Shi, G., Liu, N., Yu, X., Zhang, H., Li, S., Wu, S., et al. (2019). Bibliometric analysis of medical malpractice literature in legal medicine from 1975 to 2018: Web of Science review. *Journal of Forensic and Legal Medicine, 66*, 167–183.
Shohamy, D., & Adcock, R. A. (2010). Dopamine and adaptive memory. *Trends in Cognitive Sciences, 14*(10), 464–472. https://doi.org/10.1016/j.tics.2010.08.002
Shonkoff, J. P., & Phillips, D. A. (2000). From neurons to neighborhoods. En *National Academies Press eBooks*. https://doi.org/10.17226/9824
Somit, A., & Peterson, S. A. (2005). *The failure of democratic nation building: Ideology meets evolution*. Palgrave Macmillan.
Somit, A., & Peterson, S. A. (2012). Biopolicy: A critical linkage. *Biopolicy: The Life Sciences and Public Policy*, 3–11. https://doi.org/10.1108/s2042-9940(2012)0000010002
Taylor, M. (2011). 'The Century of the Brain?' November 15, 2011 at:
Thaler, R. H., & Sunstein, C. R. (2003). *Libertarian paternalism. American Economic Review, 93*(2), 175–179. https://doi.org/10.1257/000282803321947001
Thaler, R. H., & Sunstein, C. R. (2008). Nudge: Improving decisions about health, wealth, and happiness. *Choice Reviews Online, 46*(02), 46–0977. https://doi.org/10.5860/choice.46-0977
Thornton, D. J. (2011). *Brain culture: neuroscience and popular media*. Rutgers.
Tymoczko, M. (2012). The neuroscience of translation. *Target. International Journal of Translation Studies, 24*(1), 83–102. https://doi.org/10.1075/target.24.1.06tym
Valle-Cruz, D., Criado, J. I., Sandoval-Almazán, R., & Ruvalcaba-Gómez, E. A. (2020). Assessing the public policy-cycle framework in the age of artificial intelligence: from agenda-setting to policy evaluation. *Government Information Quarterly, 37*(4), 101509. https://doi.org/10.1016/j.giq.2020.101509
Vidal, F. (2009). Brainhood, anthropological figure of modernity. *History of the Human Sciences, 22*(1), 5–36. https://doi.org/10.1177/0952695108099133
Villarejo, A., & Camacho, A. (2009). Neuropolítica. La neurociencia visita la política. *Neurologia, 5*(1), 8–11. https://dialnet.unirioja.es/servlet/articulo?codigo=3125068
Viney, W., Callard, F., & Woods, A. (2015). Critical medical humanities: Embracing entanglement, taking risks. *Medical Humanities, 41*(1), 2–7. https://doi.org/10.1136/medhum-2015-010692
Vrecko, S. (2008). Capital ventures into biology: biosocial dynamics in the industry and science of gambling. *Economy and Society, 37*(1), 50–67. https://doi.org/10.1080/03085140701760874
Vrecko, S. (2010). Neuroscience, power and culture: an introduction. *History of the Human Sciences, 23*(1), 1–10. https://doi.org/10.1177/0952695109354395
Wall, G. (2017). 'Love builds brains': representations of attachment and children's brain development in parenting education material. *Sociology of Health & Illness, 40*(3), 395–409. https://doi.org/10.1111/1467-9566.12632
Wegner, D. M., & Bargh, J. A. (1998). Control and automaticity in social life. In D. T. Gilbert, S. T. Fiske, & G. Lindzey (Eds.), *The handbook of social psychology* (pp. 446–496). McGraw-Hill.
Westen, D. (2008). *The political brain: The role of emotion in deciding the fate of the nation*. Public Affairs.
Youdell, D., Harwood, V., & Lindley, M. R. (2017). Biological sciences, social sciences and the languages of stress. *Discourse: Studies in the Cultural Politics of Education, 39*(2), 219–241. https://doi.org/10.1080/01596306.2018.1394420
Young, D. G. (2014). Theories and effects of political humor. En *Oxford University Press eBooks*. https://doi.org/10.1093/oxfordhb/9780199793471.013.29_update_001
Yuan, B. Z., & Sun, J. (2020). Bibliometric analysis of research on the maize based on top papers during 2009-2019. *COLLNET Journal of Scientometrics and Information Management, 14*(1), 75–92.

Integrating AI and Digital Marketing for Inclusive Governance

Senka Borovac Zekan, Antonija Roje, and Andrea Russo

Introduction

There are currently 101 million people with disabilities living in the European Union. In June 2020, the European Parliament, building on the European Disability Strategy 2010–2020. In March 2021, the Commission adopted the Strategy on the Rights of Persons with Disabilities for the period 2021–2030, which includes the main recommendations of the Parliament. These include ensuring the rights of all persons with disabilities in all policies and areas. In the last decade, researchers have become increasingly interested in themes at the interface of the practice of AI in digital marketing and public governance (Kuziemski & Misuraca, 2020; Zuiderwijk et al., 2021; Okunlaya et al., 2022). Trends in scholarly literature illustrate this dynamic, where mature scholarly agendas motivate research within digital marketing, artificial intelligence (AI), and public governance departments.

In this context, an increasing number of articles on digital marketing incorporate AI, while AI research increasingly references digital marketing. For the past few years, the empirical results contribute to these trends by indicating the extent to which interdisciplinary collaboration between these fields and the broader networks of scholarship is enabled (Stone et al., 2020; Mogaji et al., 2020; Chintalapati & Pandey, 2022; Kingsnorth, 2022; Chaffey & Smith, 2022; Kopalle et al., 2022; Bag et al., 2022). AI advances at an unprecedented rate, leading to a change in decision-making, communication, service delivery norms, marketing, and data management.

S. B. Zekan (✉) · A. Roje
University of Split, University Department of Professional Studies, Split, Croatia
e-mail: sborovac@oss.unist.hr; ababic@oss.unist.hr

A. Russo
Faculty of Maritime Studies, University of Split, Split, Croatia
e-mail: andrea.russo@pfst.hr

J. R. Saura (ed.), *Global Perspectives on AI, Ethics, and Business Economics*, Contributions to Management Science,
https://doi.org/10.1007/978-3-031-88781-9_11

Public governance has yet to be spared by these developments either. We are beginning to see governments using AI, machine learning algorithms, sensor technologies, data analytics, and digital marketing tools to automate various processes, gather insights, and make evidence-based algorithms (Stone et al., 2020; Kuziemski & Misuraca, 2020; Henman, 2020; Zuiderwijk et al., 2021; Wirtz et al., 2020; Dwivedi et al., 2021). Social media marketing strategies use AI technology to influence how consumers behave. While formulating such public governance policies, rather than looking to benefit those who have the financial means to command the advanced goods and services, it is more important to promote the well-being of the larger society (Saura et al., 2022).

The scope of AI technology and marketing in governance structures raises interesting opportunities and poses significant complexities in the quest for digitalization. Aligned with the vision of the Liberato Map project, this chapter explores these dynamics when adopting technologies. The project is a real-life case of how such synergetic efforts create the possibility of using AI to design custom solutions for the needs of vulnerable populations, especially those with disability. This chapter, among others, deals with rehabilitating disabled people by providing them with technological assistance. It starts with placing the work of the association in the context of the European disability rights and inclusive governance agenda.

The chapter offers a case of the Liberato map project, which is about developing an interactive map for easy navigation as researched to be a global cooperation among students, universities, and private businesses. This chapter highlights the crucial roles students and academic institutions play in the project's success and the key features of the Liberato Map design and form. It explores the AI and digital marketing tools utilized during the project, focusing on using technologies targeting specific people. Then, it deals with managing AI resources for society's benefit while protecting rights and freedoms.

There are also ethical outcomes that such data privacy projects raise, as well as those related directly to the execution of the projects. Policies and laws that span both areas, AI and digital marketing, are also considered. This is naturally highlighted in the context of the people with disabilities rights. The case studies reconstruct the idea generation steps, decision-making factors, and barriers for the Liberato Map project and how users and impact assessments shape them. This chapter aims to highlight some of the experiences and best practices as a case study. Thus, the chapter summarizes the project's further development, additional prospects in broader governance areas, and the necessity of the interaction between academia and practice. This chapter provides a concrete explanation and reasons why it is essential for governments, industrialists, and citizens. In addition, it elaborates on how the development of data-driven approaches can be achieved in line with the considerations of privacy to promote inclusiveness. It emphasizes the opportunities of AI and digital marketing to improve public services without compromising citizens' confidence and rights. It explains how to cope with the challenges of the digital age.

The structure of the chapter is as follows: The first part, entitled "Theoretical Framework," comprehensively explores the history of the origin and evolution of AI as well as its synergy with digital marketing. The authors examine this integration's foundational principles, encompassing big data, machine learning, and consumer perspectives. This section delineates the technological evolution of AI and situates its application within governance and public service delivery. It addresses critical issues, including privacy, ethical considerations, and regulatory compliance, which are essential for a comprehensive understanding of the broader implications of AI-driven strategies. In the segment titled "The Liberato Case Study," the authors investigate the particulars of the Liberato Map initiative. This case study provides insights into the project's design, implementation, and impact, emphasizing the collaborative dynamics among universities, students, industry stakeholders, and local governments. The subsequent section concentrates on the project's technological and strategic dimensions. The authors represent how AI technologies, including machine learning, natural language processing, and geospatial analysis, were harmoniously integrated to enhance the map's functionality and user experience. This section highlights the connection between technological innovation and targeted outreach in achieving the project's objectives. Additionally, the chapter features a section titled "Policies and Regulations," where the authors examine the regulatory and ethical considerations relevant to AI and digital marketing. This part of the discussion explores frameworks such as the General Data Protection Regulation (GDPR) and the Web Content Accessibility Guidelines (WCAG), emphasizing their significance in ensuring compliance and fostering user trust. The discourse expands to include ethical concerns such as algorithmic bias and data security, illuminating the opportunities and challenges presented by AI-driven governance instruments. Integrating AI and digital marketing into governance frameworks signifies a transformative strategy to address accessibility and inclusivity challenges within public services.

Initiatives like the Liberato Map illustrate the potential to empower marginalized populations, such as individuals with disabilities while promoting equitable and effective governance. Finally, the chapter synthesizes the key findings and discusses their practical implications. The authors reflect on the future of public governance and service delivery initiatives stemming from the Liberato Map project, underscoring the importance of interdisciplinary collaboration and suggesting avenues for future research, particularly in scaling similar projects and addressing emerging challenges in AI ethics and regulation.

Literature Review

A larger historical context of technological disruption and changes in consumer behavior influences the convergence of AI and digital marketing. Digital marketing has evolved significantly from its early reliance on online advertisements and emails to engage potential customers. With advancements in data collection techniques and increased Internet accessibility, more refined strategies emerged, such as search engine optimization (SEO) and social media marketing (Bhandari & Bansal, 2018).

Concurrently, AI technology has progressed, marked by significant developments in machine learning algorithms and natural language processing (NLP).

In the 2010s, the incorporation of AI into digital marketing gained momentum, propelled by the vast amounts of big data and the rising application of automation and machine learning for personalized marketing campaigns. The marketing landscape was soon changed with AI-powered tools for customized marketing tactics, predictive analytics, and automated customer support. Its history, from a novel idea to the myriads of stages of implementation that have spread out over decades, has led to today's sophisticated, data-driven marketing practices. Viewing the timeline in hindsight offers insight into an industry's early movers and shakers that would eventually redefine marketing as we know it.

The technology landscape of digital marketing has been profoundly transformed by the integration of AI (Oanh, 2024). Even more remarkable is that machine learning (ML), this new AI technology, has changed marketing and opened new frontiers for its application and implications (Rahman et al., 2024). ML allows systems to learn and improve from experience without being programmed directly for every contingency. In digital marketing, ML algorithms scan massive data sets to discern patterns. If they can foresee how consumers behave and what will work best for marketing strategies such as chess-playing computers, calculate their next move using full board scans at every step, state-age lists, etc.

Applications include personalized recommendations, predictive analytics, and customer segmentation. For example, recommendation engines like Amazon and Netflix use ML techniques to suggest products and content tailored to users' preferences and prior choices. Natural Language Processing (NLP) app enables machines to process the natural language (Chowdhary & Chowdhary, 2020). For example, in digital marketing, NLP is used for chatbots, sentiment analysis, and content generation. Chatbots use NLP technologies to offer instant customer service and interaction on websites and social media. When customer feedback in emails is analyzed, comments or social media interactions, sentiment analysis tools can determine if the public perception of a brand or product is positive, negative, or neutral. This allows marketers to change their strategy accordingly (Saura et al., 2023). Computer vision is an AI technology that interprets visual data and finds wide application in digital marketing. They analyze visual content for image recognition algorithms that help categorize and tag images automatically, improving the user experience on social media and e-commerce sites. An example of this can be seen in Pinterest's visual search feature. It allows users to search for products using a visual representation instead of keywords (Shiau et al., 2020). This results in a higher rating and accuracy of the search results. An example of predictive analytics is evaluating historical data using statistical algorithms and machine learning techniques to measure future outcomes.

As part of digital marketing, predictive analytics predicts trends and builds long-term customer value. In this way, it optimizes marketing campaigns (Sridevi et al., 2024). By analyzing past consumer behavior, predictive models can identify customers most likely to convert, allowing marketers to allocate resources more efficiently. The advent of big data has changed the game for digital marketing

(Zwiegelaar & Stylos, 2018). The ability to collect, process, and analzse massive amounts of data in real time provides marketers with deeper insight into consumer behavior and campaign performance. Big data analytics enables hyper-targeted marketing. Quite the contrary, it allows campaigns to be adapted to individual preferences and behaviors, which results in higher engagement and conversion rates.

Therefore, predictive models help detect those customers who are most likely to convert based on their past behavior. All of this helps marketers allocate resources more efficiently. Big data represents a significant paradigm shift in digital marketing (Zwiegelaar & Stylos, 2018). The power to collect, process, and analyze massive amounts of data in real time gives marketers better insight into consumer behavior and campaign performance. With big data analytics, they can implement hyper-targeted marketing, where campaigns are designed to be specific, considering individual preferences. A few businesses have applied AI to revolutionize their marketing strategies. For example, Starbucks utilizes AI to tailor customer experiences, analyzing previous orders and preference data to suggest products and promotions (Umamaheswari, 2024). Coca-Cola, for example, is also leveraging AI-generated image recognition to analyze user-posted content on social media, providing the company with insights into how users perceive and engage with their brand (Schivinski & Dabrowski, 2016).

As this radical change escalates, we witness the onslaught of new AI-enabled solutions revolutionizing many sectors, bringing cutting-edge methodologies to solve real-world problems. From health care to transportation, AI technologies are being harnessed to enhance efficiency, improve decision-making, and offer new capabilities previously thought unattainable. AI and algorithms are revolutionizing diagnostics, treatment planning, and patient care in health care. For instance, AI algorithms can accurately analyze medical images, identifying conditions such as tumors or fractures faster and often more accurately than human clinicians. An example of this success is IBM Watson Health, which uses AI (Chaurasia, 2023) to search vast medical data. Based on them, the program makes treatment recommendations. The above recommendations are based on evidence. In this way, the accuracy and efficiency of medical care for patients increases. Another example can be seen in the financial sector. In it, AI-driven algorithms detect fraudulent activity, assess credit risks, and automate trading strategies. JPMorgan Chase companies use AI to analyze patterns like transactions and recognize suspicious activities (Zhang & Chen, 2024). Those activities result in a significant reduction in financial fraud frequency. AI is also being used to develop personalized financial products and services. The result is improved user experience and satisfaction. Despite this tremendous progress, companies are facing several challenges in using AI.

Challenges related to algorithmic transparency, bias, and ethical implications of automated decision-making are listed. Above all, the most significant challenges arise in ensuring data privacy and managing the complexity of integrating AI with existing healthcare systems. No less concerns are related to addressing the ethical issues associated with AI decision-making. The transport sector has seen significant improvements thanks to AI applications. This is particularly evident in the optimization of traffic management and the improvement of the safety and efficiency of the public transport system. Companies like Tesla and Waymo have developed autonomous vehicles that use AI algorithms for real-time sensor data to navigate complex driving environments (Jack & Jon, 2024).

The mentioned improvements reduce the number of accidents, reduce the emission of harmful gases, and increase mobility for elderly people and people with disabilities. Despite the stated successes, there are areas for improvement. They include refining algorithms to handle edge cases better, ensuring robust cybersecurity measures, and addressing regulatory and ethical issues. AI is making significant strides in environmental monitoring and sustainability initiatives. Current algorithms can analyze data from satellite imagery and Internet of Things (IoT) sensors to track deforestation, anticipate natural disasters (Saura et al., 2023a), and enhance energy efficiency. A great example is Google's AI initiative, DeepMind, which has reduced energy consumption by up to 40% at data centers. This reduction is mainly due to a machine learning algorithm designed to optimize cooling systems (Powles & Hodson, 2017). AI fosters innovation and improves efficiency across various sectors, including health care, transportation, environmental monitoring, and financial services. Applying AI and algorithmic strategies in real-world scenarios presents significant opportunities to address complex challenges and enhance daily life.

The Liberato Map project is a case study illustrating how AI can enhance accessibility for individuals with disabilities. This initiative identifies successful applications of AI and potential areas for future use. Addressing technical, ethical, and regulatory challenges will be vital in maximizing the benefits of AI and ensuring its responsible application to tackle real-world issues. The interactive map facilitates easier, quicker, and more efficient navigation for people with disabilities in public spaces. The map uses AI algorithms to evaluate and present information regarding accessible routes and facilities, empowering users to plan their journeys effectively. The success of the Liberato map underscores AI's potential to create inclusive solutions that cater to the needs of marginalized populations. Continuous efforts are essential to update data and algorithms to accommodate diverse user requirements. Furthermore, it is equally important to address privacy concerns associated with AI applications properly (Saura et al., 2024).

Role of Big Data in AI Marketing

The integration of AI into digital marketing has fundamentally transformed the field. This collaboration has facilitated greater personalization and enhanced interactions with consumers. Central to this transformation is big data, which serves as the foundation for AI algorithms by enabling the analysis of extensive data sets. The interdependent relationship between big data and AI enhances the ability to accurately predict and modify marketing strategies, refining the overall consumer experience and optimizing organizational approaches. One of the most significant advantages of this technological integration is the emergence of AI-driven personalization. AI algorithms scrutinize consumer behavior, preferences, and prior interactions to create customized marketing messages, recommended products, and promotional offers. This level of personalization fosters deeper engagement and increased satisfaction among users. For instance, online streaming platforms utilize AI to recommend films and shows based on an individual's viewing history, providing relevant suggestions that enhance the user experience.

Furthermore, tools powered by AI, such as chatbots and virtual assistants, provide immediate customer support, solving user questions and problems 24 h a day. Such tools improve operational efficiency and provide timely assistance to users, which they appreciate. Regulatory frameworks, such as the GDPR, have been instituted to mitigate concerns regarding data privacy by ensuring that users are informed about data collection practices and can access or delete their personal information. Trust and transparency are paramount in sustaining positive consumer relationships within an AI-driven marketing environment. Organizations must embrace transparent and ethical methodologies in data management and algorithmic decision-making.

According to Martin and Murphy (2017), consumers are more inclined to engage with brands that transparently communicate their use of AI and provide tools for managing privacy settings. Furthermore, transparency involves elucidating the algorithms utilized (Nabb & Pettersson, 2024), as there is a growing demand among consumers for insight into the processes behind AI-generated recommendations and advertisements. Meeting these expectations is critical for establishing trust and ensuring the ethical deployment of AI in marketing practices. AI-driven marketing strategies have significantly altered consumer behavior, shaping purchasing decisions and promoting the adoption of emerging technologies (Okeleke et al., 2024). Personalized recommendations frequently direct consumers toward particular products or services, enhancing conversion rates and fostering brand loyalty. Nonetheless, this dependence on algorithmic suggestions may also curtail the exploration of alternative options, prompting concerns regarding the potential for over-reliance on AI technologies. Additionally, consumer receptivity to AI innovations is inconsistent and frequently influenced by demographic factors and levels of technological familiarity (Gursoy et al., 2019). Typically, younger, technology-adaptable individuals are more enthusiastic about AI-driven advancements, recognizing the convenience and relevance they offer in their experiences. In contrast, older demographics or those less familiar with digital interfaces may approach such technologies with skepticism, necessitating further efforts to bridge trust gaps and promote inclusivity. Integrating AI within digital marketing presents transformative opportunities while posing challenges that demand careful attention. Addressing privacy, transparency, and consumer trust is imperative to fully harness the advantages of AI-driven personalization and ensure its responsible application within the digital marketing landscape. This complex interplay of opportunities and challenges highlights the necessity for continual dialogue among stakeholders, including marketers, technology professionals, and policymakers, to navigate the future of AI in alignment with consumer expectations and ethical principles.

Consumer Concerns and Privacy Issues

Incorporating AI into digital marketing has led to significant improvements; however, it is accompanied by various challenges. A primary concern centers around privacy, data security, and the ethical deployment of AI technologies. Given that AI systems depend heavily on collecting and analyzing vast amounts of personal data, apprehensions regarding data management have become increasingly relevant (Dawid et al., 2017). Consumers express caution regarding the risks of data breaches, unauthorized access, and the potential misuse of sensitive information. Furthermore, adhering to a spectrum of regulatory frameworks, often characterized by inconsistencies such as the GDPR in Europe and analogous legislation in other areas, necessitates an organization's proactive and adaptable approach.

Regulations like the GDPR are designed to mitigate these issues by providing individuals with enhanced control over their data and ensuring that businesses comply with rigorous data protection protocols. Trust emerges as a critical element in the efficacy of AI-driven marketing strategies (Muthuswamy & Dilip, 2024). Companies must engage in transparent practices regarding data handling and algorithmic decision-making to cultivate and sustain consumer trust. Effective communication about data collection, processing, and usage is essential to foster a reassuring consumer environment. Additionally, empowering users to manage their privacy preferences and comprehend the mechanisms behind AI-generated recommendations further solidifies this trust. Transparency in algorithmic operations tackles concerns related to bias and fairness and clarifies the function of AI within marketing, rendering it more accessible and acceptable to the public. The impact of AI on consumer behavior is immense and cannot be overlooked. AI algorithms have revolutionized how consumers engage with products and services through enhanced personalization. Companies effectively boost user engagement and drive sales by implementing targeted marketing strategies, such as individualized recommendations. For instance, Amazon's use of predictive analytics to recommend products based on a user's past behavior and preferences creates an effortless and enjoyable shopping experience (Wolniak & Grebski, 2023).

However, this high personalization raises concerns about consumers being exposed to a limited range of choices, which could lead to an over-reliance on AI-generated recommendations (Saura, 2024). The ethical implications of AI in digital marketing are substantial, extending beyond privacy and transparency to significant societal consequences. A key challenge is algorithmic bias, where AI systems may inadvertently reinforce or magnify existing inequalities found in their training data. To tackle this critical issue, we must commit to developing and testing AI models that are fair and inclusive, ensuring that technology serves the interests of everyone. Companies must emphasize accountability in their AI implementations, ensuring their decision-making processes are defensible and conform to ethical guidelines. The challenges related to scalability and integration further complicate the use of AI in digital marketing. Many organizations encounter obstacles when adjusting their systems to incorporate advanced AI technologies. Effective implementation demands significant investments in infrastructure, technical skills, and ongoing maintenance. Additionally, the financial implications of adopting AI can be considerable, especially for smaller businesses with limited resources.

The quality and quantity of data are essential for practical AI applications, as incomplete or outdated data sets can result in unreliable predictions and subpar outcomes, thus diminishing the effectiveness of AI-driven strategies. Maintaining the accuracy and consistency of data requires comprehensive data management practices, including regular updates and stringent validation procedures. Furthermore, varying global regulatory environments introduce additional challenges for organizations operating across different jurisdictions. Organizations must actively monitor changing laws and guidelines to mitigate potential legal and financial risks. Implementing AI in digital marketing brings both significant advantages and serious challenges. While it can improve personalization, efficiency, and consumer interaction, it also requires meticulous attention to privacy, ethical issues, and regulatory compliance. Organizations must pursue transparency, fairness, and inclusivity in their AI initiatives to foster consumer trust and fully leverage the transformative capabilities of this technology. As AI progresses, collaboration among marketers, technologists, and policymakers will be vital in directing its development to align with societal values and expectations.

Regulatory and Compliance Issues

Integrating AI in digital marketing poses notable regulatory and compliance challenges requiring critical examination. As AI technologies gain traction, the evolving regulatory landscape must effectively tackle data privacy issues, ethical standards, and accountability. While frameworks such as the GDPR and other regional laws have been established to regulate how organizations handle personal data, they also introduce layers of complexity that organizations must manage. These regulations protect consumer rights and foster transparency in AI operations (Sartor & Lagioia, 2020). However, compliance can be particularly daunting for multinational companies that must adhere to varying legal requirements across different regions. This situation necessitates a proactive and flexible approach, as organizations are responsible for navigating a complex web of regulations, underscoring the need for continuous vigilance and adaptability. Global compliance represents an additional challenge, as disparate standards across nations necessitate customized strategies to address local regulations effectively. For instance, while the GDPR strongly emphasizes rigorous consent and data protection protocols, other jurisdictions may prioritize different elements of AI governance.

This inconsistency compels organizations to uphold comprehensive compliance frameworks to mitigate legal risks and foster trust among their international user base. Establishing consumer trust is crucial in navigating regulatory obstacles. Organizations must exhibit accountability in their deployment of AI technologies, ensuring that decision-making processes remain transparent and adhere to ethical standards. Consumer trust is often influenced by individuals' interactions with AI systems (Glikson & Woolley, 2020), particularly regarding managing their data and whether they regard the organization as placing a premium on their privacy and interests.

Furthermore, the financial implications of adopting AI solutions exacerbate these challenges. The development and deployment of AI technologies demand significant financial investments, particularly for acquiring advanced infrastructure, hiring skilled personnel, and maintaining ongoing operations. Smaller organizations often face resource constraints that make adopting such technologies difficult. Careful financial planning is required to balance the costs of AI implementation with its potential benefits, ensuring that investments lead to meaningful outcomes. Resource allocation is another critical aspect of effectively leveraging AI. Organizations must prioritize their investments in areas where AI can deliver the most value, such as improving customer experiences, optimizing marketing strategies, or enhancing operational efficiency.

Beyond financial resources, successful AI integration requires allocating technical expertise and time to train, monitor, and refine AI systems continuously (Dwivedi et al., 2021). In the ever-evolving landscape of AI, organizations are at the crossroads of numerous challenges and opportunities. One significant hurdle is ensuring data quality, as any lapses could breed algorithmic biases that threaten the fairness and efficacy of AI applications. Alongside this, scalability emerges as a vital consideration in resource allocation. While large corporations often possess the financial leverage to implement AI technologies across many platforms and regions, smaller enterprises must navigate the delicate balance of extending their AI capabilities without straining their resources. Many organizations adopt incremental strategies to scale their efforts effectively, embarking on targeted use cases before gradually widening their scope as they achieve success and gain additional resources.

This process highlights the importance of planning and foresight when using AI. As organizations grapple with the regulatory and compliance demands of integrating these advanced technologies, they must also contend with the financial burdens and resource allocations required for effective implementation. In this intricate web of possibilities, companies can forge ahead with measured yet flexible compliance approaches, making wise investments in the necessary AI infrastructure while strategically allocating their resources. Balancing these challenges against the need to maintain consumer trust and adhere to regulations will be pivotal in unleashing AI's transformative power within digital marketing. Each decision made in this journey is critical, shaping the future of how businesses engage with technology and consumers alike.

The Case Study Liberato

The Liberato Association shines brightly as a vital source of support for individuals with disabilities, dedicated to improving their overall quality of life through targeted technical assistance and robust advocacy efforts. At the heart of its mission lies a profound commitment to making technological advancements accessible and advantageous to everyone, cultivating an inclusive society where equitable participation is a reality. The association places great importance on utilizing technological progress to promote inclusivity and social equity.

The Liberato Association's primary aspirations center around enhancing life for those with disabilities while delivering the essential technical support needed to uplift this community. With unwavering dedication to nurturing an inclusive environment, the association aims to ensure that groundbreaking technological innovations are within reach and exert a meaningful impact, especially for individuals facing disabilities. This dedication is reflected in its advocacy for the rights of disabled persons and various initiatives designed to tackle accessibility obstacles through forward-thinking solutions. The Liberato Association's mission is structured around three foundational pillars: advocacy, support, and innovation. The advocacy component prioritizes representing the rights of individuals with disabilities within policy debates and public dialogue, ensuring that their needs are acknowledged and addressed with urgency and care.

The organization provides resources, training, and tools to enhance independence and mobility. Educational programs also play a critical role in this support, equipping individuals with the necessary skills to navigate and leverage technological innovations effectively. These initiatives are consistent with the association's overarching objective of bridging the divide between accessibility and inclusion through transformative technology. Innovation is a fundamental element of the Liberato Association's mission, propelling the creation of advanced solutions tailored to meet the distinct needs of individuals with disabilities. The Liberato Map project employs AI and digital marketing to augment urban accessibility. This project is a testament to the association's unwavering belief that accessibility is a fundamental human right, showcasing its dedication to customizing technological innovations that cater to users' unique needs. Central to this mission is the spirit of collaboration. The association can cultivate and implement projects that create significant social impact by forming partnerships with universities, industry leaders, and government entities.

As we look toward the future, the Liberato Association is poised to broaden its influence and enhance its contributions. Its ambitions include scaling successful initiatives like the Liberato Map to additional cities and regions like Omiš and Trogir, addressing new accessibility challenges with innovative solutions, and persistently advocating for policies that champion the rights of individuals with disabilities. These aspirations highlight a steadfast commitment to nurturing a culture of innovation and inclusion so that everyone can reap the rewards of technological advancements. The Liberato Association is resolutely dedicated to its advocacy, support, and innovation principles. Through its tireless efforts, it strives for a more inclusive and accessible world, dismantling barriers and promoting equality by leveraging the transformative power of technology. The association's work is crucial in creating a future where everyone can participate fully and equitably in society.

Liberato Map Project Analysis

The Liberato Map project is an innovative effort to develop an interactive map that improves accessibility for people with disabilities. It is designed to engage students with disabilities and the general public, highlighting the various challenges in areas such as architecture, communication, and rehabilitation encountered by individuals with disabilities. By disseminating essential information about accessible paths, facilities, and services, the Liberato Map aspires to enhance mobility and promote independence for its users. The Liberato Map is a digital platform offering information on the accessibility of facilities, tourist attractions, and parking spaces via websites and mobile applications.

The application assesses the accessibility of various locations within the city of Split and educates tourism stakeholders on the needs of individuals with disabilities. It also compiles a comprehensive database detailing the accessibility of Split's tourist sites. Of the 100 tourist attractions and locations assessed, 52 were identified as accessible. Through this initiative, the Liberato Association has sought to encourage greater participation in daily activities among individuals with disabilities, particularly young people in higher education. Since its public launch in early 2020, the interactive map has expanded beyond Split to include locations in Omiš and Trogir.

In privately owned spaces, forging collaborations is essential to creating meaningful change. Partnerships have been established with local organizations, such as the Association of the Physically Disabled TOMS in Trogir and the Agape Association in Omiš, laying the groundwork for a collective effort. In Split, the Liberato Association has joined forces with esteemed groups like the County Association of the Blind, Info Zone, Association of Persons with Disabilities Split (UOSIS), and the ZNAKujmo svi Association. These collaborations are not just formalities; they have been key to constructing a comprehensive database vital to the project's success. The University Department of Professional Studies support has also been invaluable, providing a dedicated workspace that fosters innovation and growth. This is a testament to the power of collaboration between academia and industry, showcasing how both can come together to drive social change. Among the exciting developments emerging from these efforts is the Liberato Map mobile application.

This tool is a remarkable advancement from the initial interactive online map, designed to offer users an intuitive and efficient way to gather information about accessibility across various cities. Thus, organizing locations into specific categories—from health and public facilities to education, sports, culture, parking, and dining—the application ensures that users can swiftly find the relevant details that match their needs. Gone are the days of only accessing this information online; the Liberato Map has evolved into a mobile application, available for download on Google Play and the App Store. Users, including international travelers and young parents, have shared enthusiastic feedback about its practicality. Many have expressed relief at no longer needing to send emails or make phone calls to inquire about accessibility, as the app simplifies their travel planning process. It empowers users to discover accessible public transport, accommodations, restaurants, and other amenities, all the while offering personalized routes tailored to their unique needs and limitations. Building on the success of the Liberato Map, the initiative has broadened its horizons to include establishing a Computer Skills Center that caters specifically to students' technical aspirations. The journey of developing this application, which took flight in 2019, was a thorough and collaborative effort involving generous donors, dedicated partners, and enthusiastic external contributors. A multidisciplinary team, including university students, infused the project with AI, digital marketing, and user experience design expertise.

This collaborative spirit has resulted in a distinctive tool that offers hope for a future enriched by young innovators. The Liberato Map project demonstrates how technology can be harnessed to foster inclusivity and accessibility. Then, empowering individuals with disabilities and engaging a diverse range of stakeholders, the project illustrates the transformative potential of collective innovation. With the mobile application now in circulation, its value as a resource for those navigating urban environments with accessibility challenges is only set to grow, enriching the lives of countless users. The application analyzes the accessibility of locations in the city of Split for people with disabilities, then educates stakeholders in tourism about the needs of people with disabilities and creates a database of information on the accessibility of Split's tourist sites. Of the 100 selected tourist attractions and locations, 52 are accessible.

With it, the Liberato Association wanted to increase the number of people with disabilities in everyday activities, primarily young people in higher education. The interactive map has been available to the public since the beginning of 2020. The first locations were included in Split, and now, there are three cities. Locations in Omiš and Trogir are also included. For locations that are owned by the city, county or state, we first contact them. For the rest, we try cooperating with local associations such as the Association of the Physically Disabled TOMS from Trogir and the Agape Association from Omiš. In contrast, in Split, we cooperate with the County Association of the Blind, with Info zone, the UOSIS, and the ZNAKujmo svi Association. The Liberato Association is a significant support for the University Department of Professional Studies, which has provided them with a workspace.

The Liberato Map mobile application is a natural continuation of the interactive online map for people with disabilities, allowing easier and faster access to information on the accessibility of facilities in the city, focusing on technical infrastructure and the implementation of new areas/cities. The division into categories (health, public facilities, education, sports, culture, parking, food, drink, and others) enables more accessible and faster access to the desired information, thus meeting the individual needs of users. The map was the first to be available online, and a mobile app is now available for download. Most people who contact the Liberato Association are foreigners or young parents who point out that they no longer have to send emails, call, or beg for information about accessibility for themselves or their children. LiberatoMap is more than just a mobile app. It allows users to find and plan trips according to their needs and limitations. The app contains information on the accessibility of public transport, accommodation, restaurants, and other facilities and offers planned routes adapted to the user's needs. After the success of the Liberato Map project, an interactive map for people with disabilities intended to facilitate movement and navigation in the City of Split, the project now includes the development of the Computer Skills Center, which is focused on students and their technical needs. The development of this application was a long and arduous process. Since 2019, with the support of all project donors, partners, and external collaborators, the Liberato Association has created a unique user experience. The project involves a multidisciplinary team, including university students, who contribute their AI, digital marketing, and user experience design expertise. This instills hope for a future where young minds drive positive change.

User Experience

The Liberato Map, crafted by the dedicated team at the Liberato Association, has received widespread praise for its transformative effects on users, especially those with disabilities. This remarkable tool significantly enhances the user experience through several pivotal aspects that highlight its effectiveness and commitment to accessibility. Users have reported notable advancements in navigating public spaces with newfound ease and confidence. The Liberato Map delivers comprehensive information on accessible routes, facilities, and services, which is essential for individuals with disabilities.

This valuable data empowers users to plan their journeys intelligently, steering clear of potential obstacles while identifying the most accessible options tailored to their needs. For example, the map prominently showcases accessible entrances, ramps, and elevators—indispensable resources for those utilizing wheelchairs or mobility aids. Moreover, the map's real-time updates guarantee that the information remains fresh and trustworthy. Users express gratitude for the accuracy of the data, which is continuously updated and validated by the Liberato Association and its partners. This level of reliability alleviates the anxiety and frustration commonly linked to navigating unknown environments, reassuring users as they explore new locations. The ongoing updates instill a sense of security and awareness about their surroundings, significantly boosting confidence for outings. Furthermore, the Liberato Map features a user-friendly interface meticulously designed to meet diverse user needs. Its intuitive layout allows for straightforward searches and easy access to information about various locations. With features such as filtering options, precise categorization (including health facilities, public buildings, and dining), and engaging interactive elements, the overall user experience is seamless and enjoyable. This simplicity ensures that even those with limited technical abilities can easily navigate the map.

The Liberato Map's availability as a mobile application greatly enhances its convenience and accessibility. Users can seamlessly access the map on their smartphones or tablets, making it an invaluable resource while on the move. The mobile app offers practical tools such as route planning and real-time navigation assistance, ensuring users have the immediate information they need while traveling. With the Liberato Map, you are not just gaining access; you are gaining the freedom and confidence to explore your world. Integrating mobile devices with the Liberato Map revolutionizes how users engage with essential information, making it readily available at their fingertips, regardless of location. By offering comprehensive and dependable insights into accessibility features, this innovative map empowers individuals with disabilities to navigate public spaces with newfound independence. This boost in autonomy cultivates increased confidence and self-sufficiency, enabling users to partake more actively in daily routines and social gatherings. Users often provide glowing feedback, emphasizing how the map has transformed their experiences, granting them greater freedom and ease in their everyday lives. The positive influence of the Liberato Map extends well beyond individual experiences, enriching the community at large. Users frequently express gratitude for how the map heightens awareness of accessibility issues and champions inclusivity. Many appreciate its role in fostering a more welcoming and accessible environment. The collaboration with local associations and stakeholders enhances the map's positive impact, fostering community engagement and support. The user experience with the Liberato Map is resoundingly favurable. It is characterized by improved accessibility, real-time accuracy, a user-friendly interface, and heightened independence for those with disabilities. Its seamless integration into mobile technology and the broader community benefits underscore its effectiveness as an invaluable tool for enhancing quality of life and promoting inclusivity for all.

Collaboration Between Universities, Students, and Stakeholders

In the narrative of the Liberato Map project, one of its most remarkable aspects is the partnership forged between academia and industry. Here, students find themselves at the heart of the initiative, actively engaged in its development and execution. This involvement not only allows them to acquire invaluable hands-on experience but also enables them to contribute to a project of significant social value. The focus on systematic technological advancements aims to enhance the lives of individuals with disabilities, aiding in their educational and professional journeys and their social rehabilitation and employment prospects. Amidst this collaboration, the tourist board emerges as a vital ally, offering essential insights into the specific needs of tourists with disabilities. This partnership ensures that the Liberato Map enriches the overall experience for visitors, making it more inclusive.

In this tapestry of collaboration, academic institutions assume a crucial role by fostering innovation and tackling pressing societal issues. They bring forth the necessary research frameworks, technical know-how, and academic support essential for the project's success. Universities become vibrant centers of knowledge and creativity, where interdisciplinary collaboration thrives, uniting specialists from diverse areas such as computer science, engineering, and social sciences to pursue a common goal. Academic institutions play a crucial role in fostering collaboration by creating platforms where dialogue and exchange can thrive among various stakeholders.

Moreover, universities are vital in obtaining financial support for these initiatives, utilizing grants and research funding to ensure the development and sustainability of projects. Central to the Liberato Map project are the students who contribute meaningfully to its success with their skills, creativity, and passion. Their participation provides valuable hands-on experience and allows them to apply their academic insights to tackle real-world challenges. In a vibrant and engaging environment, students immerse themselves in a hands-on experience invaluable for their professional development. This journey significantly enhances their problem-solving abilities, nurtures their teamwork skills, and deepens their understanding of how technology can be applied within societal contexts. From diverse disciplines, students contribute their unique perspectives and expertise to the various facets of the project. For instance, computer science students lead the crafting of the AI algorithms that power the map, diligently working to ensure its accuracy and efficiency.

Meanwhile, students from the social sciences and humanities lend their insights to user experience design, striving to create a map that is not only user-friendly but also accessible to individuals with disabilities. Marketing students jump in to devise strategies that promote the map, aiming to boost its adoption among the desired audience. As they engage in the Liberato Map project, these students develop a strong sense of ownership and responsibility toward community service and social impact.

Their participation transforms them into advocates for inclusivity and accessibility, instilling these values they will carry into their future careers. Integral to the success of the Liberato Map project are the industry stakeholders, including technology companies, non-profit organizations, and the tourist board, who serve as essential partners in this collaborative endeavor. Stakeholders play a crucial role by providing essential insights, a wealth of resources, and unwavering support that significantly advance the overall execution of the project. Within this dynamic framework, the tourist board emerges as particularly important, as it offers invaluable and diverse perspectives on the specific needs of tourists with disabilities. Such critical input ensures that the meticulously crafted map caters effectively to residents and visitors alike, thereby significantly enhancing the overall inclusivity of urban spaces. Furthermore, the tourist board actively promotes the map through its well-established and extensive networks, effectively increasing its visibility and accessibility among potential tourists who may benefit from its features. In addition, technology firms contribute their invaluable expertise and financial backing, significantly facilitating the use of advanced technologies necessary for the map's effective functionality and user experience. The collaboration in the Liberato Map project, which involves universities, passionate students, and various industry stakeholders, illustrates the remarkable potency of combined efforts in actively addressing pressing societal issues. This collaboration ultimately leads to innovative solutions and notable social benefits, reinforcing the partnership's importance in advancing the community's common good.

Integration of AI and Digital Marketing

The Liberato Map utilizes AI to analyze and present data in a user-friendly format. Machine-learning algorithms process vast amounts of information to identify accessible routes and facilities, ensuring the map is accurate and up-to-date. Additionally, digital marketing strategies are employed to raise awareness about the map, encouraging widespread adoption and engagement from the community. Integrating AI and digital marketing in the Liberato Map project showcases the potential of these technologies to create impactful solutions for societal challenges. The Liberato Map project leverages several AI technologies to provide accurate, real-time information about accessible routes and facilities for people with disabilities. Key AI components include machine learning, natural language processing, and computer vision geospatial analysis. Machine Learning Algorithms analyze vast amounts of data to identify patterns and trends, enabling the map to provide reliable and up-to-date information. Machine learning models process data from various sources, including user inputs, municipal databases, and crowd-sourced information, to continuously refine and improve the accuracy of the map. NLP technologies interpret and process user queries, making it easier for individuals to find specific information about accessibility features. This ensures users can interact with the map naturally and intuitively, improving their overall experience. Computer Vision: Computer vision techniques analyze images and videos of public spaces and assess their accessibility features. For example, computer vision can identify the presence of ramps, elevators, and other accessible infrastructure, enhancing the map's comprehensiveness. Geospatial Analysis: Analytical tools integrate geographic information system (GIS) data with AI algorithms to provide detailed maps and navigation routes. These tools help users identify the most accessible paths and avoid obstacles, ensuring smoother and more efficient travel for people with disabilities. Digital marketing is crucial in promoting the Liberato Map, raising awareness about its benefits, and encouraging widespread adoption. Key strategies include social media campaigns, content marketing, search engine optimization and email marketing. The project uses social media platforms to share updates, success stories, and user testimonials.

These campaigns are designed to engage the community, highlight the map's features, and encourage individuals to share their experiences, increasing visibility and user engagement. Creating and distributing valuable content, such as blog posts, videos, and infographics, helps educate the public about the map's capabilities and accessibility. Content marketing efforts focus on storytelling, showcasing how the Liberato Map has positively impacted the lives of people with disabilities. SEO techniques ensure that information about the Liberato Map is easily discoverable through online searches. The project aims to attract more visitors and potential users by optimizing keywords and improving the website's structure. Targeted email campaigns keep stakeholders, users, and partners informed about new developments, features, and events related to the Liberato Map.

These campaigns help maintain ongoing engagement and foster community among users. Collaborating with influential organizations, such as disability advocacy groups and tourism boards, amplifies the project's reach. These partnerships help promote the map through trusted networks and channels, increasing its credibility and adoption. Effective AI and digital marketing integration require robust data analysis and user experience (UX) design. Key aspects include user feedback, user-centered design, and behavioral analytics. Collecting and analyzing user feedback is essential for improving the map's functionality and user satisfaction. Surveys, reviews, and direct user interactions provide valuable insights into how the map is used and what features need enhancement. The map is designed with a user-centered approach, ensuring it meets the needs of people with disabilities.

This involves iterative testing and refinement based on user input, focusing on accessibility, ease of use, and visual appeal. Analyzing user behavior on the platform helps identify patterns and preferences, guiding future improvements. Metrics such as user engagement, click-through rates, and navigation paths provide insights into how users interact with the map. The success of the Liberato Map depends on the accuracy and timeliness of the information it provides. Key strategies include real-time data updates, automated data verification, user contributions, and Integration of real-time data sources to ensure the map reflects the latest accessibility information. This includes updates from municipal databases, user-generated content, and live sensor data. AI algorithms verify the accuracy of the data, cross-referencing multiple sources to minimize errors. This automated verification process enhances the reliability of the information provided. Encouraging users to contribute data and report inaccuracies helps maintain the map's accuracy. Community-driven updates ensure the map stays relevant and valuable, reflecting real-world conditions. Collaborating with local governments and organizations provides access to official data and resources. These partnerships help keep the map current and comprehensive, benefiting from authoritative information sources. Integrating AI and digital marketing in the Liberato Map project exemplifies how technology can be harnessed to create inclusive solutions for societal challenges.

Policies and Regulations

As AI and digital marketing become more embedded in governance, new policies and regulatory frameworks are emerging to address the associated risks. This chapter explores these developments, highlighting how the Liberato Map project navigates the regulatory landscape to comply with privacy laws and ethical standards. The rapid Integration of AI and digital marketing in public governance necessitates the development of robust policies and regulatory frameworks to address associated risks and moral concerns. As AI technologies become more pervasive, governments and regulatory bodies increasingly focus on establishing comprehensive frameworks to govern their use. Critical areas of regulation include data privacy, algorithmic transparency, and accountability. For instance, the European Union's AI Act proposes a risk-based approach to regulate AI applications, categorizing them into different risk levels and applying corresponding regulatory requirements. High-risk AI systems, such as those used in health care and transportation, are subject to stricter regulations to ensure safety and reliability. Ethical AI use is paramount, particularly in applications affecting vulnerable populations, such as people with disabilities. Ethical guidelines emphasize principles such as fairness, transparency, and non-discrimination. AI systems must be designed to avoid biases that could disadvantage specific groups. Additionally, human oversight and intervention mechanisms should ensure that AI decisions are just and accountable.

Ethics, Privacy, and Security

Protecting user data is a critical concern in AI-driven projects. Regulations such as the EU's GDPR set stringent data collection, storage, and processing requirements. These regulations mandate that users provide informed consent for their data use and have the right to access, correct, or delete their data. For the Liberato Map project, compliance with GDPR ensures that users' personal information, such as location data and accessibility needs, is handled with the highest privacy and security standards. Data security is essential to protecting it from unauthorized access and breaches. Implementing robust encryption methods, secure data storage solutions, and regular security audits are critical. The Liberato Map project employs these measures to safeguard user data, fostering trust and confidence among its users. Regulations and standards such as the WCAG ensure digital tools and platforms are accessible to people with disabilities. The Liberato Map adheres to these standards, ensuring its interface is user-friendly and navigable for individuals with various disabilities. Features like screen reader compatibility, alternative image text, and easy-to-use navigation are integral to meeting these accessibility requirements. Policies promoting inclusivity in digital services advocate for equal access to technology for all individuals, regardless of their physical or cognitive abilities. Government initiatives and regulations encourage the development and implementation of inclusive technologies. The Liberato Map aligns with these policies by actively involving users with disabilities in the design and testing phases, ensuring the platform meets their needs.

Implications

The Liberato Map initiative illustrates that AI and digital marketing within public services significantly affects policy formulation. It highlights the need for frameworks balancing innovation with public interest protection. Policymakers are starting to see the importance of inclusive technology policies that promote accessibility and equity. Insights from the Liberato Map can help inform broader regulatory decisions, guiding the development of guidelines that support technological growth while ensuring social responsibility. New AI and digital marketing governance models stress collaborative approaches involving governments, industry, academia, and civil society, advocating for transparency, accountability, and public engagement. The Liberato Map project exemplifies collaboration, showcasing how collective efforts can lead to inclusive and impactful technologies.

However, creating effective regulations for fast-evolving technologies remains challenging. Regulations must adapt to technological progress while establishing clear ethical standards to balance innovation with public interest safeguards. Future regulatory frameworks will likely emphasize algorithmic transparency, ethical data management, and inclusivity. The involvement of technologists, ethicists, and the public is essential for developing comprehensive, forward-thinking policies that reflect changing societal values. The Liberato Map project demonstrates the importance of these frameworks, showing how technological innovation can align with privacy and inclusiveness principles.

Conclusion

The Liberato Map project combines data-driven methodologies with privacy considerations to foster trust and promote effective governance. Through collaboration among universities, students, and industry stakeholders, it aims to improve the quality of life for individuals with disabilities while providing valuable information to policymakers. This initiative underscores the importance of inclusive governance in the digital age and serves as a model for future applications of AI and digital marketing within public services. It highlights successful partnerships between academia and industry in Croatia, emphasizing innovation, knowledge transfer, and practical applications of AI.

However, it also brings attention to the necessity of addressing ethics and data privacy and aligning the objectives of academic and industrial stakeholders. The project lays a foundation for integrating AI and digital marketing into governance and invites further investigation within the rapidly evolving digital environment. A key area for future research involves evaluating the scalability of AI solutions. Although the Liberato Map excels in localized contexts, expanding these initiatives across varied regions presents challenges. Researchers are tasked with ensuring that adapted systems maintain accuracy, relevance, and user-friendliness. Another promising research direction is incorporating emerging technologies such as augmented reality (AR), the IoT, and blockchain to complement AI and create inclusive solutions. AR can improve accessibility through real-time assistance, IoT can enhance data with live information, and blockchain can facilitate secure data sharing, thereby increasing trust in public services.

The issue of algorithmic bias is critical and requires investigation to promote fairness. Biases in training data could reinforce inequalities, undermining the objectives of inclusive technology. Future research should prioritize identifying, measuring, and mitigating biases to establish equitable AI systems. Enhancing algorithmic transparency and fairness will contribute to developing ethical AI solutions. Furthermore, conducting longitudinal impact studies is essential to comprehend the long-term effects of AI initiatives on policy, behavior, and inclusivity. While immediate outcomes may be observable, thorough evaluations are necessary to assess ongoing influences on accessibility, community involvement, and policy over time.

Finally, examining collaborative governance models for technological innovation is essential. The Liberato Map underscores the importance of government, academia, industry, and civil society partnerships. Research into effective collaboration strategies can reveal best practices for engaging stakeholders and resolving conflicts in cross-sectoral situations. These findings will assist policymakers in reconciling innovation with public accountability. In summary, the Liberato Map project represents a significant achievement. It highlights the necessity for ongoing research into integrating AI into governance, particularly regarding scalability, utilizing emerging technologies, bias mitigation, long-term impact assessment, and refining collaborative strategies for more inclusive technological advancement.

References

Bag, S., Srivastava, G., Bashir, M. M. A., Kumari, S., Giannakis, M., & Chowdhury, A. H. (2022). Journey of customers in this digital era: Understanding the role of AI technologies in user engagement and conversion. *Benchmarking: An International Journal, 29*(7), 2074–2098. https://doi.org/10.1108/BIJ-07-2021-0415

Bhandari, R. S., & Bansal, A. (2018). Impact of search engine optimization as a marketing tool. *Jindal Journal of Business Research, 7*(1), 23–36. https://doi.org/10.1177/2278682117754016

Chaffey, D., & Smith, P. R. (2022). Digital marketing excellence: Planning, optimizing and integrating online marketing.

Chaurasia, A. (2023). Algorithmic precision medicine: Harnessing AI for healthcare optimization. *Asian Journal of Biotechnology and Bioresource Technology, 9*(4), 28–43. https://doi.org/10.9734/ajb2t/2023/v9i4190

Chintalapati, S., & Pandey, S. K. (2022). AI in marketing: A systematic literature review. *International Journal of Market Research, 64*(1), 38–68. https://doi.org/10.1177/14707853211018428

Chowdhary, K., & Chowdhary, K. R. (2020). Natural language processing. In *Fundamentals of AI* (pp. 603–649). https://doi.org/10.1007/978-81-322-3972-7_19

Dawid, H., Decker, R., Hermann, T., Jahnke, H., Klat, W., König, R., & Stummer, C. (2017). Management science in smart consumer products: Challenges and research perspectives. *Central European Journal of Operations Research, 25*, 203–230. https://doi.org/10.1007/s10100-016-0436-9

Dwivedi, Y. K., Hughes, L., Ismagilova, E., Aarts, G., Coombs, C., Crick, T., et al. (2021). AI (AI): Multidisciplinary perspectives on emerging challenges, opportunities, and agenda for research, practice and policy. *International Journal of Information Management, 57*, 101994. https://doi.org/10.1016/j.ijinfomgt.2019.08.002

Glikson, E., & Woolley, A. W. (2020). Human trust in AI: Review of empirical research. *Academy of Management Annals, 14*(2), 627–660.

Gursoy, D., Chi, O. H., Lu, L., & Nunkoo, R. (2019). Consumers' acceptance of artificially intelligent (AI) device use in service delivery. *International Journal of Information Management, 49*, 157–169. https://doi.org/10.1016/j.ijinfomgt.2019.03.008

Henman, P. (2020). Improving public services using AI: Possibilities, pitfalls, governance. *Asia Pacific Journal of Public Administration*. https://doi.org/10.1080/23276665.2020.1816188

Jack, W., & Jon, B. (2024). *Navigating tomorrow: Advancements and road ahead in AI for autonomous vehicles* (No. 11955). EasyChair.

Kingsnorth, S. (2022). Digital marketing strategy: An integrated approach to online marketing. gci.edu.np

Kopalle, P. K., Gangwar, M., Kaplan, A., Ramachandran, D., Reinartz, W., & Rindfleisch, A. (2022). Examining AI (AI) technologies in marketing via a global lens: Current trends and future research opportunities. *International Journal of Research in Marketing, 39*(2), 522–540. https://doi.org/10.1016/j.ijresmar.2021.11.002

Kuziemski, M., & Misuraca, G. (2020). AI governance in the public sector: Three tales from the frontiers of automated decision-making in democratic settings. *Telecommunications Policy*. https://doi.org/10.1016/j.telpol.2020.101976

Martin, K. D., & Murphy, P. E. (2017). The role of data privacy in marketing. *Journal of the Academy of Marketing Science, 45*, 135–155. https://doi.org/10.1007/s11747-016-0495-4

Mogaji, E., Soetan, T. O., & Kieu, T. A. (2020). The implications of AI on the digital marketing of financial services to vulnerable customers. *Australasian Marketing Journal*. https://doi.org/10.1016/j.ausmj.2020.05.003

Muthuswamy, V. V., & Dilip, D. (2024). Impact of AI and E-Business related factors on consumer behaviour intention: Moderating role of customer trust. *International Journal of eBusiness and eGovernment Studies, 16*(1), 162–182.

Nabb, E., & Pettersson, L. (2024). Beyond the click: An exploratory investigation of consumer privacy and trust in AI-Driven Targeted Advertising.

Oanh, V. T. K. (2024). Revolutionizing engagement: How AI is transforming the digital marketing landscape. *Journal of Electrical Systems, 20*(4s), 2504–2514.

Okeleke, P. A., Ajiga, D., Folorunsho, S. O., & Ezeigweneme, C. (2024). Predictive analytics for market trends using AI: A study in consumer behavior. *International Journal of Engineering Research Updates, 7*(1), 36–49. https://doi.org/10.53430/ijeru.2024.7.1.0032

Okunlaya, R. O., Syed Abdullah, N., & Alias, R. A. (2022). *AI (AI) library services innovative conceptual framework for the digital transformation of university education*. Library Hi Tech.

Powles, J., & Hodson, H. (2017). Google DeepMind and healthcare in an age of algorithms. *Health and Technology, 7*(4), 351–367. https://doi.org/10.1007/s12553-017-0179-1

Rahman, J., Raihan, A., Tanchangya, T., & Ridwan, M. (2024). Optimizing the digital marketing landscape: A comprehensive exploration of AI (AI) technologies, applications, advantages, and challenges. *Frontiers of Finance, 2*(2). https://doi.org/10.59429/ff.v2i2.6549

Sartor, G., & Lagioia, F. (2020). The impact of the General Data Protection Regulation (GDPR) on AI.

Saura, J. R. (2024). Algorithms in digital marketing: Does smart personalization promote a privacy paradox? *FIIB Business Review, 13*(5), 499–502. https://doi.org/10.1177/23197145241276898

Saura, J. R., Palacios-Marqués, D., & Ribeiro-Soriano, D. (2023). Privacy concerns in social media UGC communities: Understanding user behavior sentiments in complex networks. *Information Systems and e-Business Management*, 1–21. https://doi.org/10.1007/s10257-023-00631-5

Saura, J. R., Ribeiro-Navarrete, S., Palacios-Marqués, D., & Mardani, A. (2023a). Impact of extreme weather in production economics: Extracting evidence from user generated content. *International Journal of Production Economics, 260*, 108861. https://doi.org/10.1016/j.ijpe.2023.108861

Saura, J. R., Ribeiro-Soriano, D., & Palacios-Marqués, D. (2022). Assessing behavioral data science privacy issues in government artificial intelligence deployment. *Government Information Quarterly, 39*(4), 101679. https://doi.org/10.1016/j.giq.2022.101679

Saura, J. R., Škare, V., & Dosen, D. O. (2024). Is AI-based digital marketing ethical? Assessing a new data privacy paradox. *Journal of Innovation & Knowledge, 9*(4), 100597. https://doi.org/10.1016/j.jik.2024.100597

Schivinski, B., & Dabrowski, D. (2016). The effect of social media communication on consumer perceptions of brands. *Journal of Marketing Communications, 22*(2), 189–214. https://doi.org/10.1080/13527266.2013.871323

Shiau, R., Wu, H. Y., Kim, E., Du, Y. L., Guo, A., Zhang, Z., et al. (2020, August). Shop the look: Building a large scale visual shopping system at Pinterest. In *Proceedings of the 26th ACM SIGKDD International Conference on Knowledge Discovery & Data Mining* (pp. 3203–3212). https://doi.org/10.48550/arXiv.2006.10866

Sridevi, D. R. R., Saini, R., Mohideen, A. S., Natarajan, S., & Rajalakshmi, M. (2024). Predictive analytics for marketing campaign optimization. *Asian and Pacific Economic Review, 17*(2), 1–24.

Stone, M., Aravopoulou, E., Ekinci, Y., Evans, G., Hobbs, M., Labib, A., & Machtynger, L. (2020). AI (AI) in strategic marketing decision-making: A research agenda. *The Bottom Line, 33*(2), 183–200. https://doi.org/10.1108/BL-03-2020-0022

Udruga gradova. (2023). *Poziv Gradovima da Se Uključe U Liberatomap*. Udruga gradova. (2023, May 30). Retrieved from: https://www.udruga-gradova.hr/poziv-za-gradove-da-se-ukljuce-u-liberatomap/

Umamaheswari, D. D. (2024). Role of AI in marketing strategies and performance. *Migration Letters, 21*(S4), 1589–1599.

Wirtz, B. W., Weyerer, J. C., & Sturm, B. J. (2020). The dark sides of AI: An integrated AI governance framework for public administration. *International Journal of Public Administration, 43*(9), 818–829. https://doi.org/10.1080/01900692.2020.1749851

Wolniak, R., & Grebski, W. (2023). The application of business analytics in personalized customer experience. Scientific Papers of Silesian University of Technology. *Organization & Management/*Zeszyty Naukowe Politechniki Slaskiej. Seria Organizacji i Zarzadzanie, 182.

Zhang, W., & Chen, L. (2024). Real-Time Transaction Monitoring Using AI: Detecting Suspicious Activities and Money Laundering in Banking. *Asian American Research Letters Journal, 1*(3).

Zuiderwijk, A., Chen, Y. C., & Salem, F. (2021). Implications of the use of AI in public governance: A systematic literature review and a research agenda. *Government Information Quarterly*. https://doi.org/10.1016/j.giq.2021.101577

Zwiegelaar, J., & Stylos, N. (2018, September). Is Big Data the next Big game changer? Impact on customer services, marketing and ethics. In *BAM 2018 Conference Proceedings: Driving productivity in uncertain and challenging times* (p. 498). British Academy of Management.

The manufacturer's authorised representative in the EU is Springer
Nature Customer Service Centre GmbH, Europaplatz 3, 69115 Heidelberg,
Germany. If you have any concerns regarding our products, please
contact ProductSafety@springernature.com

Printed and bound by CPI Group (UK) Ltd, Croydon, CR0 4YY
30/09/2026
02225592-0013